EDVANTAGE INTERACTIVE

MW01678312

BC SCIENCE PHYSICS 12

Vancouver Island University

Authors

Lionel Sandner
Edvantage Interactive

Dr. Gordon Gore
BIG Little Science Centre (Kamloops)

Contributing Writer

Lui Zucchetto
Garibaldi Secondary School
School District 42 Maple Ridge

COPIES OF THIS BOOK MAY BE OBTAINED BY CONTACTING:

Edvantage Interactive

E-MAIL:
info@edvantageinteractive.com

TOLL-FREE FAX:
866.275.0564

TOLL-FREE CALL:
866.422.7310

OR BY MAILING YOUR ORDER TO:

P.O. Box 20001
9839 Fifth Street
Sidney, BC V8L 2X4

EDVANTAGE INTERACTIVE

BC Science Physics 12

ISBN: 978-1-77249-479-2

Vancouver Island University – 2016 Reprint

Vice-President of Marketing: *Don Franklin*
Director of Publishing: *Yvonne Van Ruskenveld*
Design/Illustration/Production: *Donna Lindenberg, Paula Gaube*
Editorial Assistance: *Rhys Sandner*

QR Code — What Is This?

The image to the right is called a QR code. It's similar to bar codes on various products and contains information that can be useful to you. Each QR code in this book provides you with online support to help you learn the course material. For example, find a question with a QR code beside it. If you scan that code, you'll see the answer to the question explained in a video created by an author of this book.

You can scan a QR code using an Internet-enabled mobile device. The program to scan QR codes is free and available at your phone's app store. Scanning the QR code above will give you a short overview of how to use the codes in the book to help you study.

Note: We recommend that you scan QR codes only when your phone is connected to a WiFi network. Depending on your mobile data plan, charges may apply if you access the information over the cellular network. If you are not sure how to do this, please contact your phone provider or us at info@edvantageinteractive.com

Contents

BC Science Physics 12

Welcome to BC Science Physics 12

BC Science Physics 12 is a print and digital resource for classroom and independent study, aligned 100% with the BC curriculum. You, the student, have two core components — this write-in textbook or WorkText and, to provide mobile functionality, an interactive Online Study Guide.

BC Science Physics 12 WorkText

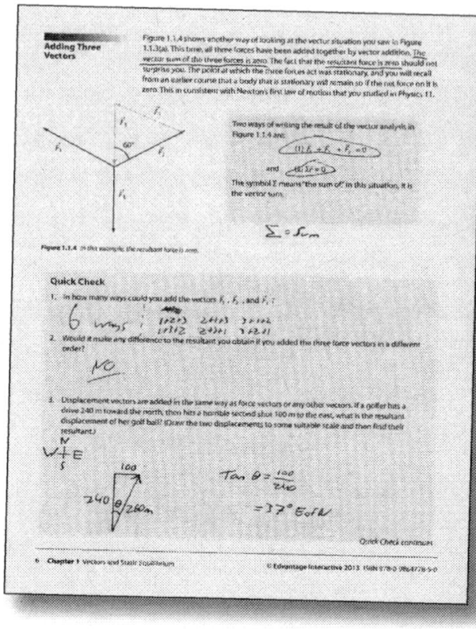

What is a WorkText?

A WorkText is a write-in textbook. Not just a workbook, a write-in **textbook**.

Like the vast majority of BC students, you will read for content, underline, highlight, take notes, answer the questions — all in this book. **Your book**.

Use it as a textbook, workbook, notebook, AND study guide. It's also a great reference book for post secondary studies.

Make it your own personal WorkText.

Why a write-in textbook?

Reading is an extremely active and personal process.

Research has shown that physically interacting with your text by writing margin notes and highlighting key passages results in better comprehension and retention.

Use your own experiences and prior knowledge to make meaning, not take meaning, from text.

How to make this book work for you:

1. Scan each section and check out the shaded areas and bolded terms.
2. Do the Warm Ups to activate prior knowledge.
3. Take notes as required by highlights and adding teacher comments and notes.
4. Use Quick Check sections to find out where you are in your learning.
5. Do the Review Questions and write down the answers. Scan the **QR codes** or go to the **Online Study Guide** to see YouTube-like video worked solutions by *BC Science Physics 12* authors.
6. Try the **Online Study Guide** for online quizzes, PowerPoints, and more videos.
7. Follow the six steps above to be successful.
8. Need extra support? ASK AN AUTHOR!

For more information on how to purchase your own personal copy or if you'd like to ASK AN AUTHOR a question — info@edvantageinteractive.com

BC Science Physics 12 Online Study Guide (OSG)

What is an Online Study Guide?

It's an interactive, personalized, digital, mobile study guide to support the WorkText.

The **Online Study Guide** or OSG, provides access to online quizzes, PowerPoint notes, and video worked solutions.

Need extra questions, sample tests, a summary of your notes, worked solutions to some of the review questions? It's all here!

Access it where you want, when you want.

Make it your own personal mobile study guide.

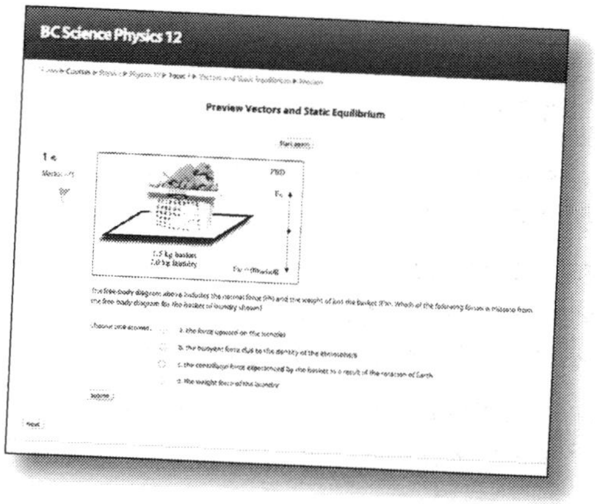

What's in the Online Study Guide?

- Online quizzes, multiple choice questions, provincial exam-like tests with instant feedback
- PowerPoint notes: Key idea summary and student study notes from the textbook
- Video worked solutions: Select video worked solutions from the WorkText

Scan this code for a quick tour of the OSG

If you have a smart phone or tablet, scan the QR code to the right to find out more. Colour e-reader WorkText version available.

Where is the Online Study Guide located?

edvantagescience.com

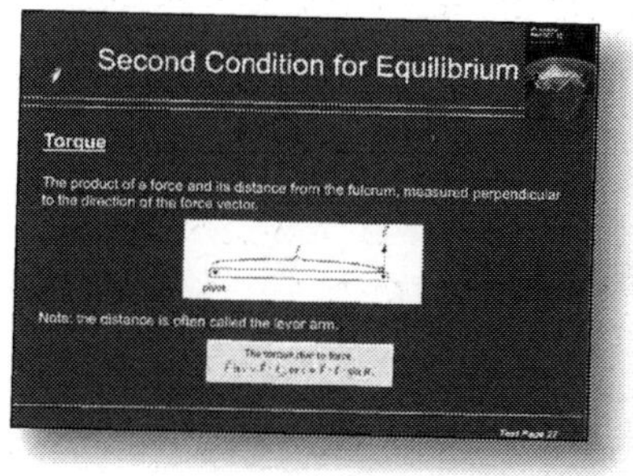

Should I use the Online Study Guide?

YES... if you want to do your best in this course.

The OSG is directly LINKED to the activities and content in the WorkText.

The OSG helps you learn what is taught in class.

If your school does not have access to the Online Study Guide and you'd like more information — info@edvantageinteractive.com

1 Vectors and Static Equilibrium

By the end of this chapter, you should be able to do the following:

- Perform vector analysis in one or two dimensions
- Apply vector analysis to solve practical navigation problems
- Use knowledge of force, torque and equilibrium to analyse various situations

By the end of this chapter, you should know the meaning of these **key terms**:

- centre of gravity
- centre of mass
- components
- equilibrium
- fulcrum
- horizontal component
- net force
- resultant force
- scalar quantities
- static equilibrium
- torque
- vector quantities
- vertical component

By the end of this chapter, you should be able to use and know when to use the following formulae:

$\tau = F \cdot \ell_{\perp}$ or $\tau = F \cdot \ell_{\perp} \sin\theta$

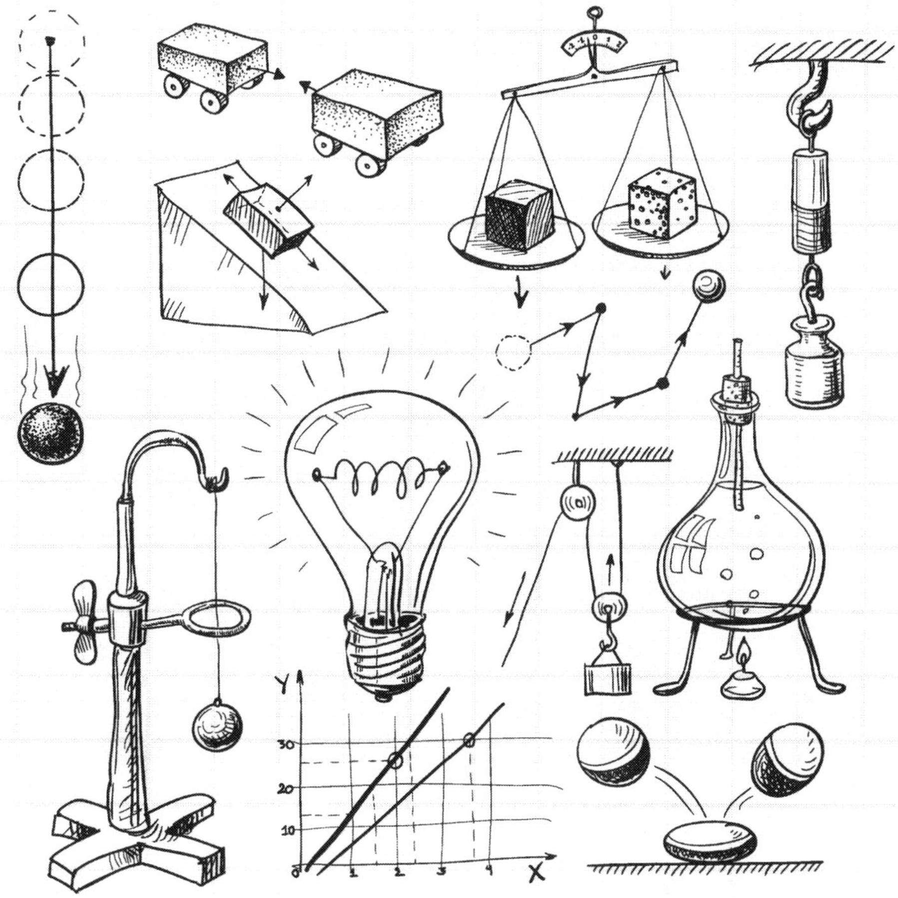

Welcome to Physics 12. In this course, you will study a variety of concepts that will help you better understand the world around you. From vector motion to dynamics to gravitational and electromagnetic fields, you will be able to use what you learn throughout your life.

1.1 Scalars and Vectors

Warm Up

Since you first learned to count and add, you have known $1 + 1 = 2$. Now as you start Physics 12, you will be learning that sometimes there is more than one way to describe physical events. For example, under what conditions could you say that $1 + 1 = \sqrt{2}$ is a true statement?

____

____

____

Scalar and Vector Quantities

If you add 5 L of water to another 5 L of water, you end up with 10 L of water. Similarly, if you add 5 kg of salt to 5 kg of salt, you will have 10 kg of salt. Volumes and masses are added by the rules of ordinary arithmetic. Volume and mass are **scalar quantities**. Scalar quantities have magnitude (size) only. Other scalar quantities with which you may be familiar are: length, energy, density, and temperature.

If you add a 5 N force to another 5 N force, the two forces together *may* add up to 10 N, but they may also add up to 0 N or to any value between 0 N and 10 N! This is because forces have *direction* as well as magnitude. Quantities that have both direction and magnitude are called **vector quantities.** Forces and other vector quantities must be added by the special rules of **vector addition,** which take into account direction as well as magnitude.

In addition to forces, other vector quantities you will encounter in this course include: velocity, displacement, acceleration, momentum, electrical field strength and magnetic field strength.

When you describe velocity, displacement, acceleration, force, momentum, or any other vector quantity, you must specify both magnitude and direction.

Watch Your Language

There are a few quantities where a different word is used for the scalar and the vector measurements. In day-to-day life, most people use one or both terms without wondering which term is correct. It is very important that you use them correctly from now on. This is important because some new concepts will seem much harder than they actually are if you use the terms incorrectly.

For now, there are two sets of scalar and vector quantities to focus on: distance and displacement, and speed and velocity. Distance and speed are scalar quantities. They only have an amount or magnitude. Think of a road sign that says 200 km to Vancouver or shows a speed limit of 30 km/h. Displacement and velocity are vector quantities and include both magnitude and direction. For example, to get to the arena, go 2 km [north].

Adding Vectors

In Figure 1.1.1, an object is hanging from a spring balance. Two forces pull on the object. Earth exerts a 10 N force of gravity downward on it, and the spring balance exerts a 10 N force up on it. Both Earth and the spring balance exert the same *size* of force on the object. The **net force** on the object is not 10 N or 20 N as one might expect. It is, in fact, 0 N!

To understand why the **net** or **resultant force** is zero in this situation, you must know (a) what a vector is and (b) how vectors are added.

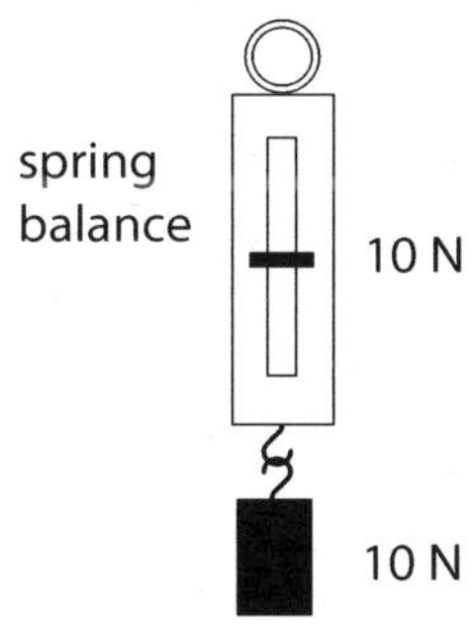

Figure 1.1.1 *The object hanging from this spring balance has forces acting on it in two directions, up and down.*

To show a vector, you must draw a line segment whose length is proportional to the magnitude of the quantity being represented. In Figure 1.1.2, this quantity is a force. You draw a segment in the direction the quantity is acting, and place an arrow tip at one end of the line segment to show its direction. The line segment, drawn to an appropriate scale complete with arrow tip, is a **vector.**

Figure 1.1.2 shows how the two forces in Figure 1.1.1 can be represented with vectors. Figure 1.1.2 (a) shows vectors representing the upward force $\vec{F}_1$ exerted by the spring balance and the downward gravitational force $\vec{F}_2$ individually. Figure 1.1.2(b) shows the two forces added together by **vector addition**.

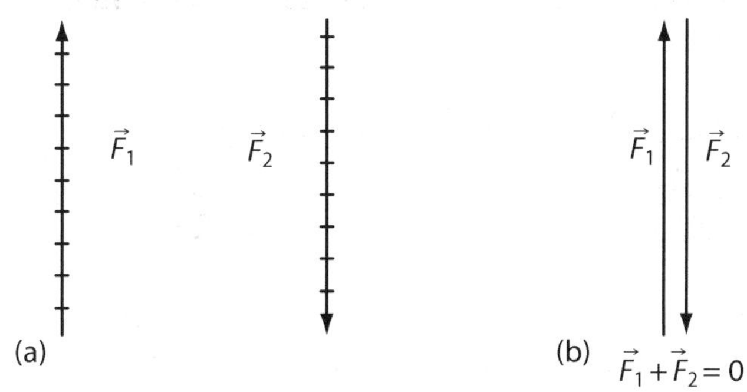

Figure 1.1.2 *Representing forces with vectors*

Note: There are two ways to indicate that a quantity is a vector quantity. In diagrams or in handwritten notes, a small arrow may be drawn above the symbol for the quantity. For example, $\vec{F}$ indicates that a force vector is being discussed. In some textbooks, the symbol for a vector quantity may be typed in ***bold italics***, like this: ***F***. This symbol also indicates that a force vector is being discussed. If only the *magnitude* of a vector is of importance, the symbol *F* (*italics*, but not bold) is used.

To add vector $\vec{F_1}$ to vector, $\vec{F_2}$ draw vector $\vec{F_1}$ first, to scale and in the proper direction. Then draw vector $\vec{F_2}$ so that its tail begins at the tip of vector $\vec{F_1}$ and the line segment of $\vec{F_2}$ points in the proper direction. Be sure to draw the tip of an arrow to show which way $\vec{F_2}$ points. The net or resultant force is the vector going from the tail of $\vec{F_1}$ to the tip of $\vec{F_2}$.

In Figure 1.1.2, the resultant is clearly zero. When two or more forces acting on a body have a resultant of zero, the body is said to be in **equilibrium.** In this example, $\vec{F_2}$ is a force that balances one or more other forces and creates a condition where there is no net force. This type of force is called the **equilibrant.**

In Figure 1.1.3(a), strings connected to two different spring balances suspend a 10 N object. The strings form an angle of 120° where they are attached to the object. Notice that *both* scales read 10 N. Can the object possibly be in equilibrium if there are *two* 10 N forces pulling it up, and just *one* 10 N force pulling it down?

To find out what the **resultant** of the two upward forces is, use the rule for adding vectors again. In Figure 1.1.3(b), vectors $\vec{F_1}$, $\vec{F_2}$, and $\vec{F_3}$ have been drawn acting at a single point where the three strings meet. The vectors are all drawn to a suitable scale and are aimed in the proper directions relative to one another.

Vector $\vec{F_1}$ (dashed line) has been added to vector $\vec{F_2}$. The tail of vector $\vec{F_1}$ starts at the tip of vector $\vec{F_2}$ and vector $\vec{F_1}$ is aimed in the direction it acts, which is 60° left of the vertical.

The resultant of $\vec{F_1}$ and $\vec{F_2}$ starts at the tail of $\vec{F_2}$, and ends at the tip of $\vec{F_1}$. The resultant is drawn with a bold line and is labeled $\vec{F_R}$. Notice that $\vec{F_R}$ is equal in magnitude but *opposite in direction* to $\vec{F_3}$. (You could call $\vec{F_R}$ the *equilibrant* of $\vec{F_3}$.)

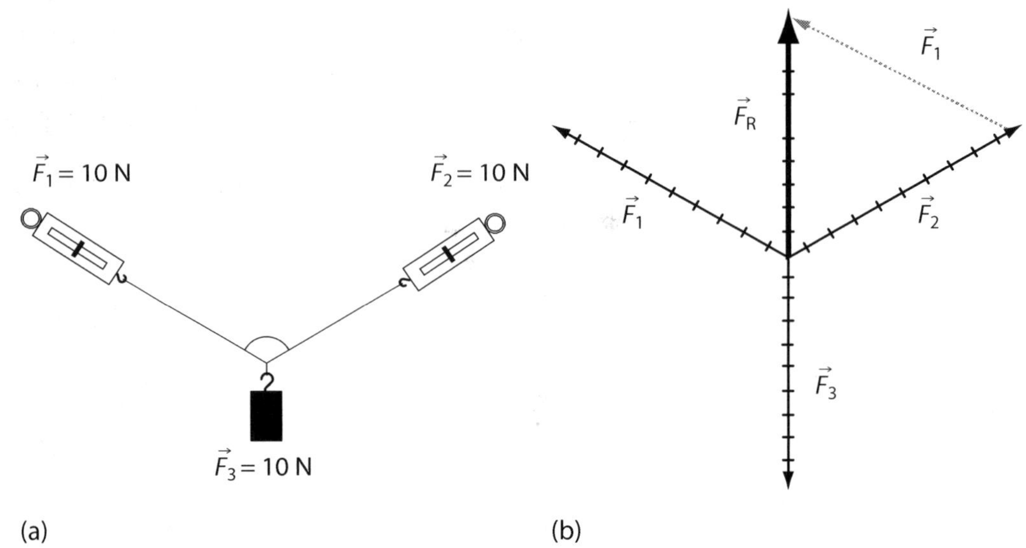

Figure 1.1.3 *Finding the resultant of two upward forces*

Quick Check

1. What would the resultant be in Figure 1.1.3(b) if you added $\vec{F}_2$ to $\vec{F}_1$ instead of $\vec{F}_1$ to $\vec{F}_2$?

2. What would the resultant be if you added $\vec{F}_R$ to $\vec{F}_3$?

3. (a) When you draw the three vectors in Figure 1.1.3(b) tip to tail, what kind of triangle do you get?

   (b) What if the three forces were 6 N [E], 8 N [S], and 10 N. What kind of triangle would they form when added together?

Adding Three Vectors

Figure 1.1.4 shows another way of looking at the vector situation you saw in Figure 1.1.3(a). This time, all three forces have been added together by vector addition. The vector sum of the three forces is zero. The fact that the resultant force is zero should not surprise you. The point at which the three forces act was stationary, and you will recall from an earlier course that a body that is stationary will remain so if the net force on it is zero. This in consistent with Newton's first law of motion that you studied in Physics 11.

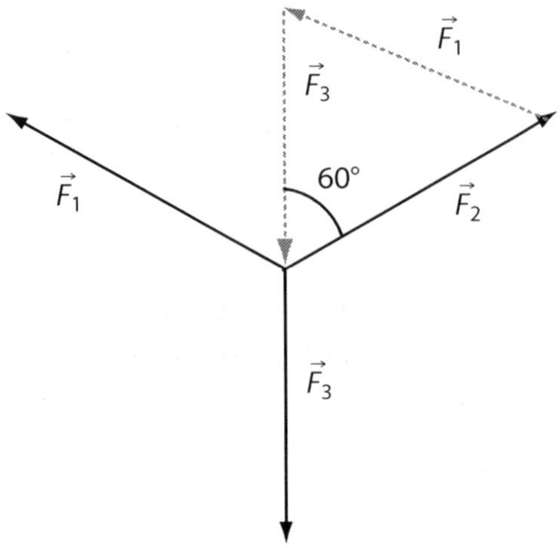

Figure 1.1.4 *In this example, the resultant force is zero.*

Two ways of writing the result of the vector analysis in Figure 1.1.4 are:

(1) $\vec{F}_1 + \vec{F}_2 + \vec{F}_3 = 0$

and (2) $\Sigma F = 0$

The symbol Σ means "the sum of." In this situation, it is the vector sum.

Quick Check

1. In how many ways could you add the vectors $\vec{F}_1$, $\vec{F}_2$, and $\vec{F}_3$?

2. Would it make any difference to the resultant you obtain if you added the three force vectors in a different order?

3. Displacement vectors are added in the same way as force vectors or any other vectors. If a golfer hits a drive 240 m toward the north, then hits a horrible second shot 100 m to the east, what is the resultant displacement of her golf ball? (Draw the two displacements to some suitable scale and then find their resultant.)

Quick Check continues

4. A dancer does the following Physics Jig move: 3 steps north, 2 steps west, 5 steps east, and 7 steps south. What is his
   (a) resultant displacement?

   (b) total distance travelled?

"Subtracting" Vectors

Method 1

Sometimes, you will have to find the difference between two vectors. For example, if the velocity of a body changes from $\vec{v}_1$ to $\vec{v}_2$, you may need to calculate the *change in velocity*, Δv. A vector *difference* is defined as the vector *sum* of the second vector and the *negative* of the first vector:

$$\Delta v = \vec{v}_2 + (-1)\vec{v}_1$$

or

$$\Delta v = \vec{v}_2 + \vec{v}_1$$

When "subtracting" vectors, simply remember that the negative of any vector is a vector of the same magnitude (size) but pointing in the opposite direction. The difference of two vectors is the sum of the first vector and the *negative* of the second vector. See Figure 1.1.5.

$$\Delta v = \vec{v}_2 - \vec{v}_1 = \vec{v}_2 + (-\vec{v}_1)$$

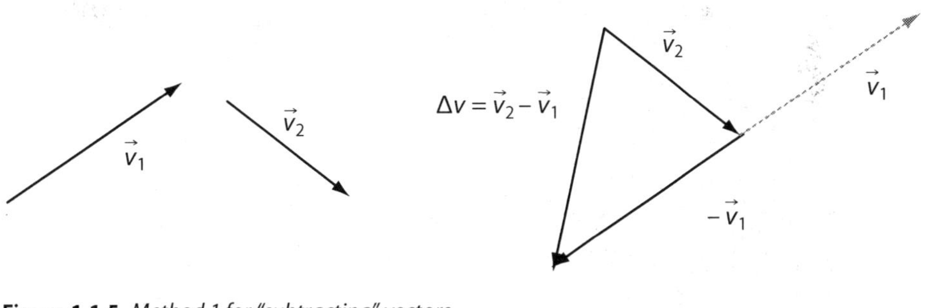

Figure 1.1.5 *Method 1 for "subtracting" vectors*

Method 2

The difference between two vectors can also be found by drawing the vectors "tail to tail," as shown in Figure 1.1.6. The resultant Δv is the vector drawn from tip to tip. From Figure 1.1.6,

$$\vec{v}_1 + \Delta v = \vec{v}_2$$

$$\therefore \Delta v = \vec{v}_2 - \vec{v}_1$$

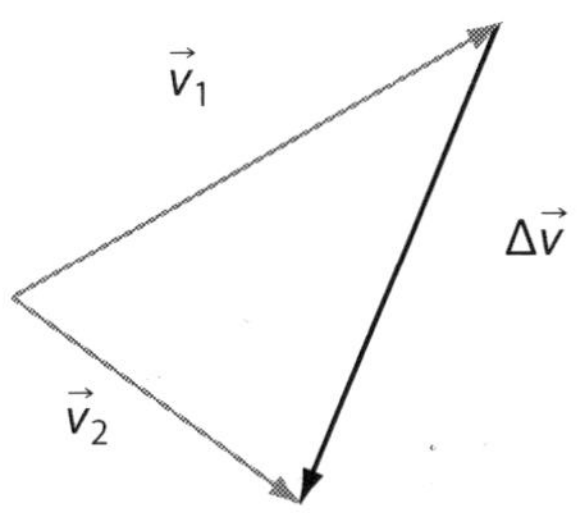

Figure 1.1.6 *Method 2 for "subtracting" vectors*

Investigation 1.1.1 Experimenting with Force Vectors

Purpose

To analyze the force vectors in situations where three forces act at a single point and no motion results from the force

Procedure

1. Set up the arrangement shown in Figure 1.1.7. Three forces act on the point where the three strings meet. The forces are 3.0 N, 4.0 N, and 5.0 N. When all the masses are hanging stationary, place a sheet of polar graph paper or a protractor behind the point where the strings meet and measure angles A, B, and C.

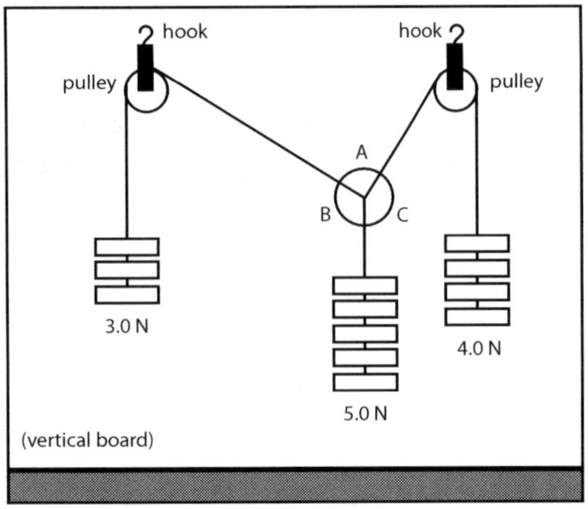

Figure 1.1.7

2. On a fresh piece of paper draw three lines meeting at a point, with the lines forming the same angles A, B, and C that were formed by the three strings. See Figure 1.1.8(a). On these lines, draw force vectors representing the forces of gravity on the three hanging masses. Use a scale of 2.0 cm for each newton of force. See Figure 1.1.8(b). Label the forces $\vec{F}_1$, $\vec{F}_2$, and $\vec{F}_3$.

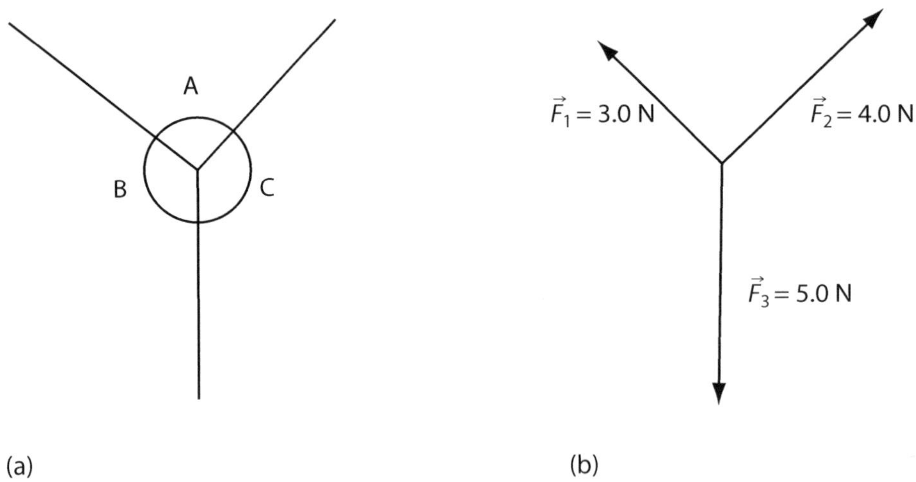

Figure 1.1.8

3. *Predict* what the resultant of these three force vectors will be. Now add them by the "head-to-tail" system.
4. Use the same arrangement as in steps 1 to 3, but change the masses used so that the force of gravity on each mass is 4.0 N. Measure the new angles A, B, and C. Draw the three forces in this new situation and use vector addition to add them.

Concluding Questions

1. Based on your observations in Procedure steps 1 to 4, what is the resultant of the forces acting on a point if the point does not move?
2. In Procedure step 1, why is angle A a right angle?
3. In Procedure step 4, why is angle A 120°?
4. If the vector sum of all the forces acting on a point were not zero, what would you observe happening to the point (in this case, the junction of the three strings)?
5. Account for any small errors you may have encountered in this activity.
6. When a body is at rest, we say it is in static equilibrium, even though there are numerous forces acting on it. According to your investigation, how would you describe the conditions needed for a point to be in static equilibrium?

1.1 Review Questions

1. Two boys are pulling a girl along on a toboggan. Each boy pulls on a rope attached to the same point on the front of the toboggan with a force of 360 N. Using a scale diagram, determine the resultant of the two forces exerted by the boys if their ropes form each of these angles with each other:

   (a) 0°

   (b) 60°

   (c) 120°

   (d) 180°

2. What is the *magnitude* of the resultant of the three forces acting at point X?

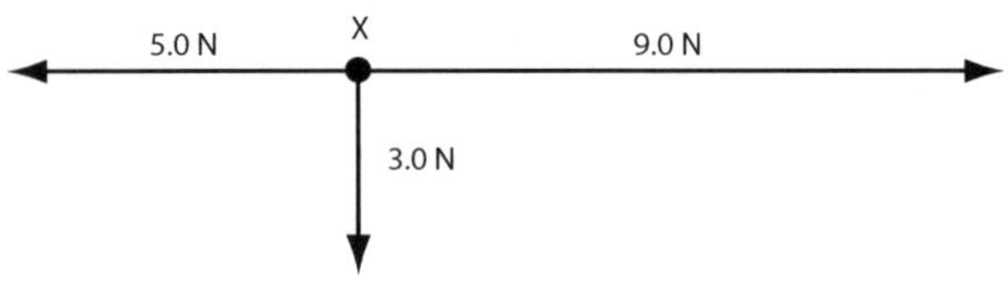

3. A football player is pushed by one opponent with a force of 50.0 N toward the east. At the same time, a second tackler pushes him with a force of 120.0 N toward the north. What is the magnitude and direction of the resultant force on the first player?

4. The following three forces act simultaneously on the same point: 100.0 N toward the north, 50.0 N toward the east, and 220.0 N toward the south. What will their resultant be?

1.2 Vectors in Two Dimensions

Warm Up

An airplane is flying north at 200 km/h. A 25 km/h wind is blowing from the east. Will this crosswind speed up, slow down, or have no effect on the plane? Defend your answer.

____

____

____

Defining Vector Components

Figure 1.2.1 shows three ways you could travel from A to B. The vectors are displacement vectors. In each of the three "trips," the resultant displacement is the same.

$$\vec{D}_1 + \vec{D}_2 = \vec{D}_R$$

Any two or more vectors that have a resultant such as $\vec{D}_R$ are called **components** of the resultant vector. A vector such as $\vec{D}_R$ can be **resolved** into an endless number of component combinations. Figure 1.2.1 shows just three possible combinations of components of $\vec{D}_R$.

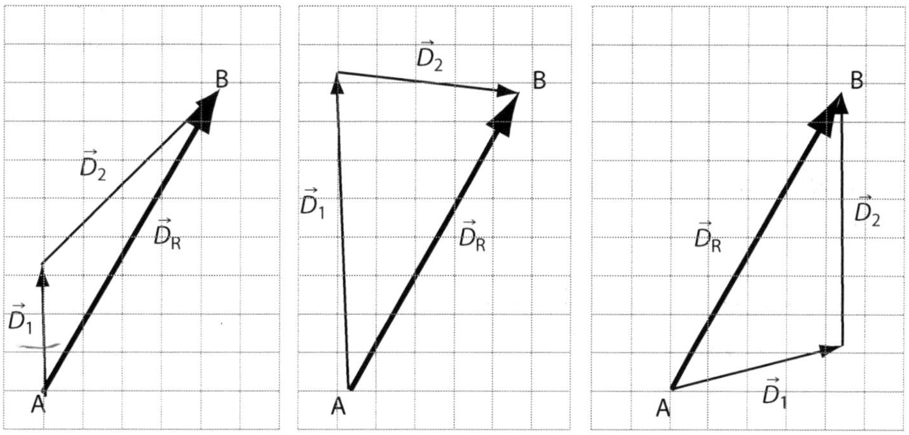

Figure 1.2.1 *Examples of possible components of* $\vec{D}_R$

Trigonometric Ratios Used in Vector Problems

In many problems, the most useful way of resolving a vector into components is to choose components that are perpendicular to each other. Let's review trigonometric ratios so you can recall how to do this.

Three trigonometric ratios are particularly useful for solving vector problems. In the right-angled triangle ABC in Figure 1.2.2, consider the angle labeled with the Greek symbol θ (theta). With reference to θ, AC is the **opposite side**, BC is the **adjacent side**, and AB is the **hypotenuse**. In any right-angled triangle, the hypotenuse is always the side opposite to the right angle.

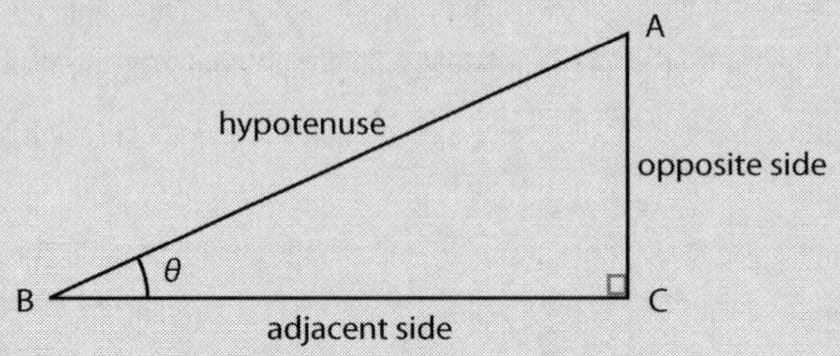

Figure 1.2.2 *A right-angled triangle with the labels you need to know for the trigonometric ratios you'll be using in vector problems*

The three most commonly used trigonometric ratios are defined as follows:

$$\textbf{sine}\ \theta = \frac{\text{opposite side}}{\text{hypotenuse}} = \frac{\text{o}}{\text{h}}$$

$$\textbf{cosine}\ \theta = \frac{\text{adjacent side}}{\text{hypotenuse}} = \frac{\text{a}}{\text{h}}$$

$$\textbf{tangent}\ \theta = \frac{\text{opposite side}}{\text{adjacent side}} = \frac{\text{o}}{\text{a}}$$

Trigonometric ratios, available with the push of a button from your calculator, can help you solve vector problems quickly. Following is a sample vector question involving velocities. The rules for adding velocity vectors are the same as those for displacement and force vectors or any other vector quantities.

Resolving Vectors into Vertical and Horizontal Components

Figure 1.2.3 shows one situation where it is wise to use perpendicular components.

In Figure 1.2.3(a), a 60.0 N force is exerted down the handle of a snow shovel. The force that actually pushes the snow along the driveway is the **horizontal component** $\vec{F}_x$. The **vertical component** $\vec{F}_y$ is directed perpendicular to the road (Figure 1.2.3(b)).

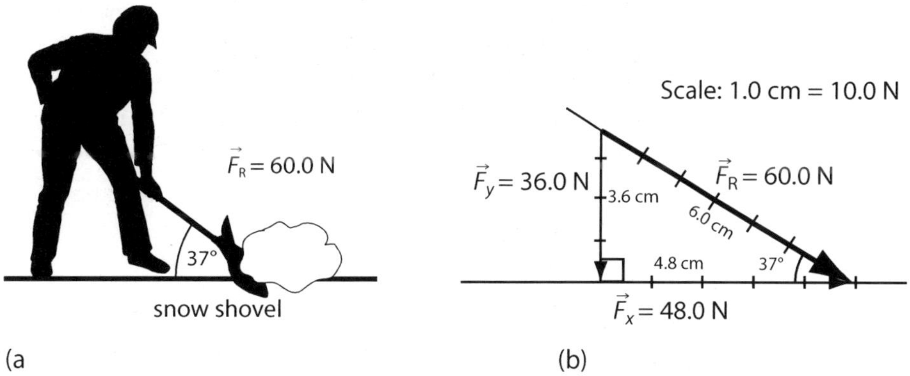

Figure 1.2.3 *The force the man exerts on the snow shovel can be resolved into horizontal and vertical components.*

Method 1: Solving By Scale Diagram

To find out what the horizontal component $\vec{F}_x$ is, you can use a scale diagram like Figure 1.2.3(b). First, draw a horizontal reference line. Then draw a line forming an angle of 37° with the horizontal reference line, because this is the angle formed by the snow shovel handle with the road.

Using a scale of 1.0 cm for each 10.0 N, draw a force vector to represent $\vec{F}_R$, where $\vec{F}_R = 60.0$ N. Next, drop a line down from the tail of $\vec{F}_R$ meeting the horizontal reference line at an angle of 90°. This gives you both the vertical and the horizontal component forces. Label these $\vec{F}_y$ and $\vec{F}_x$, and place arrows on them to show their directions.

Since the horizontal component vector has a length of 4.8 cm, and each 1.0 cm represents 10.0 N, then $\vec{F}_x = 48.0$ N. The vertical component vector is 3.6 cm long, therefore $\vec{F}_y = 36.0$ N.

Method 2: Resolve into Components

Figure 1.2.3(b) shows the force vector $\vec{F}_R = 60$ N at an angle of 37° to the surface or horizontal. This vector is then resolved into its vertical component $\vec{F}_y$ and horizontal component $\vec{F}_x$. How do we find the magnitude of these component vectors without the aid of a scale diagram?

Recall from your math class that the three angles in a triangle add up to 180°. (See, you would use that fact one day!) So, the unknown angle in Figure 1.2.3 is 53°. Remember that a right angle is 90°. So the unknown angle is equal to 180 – (90° + 37°), which is 53°.

Then to find $\vec{F}_y$, we know $\vec{F}_R$ and the angle between $\vec{F}_R$ and $\vec{F}_y$. Using cos θ, we can calculate $\vec{F}_y$:

$$\cos 53° = \frac{\vec{F}_y}{60}$$

$$\vec{F}_y = \cos 53° \times 60$$

$$\vec{F}_y = 36 \text{ N}$$

To find $\vec{F}_x$, we use sin θ to calculate the horizontal component:

$$\sin 53° = \frac{\vec{F}_x}{60}$$
$$\vec{F}_x = \sin 53° \times 60$$
$$\vec{F} = 48 \text{ N}$$

To check that we have the right answers, we use the Pythagorean theorem as the three vectors form a right angle triangle:

$$F_R = \sqrt{F_x^2 + F_y^2}$$
$$F_R = \sqrt{(36)^2 + (48)^2}$$
$$F_R = 60 \text{ N}$$

More than One Vector: Using a Vector Diagram

Figure 1.2.4 shows a typical force vector situation, where there are three forces acting, but no motion resulting. Two strings support a 36.0 N object. One string makes an angle of 30° with the vertical, and the other string is horizontal. The question is, "What is the tension in each string?" The tension in a string is simply the force exerted along the string. To find the answer to this question, we must first represent the forces in a vector diagram.

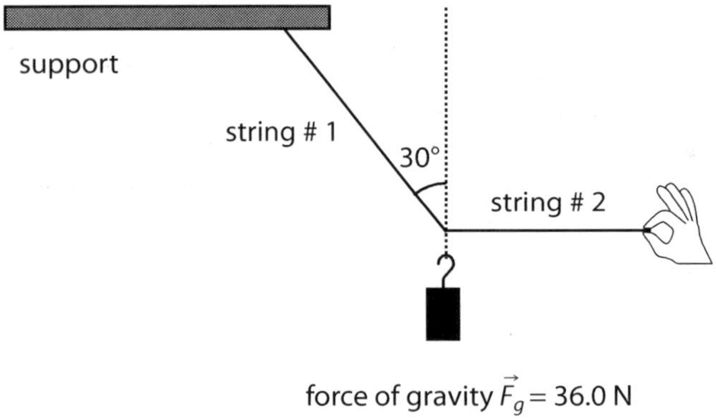

Figure 1.2.4 *Two strings support an object. You want to find the tension in each string.*

Figure 1.2.5 shows one way to look at this problem. The 36.0 N object is not moving, so the three forces acting on it must have a resultant of zero. That means the vector sum of the three forces acting on the object is zero.

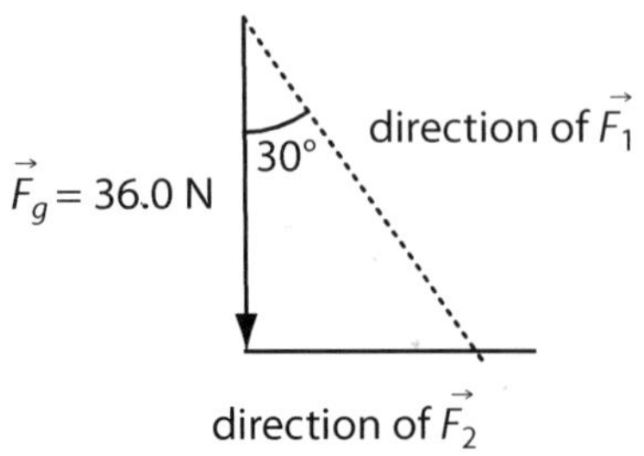

Figure 1.2.5 *Vector diagram representing the three forces acting on the object in Figure 1.2.4*

The vector to draw first is the one for which you have the most complete information. You know that the force of gravity $\vec{F}_g$ has a magnitude of 36.0 N and is directed down.

You do *not* know the *magnitude* of the tension along string #1 ($\vec{F}_1$) but you know its *direction*, which is 30° to the vertical. You do *not* know the *magnitude* of the tension in string #2 ($\vec{F}_2$), but you know that it acts in a direction *perpendicular to* $\vec{F}_g$. You also know that vectors $\vec{F}_1$, $\vec{F}_2$, and $\vec{F}_g$ form a closed triangle since their resultant is zero.

In Figure 1.2.5, dashed lines show the directions of $\vec{F}_1$ and $\vec{F}_2$. To complete the vector triangle of forces, arrows must be added to show that $\vec{F}_1$ ends at the tail of $\vec{F}_g$, and $\vec{F}_2$ starts at the tip of $\vec{F}_g$. If $\vec{F}_g$ has been drawn to scale, then both $\vec{F}_1$ and $\vec{F}_2$ will have the same scale.

Figure 1.2.6 shows what the completed vector diagram looks like. To solve for tension forces $\vec{F}_1$ and $\vec{F}_2$, you must know to what scale $\vec{F}_g$ was drawn. In the next sample problem, the tension will be found using this diagram and components.

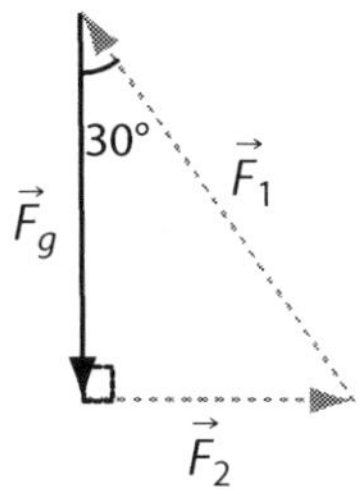

Figure 1.2.6 *Completed vector diagram from Figure 1.2.5*

Sample Problem 1.2.1 — Using a Vector Diagram

Use components to find the tension in the two strings shown in Figure 1.2.4.

What to Think About

1. Draw a vector diagram to identify all the forces in the problem.
2. Identify what to solve.
3. For $\vec{F}_1$, find the horizontal and vertical components and use the Pythagorean theorem to solve for $\vec{F}_1$.

How to Do It

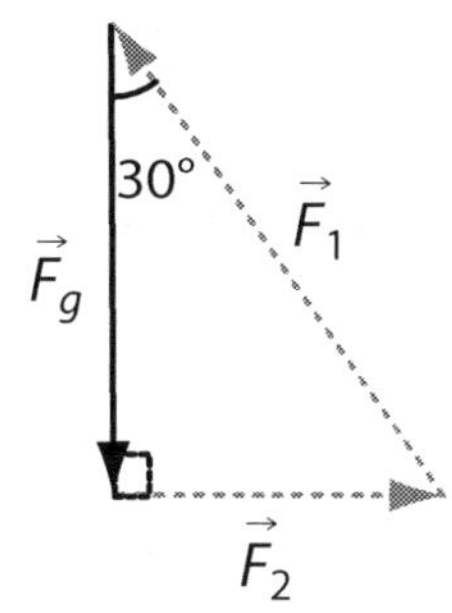

Figure 1.2.7

Find $\vec{F}_1$ and $\vec{F}_2$

$$\cos 30° = \frac{\vec{F}_g}{\vec{F}_1} = \frac{36.0\text{ N}}{\vec{F}_1}$$

$$\vec{F}_1 = \frac{36.0\text{ N}}{\cos 30°} = 41.6\text{ N}$$

Sample Problem continued

Sample Problem 1.2.1 — Using a Vector Diagram (Continued)

What to Think About	How to Do It
4. Repeat for $\vec{F}_2$.	$\tan 30° = \dfrac{\vec{F}_2}{36.0\text{ N}}$ $F_2 = (\tan 30°)(36.0\text{ N})$ $F_2 = 20.8\text{ N}$
5. Check that $\vec{F}_g = \vec{F}_1 + \vec{F}_2$.	$\vec{F}_g = \vec{F}_1 + \vec{F}_2$ $F_g = \sqrt{(41.6\text{ N})^2 - (20.8\text{ N})^2}$ $F_g = 36.0\text{ N}$

Practice Problems 1.2.1 — Using a Vector Diagram

1. Figure 1.2.8 shows three force vectors.

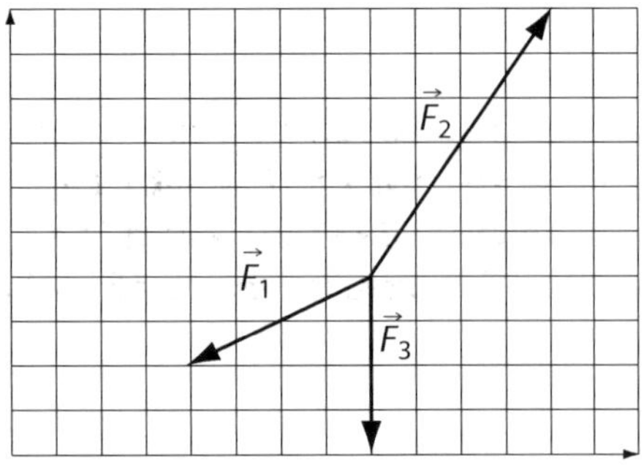

Figure 1.2.8

(a) What is the resultant of the three force vectors, added "head-to-tail"?

(b) What is the resultant of the three horizontal components?

Practice Problems continued

Practice Problems 1.2.1 — Using a Vector Diagram (Continued)

(c) What is the resultant of the three vertical components?

2. Using the empty graph in Figure 1.2.9(b) and by any logical method, find the force F_4 that must be added to F_1, F_2, and F_3 (shown in (a)) to obtain a resultant of zero.

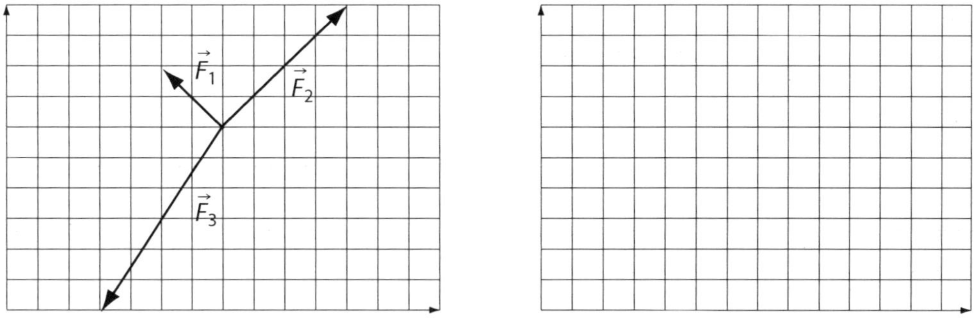

(a) (b)

Figure 1.2.9

3. A dedicated physics student pulls his brand new shiny red wagon along a level road such that the handle makes an angle of 50° with the horizontal road. If he pulls on the handle with a force of 85 N, what is the horizontal component of the force he exerts along the handle? Draw a neat, labeled vector diagram. Use a scale of 1.0 cm for every 10.0 N. Why is the horizontal component more useful information than the force he exerts along the handle?

A Velocity Vector Problem — Vectors in Action!

It might not seem at first glance to be a vector problem, but a boat crossing a river or a plane flying into a strong wind are both examples of more than one vector acting on an object. Commonly called boat or airplane vector problems in physics, these situations involve the object moving through a medium that is also moving. For a boat, this medium is the river that has a current and, for an airplane, it is the air.

Both water and air are mediums that have a velocity and can be represented with a vector. This motion is usually compared to a reference point like the ground. For example, a person watching a boat cross a river observes the boat's motion as a combination of boat speed and river speed. A person in the boat experiences only the boat's speed. This is an example of relative motion. The motion observed is relative to where the person is located.

Let's first look at a motorboat crossing a river. In Figure 1.2.10 an observer sees the boat crossing the river at an angle. This is the boat's speed relative to the ground. But a person in the boat measures the speed of the boat relative to the water. This is the boat's speed relative the water. And the current, which is pushing the boat, is the speed of the water relative to the ground. This is summarized in Figure 1.2.11. Now we can apply this to a boat vector problem.

Problem: A motorboat operator is trying to travel across a fast-moving river, as shown in Figure 1.2.10. Although he aims his boat directly across the stream, the water carries the boat to the right. If the boat's resultant velocity, as seen by an observer on the bank, is 15.0 m/s in the direction shown, how fast is the boat moving

(a) in a direction downstream?

(b) in a direction across the river?

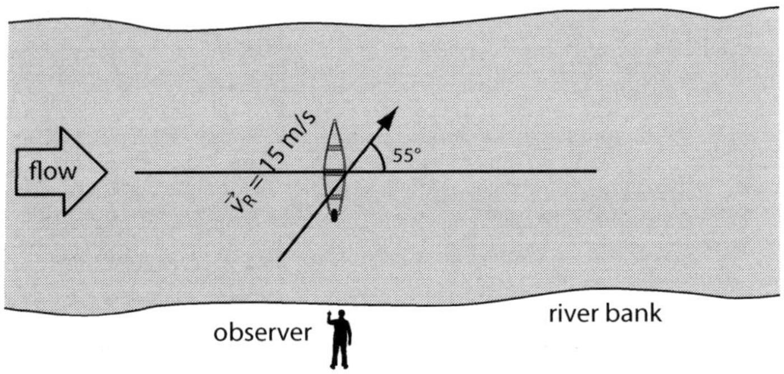

Figure 1.2.10 *The boat is aiming straight across for the shore but is moving diagonally because of the river's current.*

Solution: Consider the resultant velocity to have two component velocities: $\vec{v}_y$, the boat's velocity relative to the water, and $\vec{v}_x$, the water's velocity relative to the bank.

Component $\vec{v}_y$ is directed across the river, perpendicular to the bank, while component $\vec{v}_x$ is directed down the stream. For your vector diagram, only a neat sketch is needed, since you will be using trigonometric ratios rather than a scale diagram. See Figure 1.2.11.

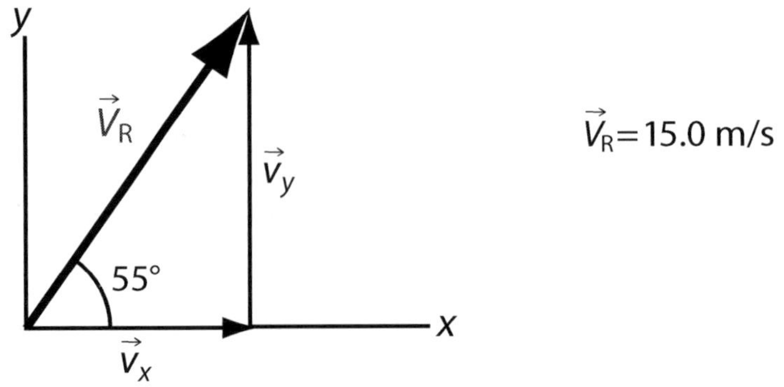

Figure 1.2.11 *Vector diagram showing the direction of the boat*

To solve for $\vec{v}_y$, use

$$\sin 55° = \frac{v_y}{15 \text{ m/s}}$$

$$\vec{v}_y = (15.0 \text{ m/s})(\sin 55°) = (15.0 \text{ m/s})(0.8192) = 12.3 \text{ m/s}$$

To solve for $\vec{v}_x$, use

$$\cos 55° = \frac{v_y}{15 \text{ m/s}}$$

$$\vec{v}_x = (15.0 \text{ m/s})(\cos 55°) = (15.0 \text{ m/s})(0.5736) = 8.60 \text{ m/s}$$

To summarize:

Velocity of the boat relative to the ground	$\vec{v}_R$	15.0 m/s
Velocity of the boat relative to the water	$\vec{v}_B$ or $\vec{v}_y$	12.3 m/s
Velocity of the water relative to the ground	$\vec{v}_C$ or $\vec{v}_x$	8.60 m/s

An airplane vector problem is similar except, instead of water flowing down a river, you must consider wind speed that can come from any direction. The simplest situation is a plane flying with the wind in the same direction (tail wind) or in the opposite direction (head wind). While the plane will have an air speed, which is the speed of the plane relative to the air around it, a person from the ground would see the ground speed being a combination of air speed and wind speed. Figure 1.2.12 demonstrates both of these situations.

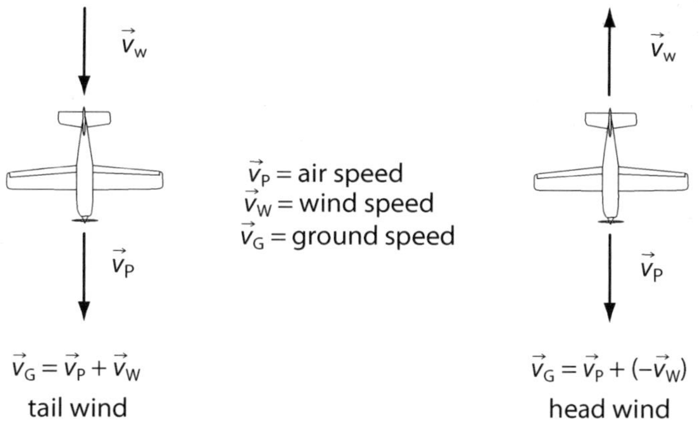

Figure 1.2.12 *The effects of a tail wind and a head wind on an airplane's velocity*

Now, what happens if the wind is moving at an angle to the plane?

Sample Problem 1.2.2 — Relative Motion

What is the ground speed of a plane flying 200 km/h north if the wind is blowing from the east at 40.0 km/h?

What to Think About

1. Identify what you know and what you are solving.
2. Represent the problem with a diagram.
3. Solve using the Pythagorean theorem.

How to Do It

1. $\vec{v}_P = 200 \text{ km/h [N]}$

   $\vec{v}_W = 40.0 \text{ km/h [W]}$

   $\vec{v}_G = ?$

2. 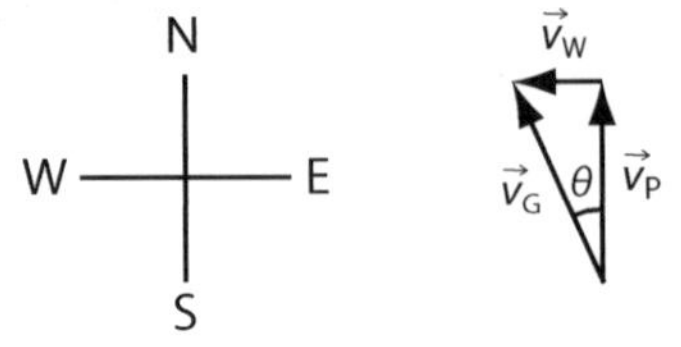

   Figure 1.2.13

3. $\vec{v}_G = \vec{v}_P + \vec{v}_W$

   $v_G = \sqrt{(200 \text{ km/h})^2 + (40 \text{ km/h})^2}$

   $v_G = 204 \text{ km/h}$

   $\text{Tan } \theta = \dfrac{40}{200}$

   $\theta = 11° \text{ W of N}$

Practice Problems 1.2.2 — Relative Motion

1. What is the tailwind a plane experiences if the groundspeed is 350 km/h and the air speed is 320 km/h?

2. A plane flying 275 km/h [W] experiences a 25 km/h [N] wind. At what angle does an observer see the plane flying?

3. What airspeed would a plane have to travel to have a groundspeed of 320 km/h [S] if there is a 50.0 km/h wind coming from the northwest?

1.2 Review Questions

1. It is 256 m across the river in Figure 1.2.11, measured directly from bank to bank.
   (a) If you wished to know how much time it would take to cross the river, which of the three velocity vectors would you use to obtain the answer most directly?

   (b) What is the magnitude of this vector?

   (c) How long would it take to cross the river?

2. You wish to calculate how far down the bank the boat in Figure 1.2.11 will land when it reaches the other side.
   (a) Which velocity vector will give you the answer most directly?

   (b) What is the magnitude of this vector?

   (c) How far down the bank will the boat travel?

3. You absolutely *must* land your boat directly across from your starting point. This time, your resultant velocity will be 15.0 m/s, but in a direction straight across the river. In what direction will you have to aim the boat to end up straight across from your starting point?

4. A girl is mowing her lawn. She pushes down on the handle of the mower with a force of 78 N. If the handle makes an angle of 40° with the horizontal, what is the horizontal component of the force she exerts down the handle?

5. A hunter walks 225 m toward the north, then 125 m toward the east. What is his resultant displacement?

6. An airborne seed falls to the ground with a steady terminal velocity of 0.48 m/s. The wind causes it to drift to the right at 0.10 m/s. What is the magnitude and direction of the resultant velocity?

7. A helium balloon is released and rises with a steady vertical velocity of 12 km/h. A wind from the east blows the balloon toward the west at 18 km/h.
(a) What is the resultant velocity of the balloon?

(b) How far west will the balloon drift in five minutes?

8. (a) In the diagram below, what horizontal force must the boy exert to hold his friend on the swing still?

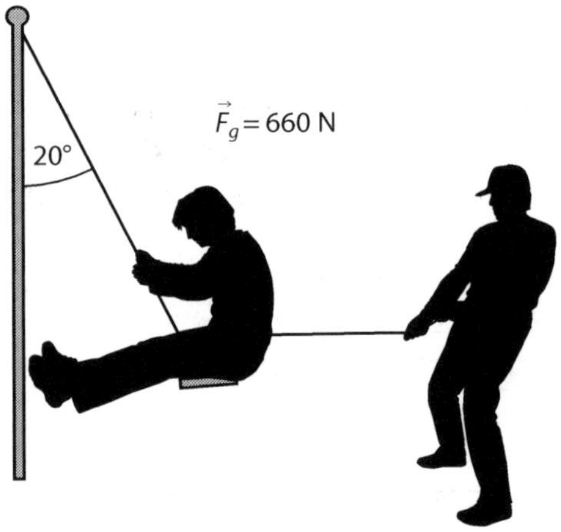

(b) What is the tension in each of the two ropes of the motionless swing, if the two ropes share the load equally?

9. A hockey player is moving north at 15 km/h. A body check changes her velocity to 12 km/h toward the west. Calculate the change in velocity of the hockey player.

1.3 Statics — Forces in Equilibrium

Warm Up

Of the three pictures hanging on a wall, which one has the greatest tension force in the two wires? Explain your reading.

____

____

____

Conditions for Static Equilibrium

You have already observed many situations where several forces acted on a body, yet the body did not move. If a body is at rest, and there are two or more forces acting on it, then the forces acting on the object must have a resultant of zero. Another way of saying this is that the *net force is zero*.

A trivial example of an object having two forces acting on it but a net force of zero is a pen sitting on a flat desk. The force of gravity pulls down on the pen, but it does not accelerate. The table exerts an equal force upward on the pen, so that the net force on the pen is zero.

If the net force on a body is zero, and the body is not moving, it is said to be in a state of **static equilibrium.** In physics, the subject of **statics** deals with the calculation of forces acting on bodies that are in static equilibrium.

First Condition for Static Equilibrium or Translational Equilibrium
For a body to be in static equilibrium, the vector sum of all the forces on it must be zero.

$$\Sigma\vec{F} = 0$$

The sum of the components of *F* must also be zero.

For forces acting in two dimensions,

$$\Sigma\vec{F}_x = 0 \text{ and } \Sigma\vec{F}_y = 0$$

Applications of Static Equilibrium

If you completed Investigation 1.1.1, you worked with force vectors in static equilibrium. This was a static condition because the masses did not move. By measuring the angles between the masses, you constructed a vector diagram that looked something like the one in Figure 1.3.1(a). In the activity, $\vec{F}_1 = 4.0$ N, $\vec{F}_2 = 5.0$ N, and $\vec{F}_3 = 3.0$ N. By adding the force vectors together, you formed a triangle that confirmed your observations that the structure was in static equilibrium.

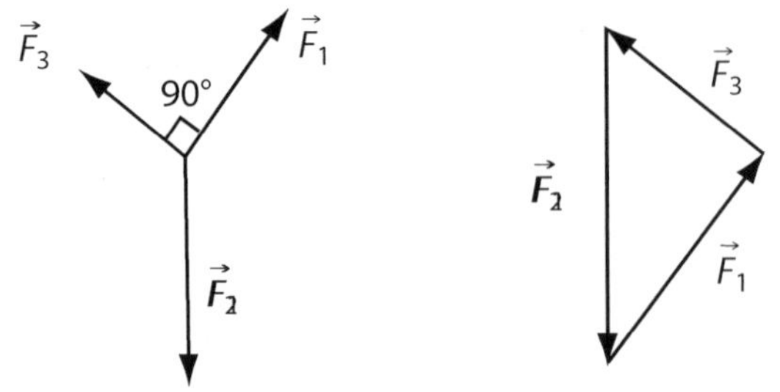

$$\Sigma\vec{F} = 0$$

$$\text{or } \vec{F}_1 + \vec{F}_2 + \vec{F}_3 = 0$$

(a) (b)

Figure 1.3.1 *Adding the force vectors confirmed that the structure was in static equilibrium.*

Another way to solve this problem is to find the *x* component and *y* component of each vector and the sum the *x* and *y* components. For the structure to be in equilibrium, both sets of components sum to zero.

First, resolve each vector into its *x* and *y* components as shown in Table 1.3.1. Using our knowledge of trigonometric ratios and geometry, we find the angle of $\vec{F}_1$ and $\vec{F}_3$ to the horizontal to be 53° and 37°. Now each vector can be resolved into *x* and *y* components. Remember to keep track of the sign of each vector. In this problem, the right direction and up are to be taken as positive.

Table 1.3.1 *Force Vector Components*

	***x* component**	***y* component**	
$\vec{F}_1$	$F_{1x} = F_1 \cos 53°$	$F_{1y} = F_1 \sin 53°$	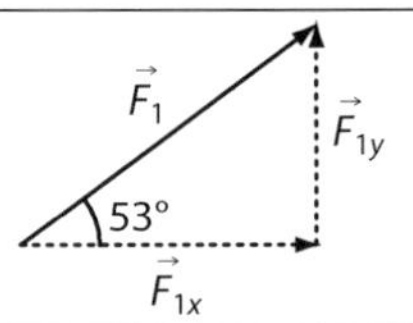
$\vec{F}_2$	No *x component*	$-F_{2y} = -mg$	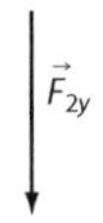
$\vec{F}_3$	$-F_{3x} = -F_3 \cos 37°$	$F_{3y} = F_3 \sin 37°$	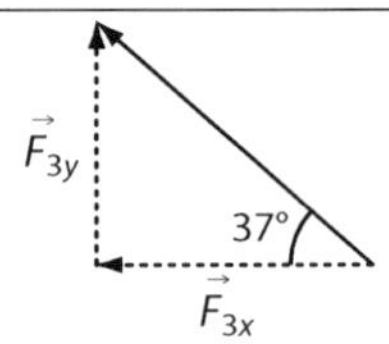
Sum	$\Sigma F_x = F_{1x} + F_{3x} = 0$ $\Sigma F_x = F_1 \cos 53° + (-F_3 \cos 37°)$ $\Sigma F_x = 4.0 \cos 53° + (-3.0 \cos 37°)$ $\Sigma F_x = 0$	$\Sigma F_y = F_{1y} + F_{2y} + F_{3y} = 0$ $\Sigma F_y = F_1 \sin 53° + (-mg) + F_3 \sin 37°$ $\Sigma F_y = 4.0 \sin 53° + (-5.0) + 3.0 \sin 37°$ $\Sigma F_y = 0$	

Based on the sum of each component, we can conclude that the first condition of static equilibrium has been met. The structure is said to be in *translational static equilibrium*, which means no acceleration or motion is occurring.

Sample Problem 1.3.1 — Static Equilibrium

A picture with a mass of 4.00 kg hangs on a wall (Figure 1.3.2). What are the magnitudes of the tension forces in the wires?

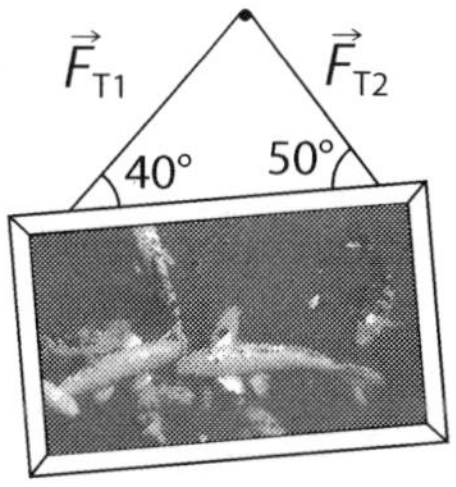

Figure 1.3.2

What to Think About

1. Represent the problem with a diagram to show forces (Figure 1.3.3).
2. All the forces are acting on one point, so this is a translational static equilibrium problem.
3. Find the *x* and *y* components of each vector.
4. Remember that the *x* and y components must sum to zero. Solve to find F_T.

NOTE: There are two variables so you will need two equations and then solve both using the substitution method you learned in Math class

How to Do It

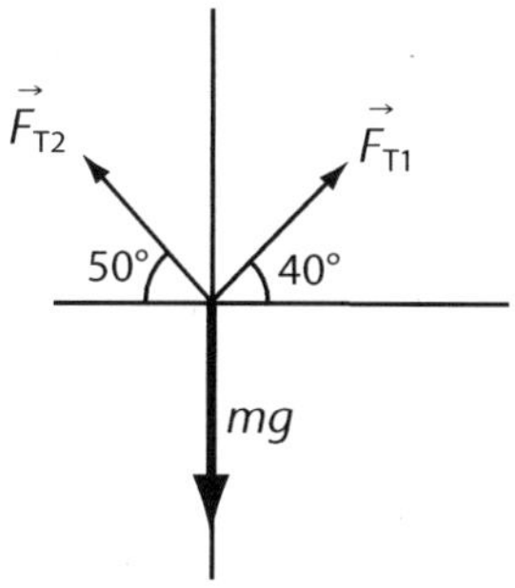

Figure 1.3.3

	x	*y*
F_{T1}	$\cos 40° = \frac{F_{1x}}{F_{T1}}$	$\sin 40° = \frac{F_{1y}}{F_{T1}}$
F_{T2}	$-\cos 50° = \frac{F_{2x}}{F_{T2}}$	$\sin 50° = \frac{F_{2y}}{F_{T2}}$
F_{T3}		$F_3 = -mg$

$\Sigma F = 0$

$F_{T1x} = F_{T2x}$

$F_{T2} \cos 50° = F_{T1} \cos 40°$

$0.643 F_{T2} = 0.766 F_{T1}$

$F_{T1} = \frac{0.643 F_{T2}}{0.766}$

$\Sigma F = 0$

$F_{T1y} + F_{T2y} = F_{T3}$

$F_{T1} \sin 40° + F_{T2} \sin 50° = mg$

$0.643 F_{T1} + 0.766 F_{T2} = mg$

$(0.643)\frac{0.643 F_{T2}}{0.766} + 0.766 F_{T2} = mg$

$F_{T2} = 30.0 \text{ N}$

Use this answer to solve for F_{T1}:

$F_{T1} = 25.2 \text{ N}$

Practice Problems 1.3.1 — Static Equilibrium

1. Two rugby players pull on a ball in the directions shown in Figure 1.3.4. What is the *magnitude* of the force that must be exerted by a third player, to achieve translational static equilibrium of the ball?

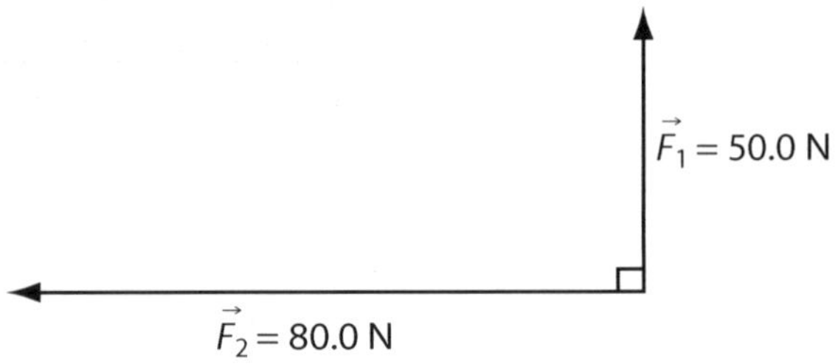

Figure 1.3.4

2. A 50.0 kg mass is supported by a rope. When a horizontal force is used to hold the mass at an angle θ with the vertical, the tension in the rope is 850.0 N. What is angle θ?

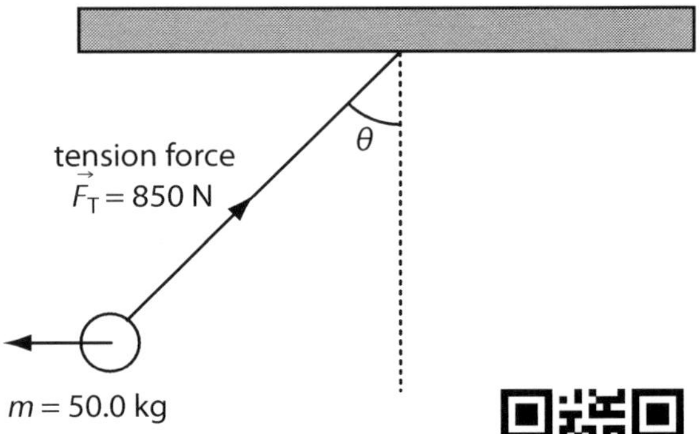

Figure 1.3.5

3. (a) A 100 kg sign is hanging from a beam and supported by a cable at a 30° angle to the beam. What is the tension in the cable if the weight of the beam is negligible?

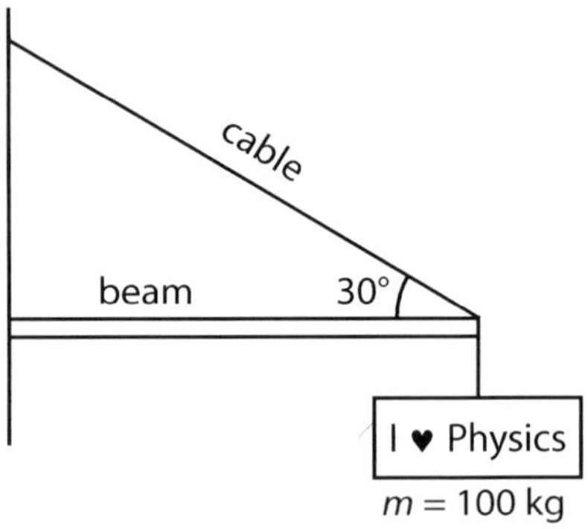

Figure 1.3.6

(b) Why is it important to assume the beam has no weight?

Second Condition for Static Equilibrium or Rotational Equilibrium

In this chapter, you have encountered situations where static equilibrium exists because the net force was zero. In these situations, all the forces acted through one point. Investigation 1.1.1 dealt with this type of static equilibrium, as did many of the examples so far in this chapter. What if the forces do NOT act through the same point?

Torque

In Figure 1.3.7, there are two forces, equal in magnitude, acting on a uniform bar. The forces act in opposite directions, and they act at *different* points on the bar. The net force is zero because the forces are equal but opposite in direction, *but the bar is not in static equilibrium.* Obviously, the bar would rotate about its mid-point. When forces on the same body do not act through the same point, there must be another condition required for static equilibrium. Investigation 1.3.1 looks at this "extra" requirement. First, here are some necessary definitions.

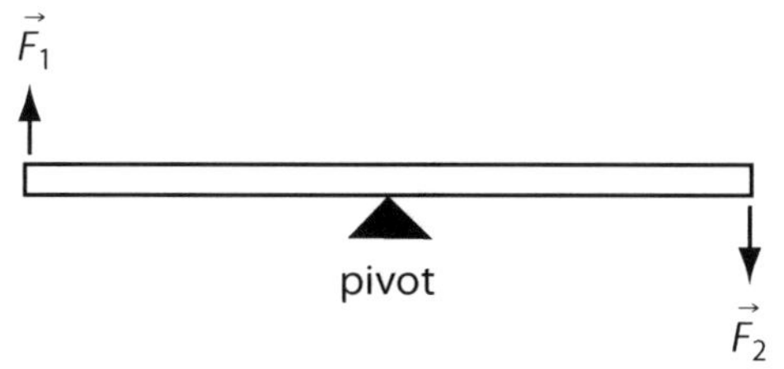

Figure 1.3.7 *The two forces acting on the bar are equal in magnitude but acting in opposite directions.*

In Figure 1.3.8, a force $\vec{F}$ is exerted at a distance ℓ from the **pivot** or **fulcrum**. The product of a force $\vec{F}$ and its distance ℓ from the fulcrum, measured perpendicular to the direction of the force vector, is called the **torque** (τ) of that force about the pivot. The distance ℓ is called the **lever arm**.

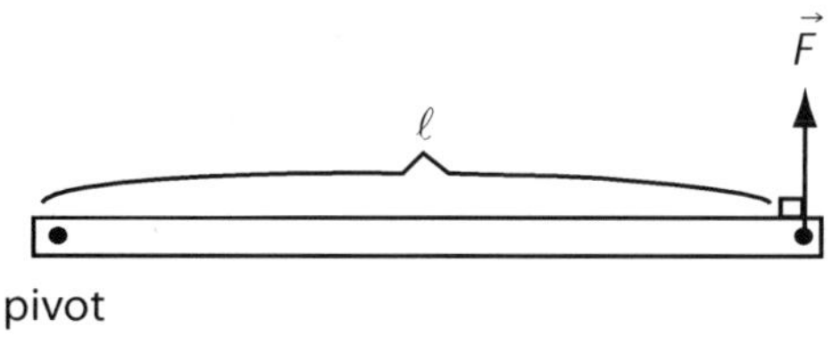

Figure 1.3.8 *The torque is calculated by multiplying a force $\vec{F}$ by its distance ℓ from the pivot.*

The force causing a torque is not always perpendicular to the line joining the pivot to the point where the force is applied. Figure 1.3.9 shows an example of this. Here, the line along which the force acts is at an angle θ to the rod. The force is applied at a distance ℓ from the pivot, but the distance you must use to calculate torque (τ) is the *perpendicular* distance from the pivot to the line of action of the force. This distance is labeled $\ell_\perp$ in Figure 1.3.9.

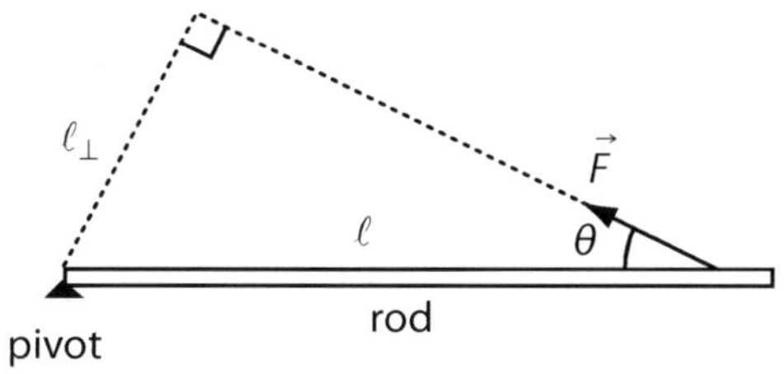

The torque due to force $\vec{F}$ is $\tau = \vec{F} \cdot \ell_\perp$, or $\tau = \vec{F} \cdot \ell \cdot \sin\theta$.

Figure 1.3.9 *The force causing a torque is not always perpendicular.*

Another way of working out the same problem is to use the lever arm ℓ "as is," but use the component of $\vec{F}$ *in a direction perpendicular to the rod*, as shown in Figure 1.3.10. This component is labeled $\vec{F}_{\perp}$.

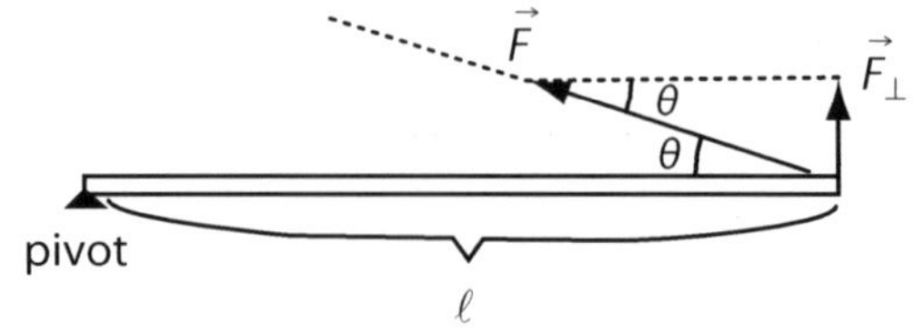

Figure 1.3.10 *A component of $\vec{F}$ perpendicular to the rod can be used to calculate torque.*

In Figure 1.3.10, the torque can be calculated as shown below.

$$\tau = \vec{F}_{\perp} \cdot \ell = [\vec{F} \cdot \sin \theta] \cdot \ell = \vec{F} \cdot \ell \cdot \sin \theta$$

As you can see, this approach gives the same answer as the first method, used in Figure 1.3.10.

Quick Check

1. What is the length of a beam that has a pivot at one end and a 10.0 N force pulling the beam in a clockwise direction so that a torque of 50.0 Nm is produced?

2. A brother and sister are on a teeter-totter at a local park. The brother is twice the weight of his sister. Where should he sit relative to the pivot so that the teeter-totter balances?

3. The rod in Figure 1.3.9 has a length of 2.5 m. A 60.0 N force is exerted at an angle of 30° to the rod, which tends to rotate in an *counterclockwise* direction. Calculate the torque produced by the force.

Centre of Gravity

Every molecule of wood in the metre stick in Figure 1.3.11 has mass and therefore experiences a force due to gravity. The figure shows a few sample vectors that represent the force of gravity on individual molecules making up the wood. The resultant of all these force vectors would be the total force of gravity on the metre stick. Where would the resultant force appear to act?

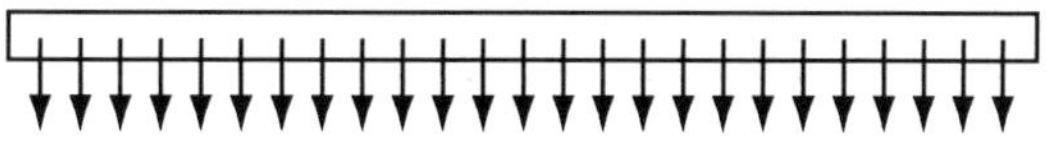

Figure 1.3.11 *The force of gravity acts on every part of the metre stick.*

You know from experience that there is a point within any rigid body where a single upward force can be used to balance the force of gravity on the body without causing any rotation of the body. For example, if you hold a metre stick with the tip of your finger at the mid-point of the uniform stick, the metre stick will remain in static equilibrium. (It will not move up, down, or sideways, and it will have no tendency to rotate.)

There is a single point in a body where the force of gravity may be considered to act. This point is called the **centre of gravity** of the body. A body supported at its centre of gravity by a force equal to the force of gravity on the body (but in the opposite direction) will experience no translational or rotational motion as a result of the supporting force.

Figure 1.3.12 shows four objects with differing shapes. The label "CG" indicates the probable location of the centre of gravity. Notice that the CG may be *outside* the solid part of the object, as is the case with the drinking glass.

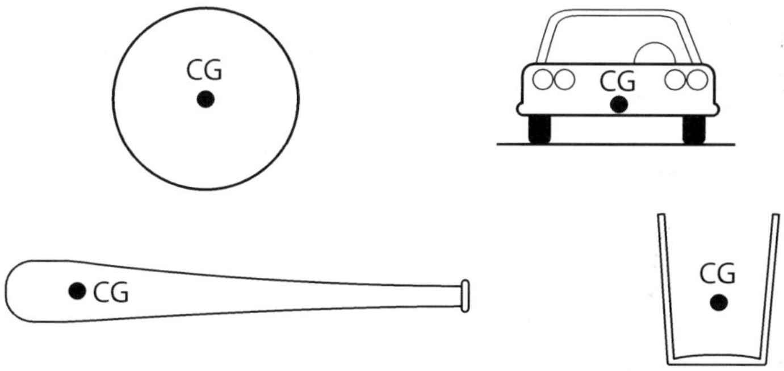

Figure 1.3.12 *Examples of the location of the centre of gravity (CG) in different objects.*

Centre of Mass

The **centre of mass** of an object is the point where the mass of the object might be considered to be concentrated for the purpose of calculation. For most situations, the centre of mass is in the same place as the centre of gravity. An exception would be when the gravitational field over the object being considered is non-uniform. This would have to be a very large object! The centre of mass of a large spherical planet would be at the centre of the planet, if its mass is uniformly distributed. Where would you expect the centre of mass of the Earth-Moon system to be located?

Earlier in this chapter, it was shown that for a body to be in translational static equilibrium, the vector sum of all the forces on it must be zero. This means that the sum of all the forces acting up must equal the sum of all the forces acting down. The sum of all the forces acting to the left must equal the sum of all the forces acting to the right. No matter how you look at it, the first condition for static equilibrium is:

$$\Sigma \vec{F} = 0$$

If you completed Investigation 1.3.1, you found that for rotational equilibrium, a second requirement must be met. Not only must the vector sum of the forces on a body be zero, but also the sum of all the clockwise torques must equal the sum of all the counterclockwise torques.

Second Condition for Static Equilibrium

$$\Sigma \tau_{\text{clockwise}} = \Sigma \tau_{\text{counterclockwise}}$$

If a torque which tends to make an object rotate counterclockwise is assigned a positive (+) value, and a clockwise torque is assigned a negative (–) value, then the second condition for static equilibrium can be written this way:

$$\Sigma \tau = 0$$

Investigation 1.3.1 Rotational Equilibrium

Purpose

To investigate the conditions necessary to prevent the rotation of a loaded beam

Procedure

1. Figure 1.3.13 shows you how to find the centre of gravity of a metre stick very quickly. Hold the metre stick on your two index fingers, as in the diagram. Slowly slide your fingers toward each other. When they meet, they will have the centre of gravity "surrounded." Try this several times.

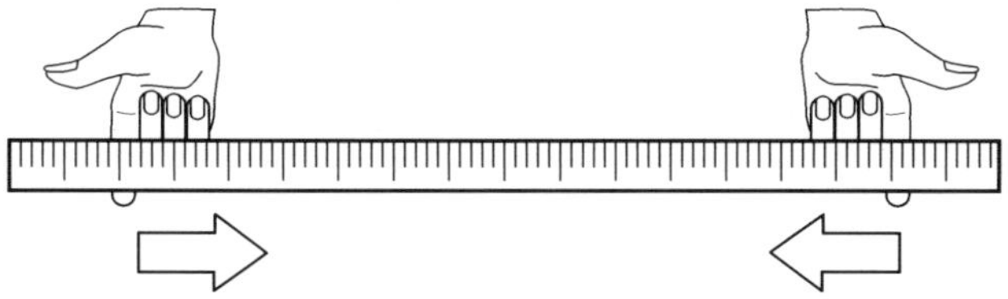

Figure 1.3.13

2. Mount your metre stick on a stand (Figure 1.3.14) with the pivot exactly at the centre of gravity. (Few metre sticks are perfectly uniform, so do not assume that the centre of gravity (CG) is at the 50.0 cm mark.) Adjust the pivot point precisely until the metre stick is in equilibrium. Record the position of the CG to the nearest millimetre.

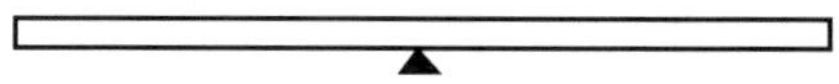

Figure 1.3.14

3. Use a very thin, light piece of wire to attach a 1.00 kg mass at a distance of 20.0 cm from the pivot. The force of gravity on this mass will be 9.80 N. This force is labeled $\vec{F}_1$ on Figure 1.3.15. The distance from the pivot to the point where $\vec{F}_1$ acts is called the lever arm and is labelled ℓ_1. The torque due to $\vec{F}_1$ produces a clockwise turning effect, so it is called a clockwise torque. It is labelled τ_1. ($\tau_1 = \vec{F}_1 \ell_1$).

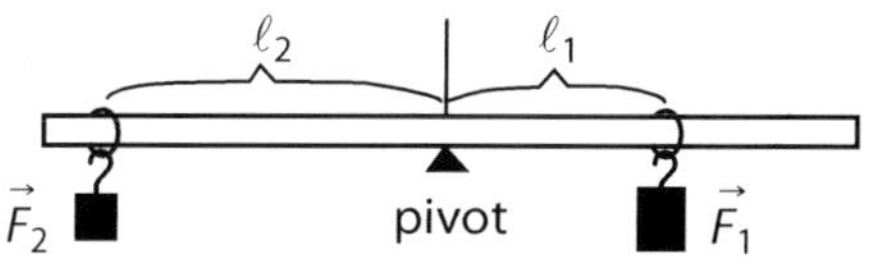

Figure 1.3.15

4. Suspend a 500 g mass by a light piece of wire on the other side of the metre stick. Adjust its lever arm until the metre stick is in a state of equilibrium. The force of gravity on the 500 g mass is 4.90 N. Call this force $\vec{F}_2$ and its lever arm ℓ_2. The torque τ_2 is a counterclockwise torque. ($\tau_2 = \vec{F}_2 \ell_2$) Record the forces and lever arms in a table like Table 1.3.2. Calculate the torques and enter them in the table for Trial 1. (Torque is expressed in N·m.)

Table 1.3.2 *Observations for Investigation 1.3.1*

Trial	$\vec{F}_1$	ℓ_1	τ_1	$\vec{F}_2$	ℓ_2	τ_2	$\vec{F}_3$	ℓ_3	τ_3	$\tau_2 + \tau_3$
	(N)	(m)	(N·m)	(N)	(m)	(N·m)	(N)	(m)	(N·m)	(N·m)
1										
2										
3										
4										

5. Repeat the experiment, but place the 1.0 kg mass 25.0 cm from the pivot. Use *two* masses to produce counterclockwise torques and adjust their positions until the metre stick is at equilibrium. Measure and record all the forces and lever arms in Table 1.3.2. Calculate torques τ_1, τ_2, and τ_3 and record them in Table 1.3.2. (Trial 2.)
6. Try another combination of at least three forces of your own choosing. Record all forces and lever arms and calculate all the torques needed to produce rotational equilibrium. (Trial 3.)
7. Finally, set up your metre stick as in Figure 1.3.16 so that the force of gravity on the metre stick produces a clockwise torque. Place the CG 20.0 cm to the right of the pivot. Use a 100 g mass (force of gravity 0.980 N) to balance the metre stick. Move the mass to a position where the metre stick stays balanced. Record all your data in Table 1.3.2 (Trial 4). Note that in this case $\vec{F}_1$ is the unknown force of gravity on the metre stick.

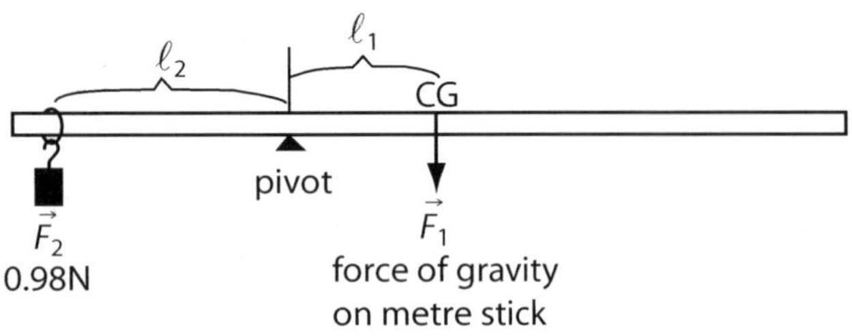

Figure 1.3.16

8. Hang the metre stick from a spring balance and measure the force of gravity on the metre stick, according to the spring balance. Keep a record of this force.

Concluding Questions

1. Examine your calculated torques for each trial. When rotational equilibrium is achieved, what can you conclude regarding the clockwise torque(s) when compared with the counterclockwise torque(s)? State a general rule describing the condition(s) required for rotational equilibrium.
2. What are some likely sources of error that might cause discrepancies in your results? What is the maximum percent difference you observed when comparing the sum of the clockwise torques with the sum of the counterclockwise torques?
3. Use the general rule you described in (1) to calculate the force of gravity on your metre stick (Procedure step 7), using only the torques involved. Calculate the percentage difference between your calculated force of gravity and the force of gravity according to the spring balance. Explain any discrepancy you observe.

Challenges

1. Explain why you can find the centre of gravity of a rod or metre stick using the method in Procedure step 1. Why do you think your fingers always meet at (or surrounding) the centre of gravity?
2. An equal-arm balance will work only if there is a gravitational field, $\vec{g}$. Explain why such a balance will "read" the same mass whether it is used on Earth or on the Moon, where $\vec{g}$ is only 1/6 of that on Earth.
3. A golfer wishes to know where the centre of gravity of his putter face is. He can find out quickly by holding the putter face horizontal and bouncing a golf ball on the face of the putter, which is held loosely in his other hand. How does he know when he is bouncing the ball off the CG?

1.3 Review Questions

1. What force $\vec{F}_1$ is needed to balance the beam in the diagram below?

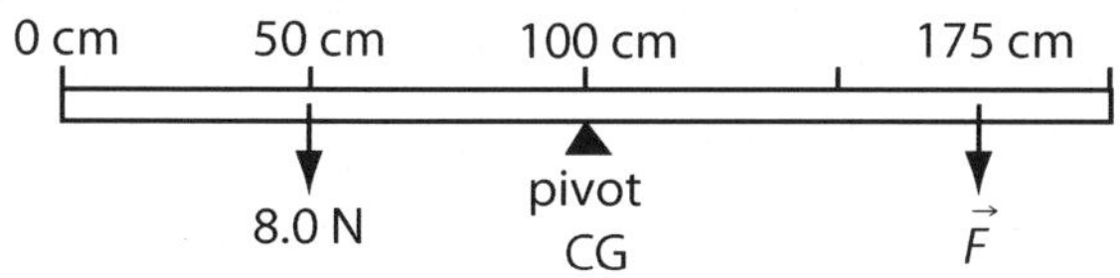

2. How far from the pivot must the 64 N object be placed to balance the beam in the diagram below?

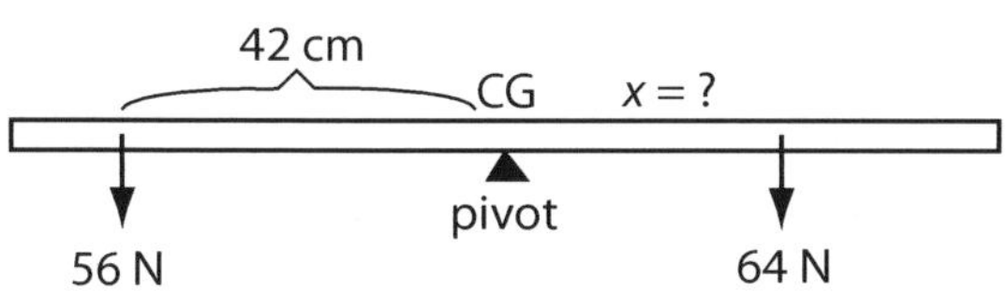

3. What upward force $\vec{F}_1$ is needed to achieve rotational equilibrium in the diagram below?

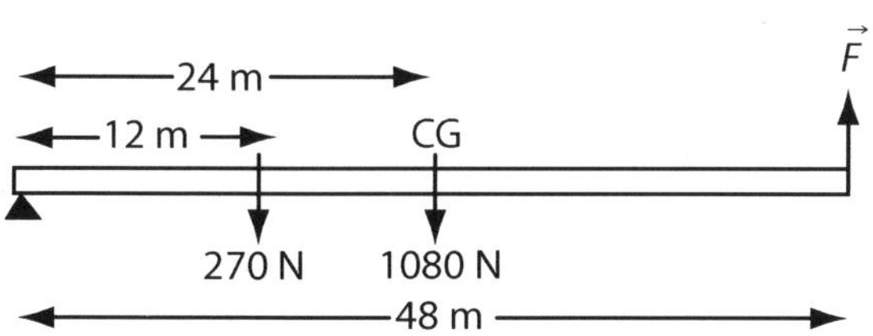

4. The force of gravity on the bridge in the diagram below is 9.60×10^5 N. What upward force must be exerted at end Q to support the bridge and the truck, if the force of gravity on the truck is 4.80×10^4 N? **Hint:** Treat the bridge as if it were a lever with an imaginary pivot at P. What torques tend to rotate the "lever" about pivot P?

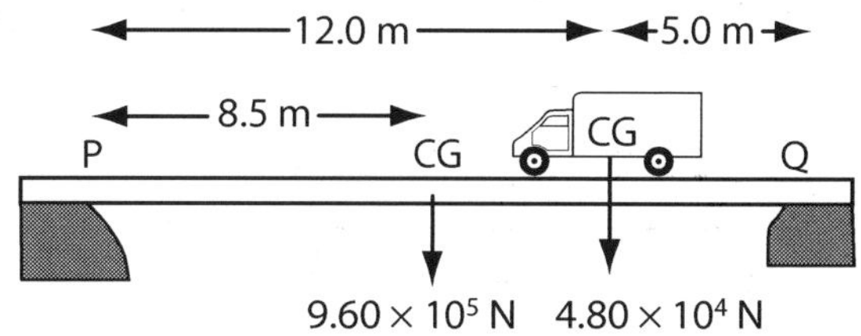

5. A small 42.0 N sign is suspended from the end of a hinged rod, which is 2.40 m long and uniform in shape as shown in the diagram below. What tension force exists in the rope holding up both the rod and the sign? The rope makes an angle of 60° with the 36.0 N rod.

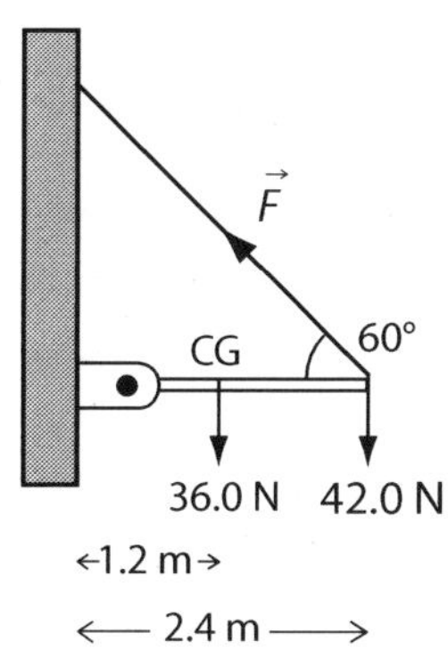

Chapter 1 Review Questions

1. What is the difference between a scalar quantity and a vector quantity?

2. A man walks 1.00×10^2 m south, then 2.4×10^2 m east. What is his resultant displacement?

3. Two forces act on point Q. One is 5.0 N toward the south and the other is 3.0 N toward the east. Find the magnitude and direction of the third force that will be needed to produce static equilibrium.

4. A girl pulls her friend across the ice on a sled with a force of 66.0 N. The rope on which she pulls makes an angle of 32° with the ice.
   (a) What is the horizontal component of the force she exerts along the rope?
   (b) If the friction force between the sled and the ice is 46.0 N, what is the unbalanced force in the horizontal direction?
   (c) Will her friend accelerate, decelerate, or move with constant velocity?

5. A plane has a velocity of 951 km/h in a direction 35° west of north. What are its west and north components?

6. A jet aircraft is aimed south and travelling 851 km/h. A wind blows the plane toward the east at 36.0 km/h. What is its resultant velocity?

7. A man is lost in the woods. He wanders 3.0 km north, then 7.0 km east, then 7.0 km south, then 4.0 km west. What is the magnitude and direction of his resultant displacement?

8. A 6.0×10^3 kg vehicle is parked on a slight down slope making an angle of 6.7° with the horizontal.
   (a) What is the force of gravity on the vehicle?

   (b) What is the component of the force of gravity acting in a direction parallel with the slope?

   (c) What friction force is needed to keep the vehicle from accelerating down the slope?

9. The heavy pendulum below is held motionless by the force on the horizontal rope.

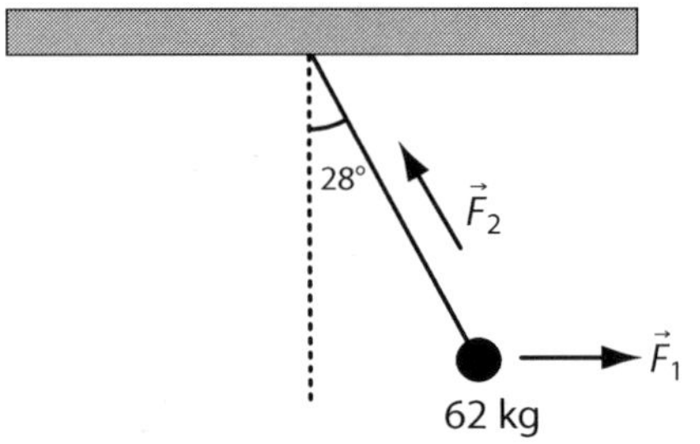

Calculate:
(a) the tension in the horizontal rope.

(b) the tension in the rope supporting the pendulum at 28° to the vertical.

10. In the diagram below, the each angle θ is formed by the two sides of the "V" made by the rope.

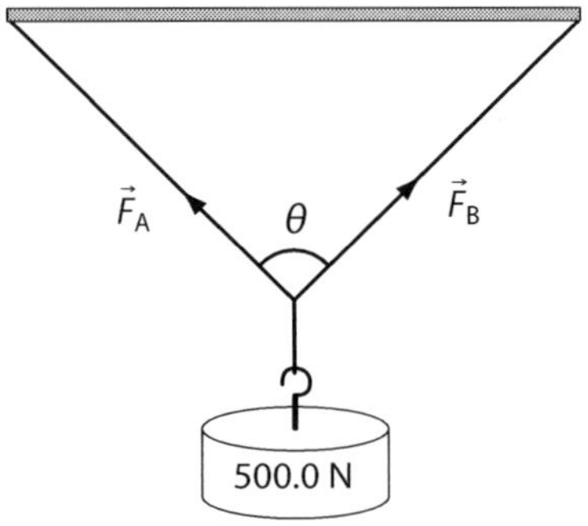

What is the tension in each supporting rope in the diagram below for is:
(a) 0°?

(b) 90°?

(c) 120°?

(d) 170°?

(e) 180°?

11. The two ropes in the diagram below support the 500.0 N load between them, but they act at different angles.

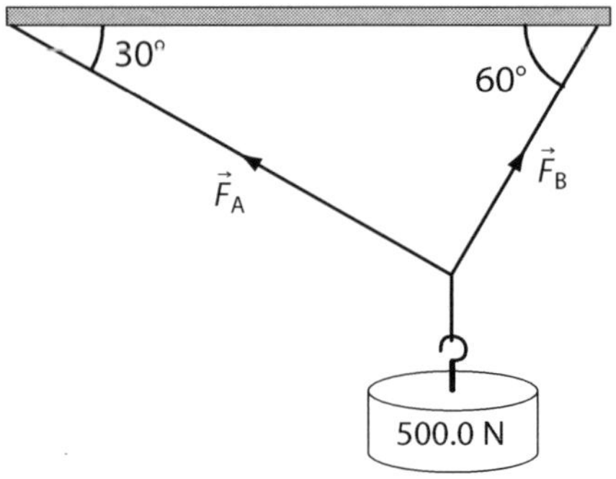

(a) What must the resultant of the two tension forces in the ropes be?

(b) What is the magnitude and direction of the tension in each of the two ropes?

12. A weather balloon rises upward at a rate of 6.4 m/s, but a wind blows it toward the east at 4.8 m/s.
(a) What is its resultant velocity?

(b) How long will it take to drift across a lake that is 12.0 km wide?

13. A 588 N mother sits on one side of a seesaw, 2.20 m from the pivot. Her daughter sits 2.00 m from the pivot on the other side of the seesaw. If the force of gravity on this child is 256 N, where must the mother's other child sit to balance the seesaw if the force of gravity on him is 412 N?

14. If the force exerted by the fish line on the tip of the rod is 4.0 N, what force must the person fishing exert in the direction and location shown in the drawing below? Ignore the rod's mass, and assume the rod is pivoted in the other hand.

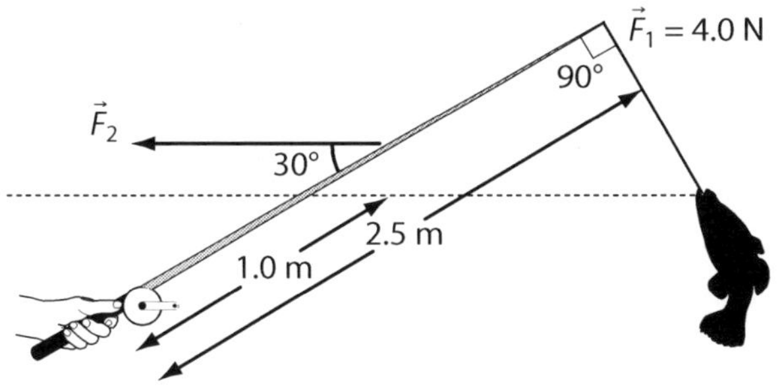

15. What upward force is exerted by the right support leg of the bench in the drawing below?

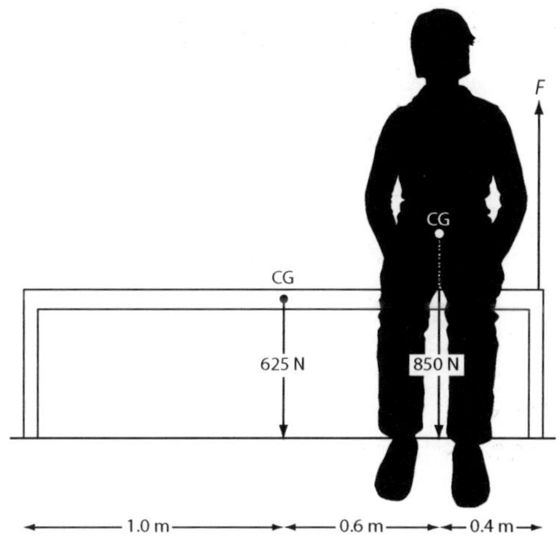

16. If the force of gravity on the beam in the diagram below is 1.2×10^3 N, what forces must be exerted at A and B to maintain equilibrium? In what direction must each force act?

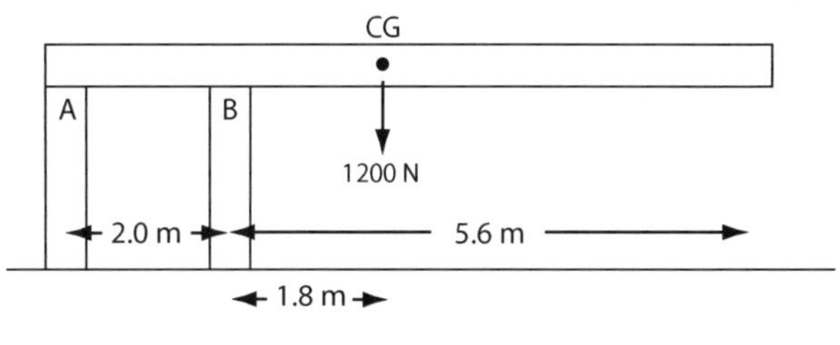

17. A golfer hits her drive 225 m in a direction 15° east of north. Her second shot is hit 175 m in a direction 20° west of north, and it ends up 3.0 m short of the hole on a direct line from the tee to the hole. How far is it from the tee to the hole?

18. If Earth's mass is 6.0×10^{24} kg and the Moon's mass is 7.4×10^{22} kg, where is the centre of mass of the Earth-Moon system? The distance from Earth's centre to the Moon's centre is 3.8×10^{5} km. Make a sketch showing approximately where the centre of mass of the Earth-Moon system would be located.

19. A uniform 15 kg ladder that is 5.0 m long stands on the floor and leans against a vertical wall, making an angle of 25° with the vertical. If the friction between the ladder and the wall is negligible, what is the minimum amount of friction between the ladder and the floor that will keep the ladder from slipping?

21. If a ladder like the one in question 20 makes an angle θ with the wall, has a mass m, and is uniform in design, show that the minimum force of friction that must exist between the ladder and floor to keep the ladder from slipping is given by

$$F_{fr} = \frac{1}{2} mg \tan \theta$$

Chapter 1 Extra Practice

1. What is the magnitude of the resultant of the three forces acting at point X?

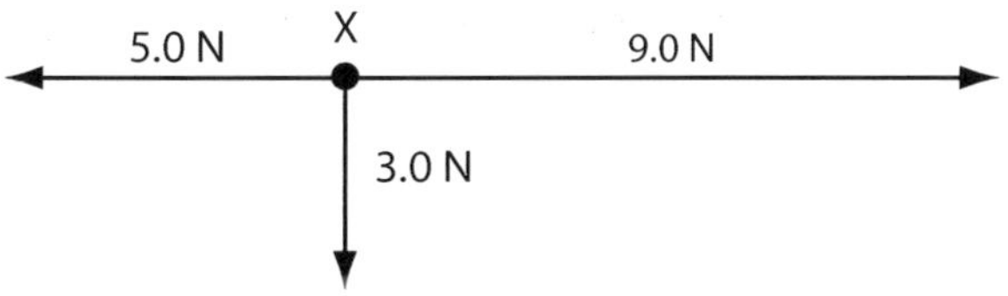

2. The current in a river is such that the water flows toward the north at 2.1 m/s. An alligator swims toward the west at 2.4 m/s relative to the water. What is the resultant direction of travel of the alligator?

3. Two rugby players pull on a ball in the directions shown in the diagram below. What is the magnitude of the force that must be exerted by a third player, to achieve translational equilibrium of the ball?

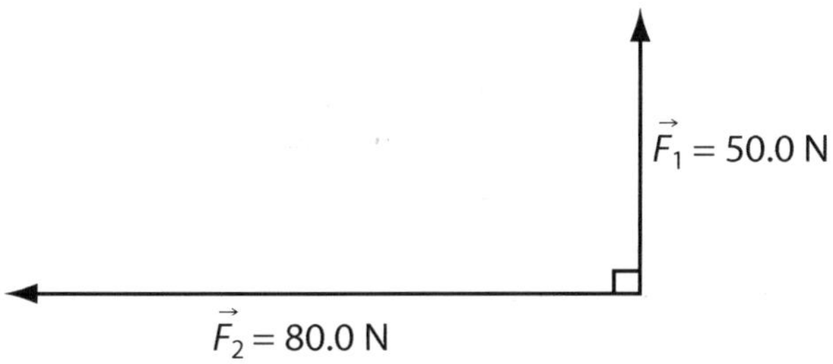

4. A 50.0 kg mass is supported by a rope. When a horizontal force is used to hold the mass at an angle θ with the vertical, the tension in the rope is 850.0 N. What is angle θ?

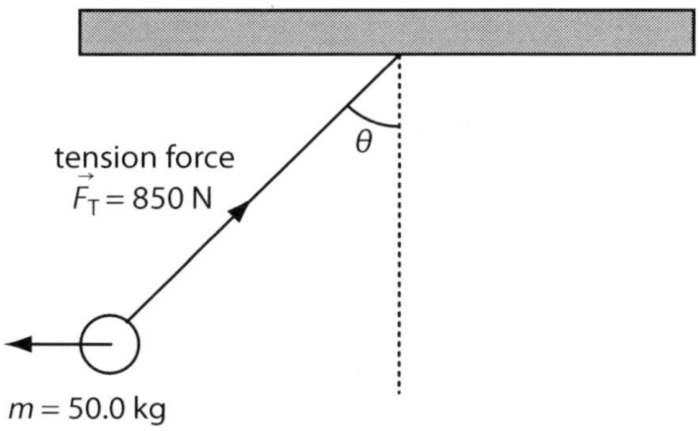

5. An airplane heads due west with an airspeed of 84 m/s. Because of a wind blowing due north, the speed of the airplane relative to the ground is 98 m/s. What is the wind speed?

6. Golfer Arnold Hacker requires three putts from position A to put his ball in the hole. His first putt, from A to B, travels 8.0 m south. His second putt, from B to C, travels 1.2 m southwest. His third putt, from C to the hole at D, travels 0.50 m northwest. What would be the magnitude and direction of the single putt that would have put the ball into the hole, from A to D?

7. A 15.0 N force is used to hold a mass on a string at an angle of 32° from the vertical, as in the above diagram. What is the mass?

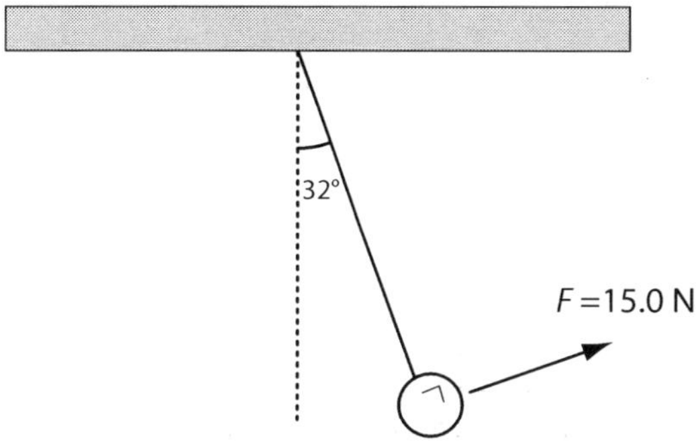

8. A 25 kg teeter-totter of uniform density is pivoted at its centre. A 35 kg girl is sitting on one side, 1.60 m from the centre. On the other side of the teeter-totter, how far from the pivot must her 54 kg boyfriend sit in order to balance the teeter-totter?

9. A traffic light is suspended midway between two supports, as shown in the diagram below.

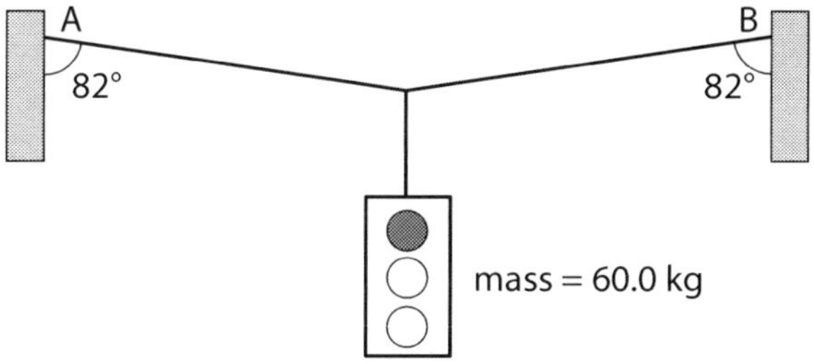

   (a) If the mass of the traffic light is 60.0 kg, what is the tension in the cord between A and B, supporting the light?
   (b) Explain why it is not possible to have the cord absolutely straight between the two supports in this static equilibrium situation.

10. A pivot is 0.50 m from end A of a 2.2 m uniform beam. A load of 8.0 kg at end A will cause the beam to be balanced on the pivot. What is the mass of the beam?

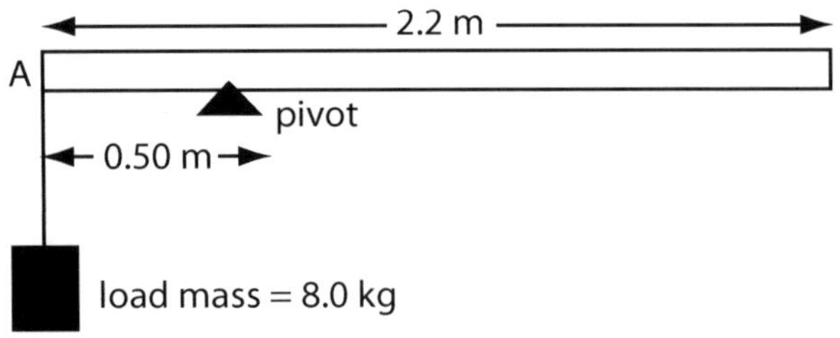

11. A horizontal beam 2.10 m long has negligible mass. If the rope exerts a 50.0 N horizontal force on the beam, what is the force of gravity on the load?

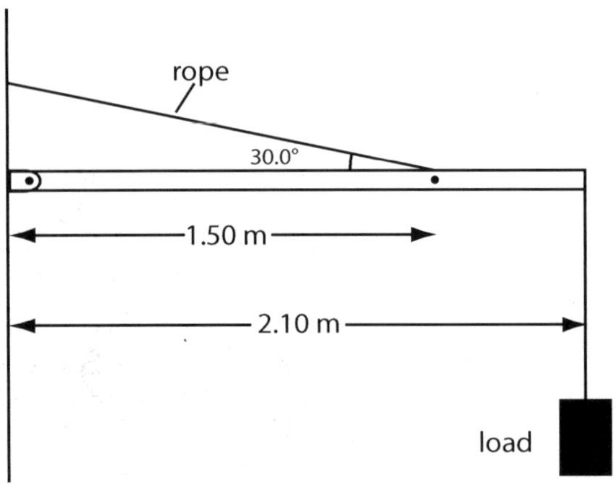

12. A cable supports a uniform boom, which is pivoted at point P. If the cable is attached two-thirds of the way along the boom from P, and the tension force in the cable is 840 N, what is the force of gravity on the boom?

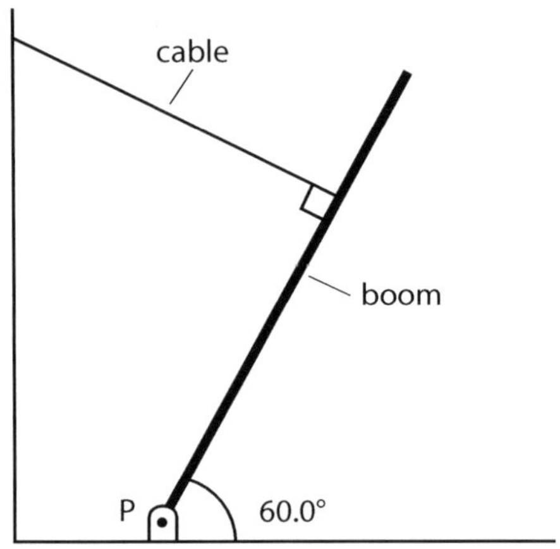

2 Kinematics

By the end of this chapter, you should be able to do the following:

- Apply the concepts of motion to various situations where acceleration is constant

By the end of this chapter, you should know the meaning of these **key terms**:

- acceleration
- acceleration due to gravity
- average speed
- average velocity
- displacement
- final velocity
- free fall
- horizontal velocity
- initial velocity
- instantaneous speed
- position
- projectile motion
- vertical velocity

By the end of this chapter, you should be able to use and know when to use the following formulae:

$v_f = v_0 + at \qquad d = \frac{v_0 + v_f}{2} \cdot t$

$d = v_0 t + ½at^2 \qquad v_f^2 = v_0^2 + 2ad$

Motocross trick rider Mike Samson of Kamloops, BC, provides a spectacular example of motion in two dimensions.

2.1 Uniform Acceleration

Warm Up

What three controls in an automobile can make it accelerate?

____

____

____

Review of Basic Definitions

Kinematics deals with the description of motion without reference to the causes of the motion. A brief review of some of the definitions you studied earlier should be helpful to you.

Position

In order to describe the motion of an object, you must first be able to describe its **position**—where it is at any particular time. More precisely, you need to specify its position relative to a convenient reference frame. Earth is often used as a reference frame, and we often describe the position of an object as it relates to stationary objects in that reference frame. For example, the location of your school is described in terms of the position of the school with respect to Earth, while your position in class could be described in terms of where you are in relation to the door. In other cases, (e.g., in vector problems), we use reference frames that are not stationary but are in motion relative to Earth. To describe the position of a person in a boat, for example, we use the boat, not Earth, as the reference frame.

Displacement

If an object moves relative to a reference frame, then the object's position changes. This change in position is known as displacement. The word "displacement" implies that an object has moved or has been displaced. **Displacement** is the change in position of an object:

$$\Delta x = x_f - x_0$$

where Δx is displacement, x_f is the final position, and x_0 is the initial position. Note that displacement has a direction as well as a magnitude. In one-dimensional motion, direction can be specified with a plus or minus sign. When you begin a problem, you should select which direction is positive. Usually that will be to the right or up, but you are free to select positive as being any direction.

For example, a student has a locker 10.0 m from the physics classroom door as in Figure 2.1.1. To walk from the locker to the door is a displacement of 10.0 m.

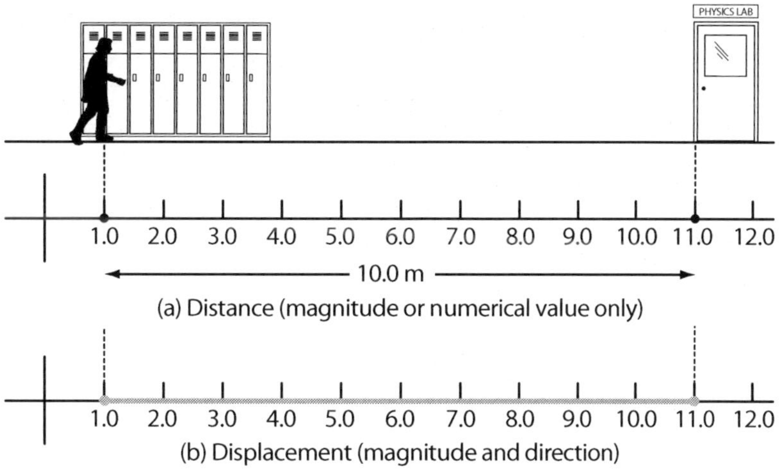

Figure 2.1.1 *Displacement is a change in position and indicates the direction of the change.*

$$\Delta x = x_f - x_0$$
$$\Delta x = 11.0 \text{ m} - 1.00 \text{ m}$$
$$\Delta x = 10.0 \text{ m}$$

Note that the plus sign indicating direction is often omitted as being understood, so the displacement is written as $\Delta x = 10.0$ m rather than $\Delta x = +10.0$ m. If the student forgot something and had to return to the locker, the displacement would be zero because the student is back in the same place from which he started.

Distance

Displacement is described in terms of direction, but distance is not. **Distance** is defined to be the magnitude or size of displacement between two positions. Note that the distance between two positions is not always the same as the distance travelled between them. Distance travelled is the total length of the path travelled between two positions. Distance has no direction and, thus, no sign. In Figure 2.1.1 the distance the student walks is 10.0 m. If he forgets something in his locker and walks back, his distance traveled is then 20.0 m

Speed

The **average speed** $\bar{v}$ of an object is defined as the **distance** *d* it travels divided by the **time** *t* it takes to travel that distance.

$$\text{average speed} = \frac{\text{distance}}{\text{time}} \quad or \quad \bar{v} = \frac{d}{t}$$

Speeds are expressed in a variety of units, such as m/s, km/h, or km/s.

A vehicle that travels 450 km in 5.5 h has an average speed of $\frac{450 \text{ km}}{5.5 \text{ h}}$, which equals 82 km/h. During the trip, the vehicle's speed would vary from minute to minute. Its speed at a particular instant, as shown on the speedometer, is called its **instantaneous speed**, *v*.

Velocity

Velocity is a vector quantity, whereas speed is a scalar. The velocity of an object is its speed in a particular direction. While speed is distance divided by time, velocity is *displacement* $\vec{d}$ divided by time. Displacement, of course, is also a vector quantity.

$$\text{average velocity} = \frac{\text{displacement}}{\text{time}} \quad \textit{or} \quad \vec{v} = \frac{\vec{d}}{t}$$

If you travel 400.0 km south, then return 400.0 km north, and the whole trip takes you 10.0 h, your average speed for the trip is 800.0 km ÷ 10.0 h or 80.0 km/h. Your average velocity, however, is zero. This is because the vector sum of the south displacement vector and the north displacement vector is zero, which means that the average velocity for the trip is zero.

Acceleration

A body **accelerates** when it changes speed or direction or both. Average acceleration is defined as the change in velocity divided by the time elapsed during the change in velocity.

$$\text{average acceleration} = \frac{\text{change in velocity}}{\text{time interval}} \quad \textit{or} \quad \vec{a} = \frac{\Delta\vec{v}}{\Delta t} = \frac{\vec{v}_f - \vec{v}_0}{t_f - t_0}$$

Generally speaking, the time interval $t_f - t_0$ is simply called t. Remember that acceleration and velocity are vector quantities, and in situations where changes in direction occur, you must use the vector difference. In many situations, we will only be concerned with the magnitudes of velocities and/or accelerations. In these situations, the symbols v and a will be used and the direction will not be reported out.

Positive and Negative Acceleration

Sometimes a moving object will have a negative acceleration and be speeding up. This can seem confusing because you may think a negative acceleration means the object is slowing down. Before you make this assumption, remember that acceleration is a vector and direction is important. Check the direction of the velocity of the object. If the velocity and acceleration are in the same direction, then the object is speeding up. This is acceleration. If the velocity and acceleration are in the different directions, the object is slowing down. This is deceleration. The sign attached to the acceleration is only indicating the direction of the acceleration. Usually acceleration to the right is positive and to the left is negative. Figure 2.1.2 summarizes the four possible combinations of velocity and acceleration.

	Speeding Up	Slowing Down
Positive Acceleration	→ $\vec{v}$ → $\vec{a}$	← $\vec{v}$ → $\vec{a}$
Negative Acceleration	← $\vec{v}$ ← $\vec{a}$	→ $\vec{v}$ ← $\vec{a}$

Figure 2.1.2 *Four instances for velocity and acceleration*

Uniform Acceleration

You will often deal with situations where acceleration is uniform or constant. A review of the laws governing uniform acceleration is provided here because these laws are used often in this course. Figure 2.1.3 is a graph showing how the speed of a uniformly accelerated object varies with time. The object is moving with speed v_0 at time t_0 and with speed v_f at the end of elapsed time *t*.

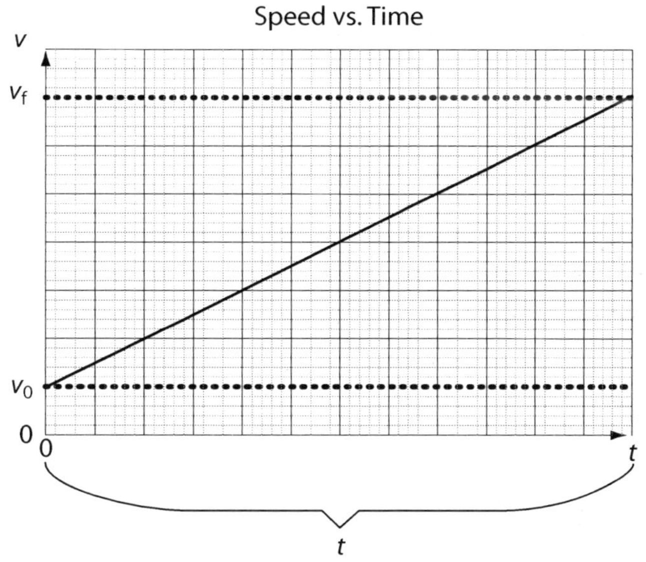

Figure 2.1.3 *Graph of speed vs. time for a uniformly accelerated object*

Consider the slope of the speed-time graph in Figure 2.1.3. Since we are interested in speeds, the symbol *v* is used. Speed is the magnitude of a velocity, so it is a scalar quantity.

$$\text{slope} = \frac{\text{rise}}{\text{run}} = \frac{v_f - v_0}{t - 0}$$

Obviously, the slope is equal to the acceleration of the body.

$$a = \frac{v_f - v_0}{t - 0}$$

The equation for the straight-line graph in Figure 2.1.3 can therefore be written as Equation I.

Equation I $\vec{v}_f = \vec{v}_0 + \vec{a}t$

Sample Problem 2.1.1 — Acceleration

What is the acceleration of a car that reaches 30 km/h in 5.0 s after the signal light turns green?

What to Think About	How to Do It
1. Is there uniform acceleration?	Yes
2. What do you know?	$v_o = 0$ m/s $v_f = 30.0 \frac{\text{km}}{\text{h}} \times \frac{1000 \text{ m}}{1 \text{ km}} \times \frac{1 \text{ h}}{3600 \text{ s}} = 8.3$ m/s $t = 5.0$ s $a = ?$
3. Solve	$\vec{v}_f = \vec{v}_o + \vec{a}t$ $\vec{v}_f - \vec{v}_o = \vec{a}t$ $\vec{a} = \frac{\vec{v}_f - \vec{v}_o}{t}$ $\vec{a} = \frac{8.3 \text{ m/s} - 0}{5.0 \text{ s}} = 1.7 \text{ m/s}^2$

Practice Problems 2.1.1 — Acceleration

1. How long does it take a car to reach 20 m/s if it starts at 2.0 m/s and accelerates at 4.5 m/s^2?

2. A motorbike takes 2.2 s to reach 35 km/h at an acceleration of 3.5 m/s^2. What was the initial velocity?

Practice Problems continued

Practice Problems 2.1.1 — Acceleration (continued)

3. A cheetah has a maximum velocity of about 100 km/h. If the animal stops in 1.20 s, what is the acceleration?

What distance *d* does a uniformly accelerating body travel during a time interval, *t*? You know that distance = average speed x time, or

$$d = \bar{v} \cdot t$$

Now, for uniformly accelerated motion, the average speed occurs halfway between v_0 and v_f, so we can write Equation II.

Equation II $$d = \frac{v_0 + v_f}{2} \cdot t$$

From Equation I, we know that $v_f = v_0 + at$, and we can substitute for v_f in Equation II.

$$d = \frac{v_0 + v_0 + at}{2} \cdot t$$

This gives us Equation III.

Equation III $$d = v_0 t + \frac{1}{2}at^2$$

Sample Problem 2.1.2 — Uniform Acceleration: Finding Displacement or Distance

A dragster racecar has an average acceleration of 25.0 m/s². How far does the car travel in 6.02 s? Can it cover a half-kilometre track in this time?

What to Think About	How to Do It
1. Is there uniform acceleration?	Yes
2. What do you know?	$v_0 = 0$ m/s $t = 5.0$ s $a = 25.0$ m/s² $d = ?$
3. Solve	$d = v_0 t + \frac{1}{2}at^2$ $d = \frac{1}{2}(25.0\ \text{m/s}^2)(6.02\ \text{s})^2$ $d = 453$ m No, the dragster will not complete the 500 m racetrack under these conditions.

Practice Problems 2.1.2 — Uniform Acceleration: Finding Displacement or Distance

1. What is the acceleration of a toy car travelling from rest 20.0 m in 14.0 s?

2. A runner decelerates at a rate of 2.50 m/s² as the end of a run. If it takes 4.00 s to stop from an initial speed of 8.00 m/s, how far did he travel?

3. How long does it take for an Olympic sprinter to run 50.0 m if we assume the average acceleration over this distance is 4.50 m/s².

If time t is not known, but the other relevant variables are known, there is a fourth equation that often comes in handy in uniform acceleration problems. It can be derived by eliminating t from Equations I and II.

According to Equation I, $v_f = v_0 + at$, therefore

$$t = \frac{v_f - v_0}{a}$$

Substituting for t in Equation II, $$d = \frac{v_0 + v_f}{2} \cdot t$$

Therefore, $$d = \frac{v_0 + v_f}{2} \cdot \frac{v_f - v_0}{a}$$

So, $$d = \frac{v_f^2 - v_0^2}{2a}$$

Therefore, we have Equation IV.

Equation IV	$\mathbf{v_f^2 = v_0^2 + 2ad}$

Thus, there are four equations you can use to solve problems involving uniform acceleration. Which equation to use will depend on the information you have available for any given problem. The key is to remember that there must be uniform acceleration to use these equations.

Sample Problem 2.1.3 — Uniform Acceleration: Without Knowing Time

At what speed must a car travel to merge onto an 80.0 km/h highway if the car accelerates at 1.10 m/s² and the merge lane is 175 m?

What to Think About	How to Do It
1. Is there uniform acceleration?	Yes
2. What do you know?	$v_0 = ?$ $v_f = 80.0 \frac{\text{km}}{\text{h}} \times \frac{1000 \text{ m}}{1 \text{ km}} \times \frac{1 \text{ h}}{3600 \text{ s}} = 22.2 \text{ m/s}$ $d = 175 \text{ m}$ $a = 1.10 \text{ m/s}^2$
3. Solve	$v_f^2 = v_0^2 + 2ad$ $v_0^2 = v_f^2 - 2ad$ $v_0 = \sqrt{v_f^2 - 2ad}$ $v_0 = \sqrt{(22.2 \text{ m/s})^2 - 2(1.10 \text{ m/s}^2)(175 \text{m})}$ $v_0 = 10.4 \text{ m/s}$ The car must be travelling at 10.4 m/s to merge onto the highway.

Practice Problems 2.1.3 — Uniform Acceleration: Without Knowing Time

1. A racecar accelerates from rest at 4.50 m/s^2 for a distance of 350 m. How fast is it going at the end of the race?

2. What is the distance a car will travel when it accelerates from 20 km/h to 80 km/h at a rate of 2.50 m/s^2?

3. What is the acceleration of a blood cell that goes from rest to 25.0 cm/s in a distance of 2.00 cm while travelling from the left ventricle of the heart out to the aorta?

Acceleration of Falling Bodies

The most commonly used example of uniform acceleration is a body that is in **free fall**, where air resistance is either zero or negligible. On Earth, a heavy body with a small surface area may approximate free fall. A falling skydiver is definitely not a good example of a body in free fall — especially when the parachute is deployed! On the Moon, there is no atmosphere to contend with, and free fall would be achieved easily, but the rate of acceleration is about 1/6 of what it is here on Earth.

The acceleration of a freely falling body is called the **acceleration due to gravity**, and is given the symbol ***g***. The magnitude of g varies slightly from place to place on Earth's surface, but rarely varies much from 9.80 m/s^2. In this book we will assume that on Earth, the magnitude of g is 9.80 m/s^2.

Acceleration is a vector quantity, of course, and in many situations where the acceleration is caused by the force of gravity you will find it necessary to consider down as the ***negative direction***. In gravitational acceleration problems where there is up and down motion, you use $\boldsymbol{a} = \mathbf{-9.80\ m/s^2}$. Figure 2.1.4 illustrates how g remains downwards when a ball is thrown up. Notice that the velocity changes, but acceleration due to gravity never changes.

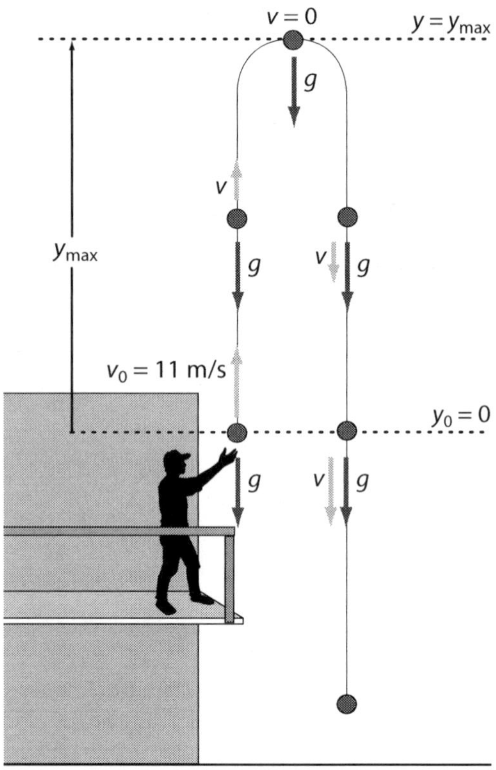

Figure 2.1.4 *If a body is thrown into the air, it accelerates downward ($a = -9.80$ m/s^2) at all times during the trajectory, whether the velocity is upward (+), zero or downward (–).*

Graphically Representing a Falling Body

You throw a baseball straight up. It leaves your hand with an initial velocity of 10.0 m/s. Figure 2.1.5 is a graph showing how the velocity of the ball varies with time, starting when you begin to throw the ball, and ending when you finish catching it. At A, the ball has just left your hand. At C, the ball has just reached the glove in which you will catch the ball. Notice that between A and C, the velocity is changing at a uniform rate. If you take the slope of this graph, you will obtain the acceleration of the ball due to gravity alone.

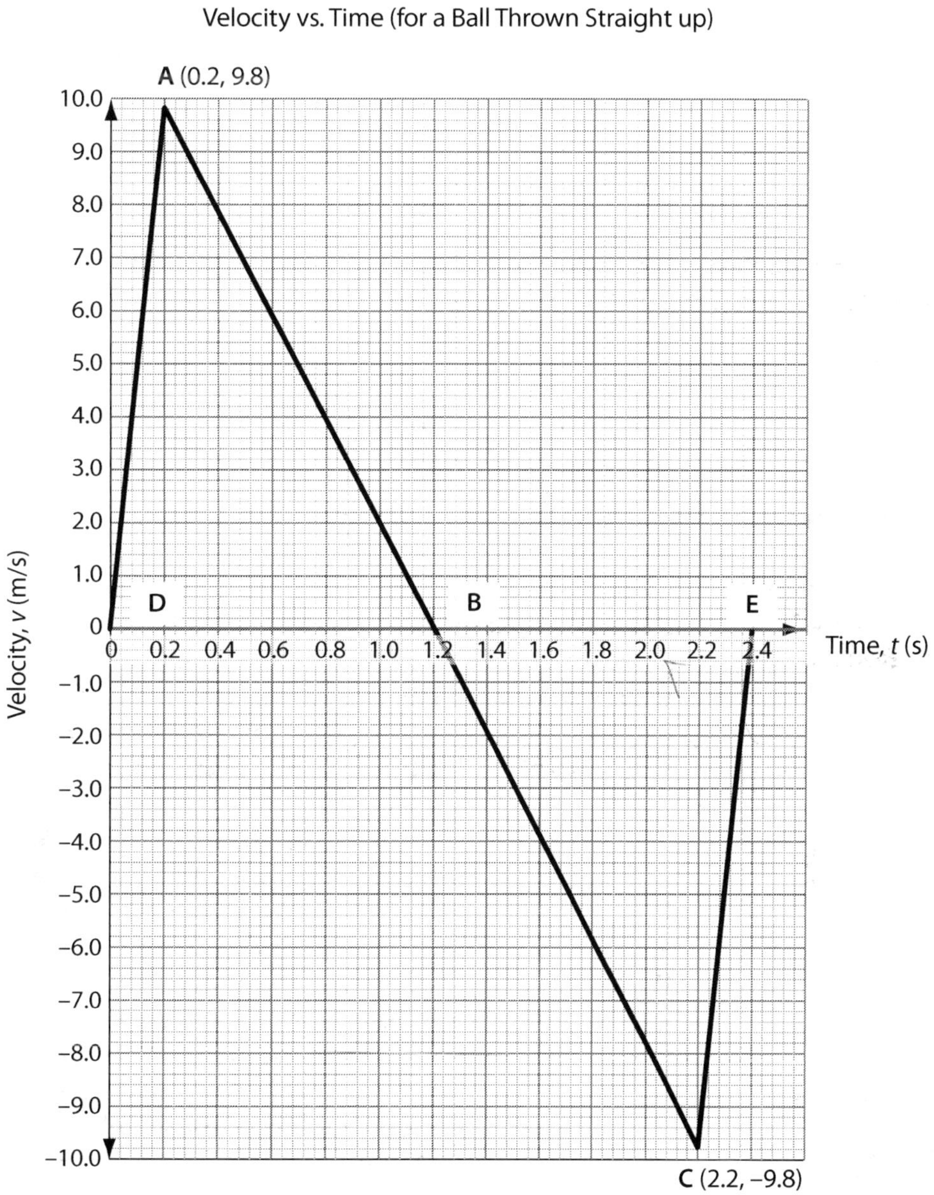

Figure 2.1.5 *The slope of this graph gives the acceleration of the ball due to gravity alone.*

Quick Check

Refer to Figure 2.1.5, which is a graph of the velocity of a ball, as a function of time when you throw a ball straight up in the air.

1. What was the acceleration of the ball
   (a) while it was being thrown?

   (b) while it was in "free fall"?

   (c) while it was being caught?

2. What point on the graph corresponds with the instant when the ball reached the "peak" of its flight? Explain how you know this.

3. What altitude did the ball reach? (**Hint**: The distance the ball travels equals the average speed multiplied by the time elapsed when it reaches its "peak" altitude.)

2.1 Review Questions

1. A tourist averaged 82 km/h for a 6.5 h trip in her car. How far did she go?

2. Change these speeds so that they are expressed in m/s:
   (a) 1 km/h

   (b) 50 km/h

   (c) 80 km/h

   (d) 100 km/h

3. An airplane has an acceleration of 15.0 m/s^2.
   (a) How fast will it be moving 2.5 s after it starts down the runway?

   (b) How far will it travel during the 2.5 s?

   (c) Minimum takeoff speed is 60.0 m/s. What length must the runway be?

4. (a) You are driving along the road at 80 km/h (22 m/s) when you see a moose 50.0 m in front of your car. Your reaction time is 0.40 s, and when you finally hit the brakes, your car accelerates at a rate of – 6.4 m/s^2. Will your car stop in time to avoid hitting the moose?

   (b) If the road is wet, and your car accelerates at a rate of just – 4.8 m/s^2, what will happen? Show your calculations.

5. Equation IV for uniform acceleration ($v_f^2 = v_0^2 + 2ad$) can be used to show that a body thrown upward with a *speed v* will return to *the same level* with the same *speed* it had when it was thrown upward.
   (a) Show mathematically why the magnitude of v_f equals the magnitude of v_0.

   (b) Will the ball have the same *velocity* when it comes down as when it was thrown up in the air? Explain your answer.

6. A skateboarder accelerates uniformly down a hill, starting from rest. During the third 1 s interval from rest, the skateboarder travels 7.5 m. What is the acceleration of the skateboarder?

7. A speeding car is traveling at a constant speed of 35.0 m/s when is passes a stopped RCMP car. If the police car accelerates at 6.0 m/s^2 how far will the police car have travelled when it catches the speeding car?

8. A frictionless air track is tilted at an angle of 2.5°.
   (a) At what rate will the glider accelerate down the sloped air track?

   (b) How long will the glider take to travel 1.5 m along the track, if its initial velocity was zero?

2.2 Projectile Motion

Warm Up

Place the bottom of a bill in line with your friend's hand as shown in the drawing. Without warning, release the bill. Can your friend grab the bill? Human reaction time is about one seventh of a second. How long would the bill have to be to make it "catchable"?

Describing Projectile Motion

If you throw a baseball, your arm exerts a force on the ball until the ball leaves your hand. Once the ball is free of your hand, it continues moving because of its inertia, and it will follow a curved path unless you throw it straight up. A baseball thrown into the air is a good example of a **projectile**. If a marble rolls off the edge of a table, it follows a curved path to the floor. The marble, too, is a projectile.

Any object (a rock, a ball, or a bullet) that is projected by some method and then continues moving because of its inertia, is a projectile. Figure 2.2.1 shows the path taken by a baseball thrown by highly skilled fielder. The dashed line shows the path the baseball would take if there were no force of gravity. The solid line shows the actual path taken by the baseball.

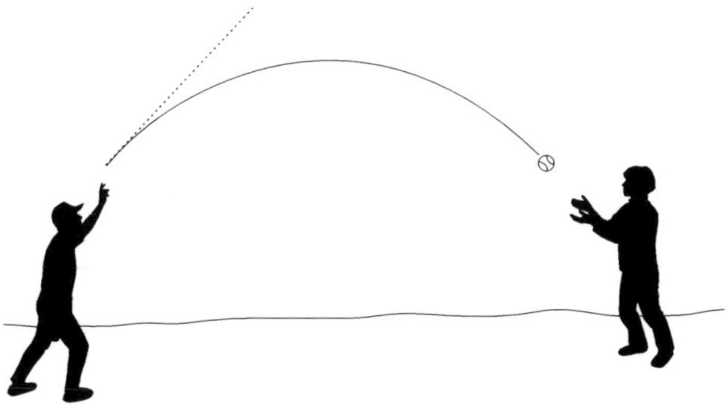

Figure 2.2.1 *The baseball follows a curved path rather than a straight one from the fielder's hand because of the force of gravity.*

At first glance, it may appear to be a complicated matter to describe the motion of a projectile. After you have done Investigation 2.1.1, you will understand that the motion of a projectile can be described very simply if you look at the vertical motion and the horizontal motion separately.

Vectors and Projectile Problems

You will use the four equations for uniform acceleration frequently when solving problems involving projectile motion. For your convenience, these laws are summarized here:

I	$\vec{v}_f = \vec{v}_0 + \vec{a}t$
II	$d = \dfrac{v_0 + v_f}{2} \bullet t$
III	$d = v_0 t + \dfrac{1}{2}at^2$
IV	$v_f^{\,2} = v_0^{\,2} + 2ad$

When solving projectile problems, you must remember that velocities, displacements, and accelerations are vector quantities. Upward motion is generally considered positive (+) and downward motion is negative (–). On or near Earth's surface, the magnitude of the acceleration due to gravity is $\vec{g} = 9.80\ \text{m/s}^2$, and since it is always acting downward, you should use

$$\vec{a} = -\,9.80\ \text{m/s}^2$$

When analyzing the motion of a projectile, the velocity is almost always resolved into its *horizontal* and *vertical* components. The laws of uniform acceleration may be applied to the vertical motion of the object. The horizontal motion is simple to deal with, since horizontal velocity is constant (ignoring air resistance).

The Parabolic Nature of Projectile Motion

When a projectile is fired, its path is *parabolic* if air resistance is negligible. This can be shown quite simply for a situation where an object is thrown horizontally (Figure 2.2.2).

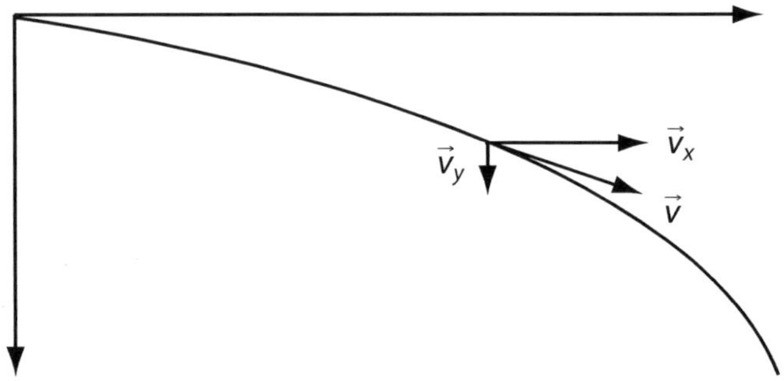

Figure 2.2.2 *Parabolic motion can be resolved into an x component and a y component for motion.*

Let the magnitude of the horizontal displacement of an object thrown horizontally be *x*. Horizontal velocity, which has magnitude v_x is constant.

$$v_x = \frac{x}{t} \text{ so } t = \frac{x}{v_x}$$

Let the magnitude of the vertical displacement be *y*. Assuming the object starts from rest so that $\vec{v}_0 = 0$, then

$$y = \tfrac{1}{2}at^2 \text{ or } y = \frac{1}{2}a\left[\frac{x}{v_x}\right]^2$$

Now, ½, a, and v_x are all constant, therefore we can say that $y = kx^2$.

This is the simplest possible equation for a *parabola*. A ball thrown out by a pitcher, or a stream of water issuing from a hose will follow a parabolic path. If air resistance is negligible, any object, given a horizontal motion in a gravitational field, will move along a parabolic path.

Sample Problem 2.2.1 — Projectile Motion

A golf ball was struck from the first tee at Lunar Golf and Country Club, a private golf course for astronauts stranded on the Moon. It was given a velocity of 48 m/s at an angle of 40° to the horizontal. On the Moon, the magnitude of $g = 1.6$ m/s².

(a) What is the vertical component of the golf ball's initial velocity?
(b) For what interval of time is the ball in flight?
(c) How far will the ball travel horizontally?

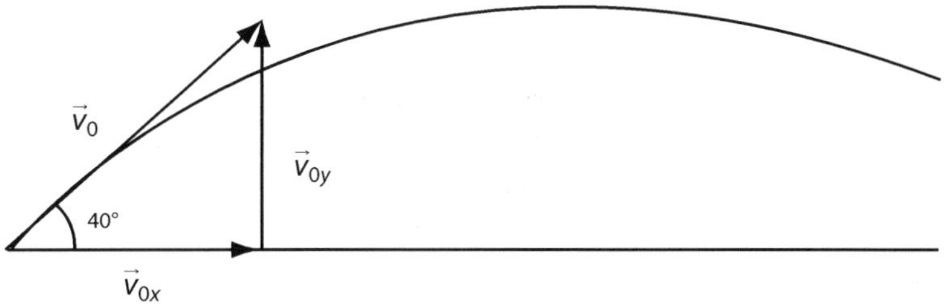

Figure 2.2.3

What to Think About	How to Do It
(a) 1. Since the velocity of the ball is initially 48 m/s, find $\vec{v}_{0y}$. (*Keep one extra significant figure for now.)	$\vec{v}_{oy} = \vec{v}_o \sin 40°$ $\vec{v}_{oy} = (48\text{ m/s})(0.6428)$ $\vec{v}_{oy} = 30.9\text{ m/s}$ *
(b) 1. The most direct way of solving for time is to use Equation III for uniform acceleration.	$d = v_o t + \frac{1}{2}at^2$
2. Since the ball will eventually return to ground level, its displacement for the entire trip, in a vertical direction, is zero ($d = y = 0$). (*Keep one extra significant figure for now.)	Therefore, $0 = (30.9\text{ m/s})t + 1/2(-1.6\text{ m/s}^2)t^2$ or $(0.80\text{ m/s}^2)t^2 = (30.9\text{ m/s})t$ $t = \frac{30.9\text{ m/s}}{0.80\text{ m/s}^2} = 38.6\text{ s}$ *
(c) 1. Horizontal displacement: $x = v_{0x}t$ Horizontal velocity remains constant: $v_{0x} = v_0 \cos 40°$	$x = (v_o \cos 40°)t$ $x = (48\text{ m/s})(0.7660)(38.6\text{ s})$ $x = 1.42 \times 10^3\text{ m}$
Summary Round the final answers to two significant figures. The golf ball would travel 1.4 km on the Moon!	(a) 31 m/s (b) 39 s (c) 1.4×10^3 m or 1.4 km

Practice Problems 2.2.1 — Projectile Motion

1. A girl throws a rock horizontally from the top of a cliff 98 m high, with a horizontal velocity of 27 m/s.
   (a) How many seconds will the rock be in the air?

   (b)How far out from the base of the cliff does the rock land?

2. A golfer gives a golf ball a velocity of 48 m/s at an angle of 45° with the horizontal.
   (a) What is the vertical component of the ball's initial velocity?

   (b) How long is the ball in the air?

   (c) What is the horizontal distance covered by the ball while in flight?

   (d) Compare your result with that for the same question on the Moon. (See Sample Problem 2.2.1.)

Investigation 2.2.1 Projectiles

Purpose

To study the two-dimensional motion of a projectile

Procedure

1. Set up the projectile apparatus in Figure 2.4.4. When the horizontal bar is released by a spring mechanism, ball A falls straight down and ball B is projected horizontally. Once "fired," both balls experience one force only (ignoring air resistance) — the force of gravity. Watch and listen as the two balls are projected simultaneously. Repeat the procedure several times.

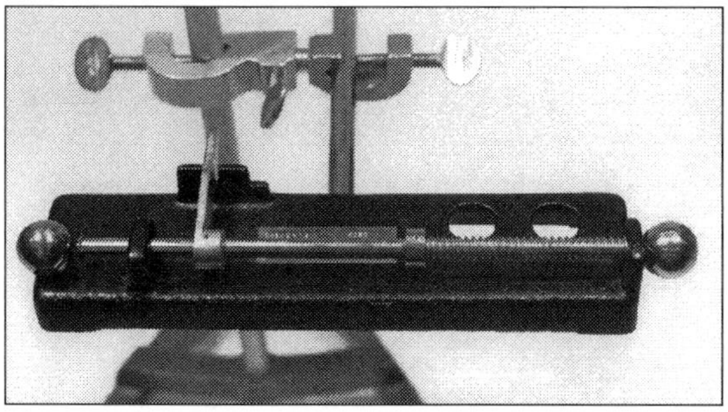

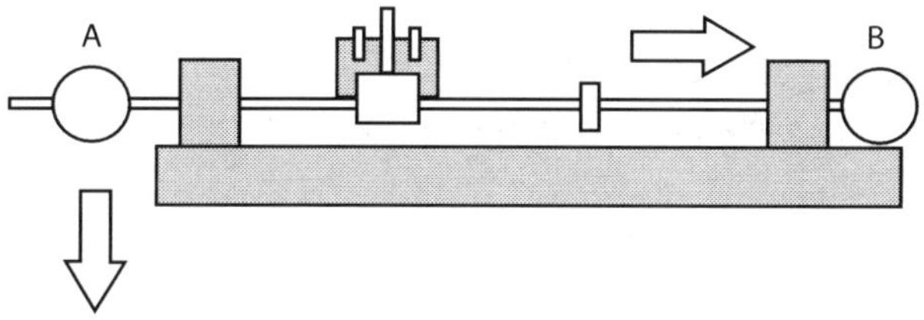

(a) (b)

Figure 2.2.4

2. Figure 2.2.5(a) could be a tracing from a strobe photograph of two balls released simultaneously by a projectile apparatus similar to the one you just used. Make or obtain a copy of this tracing. Use a sharp, penciled dot to mark the position of the centre of each image of the balls. Figure 2.2.5(b) shows what to do.

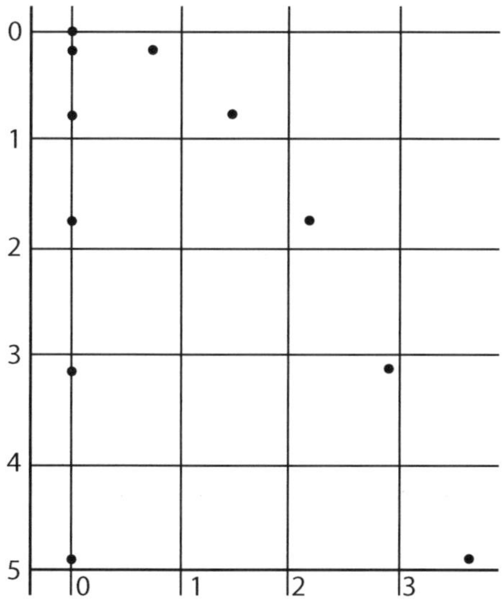

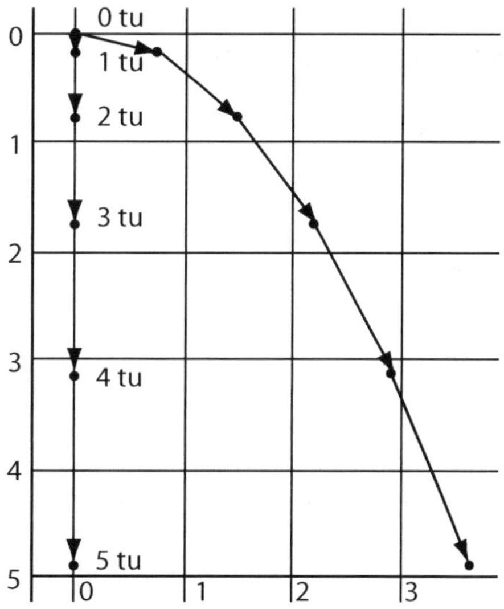

(a) (b)

Figure 2.2.5 *A tracing of a stroboscopic photograph made of a projected ball, falling simultaneously with a ball falling straight down, might look like this.*

3. Consider ball A first. (It is the one falling straight down.) Find out if its acceleration is uniform as follows: Call the time interval between images one "time unit" (tu). Measure the displacement of the ball during each successive tu. Since average velocity equals displacement divided by time, the average velocity during each successive time interval simply equals displacement divided by 1 tu.

4. Make a graph of the average vertical velocity $\bar{v}_y$ vs. time, *t*. Find out if the acceleration of falling ball A is uniform. Remember that, since this is average velocity, you should plot velocities *midway* through each time interval.
5. Now, consider ball B, which was projected horizontally. On your tracing, draw in successive velocity vectors as shown in Figure 2.2.5(b) above. These vectors are cute to look at, but they do not help you understand what is happening to ball B! Therefore, construct both horizontal and vertical components of each of the velocity vectors. See Figure 2.2.6.

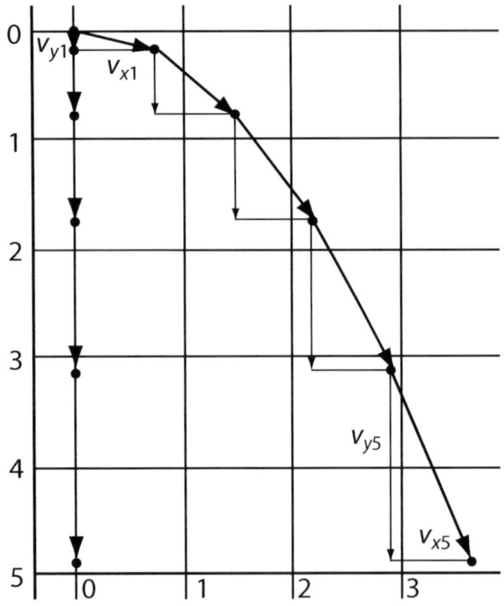

Figure 2.2.6

6. Compare successive vertical components of ball B's velocities with the corresponding vertical velocities of ball A. Plot a graph of $\bar{v}_y$ vs. *t* for ball B.
7. Compare successive horizontal components ($\bar{v}_x$) with each other. Plot $\bar{v}_x$ vs. *t*.
8. (a) Plot total vertical displacement from rest (d_y) vs. time (*t*) for the vertical motion of either ball.
   (b) Plot d_y vs. t^2.
9. Plot total horizontal displacement from rest (d_x) vs. time (*t*) for ball B.

Concluding Questions

1. A rifle fires a bullet horizontally on level ground. Just as the bullet leaves the rifle, the rifle falls to the ground. Which will hit the ground first, the bullet or the rifle? Explain your answer.
2. When a ball is projected horizontally, what conclusions do you arrive at regarding
   (a) its horizontal velocity components?
   (b) its vertical velocity components?
3. Write a simple mathematical relationship (such as $d_x = \text{k}\,t$, where k is the constant of proportionality) connecting the two variables in each of the following projectile situations:
   (a) v_y vs. *t*
   (b) v_x vs. *t*
   (c) d_y vs. *t*

Challenges

1. Build a "monkey gun" apparatus. See Figure 2.2.7. The projectile is a small marble, which is propelled by a "blow gun" made of a copper pipe, the diameter of which is just slightly larger than the marble. When the marble leaves the gun, it breaks a thin piece of aluminum foil, which opens an electric circuit. An electromagnet holding up a tin can target (the "monkey" in a tree?) is deactivated. Just as the marble leaves the gun, the "monkey" starts to fall to the ground. Will the marble hit the monkey or miss it? Explain your answer. Now test your prediction!

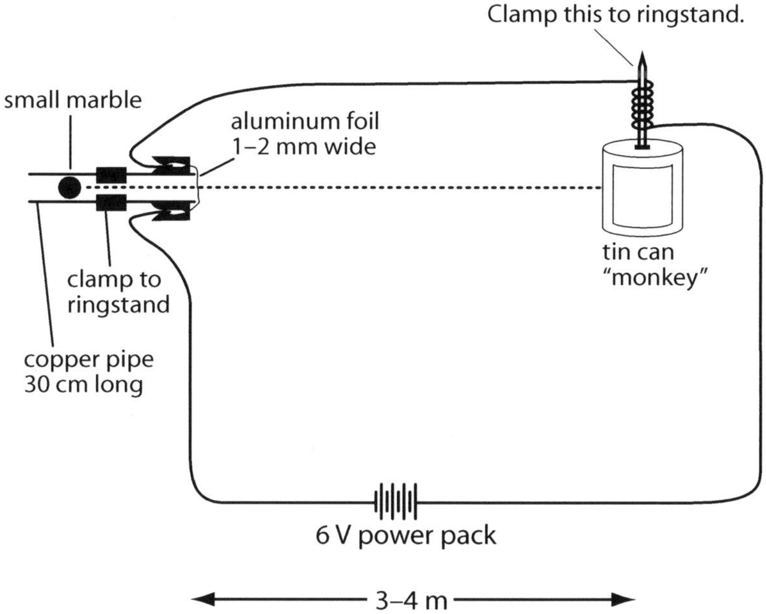

Figure 2.2.7

2. Imagine that the "blow gun" is aimed upward at some angle greater than zero relative to the horizontal. It is aimed at the "monkey" to begin with. Will it still hit the monkey if the monkey falls at the instant the marble leaves the gun? Explain your answer.

2.2 Review Questions

Use $\vec{g} = -9.80 \text{ m/s}^2$

1. A rescue pilot has to drop a package of emergency supplies so that it lands as close as possible to a downed aircraft. If the rescue plane travels with a velocity of 81 m/s and is flying 125 m above the downed craft, how far away (horizontally) from the downed craft must the rescue pilot drop his package? (Assume negligible air resistance.)

2. An archer standing on the back of a pickup truck moving at 28 m/s fires an arrow straight up at a duck flying directly overhead. He misses the duck. The arrow was fired with an initial vertical velocity of 49 m/s relative to the truck.
   (a) For how many seconds will the arrow be in the air?

   (b) How far will the truck travel while the arrow is in the air?

   (c) Where, in relation to the archer, will the arrow come down? (Ignore air friction.) Will the archer have to "duck"? Explain.

3. A bullet is fired with a horizontal velocity of 330 m/s from a height of 1.6 m above the ground. Assuming the ground is level, how far from the gun, measured horizontally, will the bullet hit the ground?

4. A ball is thrown with a velocity of 24 m/s at an angle of 30° to the horizontal.
   Assume air friction is small enough to be ignored.
   (a) What is the horizontal component of the initial velocity?

   (b) What is the vertical component of the initial velocity?

   (c) How long will the ball be in the air?

(d) What horizontal distance (range) will the ball travel?

(e) To what maximum height will the ball rise?

5. Solve question 4 for angles of (i) 45° and (ii) 60°. Which of the three angles results in the greatest range? It can be shown that, for a given initial velocity, this angle is the best of all angles for obtaining the maximum range in the ideal, "no air resistance" situation.

(i) 45°

(a) What is the horizontal component of the initial velocity?

(b) What is the vertical component of the initial velocity?

(c) How long will the ball be in the air?

(d) What horizontal distance (range) will the ball travel?

(e) To what maximum height will the ball rise?

(ii) 60°

(a) What is the horizontal component of the initial velocity?

(b) What is the vertical component of the initial velocity?

(c) How long will the ball be in the air?

(d) What horizontal distance (range) will the ball travel?

(e) To what maximum height will the ball rise?

6. A student measured the horizontal and vertical components of the velocity of a projectile in a laboratory situation. The data is given below. Times and velocities are "true" (not scaled).

Time, t (s)	Horizontal velocity, v_x (m/s)	Vertical velocity, v_y (m/s)
0.10	2.12	3.58
0.20	2.12	4.56
0.30	2.13	5.54
0.40	2.11	6.52
0.50	2.12	7.50

(a) Plot vertical velocity vs. time.

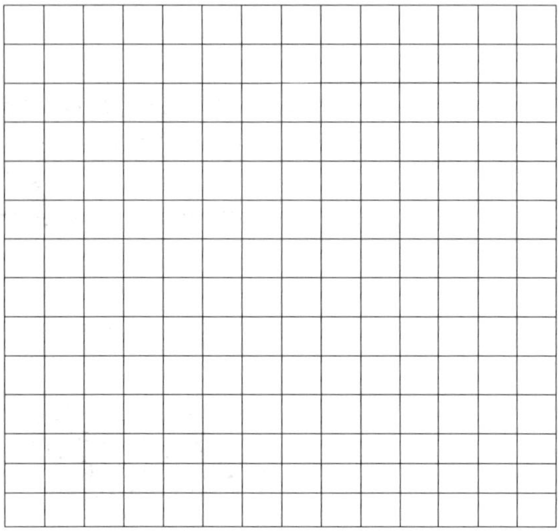

(b) Find the slope and y-intercept of your graph.

(c) Write an equation specifically describing your graph.

(d) On the same graph sheet, plot horizontal velocity vs. time.

(e) Write an equation specifically describing your second graph.

Chapter 2 Review Questions

1. Define the meaning of the following terms with a real world example for each.
   (a) speed

   (b) velocity

   (c) acceleration

2. Assuming no air resistance, how far must a small steel ball fall from rest before it reaches a speed of 100.0 km/h?

3. How far does a freely falling body travel during the fourth second of its fall?

4. A youngster hits a baseball, giving it a velocity of 22 m/s at an angle of 62° with the horizontal. Ignoring air friction, how far will the ball travel before a fielder catches it? Would this hit be a likely home run? Explain.

5. A disgruntled physics student sees the front end of his teacher's car directly below him at the base of a cliff. See the drawing below. If the student is 5.00 m above the car, which is 3.00 m long and travelling only 3.00 m/s to the right, will the apple the student drops hit the teacher's car? (Will physics be a "core" subject?) Show all details of your argument.

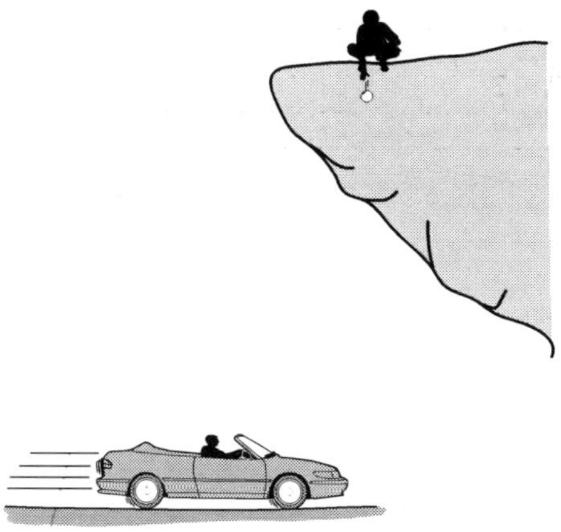

6. A pebble is fired from a slingshot with a velocity of 30.0 m/s. If it is fired at an angle of 30° to the vertical, what height will it reach? If its fall is interrupted by a vertical wall 12 m away, where will it hit the wall in relation to the starting position of the pebble in the slingshot?

7. A firefighter is standing on top of a building 20.0 m high. She finds that if she holds the hose so that water issues from it horizontally at 12.0 m/s, the water will hit a burning wall of an adjacent building, at a height of 15.0 m above the ground. What is the horizontal distance from the firefighter to the burning wall?

8. The firefighter in question 7 wants the water from the same hose to reach the burning wall at the same level above the ground as she is standing. At what angle must she aim the hose relative to the horizontal?

9. An observer records time (t), displacement (d), and velocity (v) of a skier sliding from rest down a ski slope, with uniform acceleration. Sketch graphs using the following different variables.

(a) d vs. t

(b) d vs. t^2

(c) v vs. t

(d) v^2 vs. d

(e) In which case will the observer not obtain a straight line?

10. You drop a penny down a very deep well and hear the sound of the penny hitting the water 2.5 s later. If sound travels 330 m/s, how deep is the well?

11. A stone is thrown straight up with a speed of 15.0 m/s.
    (a) How fast will it be moving when its altitude is 8.0 m above the point from which it was thrown? How much time elapses while the stone is reaching that height?

    (b) Is there one answer or are there two answers? Why?

12. A small, free-falling pebble takes 0.25 s to pass by a window 1.8 m high. From what height above the window was the pebble dropped?

Chapter 2 Extra Practice

Use the following diagram to answer questions 1 to 3. A baseball player throws a ball into the air, following the path shown. At 1, the ball has just left the thrower's hand. At 5, the ball is at its original height above the ground. Assume negligible air friction.

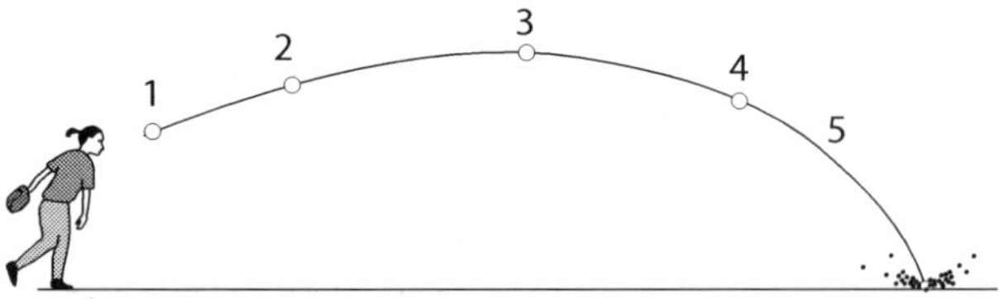

1. At what point in the ball's flight does its acceleration have magnitude g?

2. Where is the horizontal velocity of the ball at its maximum?

3. Where is the magnitude of the vertical velocity of the ball at its maximum?

4. A ball is tossed in a direction 72° above the horizontal, with a velocity of 12 m/s. What is the maximum height the ball will reach?

5. A projectile is launched with a velocity of 16.3 m/s, at an angle of 37° with the horizontal. How much time will elapse before the vertical component of the velocity is zero?

6. A daredevil BMX rider runs his bike off a cliff with a horizontal velocity of 4.5 m/s, and lands in the water 12 m from the base of the cliff.
   (a) How long does it take the rider to hit the water?
   (b) How high is the cliff?

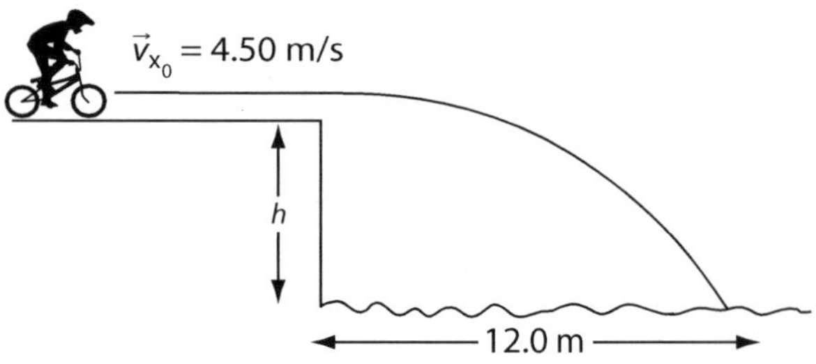

7. A marble is accelerated to a horizontal velocity of 0.50 m/s by rolling it down a small ramp. The marble rolls off the table, which is 0.78 m high. As it falls, it hits a barrier on the way down. If the barrier is 0.15 m from the edge of the table, at what height from the ground, h, will the marble hit the barrier?

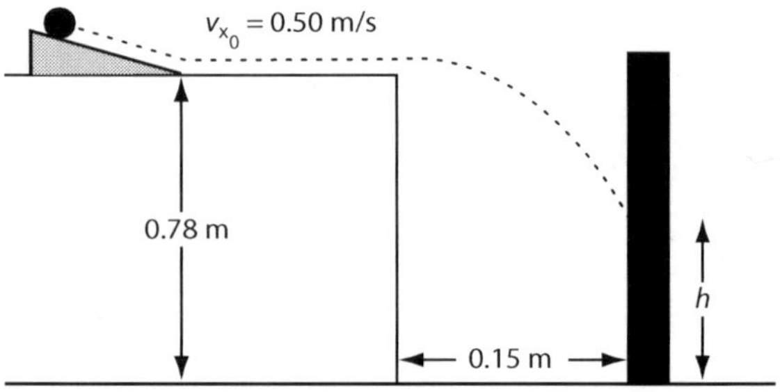

8. As part of a NASA experiment, a golfer drives a golf ball on the Moon, where $g = 1.60$ m/s^2. He "launches" the golf ball with a speed of 285 km/h, at an angle of 42° with the horizontal. What horizontal distance will his drive travel before landing back on the surface of the Moon? Ignore the curvature of the Moon.

9. A projectile is launched with a speed of 128 m/s at an angle of 60° with the horizontal.
   (a) After 2.0 s, what is the vertical component of the projectile's velocity?
   (b) After 2.0 s, what is the speed of the projectile?

3 Momentum and Energy

By the end of this chapter, you should be able to do the following:

- Apply Newton's laws of motion to solve problems involving acceleration, gravitational field strength, and friction
- Apply the concepts of dynamics to analyze one-dimensional or two-dimensional situations
- Analyze the relationships among work, energy, and power
- Use knowledge of momentum and impulse to analyze situations in one dimension

---

By the end of this chapter, you should know the meaning of these **key terms**:

- conservative forces
- elastic collisions
- energy
- force of friction
- force of gravity (weight)
- gravitational potential energy
- horsepower
- impulse
- inelastic collisions
- inertia
- kinetic energy
- law of conservation of energy
- law of conservation of momentum
- momentum
- Newton's three laws of motion
- net force
- nonconservative forces
- power
- work
- work-energy theorem

By the end of this chapter, you should be able to use and know when to use the following formulae:

$\vec{F} = m\vec{a}$ $\quad \vec{F} = m\vec{g}$ $\quad \vec{F} = \mu\vec{F}_N$ $\quad W = Fd$ $\quad E_p = mgh$ $\quad E_k = \frac{1}{2}mv^2$ $\quad P = \frac{W}{\Delta t}$ $\quad \vec{p} = m\vec{v}$ $\quad \Delta\vec{p} = F_{net}\Delta t$

The movement of a cheetah, sports car, and runner all involve force, distance, mass, velocity, and acceleration. These factors form the foundation for the study of momentum and energy in this chapter.

3.1 Dynamics

Warm Up

The drawing shows an egg balanced on a spool of thread on a cookie sheet balanced on a cup of water. If a horizontal force is applied to the edge of the cookie sheet, what will happen to the egg? Explain your reasoning.

___

___

___

Review of Newton's Laws of Motion

While Galileo was chiefly responsible for establishing the science of **kinematics** which is concerned with describing motion, without reference to its cause, it was Isaac Newton (1642-1727) who laid the foundations for the science of **dynamics.** Newton was the first to clearly explain the relationship between motion and forces, which is the basis for dynamics.

Newton's First Law of Motion
If there is no net force acting on a body, it will continue to move with constant velocity.

This means that a body at rest will stay at rest; a body moving at a certain speed will continue to move at that speed and in the same direction unless and until an unbalanced (net) force acts on it. This property, possessed by all bodies having mass, is called **inertia**.

Your own experience tells you that if you want to push a book across your desk at constant velocity, you must exert a force on the book. Does this contradict the first law? No! To move the book along at steady velocity, your force just has to balance the friction force opposing its motion. When the force you apply equals the friction force, the *net* force is zero, because the vector sum of your applied force and the friction force is zero.

Newton's Second Law of Motion

In an earlier course, you performed experiments to find out what happens when a net force acts on a body. These experiments showed you two facts about motion:

(1) A net force acting on a body causes it to accelerate in the direction of the net force. If the net force is doubled, the acceleration will double. If the net force is tripled, the acceleration will also triple. Experiments show that the acceleration is directly proportional to the net force on the object.

$$\text{acceleration} \propto \text{net force}$$

In symbols, $\vec{a} \propto \vec{F}$

(2) For a given net force, the acceleration of a body is inversely proportional to the mass of a body. For example, if a 10 N force will accelerate a 5 kg mass at a rate of 2 m/s^2, the same force will accelerate a 10 kg mass at 1 m/s^2, which is one-half the original acceleration.

$$\text{acceleration} \propto \frac{1}{\text{mass}}$$

In symbols, $\vec{a} \propto \frac{1}{m}$

Newton's second law can be summarized as written below.

Newton's Second Law
The acceleration of a body is directly proportional to the net force acting on it and inversely proportional to its mass. Acceleration is in the same direction as the net *force.*

In symbols, $\vec{a} \propto \frac{\vec{F}}{m}$ or $\vec{a} = k\frac{\vec{F}}{m}$

If units for force and mass are chosen so that k = 1, then $\vec{a} = \frac{\vec{F}}{m}$.

Rearranging terms, the familiar form of Newton's second law is obtained as shown below.

$$\vec{F} = m\vec{a}$$

Quick Check

1. What is the mass of a rocket that has an acceleration 20.0 m/s^2 at lift off and a thrust of 27 000 N?

2. A rising hot air balloon has a mass of 1000 kg and an acceleration of 3.50 m/s^2. What is the magnitude of the force lifting the balloon?

3. A 2.00 kg trout makes a sudden start to escape a predator. If the force generated to make this quick movement is 80.0 N, what is the brief acceleration of the trout?

In the Quick Check above only one unbalanced force was considered. In other situations, like Sample Problem 3.1.1 below, there are more forces to consider. Remember that in these problems it is important to identify the forces that create the unbalanced force. In a tug of war between two boys, each is pulling in the opposite direction. In the sample problem below, you need to find the net force that is causing boys to accelerate in the same direction.

Sample Problem 3.1.1 — Multiple Forces Acting on a Body and Newton's Second Law

Gareth and Owen are pulling on a 1.45 kg rope in opposite directions. If Gareth pulls with a force of 20.0 N and the rope accelerates away from him at 1.15 m/s^2, what force is Owen pulling with?

What to Think About	How to Do It
1. Identify what you know and the positive direction.	Make $\vec{F}_{Owen}$ the positive direction. $\vec{F}_{Gareth} = -20.0\ N$ $m = 1.45\ kg$ $\vec{a} = 1.15\ m/s^2$
2. Newton's second law applies so the net force is key.	$\vec{F}_{net} = \vec{F}_{Owen} - \vec{F}_{Gareth} = m\vec{a}$
3. Solve.	$\vec{F}_{Owen} = \vec{F}_{Gareth} + m\vec{a}$ $\vec{F}_{Owen} = 20\ N + (1.45\ kg)(1.15\ m/s^2)$ $\vec{F}_{Owen} = 21.7\ N$

Practice Problems 3.1.1 — Multiple Forces Acting on a Body and Newton's Second Law

1. A model rocket engine can produce an acceleration of 30.0 m/s^2. If the total mass of the rocket is 0.350 kg at lift off, what is the thrust generated?

2. A 20.0 kg rock is held up by a cable that will break if the tension in the cable exceeds 200 N. At what upward acceleration will the string break?

Types of Forces

While there are many different forces acting on objects in different situations, Table 3.1.1 lists a summary of common forces you have already encountered and will encounter in studying kinematics.

Table 3.1.1 *Common Forces*

Force	Symbol	Definition	Direction
Friction	$\vec{F}_{fr}$	The force that acts to oppose sliding motion between surfaces. Static friction occurs when an object is not moving. Kinetic friction occurs when an object is moving.	Opposite to the direction of motion and parallel to the surface
Normal	$\vec{F}_N$	The force exerted by the surface on an object	Perpendicular to and away from the surface
Tension	$\vec{F}_T$	The pull exerted by a string or rope when attached to a body and pulled tight	Away from the object and parallel to the string or rope at the point of attachment
Thrust	$\vec{F}_{thrust}$	A force for moving objects like rockets and planes	The same direction as the acceleration of the object, barring any opposing forces
Weight	$\vec{F}_g$	The gravitational force Earth exerts on a body	Straight down toward the centre of Earth

Newton's Third Law of Motion

When you do push-ups, which way do you exert your force? If you think about it, you will realize that you cannot push yourself up! You exert a force downward on the floor. What raises your body is the force exerted on you by the floor. When you climb stairs, you push down. The stairs push you up. When you swim forward, you push backward; the water pushes you forward.

Isaac Newton realized that when a force is applied to a body, it has to be applied by another body. Imagine an axe striking a block of wood. That the axe exerts a force on the wood is obvious. The force exerted by the wood on the axe might be less apparent, but if you think about it, the axe is decelerated very quickly when the wood "hits back" at it!

> **Newton's Third Law**
> When one body exerts a force on a second body, the second body exerts an equal force on the first body, but in the opposite direction. The forces are exerted during the same interval of time.

In popular literature, the third law is sometimes called the **law of action and reaction**. The first force is the 'action' force and the second is the 'reaction' force. The action force equals the reaction force, but is opposite in direction. The two forces act on different bodies. If we call the first body A and the second body B, then Newton's third law can be written symbolically as:

$$\vec{F}_{\text{A on B}} = -\vec{F}_{\text{B on A}}$$

Examples of Newton's Laws

Newton's laws are part of our everyday life. You are constantly part of examples where these laws are in action. Walking to class, driving a car, or taking the bus are all proof that Newton's laws are part of the world around you. To illustrate this point and to show you the interconnectedness of these laws, the following three sample problems combine different physics concepts you have already learned with Newton's three laws.

Sample Problem 3.1.2 — Kinematics and Newton's Law

A 110 kg motorbike carrying a 50 kg rider coasts to a stop in a distance of 51 m. It was originally travelling 15 m/s. What was the stopping force exerted by the road on the motorbike and rider?

What to Think About	How to Do It
1. The stopping force is friction, which opposes the motion of the bike. Newton's second law will permit you to solve for $\vec{F}$, if first you calculate acceleration using the appropriate uniform acceleration equation.	$\vec{v}_f^2 = \vec{v}_o^2 + 2\vec{a}d$ $\vec{a} = \dfrac{\vec{v}_f^2 - \vec{v}_o^2}{2d}$
2. The acceleration is negative because its direction is opposite to the direction of the motion of the motorbike. (It is decelerating.) Newton's second law can now be used to solve for the net force, which is the stopping force due to friction.	$\vec{a} = \dfrac{0-(15\ m/s)^2}{2(51\ m)} = -2.2\ m/s^2$
3. The negative sign simply means that the stopping force is in a negative direction relative to the motion of the motorbike.	$\vec{F} = m\vec{a}$ $\vec{F} = (160\ kg)(-2.2\ m/s^2)$ $\vec{F} = -3.5 \times 10^2\ N$

Sample Problem 3.1.3 — Kinematics, Vectors, and Newton's Laws

A truck of mass 2.00×10^3 kg is towing a large boulder of mass 5.00×10^2 kg using a chain (of negligible mass). The tension in the chain is 3.00×10^3 N, and the force of friction on the boulder is 1.20×10^3 N (Figure 3.1.1).

(a) At what rate will the boulder accelerate?

(b) How far will the boulder move in 3.0 s, starting from rest?

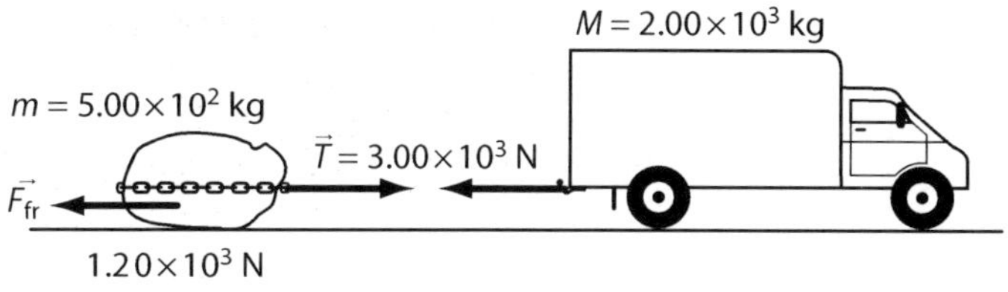

Figure 3.1.1

What to Think About

1. Draw a free body diagram, showing the forces acting on the body in question, which is the boulder.

How to Do It

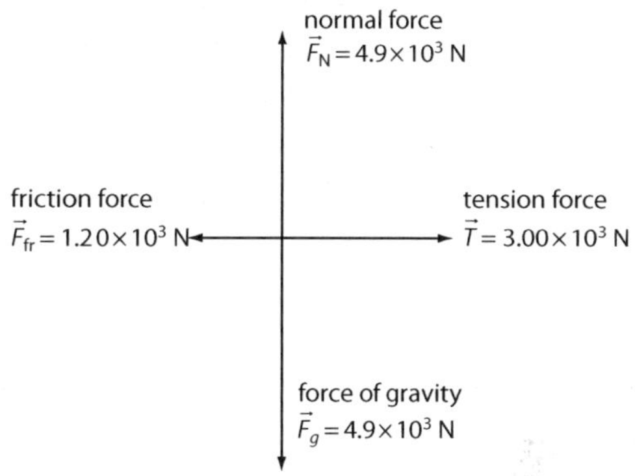

Figure 3.1.2

2. To solve for the acceleration of the boulder, you need to know the net force or resultant force acting on the boulder. Four forces are acting on the boulder:
   (1) the force of gravity ($m\vec{g}$)
   (2) the normal force ($\vec{F}_N$) exerted upward by the road (equal in magnitude but opposite in direction to mg)
   (3) the tension force ($\vec{T}$) exerted by the rope
   (4) the friction force ($\vec{F}_{fr}$) between the road and the boulder

The two y-components $m\vec{g}$ and $\vec{F}_N$ add up to zero.
The x-components $\vec{F}_{fr}$ and $\vec{T}$ have a resultant of:
$3.00 \times 10^3 \text{ N} - 1.20 \times 10^3 \text{ N} = 1.80 \times 10^3 \text{ N}$

3. Applying Newton's second law to the boulder, solve for its acceleration.

$$\vec{a} = \frac{\vec{F}}{m}$$

$$\vec{a} = \frac{1.80 \times 10^3 \text{ N}}{5.00 \times 10^2 \text{ kg}}$$

$$\vec{a} = 3.60 \text{ m/s}^2$$

4. To determine how far the boulder will move in 3.0 s, use the appropriate uniform acceleration equation. The boulder will move 16 m during the 3.0 s it is being pulled by the truck.

$$d = v_0 t + \frac{1}{2}at^2$$

$$d = 0 + \frac{1}{2}(3.6 \text{ m/s}^2)(3.0 \text{ s})^2$$

$$d = 16 \text{ m}$$

Sample Problem 3.1.4 — Forces and Newton's Laws

In Figure 3.1.3, a 5.0 kg block is connected to another 5.0 kg block by a string of negligible mass. The inclined plane down which the second block slides makes an angle of 45° with the horizontal. Friction is negligible.

(a) At what rate will the masses accelerate?

(b) What is the tension in the string joining the two masses?

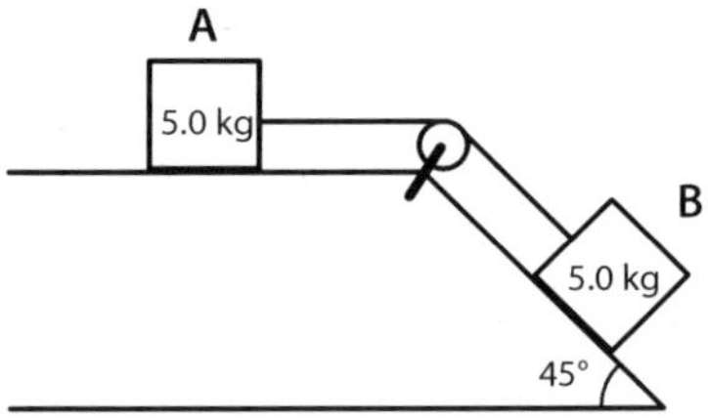

Figure 3.1.3

What to Think About / How to Do It

1. Consider block A by itself. Draw a free body diagram showing the forces acting on block A. Forces $\vec{F}_N$ and $m_A\vec{g}$ are the *y*-component forces acting on mass A. Clearly, they are equal and opposite in direction, so their vector sum is zero.

$$\Sigma \vec{F}_y = 0$$

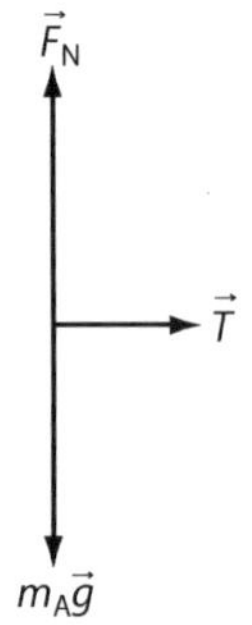

Figure 3.1.4

2. The resultant force on A will just equal the tension force $\vec{T}$ exerted on the rock by the rope. There is no friction force to oppose $\vec{T}$.

$\vec{T} = m_A\vec{a}$ (1)

$\vec{T} = (5.0 \text{ kg})\vec{a}$

3. Consider block B by itself. Draw a free body diagram showing the forces acting on B. The direction along the plane is taken as the *x*-component direction. Again, the vector sum of the *y*-component forces $\vec{F}_N$ and $\vec{F}_y$ is zero.

$$\Sigma \vec{F}_y = 0$$

The resultant force causing acceleration is $\Sigma \vec{F}_x = \vec{F}_p - \vec{T}$, where $\vec{F}_p$ is the *x*-component of the force of gravity, $m_B\vec{g}$, on mass B.

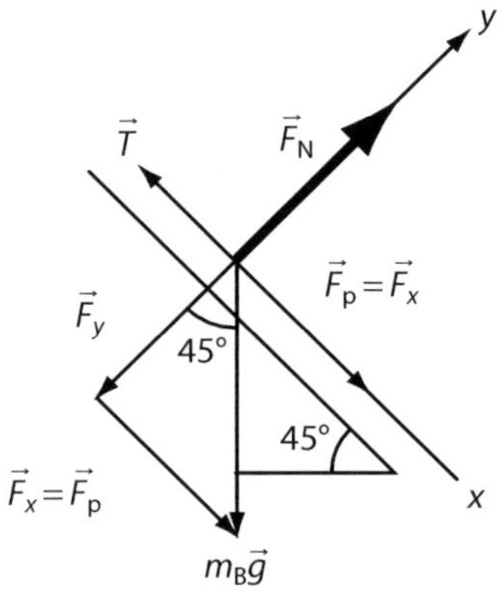

Figure 3.1.5

4. Since $\vec{F}_p = m_B\vec{g} \sin 45°$, calculate the net force causing acceleration.

$m_B\vec{g}\sin 45° - \vec{T} = m_B\vec{a}$

$(5.0 \text{ kg})(9.8 \text{ N/kg})(0.707) - \vec{T} = (5.0 \text{ kg})\vec{a}$ (2)

$34.6 \text{ N} - \vec{T} = (5.0 \text{ kg})\vec{a}$

5. To solve for acceleration $\vec{a}$ add equations (1) and (2).

Then, $34.6 \text{ N} = (10.0 \text{ kg})\vec{a}$

Therefore, $\vec{a} = 3.46 \text{ m/s}^2$

6. To solve for $\vec{T}$, use equation (1).

$\vec{T} = (5.0 \text{ kg})(3.46 \text{ m/s}^2) = 17.3 \text{ N}$

3.1 Review Questions

1. At what rate, and in which direction, will the 10.0 kg mass accelerate when the masses in the diagram below are released? Assume friction in all parts of the system may be ignored.

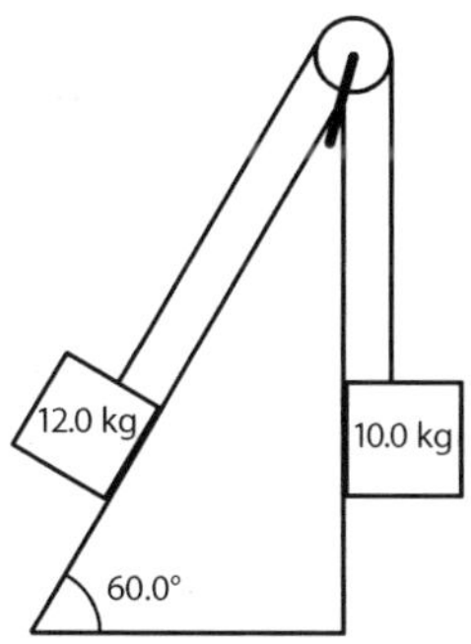

2. The two masses in the diagram below are connected by a rope of negligible mass. Friction is negligible. In what direction and at what rate will the 2.00 kg mass accelerate?

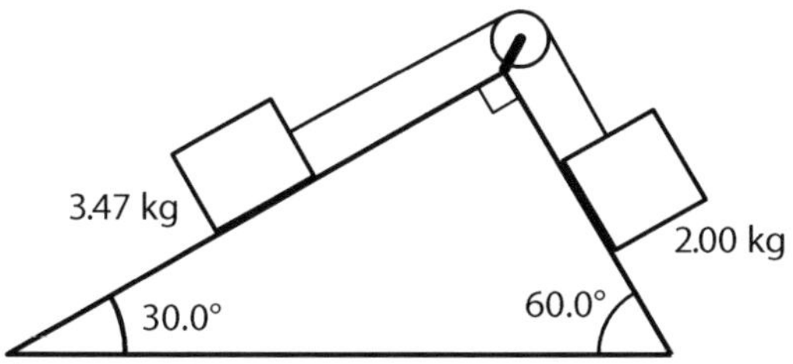

3. In the diagram below, a cord of negligible mass connects a 0.500 kg mass to a 1.00 kg mass. Friction in the system is negligible.
   (a) At what rate will the masses accelerate?
   (b) What is the tension in the cord while the masses are accelerating?

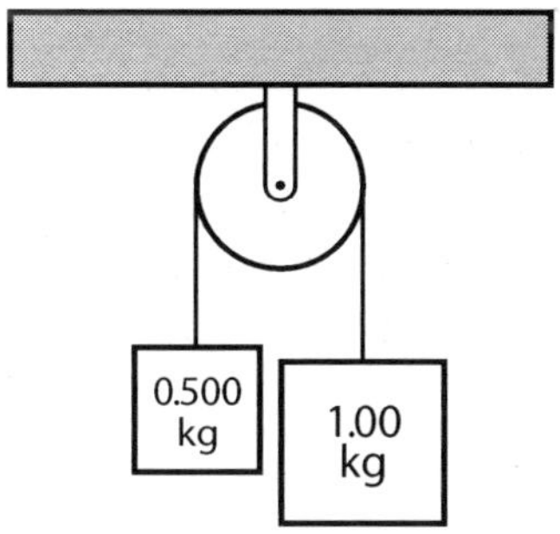

4. A criminal wants to escape from the third storey window of a jail, by going down a rope to the road below. Having taken high school physics, he thinks he can escape down the rope even though his mass is 75 kg and the rope can only support 65 kg without breaking. Explain how he can get down safely without breaking the rope.

5. The skier in the drawing below is descending a 35° slope on a surface where the coefficient of kinetic friction between his skis and the icy surface is 0.12.
   (a) If his mass (including his skis) is 72 kg, at what rate will he accelerate?
   (b) How fast is he moving after 8.0 s?

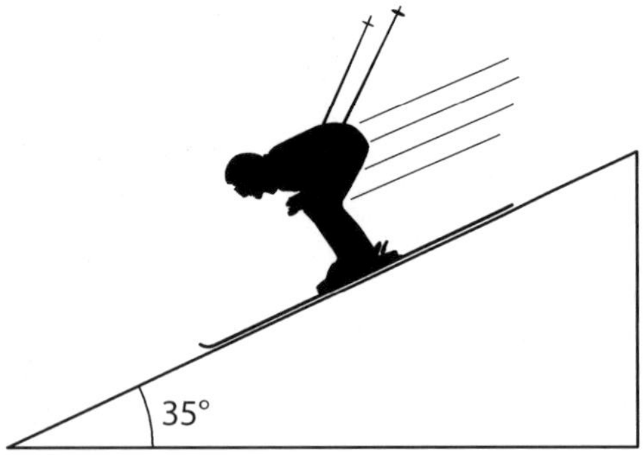

6. A 60.0 kg skydiver experiences air resistance during his jump. At one instant, the resistance is 320 N. At that instant, what is his acceleration? Describe his motion when the air resistance increases to the point where it equals the force of gravity on him.

3.2 Momentum and Impulse

Warm Up

A golf ball is placed on top of a basketball. Both are dropped from a 1.0 m height. What will happen to the golf ball after the basketball hits the ground?

____

____

____

Newton's Second Law in Terms of Momentum

One of the most important concepts in physics is the idea of **momentum.** Newton first used the concept when he formulated his second law of motion. He called the product of mass and velocity "quantity of motion" but this product has come to be known as momentum.

What makes momentum so important is that it is a conserved quantity. In an isolated system (a system in which no external forces interfere), the total momentum of the objects in the system will remain constant. This is the **law of conservation of momentum.**

Any moving object has momentum. Momentum ($\vec{p}$) is calculated by multiplying the mass of the body by its velocity.

momentum = mass × velocity

$$\vec{p} = m\vec{v}$$

Momentum is a vector quantity, and the direction of the momentum vector is the same as the direction of the velocity vector. When you add momenta (the plural of momentum), you must use vector addition.

Newton's second law can be rewritten in terms of momentum:

$$\vec{F} = m\vec{a} = m\frac{\Delta\vec{v}}{\Delta t} = m\frac{[\vec{v}_f - \vec{v}_0]}{\Delta t} = \frac{[m\vec{v}_f - m\vec{v}_0]}{\Delta t} = \frac{\Delta[m\vec{v}]}{\Delta t} = \frac{\Delta\vec{p}}{\Delta t}$$

Newton's second law can be stated in words, in terms of momentum, as given below.

An unbalanced net force acting on a body changes its motion so that the rate of change of momentum is equal to the unbalanced force.

Impulse

If the equation for net force just derived is rearranged by multiplying both sides of the equation by Δt, then

$$\vec{F}\Delta t = \Delta(m\vec{v})$$

The product of the net force and the time interval during which it acts is called the **impulse** of the force. The impulse of the force equals the change in momentum it causes. A given change in momentum can be produced by a large force acting for a short time *or* by a small force acting for a long time!

Units for Momentum and Impulse

Momentum has measuring units that have the dimensions of [mass] x [velocity], which are kg·m/s. Impulse has units with the dimensions of [force] × [time], which are N·s.

$$1\,\text{N}\cdot\text{s} = 1\,\text{kg}\cdot\frac{\text{m}}{\text{s}^2}\cdot\text{s}$$

$$1\,\text{N}\cdot\text{s} = 1\,\text{kg}\cdot\frac{\text{m}}{\text{s}}$$

Therefore, N·s is equivalent to kg·m/s. Momentum can be expressed in either units, and so can impulse.

Conservation of Momentum

Consider an isolated system consisting of two laboratory carts with a compressed spring between them. Before the spring is released by a triggering mechanism, the carts are stationary. The carts have masses m_A and m_B respectively. The total momentum is zero, since neither cart is moving.

The spring is now released. Cart A pushes on cart B and, according to Newton's third law, cart B exerts the same force on cart A, but in the opposite direction.

$$\vec{F}_{\text{A on B}} = \vec{F}_{\text{B on A}}$$

$$\frac{\Delta[m_B\vec{v}_B]}{\Delta t} = -\frac{\Delta[m_A\vec{v}_A]}{\Delta t}$$

Since the time intervals are the same for both forces, Δt can be eliminated.

Therefore $$\Delta[m_B\vec{v}_B] = -\Delta[m_A\vec{v}_A]$$

Or $$\Delta\vec{p}_B = -\Delta\vec{p}_A$$

This means that $$\Delta\vec{p}_A + \Delta\vec{p}_B = 0$$

The total change of momentum of the isolated system is zero. Since the momentum of the two-cart system was zero to begin with, it must be still zero. Both carts are moving after the spring pushes them apart, and both have momentum, but the directions are opposite. The vector sum of the momenta is still zero.

Similar arguments can be used for interacting bodies that have momentum to begin with — the change in momentum will still be zero, and the total momentum will remain constant.

The law of conservation of momentum applies to any isolated system.

> The total momentum of an isolated system of objects will remain constant.

Sample Problem 3.2.1 — Law of Conservation of Momentum

A rifle bullet of mass 0.060 kg leaves the muzzle with a velocity 6.0×10^2 m/s. If the 3.0 kg rifle is held very loosely, with what velocity will it recoil when the bullet is fired?

What to Think About	How to Do It
1. Momentum is conserved. Since before the rifle is fired the momentum of the isolated rifle-bullet system is zero, the total momentum after the bullet is fired is still zero! The subscript "r" denotes "rifle" and "b" denotes "bullet."	$\Delta\vec{p}_r + \Delta\vec{p}_b = 0$
2. Remember that momentum is the product of an object's mass and velocity.	$m_r\vec{v}_r + m_b\vec{v}_b = 0$ $(3.0\text{ kg})(\vec{v}_r) + (0.060\text{ kg})(6.00 \times 10^2\text{ m/s}) = 0$
3. The rifle will recoil with a velocity of 12 m/s in the opposite direction to the velocity of the bullet.	$\vec{v}_r = \dfrac{-(0.060\text{ kg})(6.00 \times 10^2\text{ m/s})}{3.0\text{ kg}}$ $\vec{v}_r = -12\text{ m/s}$

Practice Problems 3.2.1 — Law of Conservation of Momentum

1. A 6.0×10^3 kg railway car is coasting along the track at 7.0 m/s. Suddenly a 2.0×10^3 kg load of coal is dumped into the car. What is its new velocity?

2. A 1.2×10^3 kg car travelling 33 m/s collides head-on with a 1.8×10^3 kg car travelling 22 m/s in the opposite direction. If the cars stick together, what is the velocity of the wreckage immediately after impact?

3. A 0.060 kg rifle bullet leaves the muzzle with a velocity of 6.0×10^2 m/s. The 3.0 kg rifle is held firmly by a 60.0 kg man. With what initial velocity will the man and rifle recoil? Compare your answer with the answer to Sample Problem 3.2.1.

3.2 Review Questions

1. What is the momentum of a 0.25 g bug flying with a speed of 12 m/s?

2. (a) What is the momentum of a 112 kg football player running at 4.8 m/s?

   (b) What impulse must a tackler impart to the football player in (a) to stop him?

   (c) If the tackle is completed in 1.2 s, what average force must the tackler have exerted on the other player?

3. You are doing a space walk outside the International Space Station (ISS), with no cable between you and the ISS. Your small maneuvering rocket pack suddenly quits on you, and you are stranded in space with nothing but a $50 000 camera in your hands. What will you do to get back to the space station?

4. A rocket expels 1.2×10^3 kg of gas each second, and the gas leaves the rocket with a speed of 5.0×10^4 m/s. Will the thrust produced by the rocket be sufficient to lift it, if the force of gravity on the rocket is 5.8×10^7 N?

5. A 3.2 kg cart travelling 1.2 m/s collides with a stationary 1.8 kg cart, and the two carts stick together. What is their common velocity after the collision?

6. A bullet of mass m is fired into a steel wall with velocity $\vec{v}$, then rebounds with velocity $-1/2\,\vec{v}$. A second bullet of the same mass m is fired into a wall covered with modelling clay, and it does not rebound. Which bullet exerts a greater force on the wall: the one that rebounds or the one that does not? Show your reasoning.

7. (a) What impulse must be imparted to a 145 g baseball to change its velocity from 40.0 m/s south to 50.0 m/s north?

(b) If the collision between the baseball and the bat lasted 1.00 ms (milliseconds), what force did the bat exert on the baseball?

8. To measure the speed of a bullet, a physicist fired a 45.0 g bullet into a large block of modelling clay that rested on a metal disk floating on a large air table. The combined mass of the modelling clay and disk was 18.0 kg. By using strobe photography, the speed of the disk was measured to be 0.900 m/s immediately after the impact of the bullet. What was the speed of the bullet?

9. A 2.0×10^3 kg car travelling 15 m/s rear-ends another car of mass 1.0×10^3 kg. The second car was initially moving 6.0 m/s in the same direction. What is their common velocity after the collision if the cars lock together during the impact?

10. What impulse is needed to change the speed of a 10.0 kg body from 20.0 m/s to 12.0 m/s in a time of 5.0 s? What force is needed to do this?

3.3 Momentum in Two-Dimensional Situations

Warm Up

A firecracker bursts, sending four equal-size fragments in different directions along the compass points north, east, south, and west. Draw a vector diagram of the four momentum vectors. Explain the momentum concepts you used in creating this diagram.

Conservation of Momentum in Two Dimensions

All the examples and exercises with momentum have so far dealt with motion in a straight line. The principles involved all apply, however, to two- or three- dimensional situations as well.

When considering a collision between two or more objects, it is important to remember that momentum is a vector and that momentum is conserved. This means you always account for the direction along with the magnitude of each object's momentum. From the law of conservation of momentum, it also means that the total momentum before the collision equals the total momentum after the collision.

Three sample questions involving momentum in two dimensions will help show how useful the law of conservation of momentum can be in solving problems.

Sample Problem 3.3.1 — Collision Between Two Objects: Right Angles

A 60.0 kg hockey player travelling 2.0 m/s toward the north collides with a 50.0 kg player travelling 1.0 m/s toward the west. The two become tangled together. With what velocity will they move after the collision?

What to Think About	How to Do It
1. Momentum is a vector quantity, so you must follow the rules for vector addition.	Before the collision, the momentum of the first player is: $\vec{p}_1 = (60.0\ \text{kg})(2.0\ \text{m/s}) = 120\ \text{kg}\cdot\text{m/s}\ (\text{north})$ Before the collision, the momentum of the second player is: $\vec{p}_2 = (50.0\ \text{kg})(1.0\ \text{m/s}) = 50.0\ \text{kg}\cdot\text{m/s}\ (\text{west})$

Sample Problem continued

Sample Problem 3.3.1 — Collision Between Two Objects: Right Angles (Continued)

What to Think About	How to Do It
2. After the collision, the tangled players have a momentum equal to the vector sum of $\vec{p}_1$ and $\vec{p}_2$. Figure 3.3.1 shows how to find the vector sum. Since the vector triangle has a right angle, the Pythagorean theorem can be used to solve for $\vec{p}_R$.	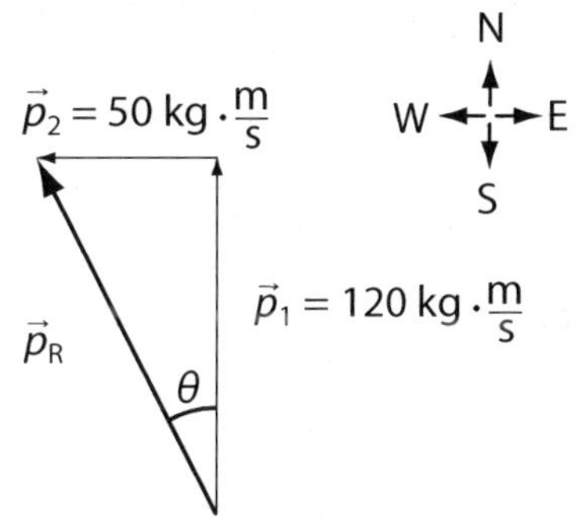 Figure 3.3.1 $\vec{p}_R^{\,2} = \vec{p}_1^{\,2} + \vec{p}_2^{\,2}$ $\vec{p}_R^{\,2} = (120\ \text{kg}\cdot\text{m/s})^2 + (50\ \text{kg}\cdot\text{m/s})^2$ $\vec{p} = 130\ \text{kg}\cdot\text{m/s}$
3. Since $\vec{p}_R = (m_1 + m_2) = \vec{v}_R$, the velocity of the tangled players will have magnitude.	$\vec{v}_R = \dfrac{\vec{p}_R}{m_1 + m_2} = \dfrac{1.3 \times 10^2\ \text{kg}\cdot\text{m/s}}{1.1 \times 10^2\ \text{kg}} = 1.2\ \text{m/s}$
4. The answer is not yet complete, since velocities have specific directions. From the momentum vector diagram, calculate the angle.	$\tan\theta = \dfrac{50\ \text{kg}\cdot\text{m/s}}{120\ \text{kg}\cdot\text{m/s}} = 0.4167$
5. The resultant velocity of the hockey players is 1.2 m/s, directed 23° W of N.	$\theta = 22.6°$ to the west of north

Sample Problem 3.3.2 — Collision Between Two Objects: Vector Components

A 0.050 kg air puck moving with a velocity of 2.0 m/s collides with an identical but stationary air puck. The direction of the incident puck is changed by 60° from its original path, and the angle between the two pucks after the collision is 90°. What are the speeds of the two pucks after they collide?

What to Think About	How to Do It
1. Momentum is conserved, so the resultant momentum after the collision must equal the momentum of the incident puck. The directions of the momenta of the two pucks are known. The resultant momentum must equal $\vec{p}_{io}$	$\vec{p}_{io} = (0.050\ \text{kg})(2.0\ \text{m/s}) = 0.10\ \text{kg}\cdot\text{m/s}$

Sample Problem continued

Sample Problem 3.3.2 — Collision Between Two Objects: Vector Components (Continued)

What to Think About

2. In Figure 3.3.2, the resultant momentum ($\vec{p}_R = \vec{p}_{io}$) was drawn first. Then the directions of $\vec{p}_{if}$ and $\vec{p}_{sf}$ were constructed. As you can see, it is then a simple task to complete the momentum vector triangle.

How to Do It

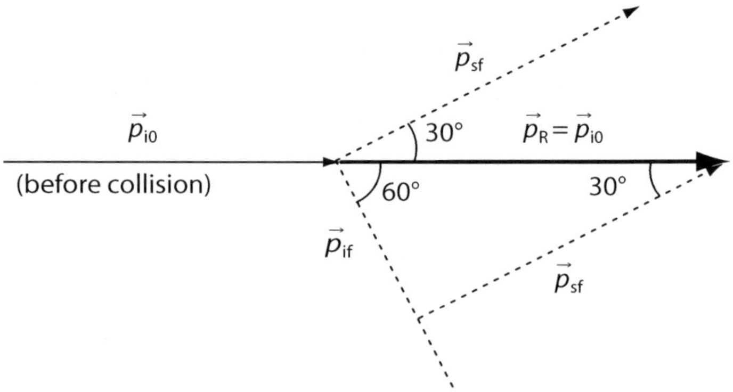

Figure 3.3.2

3. After the collision, $\vec{p}_R = \vec{p}_{io} = 0.10$ kg·m/s in the direction shown. Use trigonometry to solve for the magnitudes of $\vec{p}_{if}$ and $\vec{p}_{sf}$.

$$\vec{p}_{if} = \vec{p}_R \cos 60^\circ$$

$$\vec{p}_{if} = (0.10 \text{ kg}\cdot\text{m/s})(0.500)$$

$$\vec{p}_{if} = 0.050 \text{ kg}\cdot\text{m/s}$$

$$\vec{v}_{if} = \frac{\vec{p}_{if}}{m_i} = \frac{0.050 \text{ kg}\cdot\text{m/s}}{0.050 \text{ kg}} = 1.0 \text{ m/s}$$

Similarly,

$$\vec{p}_{sf} = \vec{p}_R \sin 60^\circ$$

$$\vec{p}_{sf} = (0.10 \text{ kg}\cdot\text{m/s})(0.866)$$

$$\vec{p}_{sf} = 0.087 \text{ kg}\cdot\text{m/s}$$

$$\vec{v}_{sf} = \frac{\vec{p}_{sf}}{m_s} = \frac{0.087 \text{ kg}\cdot\text{m/s}}{0.050 \text{ kg}} = 1.7 \text{ m/s}$$

Challenge: Can you see a shorter way to solve this particular problem?

Sample Problem 3.3.3 — Collision Between Two Objects: Vector Addition

A metal disk explodes into three pieces, which fly off in the same geometric plane. The first piece has a mass of 2.4 kg, and it flies off north at 10.0 m/s. The second piece has a mass of 2.0 kg and it flies east at 12.5 m/s. What is the speed and direction of the third piece, which has a mass of 1.4 kg?

What to Think About	How to Do It
1. Before the explosion, total momentum was zero. After the explosion, the vector sum of the three momenta must be zero, as well, since momentum is conserved. Begin by drawing momentum vectors for the two fragments for which you have full information. The momentum of the third fragment must be such that the three momenta have a vector sum of zero. They must form a closed triangle (Figure 3.3. 3).	The momentum of the first fragment, $\vec{p}_1 = (2.4\ \text{kg})(10.0\ \text{m/s}) = 24\ \text{kg·m/s (north)}$ The momentum of the second fragment, $\vec{p}_2 = (2.0\ \text{kg})(12.5\ \text{m/s}) = 25\ \text{kg·m/s (east)}$ 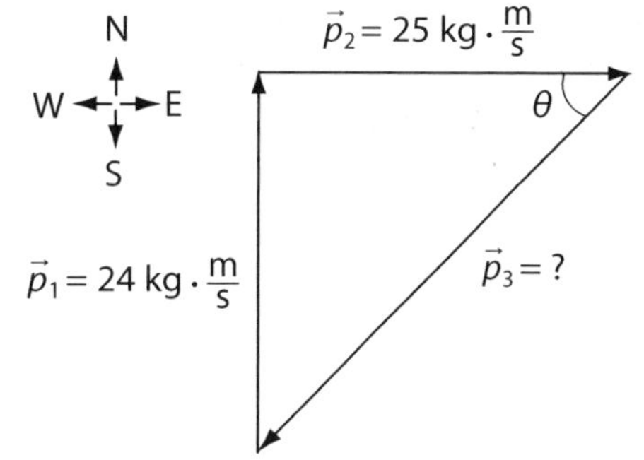 Figure 3.3.3
2. Since these momentum vectors form a right-angled triangle, use the Pythagorean theorem to solve for the magnitude of $\vec{p}_3$.	$\vec{p}_1 = \sqrt{(24\ \text{kg·m/s})^2 + (25\ \text{kg·m/s})^2} = 35\ \text{kg·m/s}$ $\vec{v}_3 = \frac{\vec{p}_3}{m_3} = \frac{35\ \text{kg·m/s}}{1.4\ \text{kg}} = 25\ \text{m/s}$
3. Therefore, the velocity of the third fragment is 25 m/s in a direction 44° south of west.	$\tan\theta = \frac{24\ \text{kg·m/s}}{25\ \text{kg·m/s}}$ $\tan\theta = 0.9600$ $\theta = 44°$

Special Note: In each of the three examples, the angle between vectors has been a right angle. If there is no right angle, the problem may be solved using a scale diagram or by using sine law or cosine law. Another method is to use *x*- and *y*-components of velocities or momenta.

Investigation 3.3.1 Momentum in Explosions and Collisions

Purpose

To measure and compare momentum before and after "explosions" and "collisions"

Part 1 An "Explosion" of Two Carts (Demonstration)

Procedure

1. Two laboratory carts of equal mass are equipped with spring bumpers (Figure 3.3.4). Predict how the speeds of the carts will compare when the springs are compressed, and the two carts are allowed to "explode" apart. Design a way to compare speeds using only a metre stick. Test your prediction.

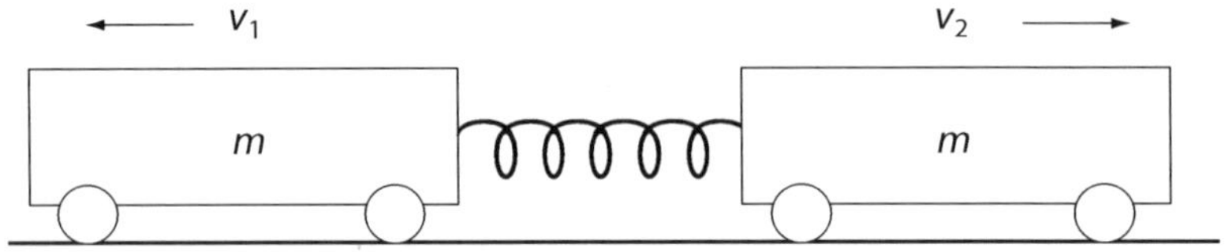

Figure 3.3.4

2. Place an extra laboratory cart on top of one of the identical carts, so that you double the mass of the bottom cart. Again, predict how the speeds will compare after the carts "explode" apart. Test your prediction.

Concluding Question

1. On what basis did you make your predictions? Were they correct? If not, explain why they were not.

Part 2 Straight-Line Collisions of Carts of Equal Mass (Demonstration)

Procedure

1. (a) Predict what will happen if a spring-bumpered cart moving with a speed v is made to collide head-on with a second cart of equal mass, which is initially at rest. Test your prediction.
   (b) Repeat the procedure in (a), but this time attach a strip of Velcro to two identical carts so that when they collide they will stick together when they collide. Predict what the speed of the combined carts will be after the collision, if the incoming cart has speed v.
2. (a) Predict what will happen if two identical spring-loaded carts, travelling toward each other at speed v, collide head-on. Test your prediction.
   (b) Predict what will happen if two identical carts, equipped with Velcro bumpers, approach each other, both at speed v, and stick together following the collision. Test your prediction.

Concluding Question

1. On what basis did you make your predictions in procedure steps 1 and 2? Were they correct? If not, explain why they did not work out.

Part 3 Oblique Collisions of Pucks on an Air Table (Demonstration)

Procedure

1. Place two pucks of identical mass on an air table (Figure 3.3.5). Observe what happens when a moving puck collides with a stationary puck (a) head-on and (b) at an oblique angle. Pay particular attention to the angle between the incident puck and the struck puck.

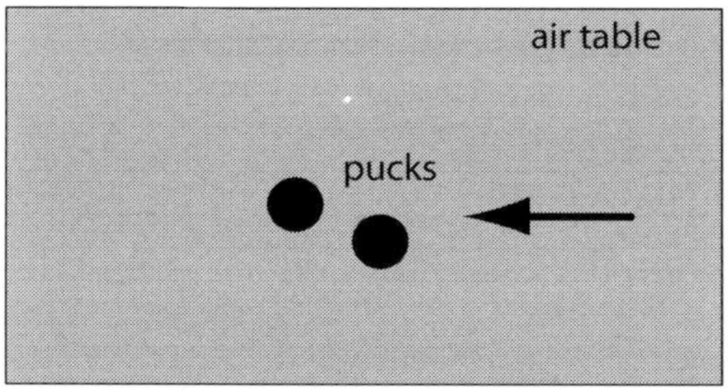

Figure 3.3.5

If you have the equipment, take a strobe photograph of these two types of collision and measure the angles from the photograph. You may substitute Part 3 for Part 4 if you use this method for Part 3.

2. Try varying the masses of the pucks. Observe whether the angle between the incident puck and the struck puck is the same as it was when the pucks had identical mass.

Concluding Questions

1. What do you conclude about the angle between the incident puck and the struck puck after they collided (a) head-on and (b) obliquely, when their masses are identical?
2. Does this conclusion hold true when the masses are different?

Part 4 Collisions of Steel Balls of Equal Mass (Student Experiment)

If one sphere of mass *m* collides with a second sphere of equal mass *m*, we expect momentum to be conserved, and therefore

$$m\vec{v}_{io} + m\vec{v}_{so} = m\vec{v}_{if} + m\vec{v}_{sf}$$

where $\vec{v}_{io}$ is the velocity of the incident *ball before the collision;*
$\vec{v}_{so}$ is the velocity of the struck ball before the collision;
$\vec{v}_{if}$ is the velocity of the incident ball after the collision; and
$\vec{v}_{sf}$ is the velocity of the struck ball after the collision.

Keep in mind that velocity and momentum are vector quantities.

Figure 3.3.6 shows the arrangement for this experiment. From your study of projectile motion, you know that no matter what the horizontal velocity of a ball coming off the ramp is, it will take the same time to fall to the floor. This means that you can use the horizontal displacement of the ball from its position during the collision as a measure of its velocity. Since the time taken to fall for either ball will always be the same, let that time be one arbitrary time unit (tu). If, for example, the horizontal displacement of the struck ball was 32 cm, then its velocity is $\vec{v}_{sf} = 32$ cm/tu.

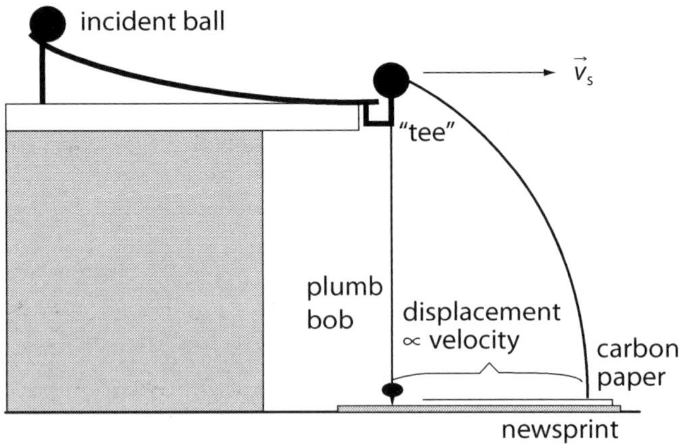

Figure 3.3.6

In addition, since the incident ball and the struck ball are of equal mass *m*, mass cancels out of the momentum equation, and you can compare momenta simply by comparing velocities (or, in this case, displacements). This only works when the colliding balls are of equal mass.

Procedure

1. Set up the apparatus in Figure 3.3.6. Place several sheets of carbon paper with the carbon side *down* on top of a large sheet of newsprint paper, so that when a ball lands on the floor it will leave a black mark showing where it landed.
2. The plumb bob shows the exact location of the centre of the struck ball. Make a pencil mark at this location. Also, make a pencil mark where the centre of the incident ball will be at the moment of collision. (It should be one ball diameter in front of the struck ball's centre.)
3. To measure the velocity (displacement) of the incident ball, let it run down from the very top of the ramp at least five times. Measure the *average displacement* using the close cluster of ball marks. Record this average as the value of $\vec{v}_{io}$.
4. Set the target ball on its "tee," making sure that the collision will be truly head-on. Allow the incident ball to run down the ramp from the very top again, but let it collide with the target ball, which should be identical with the incident ball. Repeat this four more times and measure the *average displacement* of the target (struck) ball from the cluster of ball marks. Record this average as the value of $\vec{v}_{sf}$. Why can the displacement of the incident ball after the collision be disregarded in this particular type of collision? (Remember Parts 2 and 3.)
5. Draw vector diagrams (scaled down if necessary) showing the following:
   (a) the momentum of the incident ball before the head-on collision
   (b) the momentum of the incident ball after the collision
   (c) the momentum of the struck ball after the collision

   Label these vectors $\vec{p}_{io}, \vec{p}_{if}$, and $\vec{p}_{sf}$.

6. Arrange the target ball so that the collision will be oblique (i.e., the incident ball will strike the target ball at an angle other than head-on). Let the incident ball run down from the very top of the ramp and collide with the target ball. Mark the landing positions of both balls. Repeat four more times and average the displacement of each ball after the collision. Be sure to record the angles between the two balls after the collision. Also record the angle between their displacement vectors and the displacement vector the incident ball would have had if it had not collided with the struck ball. You need to know the direction of the initial momentum vector.
7. Draw a vector diagram (scaled down if necessary) showing the following:
   (a) the momentum of the incident ball before the oblique collision
   (b) the momentum of the incident ball after the collision
   (c) the momentum of the struck ball after the collision
   (d) the vector sum of the momenta of the incident ball after collision and the struck ball after the collision

   Label these vectors respectively: $\vec{p}_{io}$, $\vec{p}_{if}$, $\vec{p}_{sf}$, and $\vec{p}_R$.

Concluding Questions

1. Compare the total momentum before with the total momentum after a head-on collision of two steel balls of equal mass. Calculate the percent difference between the two, and discuss sources of error.
2. Compare the resultant momentum of the incident and struck balls after an oblique collision, with the momentum of the incident ball before the collision.
   If there is a difference, remember you must use the vector difference.
3. What percent is the magnitude of the vector difference between $\vec{p}_R$ and $\vec{p}_{io}$ of the initial momentum, $\vec{p}_{io}$ of the incident ball? Discuss sources or error.

Challenge

1. Repeat procedure steps 1 to 7, using a steel ball colliding with a less massive glass ball. Note that you can no longer use just displacement vectors to compare momenta. Each displacement (velocity) must be multiplied by the appropriate mass.

3.3 Review Questions

1. A hockey player of mass 82 kg is travelling north with a velocity of 4.1 m/s. He collides with a 76 kg player travelling east at 3.4 m/s. If the two players lock together momentarily, in what direction will they be going immediately after the collision? How fast will they be moving?

2. A 2.5×10^3 kg car travelling west at 6.0 m/s is hit by a 6.0×10^3 kg truck going south at 4.0 m/s. The two vehicles lock together on impact. What is the speed and direction of the wreckage immediately after impact?

3. A frustrated physics student blew up her physics textbook, using a small amount of an explosive. It broke into three pieces, which miraculously flew off in directions that were all in the same geometric plane. A 0.200 kg piece flew off at 20.0 m/s, and a 0.100 kg piece went off at 90° to the first piece at 30.0 m/s.
   (a) What was the momentum of the third piece?

   (b) If the mass of the third piece was 0.150 kg, what was its velocity right after the explosion?

4. A proton of mass m collides obliquely with another proton. The first proton is moving with a speed of 6.0×10^6 m/s before it hits the second, stationary proton. Assuming the collision is perfectly elastic (no kinetic energy is lost), and using the fact that the first proton is moved 30° from its initial path after the collision, figure out the speed and direction of each proton after the collision.

5. A 0.40 kg model airplane is travelling 20 km/h toward the south. A 0.50 kg model airplane, travelling 25 km/h in a direction 20° east of south, collides with the first model airplane. The two planes stick together on impact. What is the direction and magnitude of the velocity of the combined wreckage immediately after the collision?

6. What impulse is needed to change the velocity of a 90.0 kg football player from 3.6 m/s toward the north and make it 1.2 m/s toward the northeast? In what direction must the force be exerted?

3.4 Energy

Warm Up

If you were designing a roller coaster, where would you put its highest point? Defend your answer.

____

____

____

Work

Imagine you have just spent the past hour finishing a physics experiment, writing a quiz, and then solving five difficult problems from your physics textbook. After all this, your physics teacher says, "You people have done very little work this period!" Your reaction to this statement would be predictable. You would be very annoyed with your teacher — unless you know what a physics teacher really means by *work*. In physics, work has a very special meaning.

Work is done on a body when a force or a component of that force acts on the body, causing it to be displaced. Work is calculated from the product of the force component in the direction of motion and the distance moved.

work = (force component in direction of motion) × (distance)

$$W = F_d \cdot d$$

The measuring unit for work is the newton•metre, which is called a **joule.**

$$1\ J = 1\ N{\cdot}m$$

Sample Problem 3.4.1(a) — Work in the Physics Way

How much work does the man in Figure 3.4.1 do to lift the 150 N of firewood from the ground up to a height of 1.2 m?

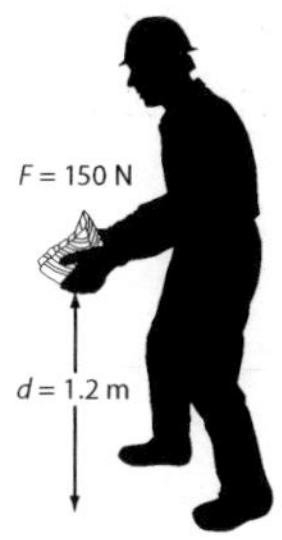

Figure 3.4.1

What to Think About	How to Do It
1. Lifting the wood at a steady speed, he will exert a force equal to the force of gravity on the wood. The direction of the force is straight up.	$W = Fd = (150\ N)(1.2\ m) = 180\ J$
2. Solve.	The man does 1.8×10^2 J of work on the wood.

Sample Problem 3.4.1(b) — Work and Direction

How much work does the hiker in Figure 3.4.2 do on the 90.0 N backpack she carries to the top of the 850 m high hill?

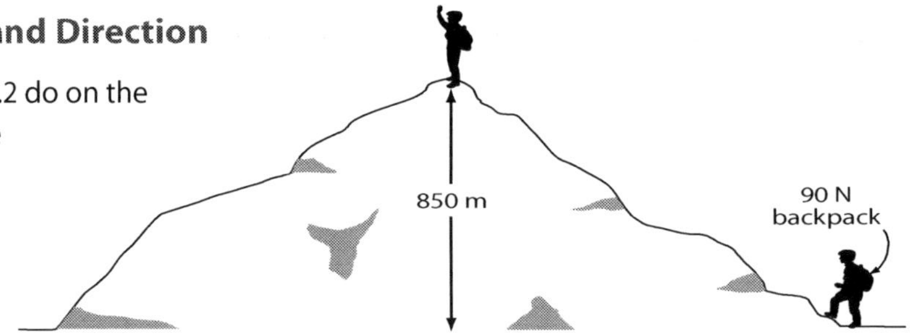

Figure 3.4.2

What to Think About	How to Do It
1. When the hiker reaches the top of the hill, her vertical displacement is 850 m. The force component in the vertical direction is equal to the force of gravity on the backpack, but in the opposite direction, assuming the vertical velocity component is constant.	$W = Fd$ $W = (90.0\text{ N})(850\text{ m})$ $W = 7.7 \times 10^4\text{ J}$
2. Solve.	The work done on the backpack is 77 kJ.

Sample Problem 3.4.1(c) — Work and Components

A child is pulling a wagon along a driveway, exerting a force $\vec{F}$ along the handle of the wagon. How would you calculate the work done by the child on the wagon?

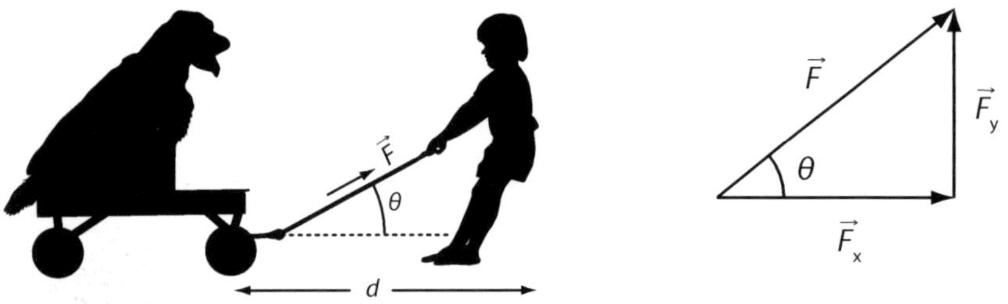

Figure 3.4.3

What to Think About	How to Do It
1. The component of the force exerted by the child in the direction of motion is $\vec{F}_x$, the horizontal component.	$\vec{F}_x = F \cdot \cos\theta$
2. Solve.	The work done is therefore $W = F \cdot \cos\theta \cdot d$.

Practice Problems 3.4.1 — Work and Components

1. (a) How much work must be done to lift a 110 kg motorbike directly up 1.1 m to the back of a truck?

   (b) If a 2.6 m ramp is used to push the bike up to the back of the truck, the force needed is 550 N. Does this ramp "save" you work? Why is it used?

2. In Figure 3.4.3, if the force exerted on the handle of the wagon is 45 N, and the angle θ is 28°, how much work will be done pulling the wagon 17 m along the driveway?

3. A ball on the end of a rope is following a circular path because of a constant force exerted on the ball by the rope in a direction toward the centre of the circle. How much work is done on the ball by this force?

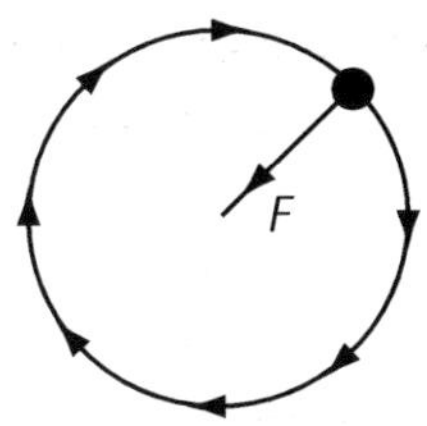

Figure 3.4.4 (top view)

Work Done by a Changing Force

Often, the force acting on an object is not constant over the distance it is exerted. The three examples below involving changing forces illustrate how to calculate the work done in these situations.

1. Area under a force–distance graph with varying force

A girl is pushing a laboratory supply cart down the hallway of a school. She pushes in a direction parallel with the floor. On a linoleum floor, she exerts a force of 30.0 N over a distance of 10.0 m. She then has to push the cart over a carpeted floor for a distance of 10.0 m, and this requires a force of 50.0 N. Finally, she must push it another 7.5 m on another stretch of linoleum floor, again with a force of 30.0 N. How much work does she do on the cart during the whole trip?

This situation can be represented in a force–distance graph as shown in Figure 3.4.5.

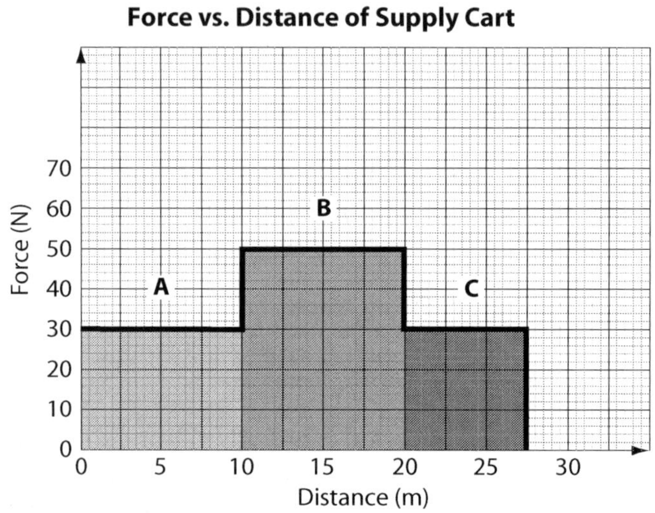

Figure 3.4.5 *A force vs. distance graph representing the girl's travels with the supply cart*

The total work done will be the sum of the work done on each stretch of floor or the sum of the areas under the graph line:

$$
\begin{aligned}
W &= A + B + C \\
&= (30.0\ \text{N})(10.0\ \text{m}) + (50.0\ \text{N})(10.0\ \text{m}) + (30.0\ \text{N})(7.5\ \text{m}) \\
&= 300\ \text{J} + 500\ \text{J} + 225\ \text{J} = 1025\ \text{J}
\end{aligned}
$$

The total work done is 1.025×10^3 J. If you examine Figure 3.4.5, you will see that this work is equal to the area under the force–distance graph. As a rule, where the force is parallel to the displacement of the object, the area under the force–distance graph is equal to the amount of work done.

2. Area under a force–distance graph with average force

A coiled spring is stretched by hanging known weights from its end, and the stretch is measured in metres. Figure 3.4.6 is a graph showing how the force on the spring varies with the amount of stretch. How much work must be done to stretch the spring 0.50 m?

Since the force is changing all the time the spring is being stretched, the average force must be used. From the graph, the average force is 3.0 N, so the work done while stretching the spring is

$$W = \bar{F} \cdot x = (3.0\ \text{N})(0.50\ \text{m}) = 1.5\ \text{J}$$

Force vs. Distance of Stretched Spring

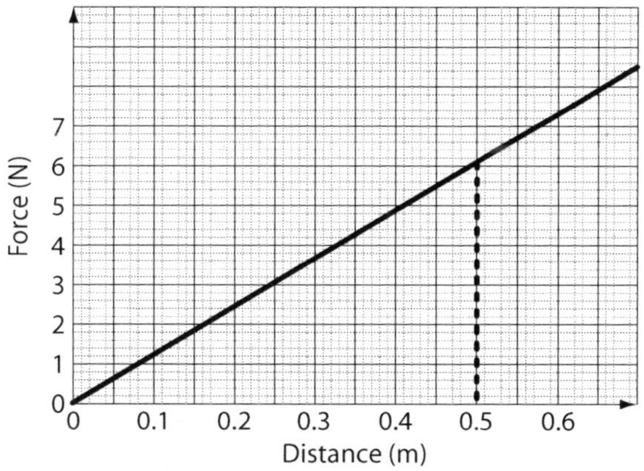

Figure 3.4.6 *Graph representing the variation in force with the amount of stretch in a spring*

The work done to stretch the spring is 1.5 J. Notice that this is the area under the force–distance graph. The area of the triangle underneath the line on the graph is [1/2•height•base], which is 1/2• $\bar{F} \cdot x$. This is the same as $\bar{F} \cdot x$.

3. Area under a force–distance graph with force changing radically with distance

Figure 3.4.7 shows a common situation in physics. The force in this case changes radically with distance. In fact, if you study the graph carefully you will notice that as the distance doubles, the force is reduced to one-quarter of what it was. If the distance triples, the force is reduced to one-ninth of its original value. You will encounter at least two situations where this happens. The gravitational attraction between any two masses is one example of a force that varies as the inverse of the square of the distance between the two bodies.

Force vs. Distance for Gravitational Force Between Two Objects

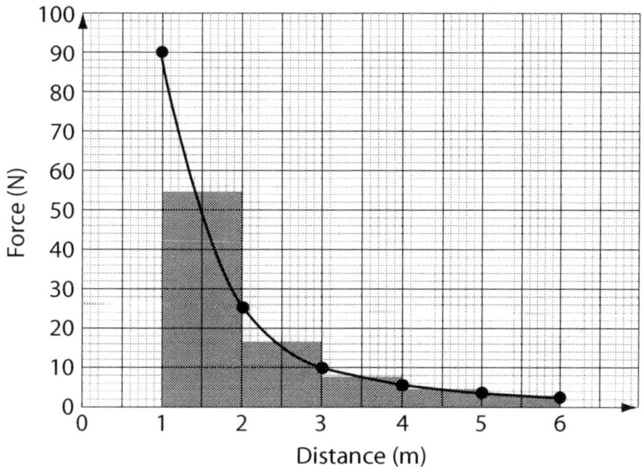

Figure 3.4.7 *Graph showing major changes in force over distance*

How much work would be done moving an object from a distance of 1.0 m to a distance of 5.0 m (Figure 3.4.7)? If you knew the average force between these two distances, you could use it to calculate the work done. Obviously, that is not a simple thing to determine. You could draw a series of rectangles that average the force over a sequence of short distances, and then total their areas. Or, you can wait until you learn the calculus method of finding the area under such a curve. This area is what will give you the amount of work done.

Quick Check

1. In Figure 3.4.6, how much work is done to stretch the spring from a starting stretch of 0.20 m to a new stretch of 0.40 m?

2. If 1.0 J of work is done to stretch the spring in Figure 3.4.6 from its relaxed position, by how much will the spring be extended?

Kinetic Energy

A moving object can do work. A falling axe does work to split a log. A moving baseball bat does work to stop a baseball, momentarily compressing it out of its normal shape, then reversing the ball's direction and sending it off at high speed. Since a moving object has the ability to do work, it must have energy. We call the energy of a moving object its **kinetic energy**.

A body that is at rest can gain kinetic energy if work is done on it by an external force. To get such a body moving at speed *v*, a net force must be exerted on it to accelerate it from rest up to speed *v*. The amount of work *W* which must be done can be calculated as follows:

$$W = F \cdot d = (ma)d = m(ad)$$

Remember that for an object accelerating from rest at a uniform rate $v_f^2 = 2ad$. Therefore,

$$(ad) = \frac{v_f^2}{2} \text{ and}$$
$$W = m(ad) = m\frac{v_f^2}{2} = \frac{1}{2}mv_f^2$$

The work done on the object to accelerate it up to a speed *v* results in an amount of energy being transferred to the object, which is equal in magnitude to $\frac{1}{2}mv^2$. The energy an object has because of its motion is called kinetic energy, E_k.

$$E_k = \frac{1}{2}mv^2$$

Once an object has kinetic energy, the object itself can do work on other objects. This is called the work-energy theorem and is written:

$$W = \Delta E_k$$

Quick Check

1. A golfer wishes to improve his driving distance. Which would have more effect, (a) doubling the mass of his golf club or (b) doubling the speed with which the club head strikes the ball? Explain your answer.

2. How much work must be done to accelerate a 110 kg motorbike and its 60.0 kg rider from 0 to 80 km/h?

3. How much work is needed to slow down a 1200 kg vehicle from 80 km/h to 50 km/h? What does this work?

Potential Energy

Potential energy is sometimes referred to as *stored* energy. A skier has potential energy at the top of a hill, because work has been done (by the skier or by a ski tow) to raise the skier from the bottom of the hill to the top. If the skier has been lifted a height *h* from the bottom of the hill, and the force of gravity on the skier is *mg,* then the amount of *work* done on the skier is $W = mgh$.

The energy transferred to the skier because of this amount of work done on the skier is now potentially available to do work. In this situation, it can be said that the skier has **gravitational potential energy**.

$$\text{gravitational } E_p = mgh$$

A stretched spring or a compressed spring has potential energy. Work must be done to stretch or compress a spring. In the example of Figure 3.4.6 the work done to stretch the spring a distance *x* is $\frac{1}{2}F \cdot x$. For this particular spring, force is directly proportional to extension (stretch), so $F = kx$.

The work done to stretch the spring is, therefore, $W = \frac{1}{2}(kx)x = \frac{1}{2}kx^2$.

The amount of energy transferred to the spring because of the work done on it is potentially available to do work. In this case, the stored energy is called **elastic potential energy**.

$$\text{elastic } E_p = \frac{1}{2}kx^2$$

An object has kinetic energy because of its motion. It has potential energy because of its position (in the case of gravitational potential energy) or its shape (elastic potential energy).

Quick Check

1. How much gravitational energy is gained by a 45 kg girl if she climbs 6.0 m up a flight of stairs?

2. (a) A spring in a toy gun requires an average force of 1.2 N to compress it a distance of 3.0 cm. How much elastic potential energy is stored in the spring when it is fully compressed?

   (b) If all the elastic potential energy is transferred to a 10.0 g "bullet" (a plastic rod with a suction cup on the end), how fast will the "bullet" move as it leaves the gun?

3. Discuss the forms of energy involved when a basketball is dropped from your hand, bounces on the floor, and moves back up into your hand.

Power

The word **power** is used in a variety of ways in everyday language, but in physics it has a specific meaning. Power is the rate at which work is done or the rate at which energy is transformed from one form to another.

$$\text{power} = \frac{\text{work done}}{\text{time}} = \frac{\text{energy transformed}}{\text{time}}$$

Power is measured in watts (W), where $1\ \text{W} = 1\ \frac{\text{J}}{\text{s}}$.

A typical household light bulb transforms energy at the rate of 60 W. Most of the electrical energy, unfortunately, is transformed into heat instead of light. Approximately 57 W of heat and 3 W of light are produced by the bulb. An incandescent light bulb is only about 5 percent efficient. A kettle might transform electrical energy into heat at the rate of 1500 W. The power rating of an electrical appliance is usually printed somewhere on the appliance.

A commonly used unit for power is the **horsepower (hp)**. In the metric system, the hp is defined as 750 W. (The electrical kettle just described is 2 hp.) The hp was originally defined by James Watt, who was looking for a way to describe the power of his newly invented steam engines, in terms that people accustomed to using horses to do their work could understand.

Quick Check

1. How much work can a 5.00 hp motor do in 10.0 min?

2. A 60.0 kg boy runs up a flight of stairs 3.32 m high in 2.60 s.
   What is his power output (a) in watts? (b) in hp?

3. How long would it take a 5.0 hp motor to lift a 500.0 kg safe up to a window 30.0 m above the ground?

Investigation 3.4.1 Energy Changes of a Swinging Pendulum

Purpose

To predict the maximum speed reached by a pendulum swinging from a known height above its rest position, and to check the prediction by measurement

Procedure

1. Attach a massive pendulum bob (1 kg) by a sturdy cable to a support on the ceiling of your classroom.
2. Design a system so that you can raise the bob to the same height *h* repeatedly. Measure *h* from the lowest position the bob reaches during each swing (Figure 3.4.8).

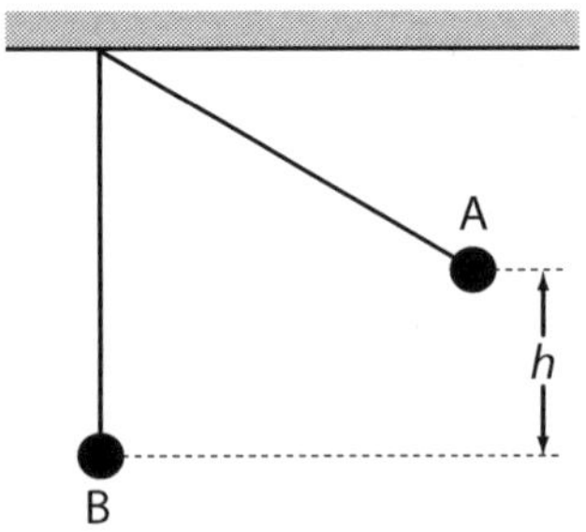

Figure 3.4.8

3. Choose the value of *h* you are going to use, then calculate how much gravitational potential energy (E_p) the bob will have at height *h*.
4. Let the bob swing once, and record the height *h*′ reached by the bob on its *return swing*. Repeat this measurement four more times and average your five measurements of *h*′. Calculate the loss of E_p during one full swing (*mgh* – *mgh*′).
5. The loss of energy during one complete swing can be accounted for by assuming work is done by the bob and string to overcome the force of friction due to the air. As the bob moves from its starting position A to the bottom of its swing at B, it will lose an amount of energy equal to one-quarter of the loss for one full swing, which you calculated in procedure step 4. What happens to the rest of the potential energy the bob has when it is at A?

   Let us assume that all the remaining potential energy is changed into kinetic energy. At the bottom of the swing, all the bob's energy is kinetic energy, $E_k = \frac{1}{2}mv^2$. This energy was initially the potential energy of the bob at A. If there was no air friction (or other forms of friction), we could predict that

$$E_k \text{ (bottom of swing)} = E_p \text{ (top of swing)}$$

   Since there *is* a loss of potential energy due to friction, this loss must be taken into account. The loss of energy during the swing from A to B is $\frac{1}{4}(mgh - mgh')$.

   To predict the speed of the bob at B, calculate *v* using the following equation:

$$\frac{1}{2}mv^2 = mgh - \frac{1}{4}(mgh - mgh')$$

6. Attach a short length of ticker tape (no longer than needed) to the 1 kg mass, and use a recording timer to measure the maximum speed reached by the swinging mass. (If your timer vibrates with a frequency of 60 Hz, the time between dots is 1/60 s.) When several groups have duplicated the same measurement using the same starting height, average the values of v.

Concluding Questions

1. What is the percent difference between your predicted speed and your measured speed?
2. What are some sources of error in this experiment?
3. If you had used a bob with a different mass, how would that affect the predicted speed? Explain your answer.
4. Do your results suggest that the total energy of the bob (potential and kinetic) remains constant during a full swing? Discuss your answer.

Challenge

1. Predict what these graphs would look like, for one-half swing of the pendulum:
   (a) v vs. x
   (b) E_p vs. x
   (c) E_k vs. x
   (d) total E vs. x
2. Design and carry out an experiment to test your predictions in question 1.

3.4 Review Questions

1. A worker does 100 J of work in moving a 20 kg box over a 10 m distance. What is the minimum force required to do this?

2. Another worker moves another 20 kg box over a 10 m distance. If the coefficient of friction between the box and the floor is 0.25, what is the work done by the frictional force.

3. In a baseball game, the pitcher throws a ball and the catcher catches the ball in her mitt. With reference to the catchers mitt, was positive work done, was negative work done, or was the net work zero?

4. In the drawing below, how much work is done by the person mowing the lawn if the force pushing the lawn mower is 100 N at an angle of 30° below the horizontal and moves the mower 40.0 m?

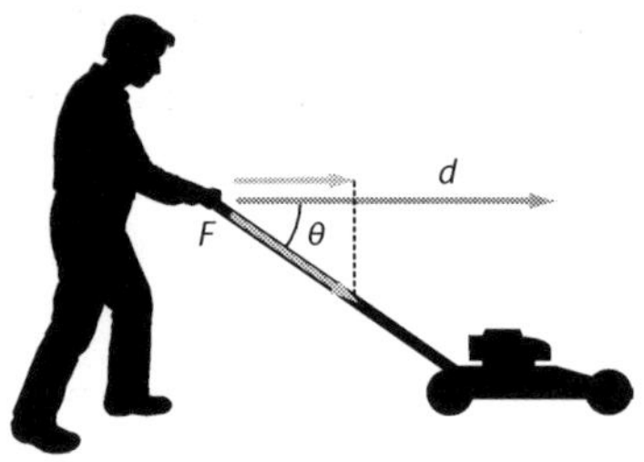

5. Find the work done for the first 5.00 s by the variable force in the graph below.

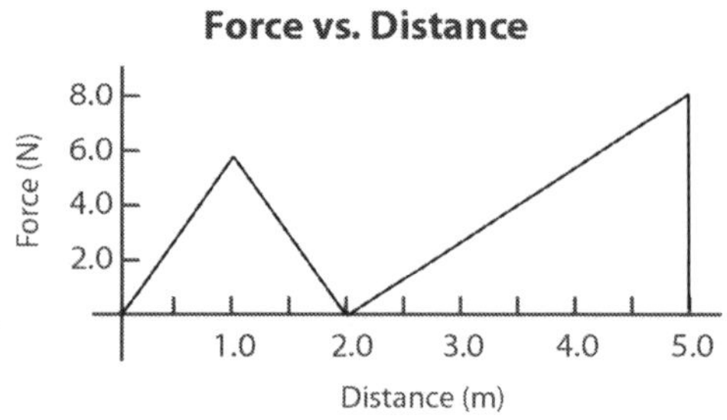

6. Truck A is traveling twice as fast as truck B, but truck B has four times the mass of truck A. Which truck has more kinetic energy?

7. How much work is needed to accelerate a 1.0 g insect from rest up to 12 m/s?

8. If the speed of a proton is tripled by a particle accelerator, by how much will its kinetic energy increase? (Ignore relativistic effects.)

9. A 1500 kg car travels at 80 km/h. What is the kinetic energy of the car? What net work would it take to stop the car?

10. A car travelling at 50 km/h stops in 70.0 m. What is the stopping distance if the car's speed is 90 km/h?

11. You and your friend are sitting at the table looking at your physics book. Your friend says the book has 0 J of potential energy. You say because the book weighs 1 kg and is 1 m off the ground, it has 9.8 J. Who is correct?

12. How much more gravitational potential energy does a 4.0 kg box have when it is on a shelf 1.5 m high than when it is on a shelf that is 75 cm high?

13. Five books of mass 0.750 kg and 5 cm thick are placed separately on a table. How much work must be done to stack the books one on top of the other?

14. A man slides a 100.0 kg box along the floor for a distance of 4.0 m. If the coefficient of kinetic friction is 0.250, and the man does the job in 3.6 s, what is his power output (a) in watts? and (b) in hp?

15. A certain automobile engine is rated at 350 hp. What is its power (a) in watts? (b) in kilowatts (1 kW = 1000 W)?

16. Describe an experiment you could carry out to determine your power output in climbing a flight of stairs that is 10.0 m high (vertical distance from bottom to top).

3.5 The Law of Conservation of Mechanical Energy

Warm Up

Your teacher sets up a pendulum in the classroom with a 5 kg bob on the end and stands to one side of it so the bob is next to his nose. If the bob is released, will it swing back and touch your teacher's nose? Explain your thinking.

____

____

____

Conservation of Mechanical Energy

Consider a frictionless pendulum as it makes a swing from one side to the other. If we decide to assign the bob zero potential energy at the bottom of its swing, as we did in Investigation 3.4.1, then it gains potential energy equal to *mgh* when it reaches the highest point in its swing. When it swings through the lowest part of its swing, its potential energy returns to zero, but it still has the same total energy. At the bottom of the swing, all the potential energy the bob had at the top of its swing has been transformed into kinetic energy. Ignoring energy lost because of friction in the system,

$$E_k \text{ (bottom of swing)} = E_P \text{ (top of swing)}$$

At any point in the swing, ignoring energy losses because of work done overcoming friction, the *total mechanical energy* $(E_k + E_P)$ is constant.

$$\text{total mechanical energy} = E_k + E_P = \text{constant}$$

If the subscripts 1 and 2 are used to represent any two positions of the pendulum, the **law of conservation of mechanical energy** for this situation can be written:

$$\frac{1}{2}mv_1^2 + mgh_1 = \frac{1}{2}mv_2^2 + mgh_2$$

This description would also apply to a body falling under the influence of the force of gravity, from an initial height *h*.

Although we have looked at only a single example of a mechanical situation (the pendulum), the law of conservation of energy applies in a very general way to all similar energy transformations. Taking all forms of energy into account, a broader statement can be made about energy in general.

Energy can be transformed from one form to another, but it is never created and it is never destroyed. Total energy remains constant.

Sample Problem 3.5.1 — Conservation of Mechanical Energy

A 45.93 g golf ball is struck by a golf club, and it leaves the face of the club with a speed of 75.0 m/s.

(a) How much kinetic energy does the golf ball have as it leaves the face of the club?

(b) If air friction is ignored, from what height would the same golf ball have to be dropped to gain this much kinetic energy?

What to Think About	How to Do It
(a) 1. When the ball is struck, all the energy in the ball is kinetic. Find the total kinetic energy.	$E_k = \frac{1}{2}mv^2$ $E_k = \frac{1}{2}(0.04593\ \text{kg})(75.0\ \text{m/s})^2$ $E_k = 129\ \text{J}$
(b) 1. The question is really asking how high the ball will go when kinetic energy is zero and all the kinetic energy has been converted to potential energy. We know at top of ball's flight, $E_k = E_P$ Find h from E_P	$E_k = E_p = mgh$ $h = \frac{E_P}{mg}$ $h = \frac{129\ \text{J}}{(0.04593\ \text{kg})(75.0\ \text{m/s})}$ $h = 37.4\ \text{m}$

Practice Problems 3.5.1 — Conservation of Mechanical Energy

1. A 1.00 kg pendulum bob is released from a height of 0.200 m. Its speed at the bottom of its swing is 1.95 m/s on the first pass. How much energy is lost due to friction during one complete swing of the pendulum?

2. A rope is hanging from the roof of the gymnasium. You are going to run at the rope, grab it, and see how high you are carried off the floor by the swinging rope. How fast must you run if you want to swing to a height of 1.5 m off the floor? Does your mass matter? Does the length of the rope matter? Discuss your answers.

Practice Problems continued

Practice Problems 3.5.1 — Conservation of Mechanical Energy (Continued)

3. A skier slides down a frictionless 25° slope from a height of 12 m. How fast is she moving at the bottom of the hill? Does the slope of the hill matter? Explain.

Categorizing Forces in a System

Using the law of conservation of energy can be a powerful tool in your problem solving tool kit. Before examining a specific problem, you need to consider two additional concepts. First, you should consider the type of system based on the two categories of forces that may act within or on it: conservative and nonconservative forces. Second, if there is a collision, you need to know if the collision was elastic or inelastic.

A force is **conservative** if the work done by it in moving an object is independent of the object's path. This means only the initial and final positions of an object are used when determining the amount of work done on the object. For example, gravity is a conservative force. In calculations of gravitational potential energy, an object gains from work being done on it. You only need to know the starting and finishing positions of the object. A force is **nonconservative** if the work done by it in moving an object depends on the object's path. For example, friction is a nonconservative force. The longer an object is pushed, the longer the frictional force is acting on that object.

Types of Collisions in a System

Whenever two or more objects interact in a way that energy and/or momentum are exchanged, a collision has occurred. In an **elastic collision**, the total kinetic energy is conserved. In an **inelastic collision**, the total kinetic energy in not conserved. Some of the kinetic energy is lost. In everyday collisions, this is the common type that occurs. Another form of an inelastic collision is when a moving object hits and sticks to another object. This is called a **completely inelastic collision**.

Regardless of the type of collision, for isolated systems, the momentum is always conserved. Remember that momentum is a vector quantity. This difference between momentum and energy, a scalar quantity, is an example of the difference between vector and scalar quantities.

Applying the Law of Conservation of Energy

A ballistic pendulum, used to measure the speed of a bullet indirectly, is a good illustration of the use of both the law of conservation of momentum and the law of conservation of mechanical energy.

A bullet of mass *m* is fired at an unknown speed *v* into a sand-filled pendulum bob of mass *M*, causing the bob to swing to the right and rise to a height *h* (Figure 3.5.1). How can the speed *v* be calculated?

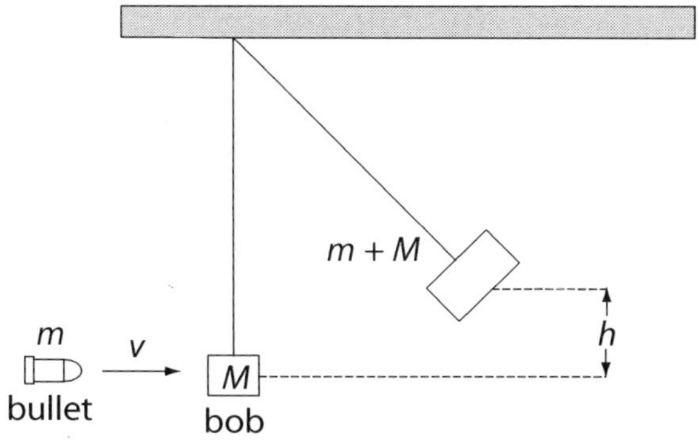

Figure 3.5.1 *A ballistic pendulum*

The bullet entering the bob transfers its momentum to the bob, and the combined masses continue on at initial speed v'. Since momentum is conserved,

$$mv = (m + M)v' \qquad \text{(I)}$$

The bob and bullet together now have kinetic energy due to their motion.

$$E_k = ½(m + M)v'^2 \qquad \text{(II)}$$

The bob and bullet rise and momentarily come to rest at height *h,* where all the mechanical energy is in the form of gravitational potential energy.

$$E_p = (m + M)gh \qquad \text{(III)}$$

If we assume that mechanical energy is conserved (energy loss due to friction is negligible), then

$$½(m + M)v'^2 = (m + M)gh$$

Therefore, $$v'^2 = 2gh$$

According to equation I, $$v' = \frac{m}{m + M} \cdot v'$$

However, $$v' = \sqrt{2gh}$$

Therefore, $$\frac{m}{m + M} \cdot v = \sqrt{2gh}$$

and $$v = \frac{m + M}{m} \cdot \sqrt{2gh}$$

Quick Check

1. A 5.0 g bullet is fired into the ballistic pendulum described in Figure 3.5.1. If the bob has a mass of 2.0 kg and the bob rises a vertical distance of 8.0 cm, how fast was the bullet moving? (Use $g = 9.80 \text{ m/s}^2$.)

2. In designing a ballistic pendulum, you want a bullet of mass 6.0 g and speed 6.0×10^2 m/s to make the pendulum bob rise 3.0 cm. What mass must the bob have?

3. A 56 kg boy jumps down from a 2.0 m high ladder. Using only the law of conservation of mechanical energy, determine his kinetic energy and his speed when he is half-way down.

3.5 Review Questions

1. Which best describes an *elastic collision* between two objects?

	total energy	total momentum	kinetic energy
A	conserved	conserved	conserved
B	conserved	conserved	not conserved
C	conserved	not conserved	not conserved
D	not conserved	not conserved	not conserved

2. A 50 g golf ball is thrown upward with an initial velocity of 12 m/s. Assume the initial potential energy is zero. Find the potential energy, kinetic energy and total energy of the system at each of the following:
   (a) the initial position

   (b) at a point 2.75 m above the initial position

   (c) at the maximum height the ball reaches

3. A new roller coaster has come to the PNE in Vancouver as shown in the diagram below. The speed of the roller coaster at point A is 4.0 m/s.

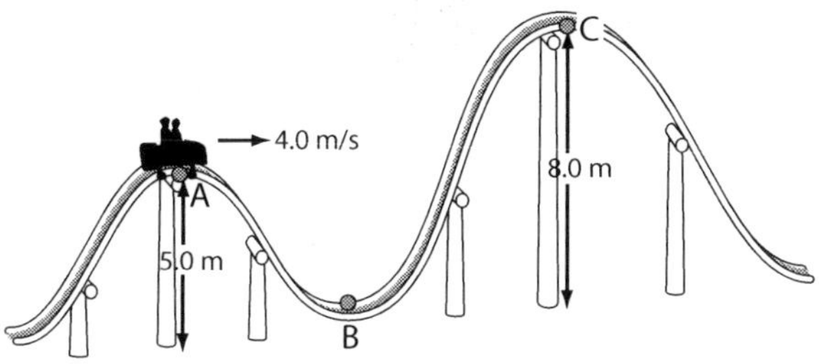

   (a) What is its speed at point B?

   (b) Is the roller coaster going fast enough to get to the top of the second hill (point C)?

   (c) How fast does the roller coaster have to be going at point B to make it to the top of the second hill?

   (d) Why don't you need to know the mass of the roller coaster car?

4. A 45 kg youngster slides down a homemade snowslide, which is 3.0 m high. At the bottom of the slide she is moving 7.0 m/s. How much energy was lost during the trip down the slide? What would account for this loss?

5. A skier slides down the ice-covered hill on the left, passing P, and coasts up the hill on the right to a vertical height h of 12 m. How fast was the skier moving when passing point P? Assume that frictional effects are negligible.

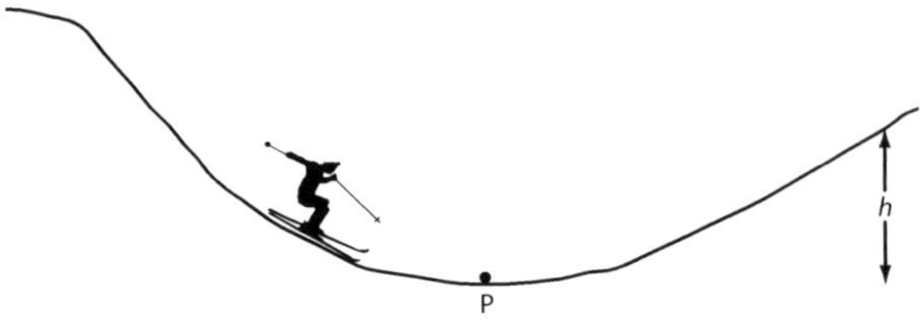

6. A 0.50 kg ball with a speed of 1.5 m/s in the positive direction has a head-on elastic collision with a stationary 0.80 kg ball. What are the velocities of the balls after the collision?

7. The pendulum bob in the diagram below has a mass of 0.500 kg. The pendulum is 1.20 m long. The bob is raised up a vertical distance of 0.150 m relative to its starting height. If friction is ignored, how fast will the bob be moving as it swings through A?

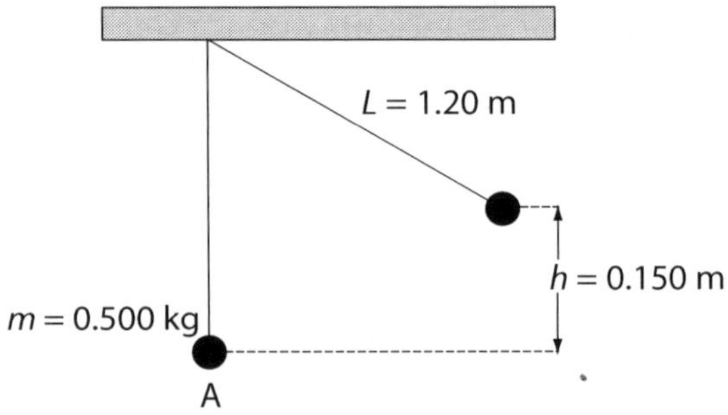

Chapter 3 Review Questions

1. Two monkeys are connected by a rope of negligible mass, which passes over a pulley. Friction in the pulley is negligible. One monkey has a mass of 20.0 kg while the other has a mass of 22.0 kg. At what rate will the monkeys accelerate? What will be the tension in the rope connecting the monkeys?

2. The following system is set up in your science lab.

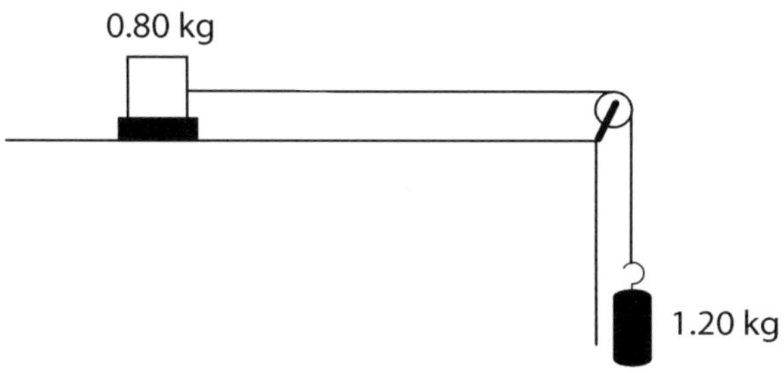

   (a) At what rate will the system accelerate, assuming no friction?

   (b) What is the tension in the string while the system accelerates?

3. How much momentum does a 0.500 kg rock have when thrown at 25.0 m/s?

4. What impulse must be imparted to a 100.0 g ball to get it moving at 40.0 m/s?

5. A 2.4 kg cart moving 0.64 m/s collides with a stationary 1.8 kg cart. The carts lock together. What is their combined velocity after the collision?

6. A 1.5×10^3 kg car collides head-on with a 1.2×10^3 kg car. Both cars were travelling at the same speed, 20.0 m/s, but in opposite directions. What will the velocity of the combined wreckage be immediately after the collision?

7. A 52 kg girl is coasting along the floor on a large 2.0 kg skateboard. If she is moving 1.8 m/s when a 46 kg boy jumps on to the same skateboard, what is the speed of the skateboard immediately after the boy jumps on it?

8. A 30.0 kg hockey player travelling 1.0 m/s toward the south collides with a 25.0 kg hockey player moving 0.50 m/s toward the west. They become tangled and they move off together. With what speed and in what direction will the two players move immediately after the collision?

9. A 5.00×10^{-3} kg steel ball moving 1.20 m/s collides elastically (i.e., with no loss of kinetic energy) with an identical, stationary steel ball. The incident ball is deflected 30° from its original path.
   (a) Draw a vector diagram showing the paths of both balls after the perfectly elastic collision.
   (b) What is the velocity of the incident ball after the collision?
   (c) What is the velocity of the struck ball after the collision?
   (d) How much of the incident ball's kinetic energy was transferred to the struck ball?

10. If an amateur astronomer carries a 5.0 kg telescope to the top of a 250 m hill, how much work will she do on the telescope?

11. A child pulls a toy wagon along the road for a distance of 250 m. The force he exerts along the handle is 32 N. The handle makes an angle of 30° with the horizontal road. How much work does the child do on the wagon? Express your answer in kJ.

12. How much kinetic energy does a 1.0×10^3 kg car, travelling at 90 km/h, have?

13. How much gravitational potential energy does a 75 kg skier have when at the top of a hill 2.0×10^3 m high?

14. A large ball of modelling clay is dropped from a height of 2 m to the floor. The ball does not bounce back up in the air. Explain this in terms of the conservation laws discussed in this chapter.

15. A girl lifts a 30. kg box from the ground up to a table 1.0 m high in a time of 1.5 s. A weightlifter friend carries a 100. kg load across the gym in 5.0 s, without dropping it or lifting it higher. Who has the greater power output? Explain.

16. How much work can a 6.0 hp motor do in an 8.0 h working day? Express your answer in megajoules. (1 MJ = 10^6 J)

17. An 80 kg rider on a 120 kg motorbike, travelling 25 m/s in a direction 12° west of north, enters a highway without properly checking that the road is clear. He collides with a 1200 kg car travelling north at 20 m/s. The two vehicles and rider become entangled. In what direction and at what speed will the wreckage move immediately after the collision? (Assume the car's mass includes its occupants.)

18. A 9.6 kg box slides down a ramp inclined at 32° to the horizontal. At what rate will it accelerate if the coefficient of kinetic friction is 0.28?

19. Agatha Physics is travelling on a jet. As it accelerates down the runway, she holds a pendulum (consisting of a small washer on the end of a thread) in front of her and observes that the pendulum is displaced 10.0° from its usual vertical alignment. Help her by calculating the acceleration of the aircraft.

20. A block slides down a smooth inclined plane at steady speed when one end of the plane is raised to form an angle θ with the horizontal. Show that the coefficient of kinetic friction, μ, can be calculated as follows:

$$\mu = \tan \theta$$

21. A 5.00 g bullet is fired into a 6.00 kg block, which is suspended from a string 1.00 m long. The string deflects through an angle of 12.0°. How fast was the bullet moving?

Chapter 3 Extra Practice

1. A 5.00 kg block is accelerated along a level surface at 4.00 m/s². The applied force is 30.0 N.

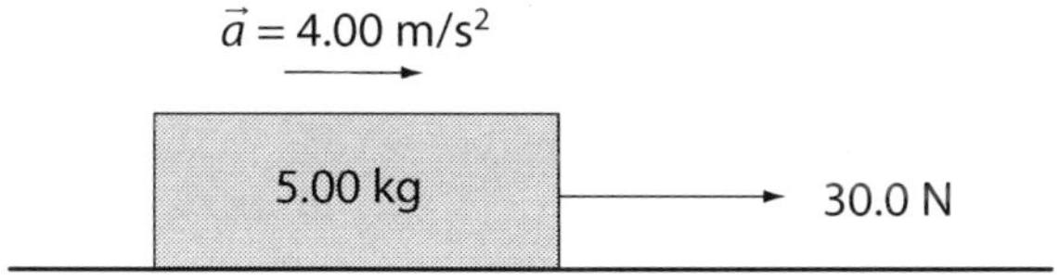

   (a) What is the net force?
   (b) What is the friction force?
   (c) What is the coefficient of friction μ between the block and the surface?

2. If the two forces $\vec{F}_1$ and $\vec{F}_2$ act simultaneously on the 5.00 kg mass in the diagram below, what will the magnitude of the acceleration be?

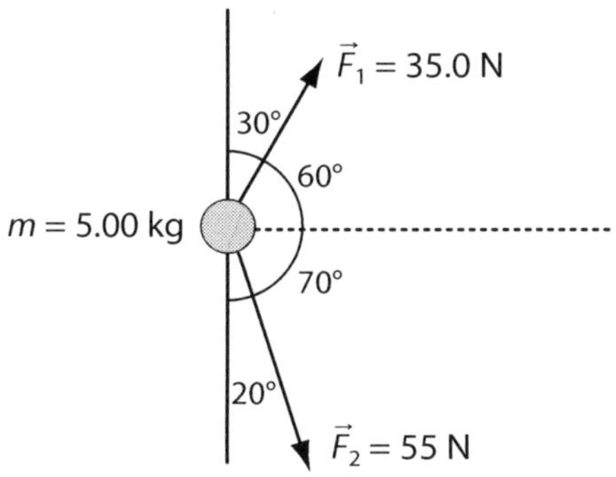

3. Spring-loaded cart A is moving with a speed of 50.0 cm/s when it collides with stationary cart B. After the collision, cart A is moving 30.0 cm/s. How fast is cart B moving after the collision?

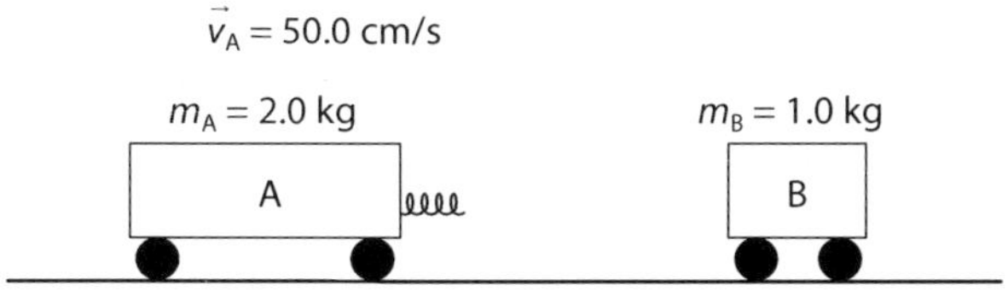

4. In the diagram below, is it easier to push a lawnmower up a slope or to pull it up the same slope? Explain your answer using sketched vector diagrams.

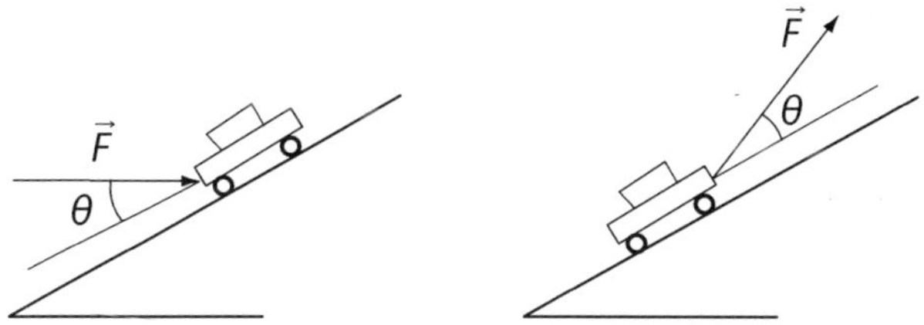

5. The 3.50 kg block in the diagram below starts to slide at steady speed down the ramp when the ramp is raised to an angle of 42° with the horizontal. What is
   (a) the normal force?
   (b) the force of friction?
   (c) the coefficient of kinetic friction, μ?

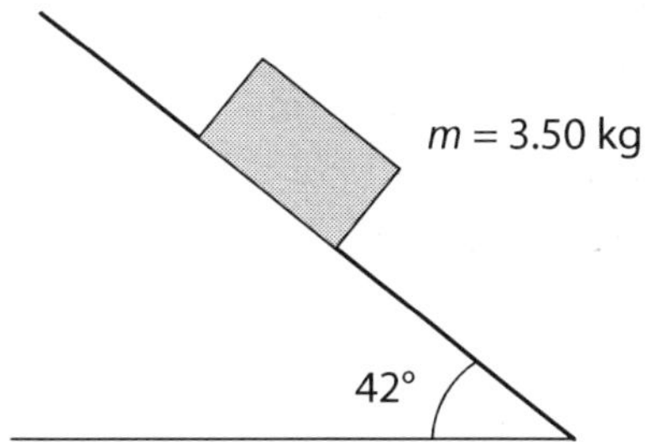

6. A gun fires 10 bullets per second, each of mass 0.020 kg, travelling 400 m/s. What is the average recoil force exerted on the gun?

7. Two objects are connected by a light string, as in the diagram below. The horizontal surfaces and the pulley are frictionless.
   (a) At what rate will the 12 kg mass accelerate?
   (b) What is the tension in the connecting string?

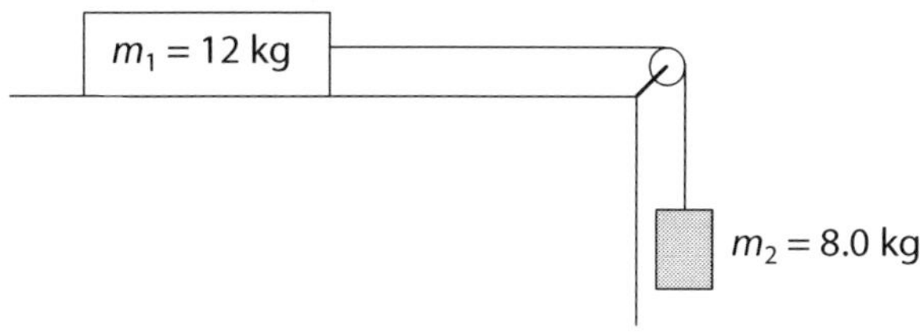

8. A 10.0 kg pumpkin explodes into three fragments. The first fragment has a mass of 4.00 kg, and it travels north at 2.0 m/s. The second fragment has a mass of 1.5 kg, and it travels east at 4.0 m/s. In what direction and at what speed will the third fragment travel?

9. A 0.050 kg bullet leaves the muzzle of a 2.0 kg rifle with a velocity of 6.0×10^2 m/s. With what velocity will the rifle start to recoil if the rifle is (a) held loosely? (b) held firmly against the shoulder of a 98.0 kg man?

10. A large superball and a small superball are dropped from the same initial height *H*. Both balls bounce back up to a height *h*, which is just a bit less than *H*. If, however, the small superball is placed immediately above the large superball and both are dropped to the ground simultaneously from height *H*, the small superball rebounds to a height $h' >>> H$! Explain this in terms of the conservation laws discussed in this chapter.

11. A conveyor belt lifts 15 large 75 kg boxes from the road up to a window 4.2 m high, in a time of 8.2 s. What is the power rating of the conveyor in this situation?

12. A girl pushes a 3.0×10^2 N box along the floor for a distance of 4.0 m. The coefficient of kinetic friction is 0.33. She then lifts the box straight up 1.2 m. What is the total amount of work she has done?

13. A spring with a force constant, k, of 12 N/m is compressed horizontally by a distance of 0.30 m. A 0.100 kg mass is then placed at the end of the compressed spring. When the spring is released, with what speed will the mass be thrown by the spring?

4 Circular Motion and Gravitation

By the end of this chapter, you should be able to do the following:

- Use knowledge of uniform circular motion to analyze various situations
- Analyze the gravitational attraction between masses

By the end of this chapter, you should know the meaning of these **key terms**:

- centripetal acceleration
- centripetal force
- free fall
- Newton's law of universal gravitation
- uniform circular motion

By the end of this chapter, you should be able to use and know when to use the following formulae:

$T = \frac{1}{f}$ $\quad a_c = \frac{v^2}{r} = \frac{4\pi^2 r}{T^2}$ $\quad F_c = ma_c$ $\quad F_g = G\frac{m_1 m_2}{r^2}$

This Canadian stamp from 1965 commemorates Alouette II, *Canada's second research satellite. Used to study the atmosphere,* Alouette II *like all other orbiting objects demonstrates the concepts of circular motion and gravitation that you will study in this chapter.*

4.1 Motion in a Circle

Warm Up

Imagine you are swinging a tin can on a string in a circle above your head as shown in the diagram. Suddenly, the string breaks! Draw on the diagram the direction in which the can will move.

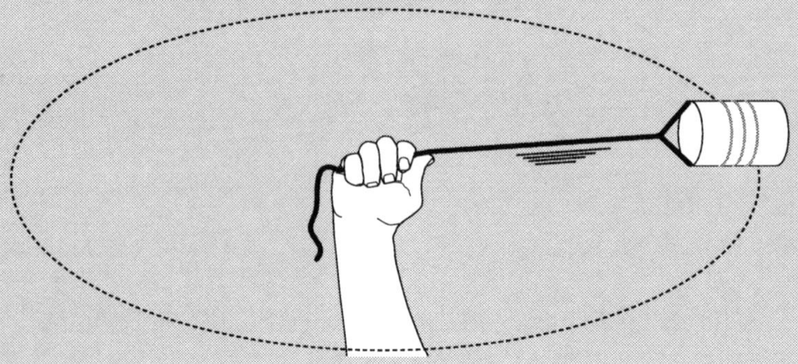

Gravity and Motion

In a previous course, you may have solved problems involving the force of gravity and the acceleration due to gravity ($\vec{g}$). You assumed g remains constant as a body falls from a height, and you considered many situations, most of which happened on or near the surface of Earth. Here are some questions you should be able to answer after you study this chapter:

- Is $\vec{g}$ the same for a satellite orbiting Earth several hundred kilometres above the surface as it is at Earth's surface?
- Does Earth exert a force of gravity on the Moon?
- Why does the Moon not "fall down" to Earth?

The force that keeps you firmly attached to this planet is the type of force that keeps Earth in orbit around the Sun. The force of gravity exists between any two masses in the universe.

All the planets orbit the Sun in elliptical orbits. Satellites (both artificial and our Moon) orbit Earth in elliptical paths. The ellipses are usually very close to being circular, however, so we begin our study of gravity by learning about objects moving in circular paths.

Uniform Circular Motion

Imagine you are driving a car around a circular track, maintaining the same speed all the way around the track. Any object that moves in a circle at steady speed is said to be in **uniform circular motion.** Is such an object accelerating? It may seem to have zero acceleration, but in fact an object moving in a circle has a constant acceleration —not because of a change in speed, but because of its constantly changing direction. Remember: acceleration is defined as change in velocity divided by change in time, and velocity is a vector quantity.

$$\vec{a} = \frac{\Delta \vec{v}}{\Delta t}$$

Identifying Centripetal Acceleration

If a body is moving in a circular path, in what direction does it accelerate? Figure 4.1.1 shows two consecutive positions of a body moving in a circle. Velocity vectors are labelled $\vec{v}_0$ and $\vec{v}_1$. To find out the direction of the acceleration, we need the direction of $\Delta\vec{v}$. Since $\Delta\vec{v}$ is the vector difference between $\vec{v}_1$ and $\vec{v}_0$, we use the rules for vector subtraction.

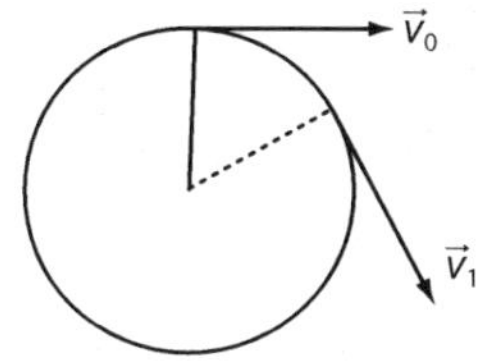

Figure 4.1.1 *Two consecutive positions of a body moving in a circle*

Figure 4.1.2 shows how to find the vector difference, $\Delta\vec{v}$, between $\vec{v}_1$ and $\vec{v}_0$.

$$\Delta\vec{v} = \vec{v}_1 - \vec{v}_0$$

$$\Delta\vec{v} = \vec{v}_1 + (-\vec{v}_0)$$

Vector $\Delta\vec{v}$ is the resultant of $\vec{v}_1$ and ($-\vec{v}_0$).

In Figure 4.1.2, the velocity vectors chosen represent the velocity of the body at two different times. The time interval between the occurrences of the velocities is relatively long.

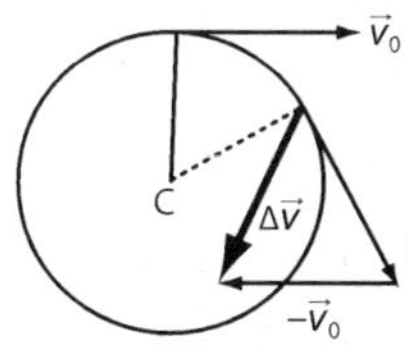

Figure 4.1.2 *The vector difference, $\Delta\vec{v}$, between $\vec{v}_1$ and $\vec{v}_0$*

If this time interval (Δt) is shortened, the direction of $\Delta\vec{v}$ becomes closer and closer to being toward the centre of the circle as in Figure 4.1.3.

In fact, as $\Delta t \rightarrow 0$, the direction of $\Delta\vec{v}$ and therefore the direction of the acceleration $\vec{a}$ for all practical purposes, is toward the centre of the circle.

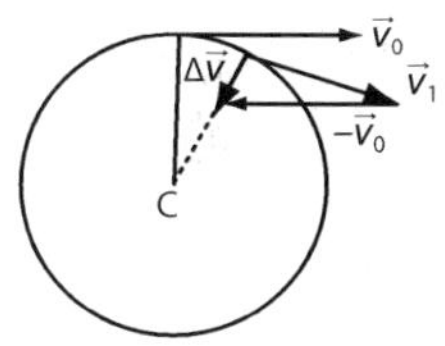

Figure 4.1.3 *As Δt is shortened, the direction of $\Delta\vec{v}$ becomes closer and closer to being toward the centre of the circle.*

Direction of Centripetal Acceleration

Since the direction of the acceleration of a body moving at uniform speed in a circle is toward the centre of the circle, the acceleration is called **centripetal acceleration**. **Centripetal** means directed toward a centre.

A device called an **accelerometer** can be used to show that a body moving in a circle accelerates toward the centre of the circle (Figure 4.1.4). If the accelerometer is attached to a lab cart accelerating in a straight line, the coloured water inside the cart forms a wedge pointing in the direction of the acceleration. If the same accelerometer is attached to a toy train travelling at constant speed on a circular track, the accelerometer shows no acceleration in the direction of travel, but a definite acceleration perpendicular to the direction of travel (Figure 4.1.5). In other words, the train on the circular track accelerates toward the centre of the track.

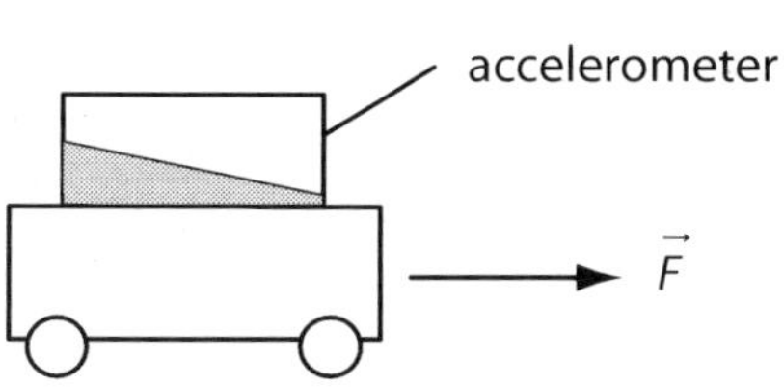

Figure 4.1.4 *An accelerometer on a lab cart*

Figure 4.1.5 *An accelerometer on a train going around a curve. Note the direction of the force is pointed inward to the centre of the circle.*

In Figure 4.1.6, a body is moving in a circle of radius $\vec{R}_0$. The radius is a displacement vector. The velocity of the body is $\vec{v}_0$. Following a very short time interval Δt, the body has moved through a small angle θ, and the body has a new velocity $\vec{v}_1$, the same magnitude as $\vec{v}_0$, but in a new direction.

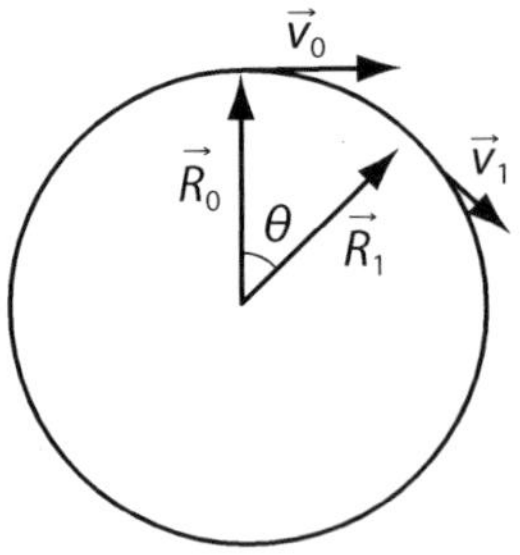

Figure 4.1.6 *A body moving at $\vec{v}_0$ in a circle of radius $\vec{R}_0$*

Defining Centripetal Acceleration

In Figure 4.1.7(a), $\Delta\vec{R}$ is the vector difference between $\vec{R}_1$ and $\vec{R}_0$.

$$\vec{R}_1 + (-\vec{R}_0) = \Delta\vec{R}$$

or

$$\vec{R}_0 + \Delta\vec{R} = \vec{R}_1$$

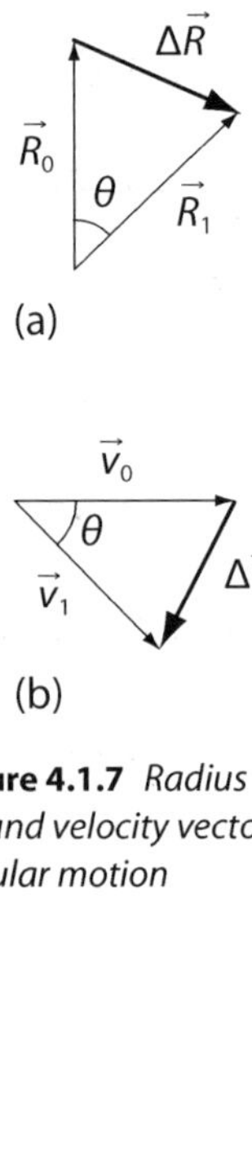

Figure 4.1.7 *Radius vectors (a) and velocity vectors (b) in circular motion*

Figure 4.1.7(b) shows vector subtraction of the velocity vectors. Vector $\Delta\vec{v}$ is the vector difference between $\vec{v}_1$ and $\vec{v}_0$.

$$\vec{v}_1 + (-\vec{v}_0) = \Delta\vec{v}$$

or

$$\vec{v}_0 + \Delta\vec{v} = \vec{v}_1$$

Now, consider the triangles formed by the radius vectors in Figure 4.1.7(a) and the velocity vectors in Figure 4.1.7(b). Both are isosceles triangles with a common angle θ, so they are similar triangles. Corresponding sides of similar triangles are proportional; therefore,

$$\frac{\Delta v}{\Delta R} = \frac{v}{R}$$

(The subscripts have been dropped because the magnitudes of the speeds and the radii do not change.)

$$\Delta v = \frac{v}{R}\Delta R$$

During a time interval Δt, the average acceleration is $\frac{\Delta v}{\Delta t}$, so

$$\bar{a} = \frac{\Delta v}{\Delta t} = \frac{v}{R} \bullet \frac{\Delta R}{\Delta t}$$

Consider what happens during the motion of one complete circle of the body in Figures 4.1.6 and 4.1.7.

If the time interval Δt is chosen to be very small ($\Delta t \to 0$), Figure 4.1.8 shows that each $\Delta\vec{R}$ becomes closer to being equal to the section of corresponding arc Δs on the circumference of the circle. If Δs is the arc in question, then $\Delta\vec{R} \to \Delta s$ as $\Delta t \to 0$.

The speed v of the body as it moves around the circle is $v = \frac{\Delta s}{\Delta t}$, and if $\Delta t \to 0$,

$$v = \frac{\Delta R}{\Delta t}$$

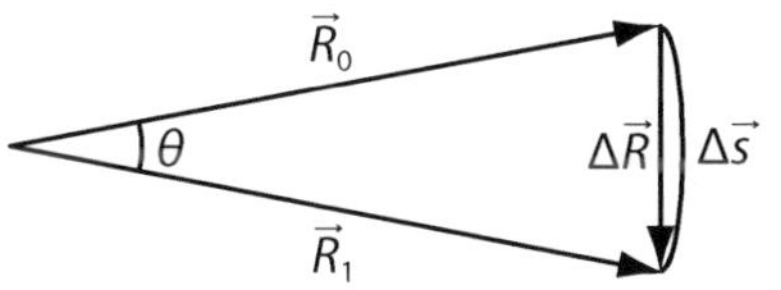

Figure 4.1.8 *If $\Delta t \to 0$, $\Delta\vec{R} \to \Delta s$.*

It can therefore be said that the average acceleration during time Δt is

$$\bar{a} = \frac{\Delta v}{\Delta t} = \frac{v}{R} \bullet \frac{\Delta R}{\Delta t} = \frac{v}{R} \bullet v = \frac{v^2}{R}$$

If $\Delta t \to 0$, the magnitude of the average acceleration approaches the instantaneous centripetal acceleration, $\vec{a}_c$. The magnitude of the **centripetal acceleration** is, therefore,

$$a_c = \frac{v^2}{R}$$

To summarize: when a body moves in a circle with uniform speed, it accelerates toward the centre of the circle, and the acceleration has a magnitude of $\frac{v^2}{R}$.

Another Way to Calculate Centripetal Acceleration

Newton's second law suggests that since the acceleration is toward the centre of the circle, the net force causing it should also be a centripetal force**.** If the centripetal force causing the centripetal acceleration is "turned off," the body will travel off in a direction that is along a tangent to the circle.

Another useful equation for calculating centripetal acceleration can be derived from $a_c = \frac{v^2}{R}$. If one full revolution of the body is considered, its speed will equal the circumference of the circle divided by the period of the revolution; that is, $v = \frac{2\pi R}{T}$, where R is the radius of the circle, and T is the period of one revolution.

Since $a_c = \frac{v^2}{R}$, then $a_c = \left(\frac{2\pi R}{T}\right)^2 \frac{1}{R}$, therefore,

$$a_c = \frac{4\pi^2 R}{T^2}$$

Both equations for centripetal acceleration are useful in many situations. You will use them when studying the motion of planets around the Sun, satellites around Earth, electrons in a magnetic field, and any kind of circular motion.

Quick Check

1. What is the centripetal acceleration of the Moon toward Earth?
   Given: $R = 3.84 \times 10^8$ m and $T = 2.36 \times 10^6$ s

2. A skater travels at 2.0 m/s in a circle of radius 4.0 m. What is her centripetal acceleration?

3. A 20.0 g rubber stopper is attached to a 0.855 m string. The stopper is spun in a horizontal circle making one revolution in 1.36 s. What is the acceleration of the stopper?

Centripetal Force

The net force that causes centripetal acceleration is called centripetal force. Acceleration and net force are related by Newton's second law, which says that $F = ma$. So the magnitude of the centripetal force can be calculated by:

centripetal force $F_c = ma_c$

Therefore, $F_c = m\dfrac{v^2}{R}$ or $F_c = m\dfrac{4\pi^2 R}{T^2}$

Sample Problem 4.1.1 — Centripetal Force

In a local playground a merry-go-round is turning at 4.50 m/s. If a 50.0 kg person is standing on the platforms edge, which is 5.80 m from the centre, what force of friction is necessary to keep her from falling off the platform?

What to Think About	How to Do It
1. This is a circular motion question and the force of friction between the person and the platform is the centripetal force.	$a_c = \dfrac{v^2}{R}$
2. Find the centripetal acceleration.	$a_c = \dfrac{(4.50\text{ m/s})^2}{5.80\text{ m}}$ $a_c = 3.49\text{ m/s}^2$
3. Find the centripetal force, which is the frictional force keeping her on the platform as it spins.	$F_{fr} = F_c = ma_c$ $F_{fr} = (50.0\text{ kg})(3.49\text{ m/s}^2)$ $F_{fr} = 175\text{N}$

Practice Problems 4.1.1 — Centripetal Force

1. A 61 kg skater cuts a circle of radius 4.0 m on the ice. If her speed is 4.00 m/s, what is the centripetal force? What exerts this force?

2. What centripetal force is needed to keep a 12 kg object revolving with a frequency of 5.0 Hz in an orbit of radius 6.0 m?

3. A 1.2×10^3 kg car rounds a curve of radius 50.0 m at a speed of 80.0 km/h (22 m/s).
   (a) What is the centripetal acceleration of the car?

   (b) How much centripetal force is needed to cause this acceleration?

   (c) If the coefficient of kinetic friction μ is 0.25 on a slippery road, will the force of friction between the road and the wheels of the car be enough to keep the car from skidding?

Investigation 4.1.1 Circular Orbits

Purpose

To investigate factors involved in the uniform circular motion of a mass revolving at the end of a string

Introduction

Some aspects of circular motion can be studied using the simple equipment shown in Figure 4.1.9. A small mass m (a bundle of three washers) "orbits" on the end of a string. A large mass M experiences a force of gravity Mg. In this investigation, M is chosen to be a bundle of nine identical washers, so that $M = 3m$.

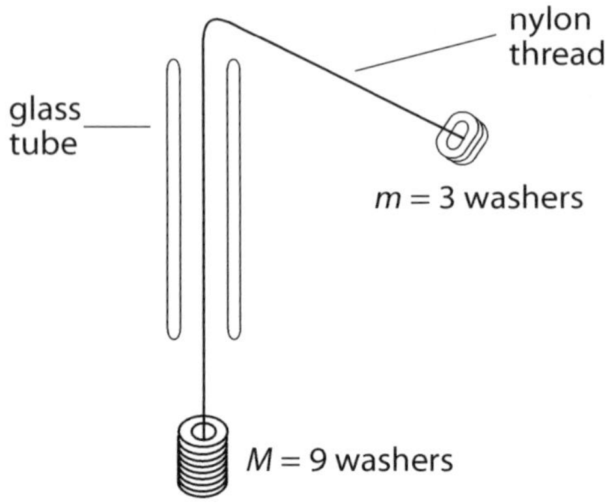

Figure 4.1.9

The glass tube is smoothly polished at the top, and strong, smooth nylon thread joins the two masses. In effect, the edge of the tube acts like a pulley, changing the direction of the tension force in the string without changing its magnitude.

When the small mass m is made to "orbit" around the top end of the glass tube, mass M remains static, so the tension in the string along its length L is equal to the downward force of gravity on M, which is Mg.
The radius of the orbit is not L, however, but R (the horizontal distance from m to the vertical glass tube). See Figure 4.1.10.

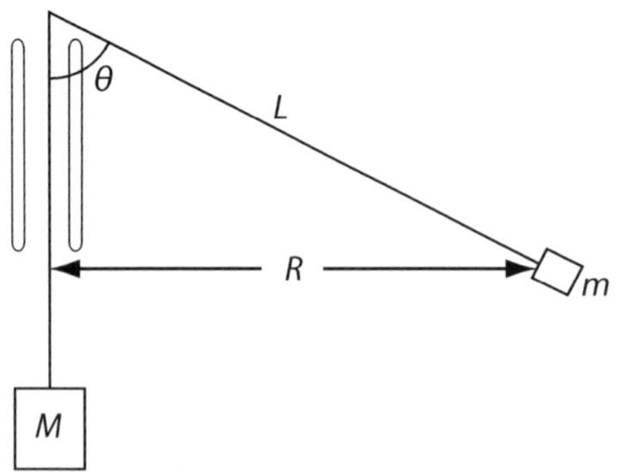

Figure 4.1.10

When the small mass m is made to "orbit" the top of the glass tube, we will assume the upward force on the stationary mass M has a magnitude of Mg. The reaction force exerted on m through the string has the same magnitude (Mg), but is exerted in the opposite direction. In Figure 4.1.11, this tension force is labelled $T = Mg$.

Consider the two components of $\vec{T}$. The vertical component $\vec{F}_y$ balances the downward force of gravity on m, so $\vec{F}_y = mg$. The horizontal component of $\vec{T}$ is the centripetal force, so $\vec{F}_x = \vec{F}_c$.

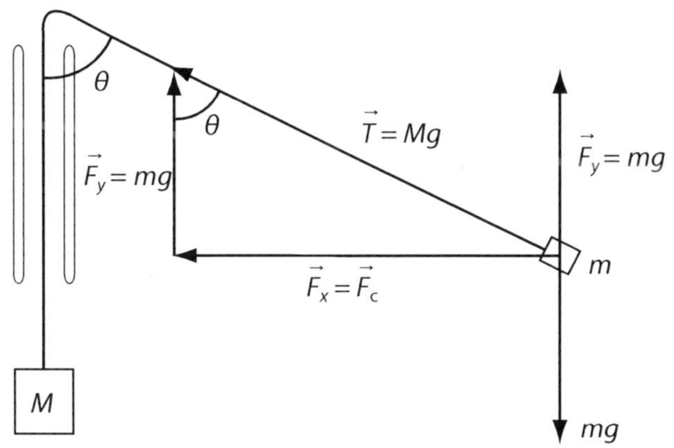

Figure 4.1.11

Procedure

1. Prepare the apparatus, using three identical washers for the orbiting mass and nine washers for the large mass. Predict what the angle θ between the thread and the vertical glass tube will be, using the fact that

$$\cos\theta = \frac{F_y}{T} = \frac{mg}{Mg} = \frac{m}{M}$$

2. In this investigation, you will vary L and measure the period of revolution T for each length L. Measure from the centre of gravity of the mass m along the string, and mark off distances of 20 cm, 40 cm, 60 cm, 80 cm, and 100 cm with chalk or a small dab of correction fluid.
3. Hold the glass tube vertically in your hand, and swing mass m until it achieves a stable orbit such that length L is 20.0 cm. While you keep the orbiting mass revolving, have your partner make the following measurements (as best they can, for it will be difficult!):
   (a) The radius of the orbit R: Your partner will have to hold a metre stick as near to the orbiting mass as they dare (to avoid decapitation) and estimate R as closely as possible;
   (b) The period of revolution T: Your partner will time how long the mass takes to make 10 revolutions; then divide the total time by 10.
4. Repeat step 3 for lengths of 40.0 cm, 60.0 cm, 80.0 cm, and 100.0 cm. Record all your measurements in a table like Table 4.1.1.
5. Calculate the ratio of R/L. From Figure 4.1.10 you can see that this ratio equals sin θ. Calculate θ knowing sin θ.

Table 4.1.1 *Data for Investigation 4.1.1*

Length of String, L [cm]	Radius of Orbit, R [cm]	Period of Revolution, T [s]	sin θ $= \frac{R}{L}$	θ [°]	cos θ $= \frac{m}{M}$	θ [°]
20.0						
40.0						
60.0						
80.0						
100.0						

6. Plot a graph with *T* on the *y*-axis (since it is the dependent variable) and *L* on the *x*-axis (since it is the independent variable).
7. Examine the shape of your graph of *T* vs. *L*, and make an educated guess at what the power law might be. For example, if you think the power law is most likely $T^n = k \cdot L$, then plot a graph of T^n vs. *L*. If you choose the correct value of *n*, your graph should be a straight line passing through (0,0).
8. Determine the slope of your final, straight-line graph, and express it in appropriate units. Then write an equation for your straight line, incorporating the slope.

9. You can use the results of your experiment to do a check on the formula for centripetal force.

$$\text{Since } F_c = \frac{m4\pi^2 R}{T^2}, \text{ therefore } T^2 = \frac{m4\pi^2 R}{F_c}.$$

Figure 4.1.10 shows you that $R = L\sin\theta$, and Figure 4.1.11 makes it clear that

$F_c = F_x = Mg\sin\theta$. Therefore, we can write

$$T^2 = \frac{m4\pi^2 L\sin\theta}{Mg\sin\theta} = \frac{m4\pi^2}{Mg}L$$

Thus, the theoretical slope of a graph of T^2 vs. *L* should be $\frac{m4\pi^2}{Mg}$.

Concluding Questions

1. Compare the average value of angle θ calculated from $\sin\theta = R/L$ with the value of θ predicted using $\cos\theta = m/M$. What is the percent difference between the two results?
2. According to your results, how does the period *T* of the orbiting mass vary with the length *L*? Write a specific equation for your graphical result.
3. What is the theoretical value of your slope for the graph in Concluding Question 2? What is the percent difference between your graph's actual slope and the theoretical slope?
4. Discuss sources of error in this experiment and how you might be able to reduce their effects.

Challenges

1. Discuss how the results of your experiment would be affected if the ratio of the masses used was 1:2 instead of 1:3. How would this affect
   (a) the angle θ made by the string with the vertical glass tube?
   (b) the relationship between the period of revolution and the length of the string?
2. Design a way of testing out the centripetal force formula using an air puck on an air table. See if you can design a way of showing that Newton's second law really does apply to centripetal acceleration.

4.1 Review Questions

Use $g = 9.80\ \text{m/s}^2$

1. A 1.00 kg rock is swung in a horizontal circle of radius 1.50 m, at the end of a rope. One complete revolution takes 0.80 s.
   (a) What is the speed of the rock?

   (b) What is the centripetal acceleration of the rock?

   (c) What is the centripetal force exerted on the rock?

   (d) What exerts the centripetal force?

   (e) The circle traced out by the rock was described as being horizontal. Would the rope, as it swings, be horizontal too? Explain.

2. A spider that could not find its web site (because its computer crashed?) is on the outside edge of an old phonograph record. It holds on for dear life, as the record rotates at 78 rpm. The radius of the record is 15 cm.
   (a) What is the linear speed *v* of the record at its outside edge?

   (b) What is the centripetal acceleration of the spider?

   (c) How much frictional force must there be to keep the spider from flying off the spinning record, if its mass is 1.0 g?

3. A satellite is orbiting Earth at a distance of 6.70×10^6 m from the Earth's centre. If its period of revolution around Earth is 5.45×10^3 s, what is the value of *g* at this distance?

4. A pendulum 1.00 m long and with a 1.20 kg bob is swinging with a maximum speed of 2.50 m/s. Calculate the total force exerted by the string on the swinging mass when the mass is at the bottom of its swing.

5. A motocross rider at the peak of his jump has a speed such that his centripetal acceleration is equal to g. As a result, he does not feel any supporting force from the seat of his bike, which is also accelerating at rate g. Therefore, he feels as if there is no force of gravity on him, a condition described as apparent weightlessness. If the radius of the approximately circular jump is 75.0 m, what was the speed of the bike?

6. Planet Earth has a period of rotation of 24 h and a radius of 6.4×10^6 m.
   (a) What is the centripetal acceleration toward Earth's centre of a person standing on the equator?

   (b) With what frequency f, in hertz, would Earth have to spin to make the centripetal acceleration a_c equal in magnitude to g? Compare this with Earth's normal frequency of rotation. (1 rotation in 24 h = 1.16×10^{-5} Hz)

   (c) If Earth could be made to spin so fast that $a_c = g$, how would this affect the apparent force of gravity on you? Explain.

7. A 25 kg child is on a swing, which has a radius of 2.00 m. If the child is moving 4.0 m/s at the bottom of one swing, what is the centripetal force exerted by the ropes of the swing on the child? What is the total force exerted by the ropes when the swing is at its lowest point?

8. At the bottom of a power dive, a plane is travelling in a circle of radius 1.00 km at a speed of 2.50×10^2 m/s. What is the total force exerted upward on the 90.0 kg pilot by his seat?

9. Tarzan is swinging through the jungle on a vine that will break if the force exceeds 2.0×10^3 N. If the length of the vine is 5.0 m and Tarzan's mass is 1.00×10^2 kg, what is the highest speed he can safely travel while swinging on the vine? **Hint:** At what point in the swing will the tension in the vine be greatest?

10. Earth orbits the Sun at a distance of 1.5×10^{11} m.
    (a) What is its centripetal acceleration toward the Sun?

    (b) If the mass of Earth is 6.0×10^{24} kg, what is the centripetal force exerted by the Sun on Earth? What provides this force?

11. A roller coaster loop has a radius of 12 m. To prevent the passengers in a car from not falling out at the top of the loop, what is the minimum speed the car must have at the top?

12. A highway curve is designed to handle vehicles travelling 50 km/h safely.
    (a) Assuming the coefficient of kinetic friction between the rubber tires and the road is 0.60, what is the minimum radius of curvature allowable for the section of road?

    (b) For added safety, the road might be built with "banking." In what direction should the road be banked? Why does this help?

4.2 Gravity and Kepler's Solar System

Warm Up

If you drop a piece of paper and a book from the same height, which object will hit the ground first? If you put the piece of paper on top of the book and drop them together, why does the paper fall at the same rate as the book? What can you conclude about the rate at which objects fall?

___

___

___

Falling Objects

If gravity is the only force acting on a body, the body is in **free fall**. If there is no friction, each of the bodies in Figure 4.2.1 is in free fall. Each is accelerating downward at rate $\vec{g}$, which is independent of the mass of the body and has a magnitude of 9.80 m/s^2 near Earth's surface.

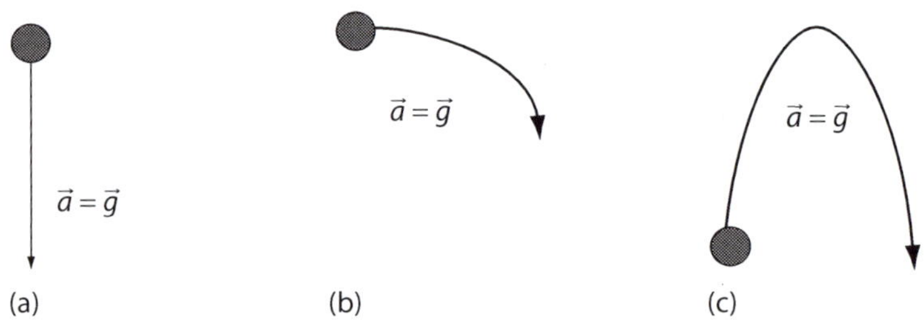

Figure 4.2.1 *In all three situations, the only force causing the acceleration of the free-falling body is gravity.*

"What goes up must come down." This simple truth has been known for centuries. Any unsupported object will fall to the ground. According to legend, Isaac Newton (1642–1727) was sitting under an apple tree when he saw an apple fall to the ground. He looked up at the Moon and wondered, "Why should the Moon not fall down, as well?"

The Moon in Free Fall

Might the Moon be in "free fall"? If it is, then why does it not fall to Earth like other unsupported bodies? Newton created a diagram like the one in Figure 4.2.2 to explain why the Moon circles Earth without "falling down" in the usual sense.

Imagine you are at the top of a mountain that is high enough so that there is essentially no air to offer resistance to the motion of a body projected horizontally from the top of the mountain. If a cannon is loaded with a small amount of gunpowder, a cannonball will be projected horizontally at low speed and follow a curved path until it strikes the ground at A. If more gunpowder is used, a greater initial speed will produce a curved path ending at B.

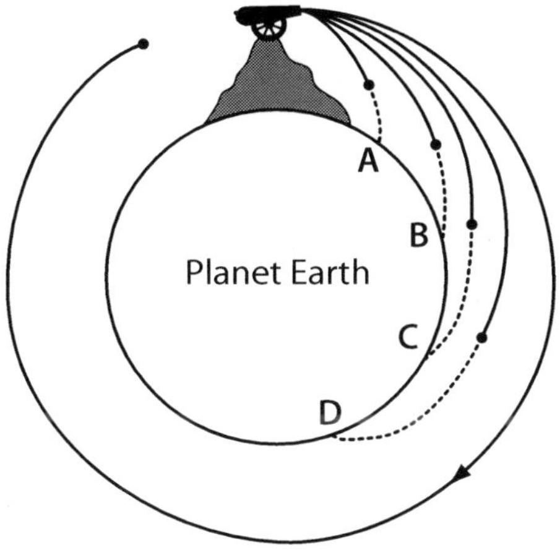

Figure 4.2.2 *Newton's diagram explaining why the Moon doesn't fall to Earth.*

With increasing initial speeds, paths ending at C and D will be achieved. If the initial speed is just high enough, the path will have a curvature parallel with Earth's curvature, and the cannonball will circle Earth for an indefinite period. The cannonball will orbit Earth, just like the Moon.

Isaac Newton actually anticipated artificial Earth satellites. Of course, the technology for sending a satellite into orbit was not available 300 years ago. To place an artificial satellite in orbit 500 km above Earth's surface requires a horizontal speed of approximately 7.6 km/s. It will take such a satellite approximately 90 minutes to complete one orbit.

The Moon was our first satellite. No one knows how or why it attained its orbit, but it is in a nearly circular path around this planet. The Moon is, indeed, in free fall. It does "fall toward Earth." Its horizontal speed is great enough that it completes its orbit with no danger of colliding with Earth's surface — just like the cannonball in Figure 4.2.2 but at a much greater altitude. The Moon's mean distance from Earth is 3.84×10^5 km. The orbit is actually slightly elliptical; hence mean (average) distance.

Gravitational Force, Earth, and the Moon

Could the centripetal force needed to keep the Moon in a near-circular orbit around Earth be the same force that makes an apple fall from a tree? What would exert this force of gravity on the Moon?

Since every known thing on Earth experiences the pull of gravity, Newton was certain that Earth itself exerted a gravitational force on objects near its surface. At Earth's surface, gravity makes objects accelerate at a rate of 9.8 m/s^2. What would the acceleration due to gravity be at a distance as far away as the Moon?

Treating the Moon as a body in circular orbit, the acceleration due to gravity is just the centripetal acceleration of the Moon. Therefore,

$$a_c = \frac{4\pi^2 R}{T^2} = \frac{4\pi^2(3.84 \times 10^8 \text{ m})}{[(27.3 \text{ d})(24 \text{ h/d})(3600 \text{ s/h})]^2} = 2.7 \times 10^{-3} \text{ m/s}^2$$

If this value of a_c was really the magnitude of g at the Moon's distance from Earth, it is much smaller than the value of g at Earth's surface. Newton was convinced that, since $F = ma$, the force of gravity causing this acceleration must decrease rapidly with distance from Earth.

In Investigation 4.2.1, you will be provided with data about most of the planets in the solar system. Given their orbital radii and their periods of revolution, you will calculate their centripetal accelerations toward the Sun. You will then use graphical analysis to determine the nature of the relationship between a_c, caused by the force of gravity of the Sun on the planet, and distance R from the Sun.

Johannes Kepler

Johannes Kepler (1571–1630) was a German mathematician who had worked in the astronomical laboratory of Danish astronomer Tycho Brahe (1546–1601). Brahe is famous for his precise observations of the positions of almost 800 stars and his accurate records of the positions of planets over a period of two decades. Brahe did all his work without a telescope! The telescope had not yet been invented.

Kepler was fascinated with planetary motions, and devoted his life to a search for mathematical patterns in their motions. To find these patterns he relied completely on the observations of Tycho Brahe. Kepler formulated three laws describing the orbits of the planets around the Sun.

Kepler's Three Laws of Planetary Motion

1. Each planet orbits the Sun in an elliptical path, with the Sun at one of the two foci of the ellipse.
2. A line joining the centre of the Sun and the centre of any planet will trace out equal areas in equal intervals of time (Figure 4.2.3). If time intervals $T_2 - T_1$ and $T_4 - T_3$ are equal, the areas traced out by the orbital radius of a planet during these intervals will be equal. (The diagram is not to scale.)

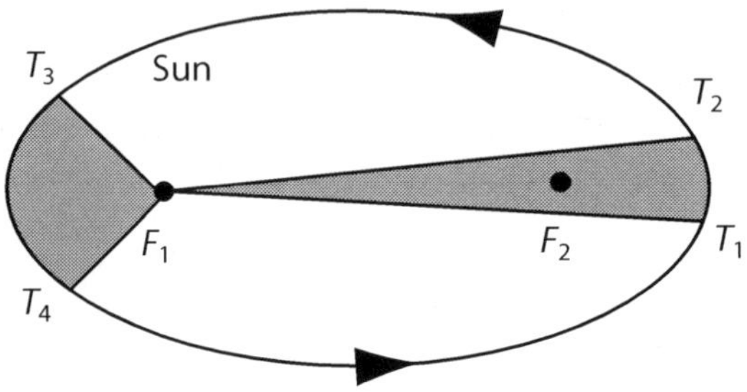

Figure 4.2.3 *Kepler's second law*

3. For any planet in the solar system, the cube of its mean orbital radius divided by the square of its period of revolution is a constant.

$$\frac{\bar{R}^3}{T^2} = K$$

Kepler's three laws can be neatly summarized in half a page of this text, but remember that to arrive at these laws required many years of work by this dedicated mathematician, not to mention the 20 years spent by Tycho Brahe making his painstaking observations of the heavenly wanderers, the planets.

In Investigation 4.2.2, you will calculate Kepler's constant K for the solar system.

Sample Problem 4.2.1 — Kepler's Laws

Planet Xerox (a close copy of planet Earth) was discovered by Superman on one of his excursions to the far extremes of the solar system. Its distance from the Sun is 1.50×10^{13} m. How long will this planet take to orbit the Sun?

What to Think About	How to Do It
1. Collect data needed to answer the question.	Earth's orbital radius, $R_e = 1.5 \times 10^{11}$ m Earth's period of revolution, $T_e = 1.0$ a Xerox's orbital radius, $R_X = 1.50 \times 10^{13}$ m
2. You could solve the problem using Kepler's constant derived in Investigation 4.2.2. Using Kepler's third law, you would simply solve for T_X. Another way to solve the problem is to use data for Earth (above) and the fact that $\frac{R_X^3}{T_X^2} = \frac{R_e^3}{T_e^2} = K_{Sun}$	$T_x^2 = \frac{R_x^3}{R_e^3} \cdot T_e^2$ $T_x^2 = \frac{[1.5 \times 10^{13}\ m]^3}{[1.5 \times 10^{11}\ m]^3} \cdot [1.0a]^2$ $T_x^2 = 1.0 \times 10^6\ a^2$ $T_x = 1.0 \times 10^3\ a$
3. The planet Xerox has a period of revolution around the Sun of 1.0×10^3 a.	

Practice Problems 4.2.1 — Kepler's Laws

1. A certain asteroid has a mean orbital radius of 5.0×10^{11} m. What is its period of revolution around the Sun?

2. A satellite is placed in orbit around Earth with an orbital radius of 2.0×10^7 m. What is its period of revolution? Use the facts that the Moon's period of revolution is 2.36×10^6 s and its orbital radius is 3.84×10^8 m.

Investigation 4.2.1 Centripetal Acceleration of Planets

Purpose

To use planetary data to determine how the centripetal acceleration of planets varies with their distances from the Sun

Procedure

1. Prepare a table similar to Table 4.2.1. Calculate values of a_c for each of the planets listed, using $a_c = \frac{4\pi^2 R}{T^2}$.
   Note: The orbits of the planets are actually elliptical, but they are close to being circular. The radii given in Table 4.2.1 are mean orbital radii.
2. Plot a graph of a_c (on the y-axis) vs. R (on the x-axis). Label your graph using appropriate units.
3. Make an educated guess at the power law involved. Plot a_c vs. R^n, where n is your reasoned best choice. Repeat this procedure if necessary until you obtain a straight line.

Table 4.2.1 *Planetary Data: Mean Orbital Radii and Periods*

Planet	Mean Orbital Radius, R	Period of Revolution, T	Centripetal Acceleration, a_c
	[m]	[s]	[m/s^2]
Mercury	0.58×10^{11}	7.60×10^{6}	
Venus	1.08×10^{11}	1.94×10^{7}	
Earth	1.49×10^{11}	3.16×10^{7}	
Mars	2.28×10^{11}	5.94×10^{7}	
Jupiter	7.78×10^{11}	3.74×10^{8}	
Saturn	14.3×10^{11}	9.30×10^{8}	
Uranus	28.7×10^{11}	2.66×10^{9}	

Concluding Question

1. Write an equation for your final, straight-line graph, complete with a numerical value for the slope in appropriate units. Describe the nature of the relationship between centripetal acceleration and distance in words.

Investigation 4.2.2 Determining Kepler's Constant for the Solar System

Purpose

To use astronomical data for the planets in the solar system to calculate the value of K, Kepler's constant

Procedure

1. Table 4.2.1 in Investigation 4.2.1 lists the mean orbital radii and periods for seven planets. Use this information to prepare a data table and calculate $K = \frac{R^3}{T^2}$ for each planet. Express K in appropriate units.
2. In Investigation 4.2.1, you obtained a straight-line graph when you plotted a_c vs. $\frac{1}{R^2}$. Therefore, $a_c = k \cdot \frac{1}{R^2}$, where k is the slope of your graph.

   As you know, $a_c = \frac{4\pi^2 R}{T^2}$. The slope of your graph was:

$$k = \frac{\Delta a_c}{\Delta \frac{1}{R^2}} = \frac{a_c - 0}{\frac{1}{R^2} - 0} = a_c R^2 = \frac{4\pi^2 R}{T^2} \cdot R^2 = 4\pi^2 \cdot \frac{R^3}{T^2} = 4\pi^2 K$$

   where K is Kepler's constant.

   Slope $k = 4\pi^2 K$, where K is Kepler's constant for the solar system. Calculate K using the slope k of your graph from Investigation 4.2.1. $K = \left(\frac{k}{4\pi^2}\right)$

Concluding Questions

1. What is the mean value of K, according to Procedure step 1? Procedure step 2?
2. Planet Neptune has a mean orbital radius of 4.50×10^{12} m. What is its period of revolution according to Kepler's third law? How many Earth years is this?
3. Pluto has a period of revolution of 7.82×10^9 s. What is its mean orbital radius?

4.2 Review Questions

1. What is the period of revolution of a planet that is 5.2 times as far away from the Sun as Earth?

2. The diagram below shows the orbit of a comet around the Sun. Mark on the diagram where the comet will be moving fastest. Explain in terms of Kepler's second law.

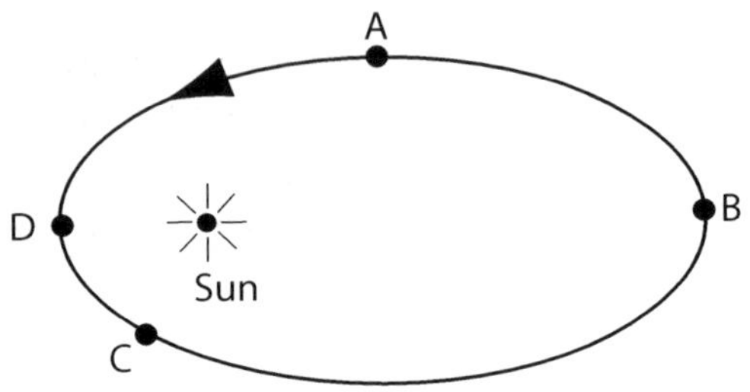

3. A satellite has period *T* and orbital radius *R*. To increase the period to 8*T*, what must the new orbital radius be?

4. The Earth orbits the Sun once a year, so its period of revolution is 1.0 a. If a space probe orbits the Sun with an orbital radius nine times that of Earth, what is the space probe's period of revolution?

5. For satellites of Earth, Kepler's law applies, but a different constant K must be used. Calculate what K would be for Earth's satellites, using only the fact that the Moon has a mean orbital radius of 3.84×10^8 m and a period of revolution of 2.36×10^6 s.

6. Using K for Earth's satellites, calculate the mean orbital radius of an Earth satellite that is in geosynchronous orbit. (A communications satellite in geosynchronous orbit orbits Earth in the plane of the equator in a period of 24 h, and therefore stays above one point on Earth's surface as Earth completes its daily rotation).

7. Halley's comet is a satellite of the Sun. It passed Earth in 1910 on its way around the Sun, and passed it again in 1986.
   (a) What is the period of revolution of Halley's comet, in years (a)?
   (b) What is the mean orbital radius of Halley's comet?
   (c) The mean orbital radius equals the average of the orbiting comet's closest and farthest distances from the Sun. If the closest Halley's comet gets to the Sun is 8.9×10^{10} m, what is its farthest distance from the Sun?
   (d) When Halley's comet is at its farthest distance from the Sun, where is it located in relation to the orbits of the outer planets?

8. The Earth is 1.49×10^8 km from the Sun, and its period of revolution is 1.0 a. Venus is 1.08×10^8 km from the Sun, on average. Use Kepler's third law to calculate the length of a Venus year in Earth years (a).

4.3 Newton's Law of Universal Gravitation

Warm Up

The Moon orbits Earth about once every 28 days. Why doesn't the Moon crash into Earth?

From Kepler to Newton

Kepler's three laws describe the orbits of the planets around the Sun. Newton used Kepler's laws to derive a law describing the nature of the gravitational forces that cause the planets to move in these orbits.

Newton concluded that the force that keeps planets in orbit is the same force that makes an apple fall to the ground. He stated that there is a gravitational force between any two bodies in the universe. Like all other forces, gravity is a mutual force. That is, the force with which Earth pulls on a falling apple is equal to the force with which the apple pulls on Earth, but in the opposite direction. Earth pulls on your body with a force of gravity that is commonly referred to as your "weight." Simultaneously, your body exerts a force on planet Earth of the same magnitude but in the opposite direction. Relative to each other, Earth "weighs" the same as your body!

Newton was able to use Kepler's laws as a starting point for showing that the force of gravity between the Sun and the planets varied as the inverse of the square of the distance between the Sun and the planets. He was convinced that the inverse square relation would apply to everyday objects near the surface of Earth as well. He produced arguments suggesting that the force should depend on the product of the masses of the two bodies being attracted to one another. The mathematical details of how Newton arrived at his famous **law of universal gravitation** can be found in many references, but are too lengthy to reproduce here.

Newton's Law of Universal Gravitation

Every body in the universe attracts every other body with a force that is (a) directly proportional to the product of the masses of the two bodies and (b) inversely proportional to the square of the distance between the centres of mass of the two bodies.

The equation for Newton's law of universal gravitation is:

$$F = G\frac{Mm}{R^2}$$

The constant of proportionality G is called the universal gravitation constant. Isaac Newton was unable to measure G, but it was measured later in experiments by Henry Cavendish (1731–1810).

The modern value for G is 6.67×10^{-11} Nm^2/kg^2.

Cavendish's Experiment to Measure G

You can imagine how difficult it is to measure the gravitational force between two ordinary objects. In 1797, Henry Cavendish performed a very sensitive experiment, which was the first "Earthbound" confirmation of the law of universal gravitation. Cavendish used two lead spheres mounted at the ends of a rod 2.0 m long. The rod was suspended horizontally from a wire that would twist an amount proportional to the gravitational force between the suspended masses and two larger fixed spherical masses placed near each of the suspended spheres (Figure 4.3.1).

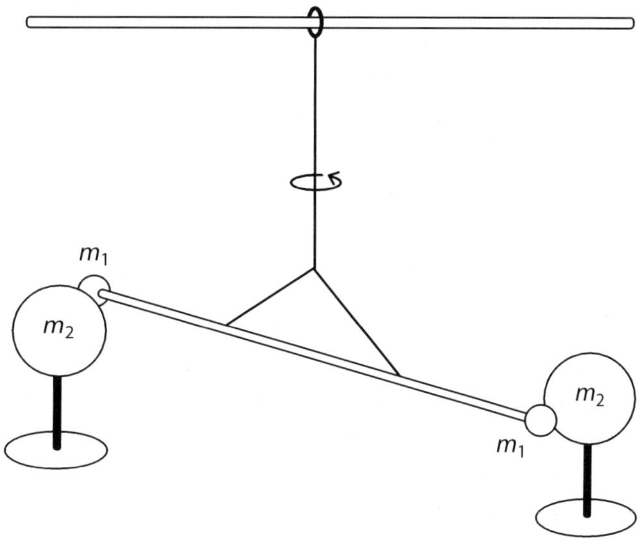

Figure 4.3.1 *Cavendish's apparatus for confirming Newton's law of universal gravitation*

The forces involved in this experiment were extremely small (in the order of 10^{-6} N), so great care had to be taken to eliminate errors from air currents and static electricity. Cavendish did manage to provide confirmation of the law of universal gravitation, and he arrived at the first measured value of G.

Gravitational Field Strength of the Earth

To calculate the force of gravity on a mass *m*, you simply multiply the mass by the gravitational field strength *g* ($F = mg$.) You could also use the law of universal gravitation:

$$F = G\frac{Mm}{R^2}, \text{ where } M \text{ is the mass of Earth.}$$

This means that $mg = G\frac{Mm}{R^2}$ and, therefore,

$$g = G\frac{M}{R^2}$$

Thus, the gravitational field strength of Earth depends only on the mass of Earth and the distance, R, from the centre of Earth to the centre of mass of the object that has mass m.

Sample Problem 4.3.1 — Newton's Law of Universal Gravitation

What is the force of gravity on a 70.0 kg man standing on Earth's surface, according to the law of universal gravitation? Check your answer using $F = mg$.

What to Think About	How to Do It
1. What data do you need?	$G = 6.67 \times 10^{-11}\ \text{Nm}^2/\text{kg}^2$ $g = 9.80\ \text{N/kg}$ Earth's mass $= 5.98 \times 10^{24}$ kg Earth's radius $= 6.38 \times 10^{6}$ m
2. Find the force of gravity using the law of universal gravitation.	$F_g = G\frac{m_1 m_2}{r^2}$ $F_g = (6.67 \times 10^{-11}\ \text{Nm}^2/\text{kg}^2)(\frac{(70.0\ \text{kg})(5.98 \times 10^{24}\ \text{kg})}{(6.38 \times 10^{6}\ \text{m})^2}$ $F_g = 686$ N
3. Calculate the force of gravity using $F = mg$.	$F_g = mg$ $F_g = (70.\ \text{kg})(9.80\ \text{m/s}^2)$ $F_g = 686$ N

Practice Problems 4.3.1 — Newton's Law of Universal Gravitation

1. What is the force of gravitational attraction between a 75 kg boy and a 60.0 kg girl
   (a) when they are 2.0 m apart?

   (b) when they are only 1.0 m apart?

Practice Problems continued

Practice Problems 4.3.1 — Newton's Law of Universal Gravitation (Continued)

2. What is the force of gravity exerted on you if your mass is 70.0 kg and you are standing on the Moon? The Moon's mass is 7.34×10^{22} kg and its radius is 1.74×10^{6} m.

3. What is the force of gravity exerted on you by Mars, if your mass is 70.0 kg and the mass of Mars is 6.37×10^{23} kg? The radius of Mars is 3.43×10^{6} m, and you are standing on its surface, searching for Mars bars.

Weightlessness

According to Newton's law of universal gravitation, the force of gravity between any two bodies varies *inversely* as the square of the distance between the centres of mass of the two bodies.

Figure 4.3.2 is a graph showing how the force of gravity (commonly called "weight") changes with distance measured from Earth's centre. To be truly "weightless" (experience no force of gravity) an object would have to be an infinite distance from any other mass. According to the law of universal gravitation, as $R \to \infty$, $F \to 0$.

Figure 4.3.2 *The force of gravity decreases dramatically with distance from Earth.*

Obviously, true weightlessness is not likely to be achieved! When people talk about "weightlessness," they usually are referring to *apparent* weightlessness. Apparent weightlessness is experienced when you feel zero force from supporting structures like your seat, the floor, or Earth's surface. This will happen when your supporting structure has the same acceleration as you have. Of course, if there is no supporting structure as when you jump off a cliff or a ladder or when you are in the middle of a jump you will also experience apparent weightlessness.

Examples of Apparent Weightlessness

1. A Falling Elevator

Imagine a person standing on a scale in an elevator (Figure 4.3.3(a)). When the elevator is standing still, the scale will give the true weight of the person, which is the force of gravity exerted by Earth on the person ($F = mg$). In the illustration, this is shown as the pair of forces of the person's weight ($w = mg$) and the normal force (N) from the scale exerting a force back on the person. With no acceleration, the scale reads the true weight: $w = N = mg$.

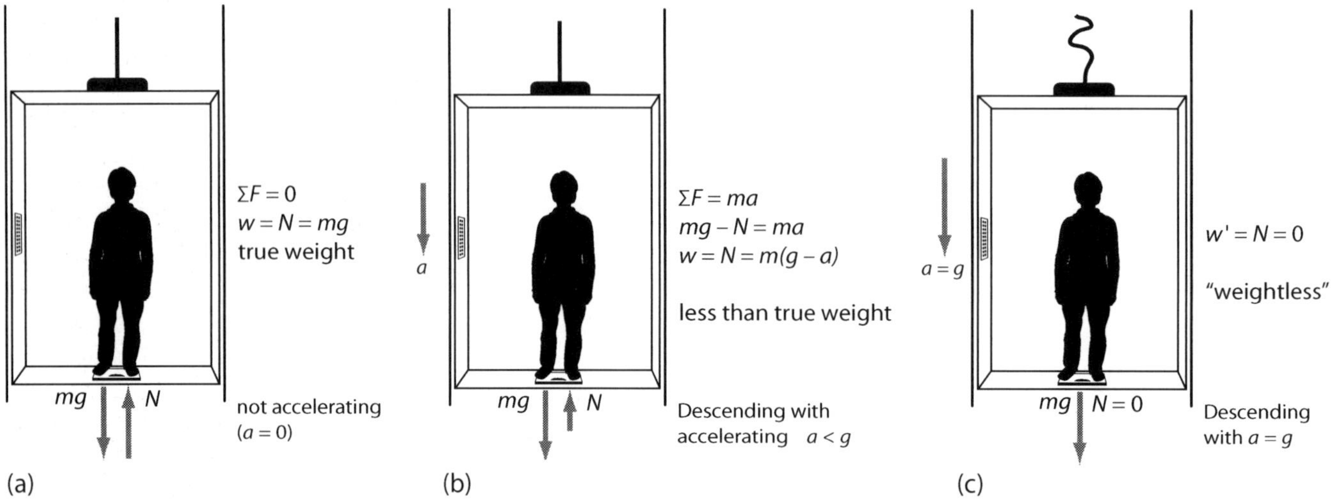

Figure 4.3.3 *A person in an elevator can experience apparent weightlessness.*

In Figure 4.3.3(b) the elevator is accelerating down at a rate less than gravity. Now the person's weight is greater than the normal force being exerted back, so the person appears to be lighter than their true weight based on the reading on the weigh scale.

Imagine now that the cable breaks, as in Figure 4.3.3(c). The elevator will accelerate down at rate $a = g$. The person in the elevator will also fall, accelerating at rate $a = g$. The scale, placed in the elevator by the person, will read the apparent weight of the person, which is zero. In this situation, $w = N = 0$. At this moment, the person experiences true weightlessness. You get a similar feeling when you go over a large bump while driving in a car or take a quick drop on an amusement park ride.

2. Orbiting Astronauts

Astronauts in an orbiting space vehicle feel weightless for the same reason as a person in a falling elevator. Both the astronauts and the vehicle they occupy are in free fall. The astronauts feel no resistance from any supporting structure, so they feel weightless.

3. Momentary Weightlessness

You experience brief sensations of weightlessness during everyday activities. If you are running, you will experience apparent "weightlessness" during those intervals when both feet are off the ground, because you are in a momentary free fall situation. Jumping off a diving board or riding your bike swiftly over a bump, you will experience brief moments of apparent weightlessness.

Quick Check

1. Why would a BMX rider feel momentarily "weightless" during a jump?

2. A 70.0 kg man is in an elevator that is accelerating downward at a rate of 1.0 m/s^2. What is the man's *apparent weight?*

3. How fast would Earth have to move at the equator before a person standing on the equator felt "weightless"? Earth's radius is 6.37×10^6 m.

4. Earth is in free fall toward the Sun. Why do you not feel "weightless" when you are an occupant of this satellite of the Sun?

Satellites in Circular Orbits — Orbital Velocity

What orbital (tangential) speed must a space vehicle have to achieve a circular orbit at a given altitude (Figure 4.3.4)? Since the centripetal force (mv^2/R) is provided by gravity, we can write:

$$\frac{mv^2}{R} = \frac{GMm}{R^2}$$

Therefore, $$v^2 = \frac{GM}{R}, \text{ and}$$

$$v_{\text{orbital}} = \sqrt{\frac{GM}{R}}$$

where M is the mass of Earth, R is the distance from Earth's centre to the space vehicle, and G is the universal gravitation constant.

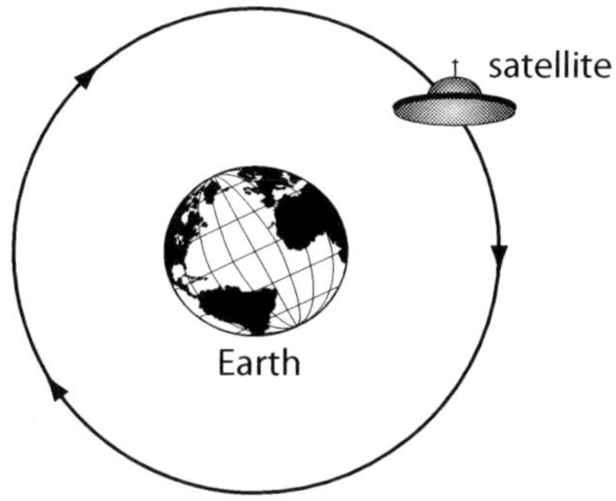

Figure 4.3.4 *A space vehicle must achieve and maintain a minimum speed to remain in orbit.*

Quick Check

1. What orbital speed is required by an Earth satellite in orbit 1.0×10^3 km above Earth's surface? Does it make a difference what the mass of the satellite is? Explain your answer. Earth's mass = 5.98×10^{24} kg — Earth's radius = 6.37×10^6 m

2. What is the speed of a satellite orbiting Earth at a distance of 9.0×10^5 m above Earth's surface?

Gravitational Potential Energy

Newton's law of universal gravitation tells us the force between a space vehicle and planet Earth at any distance R from the centre of mass of Earth:

$$F = G\frac{Mm}{R^2}$$

where M is the mass of Earth, m is the mass of the space vehicle, and R is the distance from Earth's centre to the space vehicle.

If a space vehicle is to travel to other parts of the solar system, it must first escape the grasp of Earth's gravitational field. How much energy must be supplied to the vehicle to take it *from Earth's surface* (where $R = R_e$) to a distance where the gravitational force due to Earth is "zero" ($R \rightarrow \infty$)?

The force on the space vehicle is continually changing. Figure 4.3.5 shows how the force changes with distance. To get the vehicle out of Earth's gravitational field, enough energy must be supplied to the space vehicle to equal the amount of work done against the force of gravity over a distance between Earth's surface and infinity where the force approaches zero.

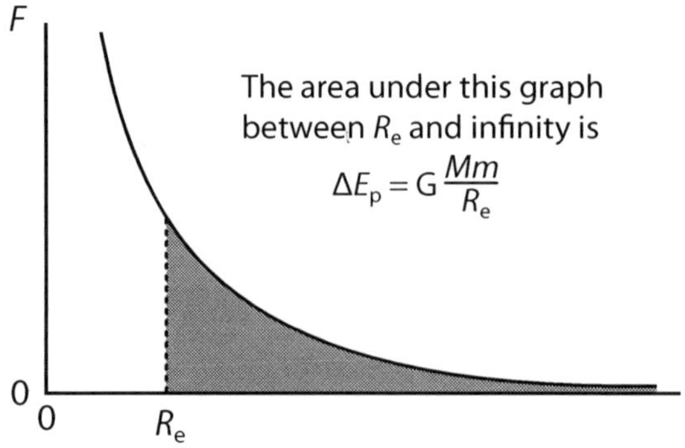

Figure 4.3.5 *A large force is needed at first to move the space vehicle out of Earth's gravitational field.*

The amount of work that must be done to escape Earth's gravitational field is equal to the area underneath the force vs. distance graph, between $R = R_e$ and $R \rightarrow \infty$ (Figure 4.3.5). Using calculus, it can be shown that the area under the graph (shaded portion) is equal to GMm/R_e. This area represents the change in gravitational potential energy of the vehicle as it moves from distance R_e out to infinity.

$$\Delta E_p = G\frac{Mm}{R_e}$$

In routine, Earthbound problems involving gravitational potential energy, we often arbitrarily take the "zero" level of potential energy to be at Earth's surface. In situations involving space travel, it is conventional and convenient to the let the "zero" of E_p be at infinity.

Since the change in E_p between $R = R_e$ and $R \rightarrow \infty$ is $+G\frac{Mm}{R_e}$, the E_p at Earth's surface is negative.

$$E_p \ (at\ R = R_e) = -G\frac{Mm}{R_e}$$

Escape Velocity

How fast must a spaceship travel to escape the gravitational bond of the planet Earth? In order to escape Earth's gravitational pull, the space vehicle must start with enough kinetic energy to do the work needed to bring its potential energy to zero. Sitting on the launch pad, the total energy of the space vehicle is

$$E_p = -G\frac{Mm}{R_e}$$

If the space vehicle is to escape Earth's field, it must be given sufficient kinetic energy so that:

$$-G\frac{Mm}{R_e} + E_k = 0$$

$$-G\frac{Mm}{R_e} + \frac{1}{2}mv^2 = 0$$

$$\frac{1}{2}mv^2 = G\frac{Mm}{R_e}$$

$$v^2 = 2G\frac{M}{R_e}$$

$$v = \sqrt{\frac{2GM}{R_e}}$$

This means that $v_{escape} = \sqrt{\frac{2GM}{R_e}}$ is the minimum speed the space vehicle must be given in order to escape Earth's gravitational pull.

This minimum speed for escape is called the escape velocity for planet Earth. It depends only on Earth's mass and Earth's radius. Obviously different planets or moons would have different escape velocities, as questions in the rest of the chapter will show.

Quick Check

1. A 2.0×10^4 kg satellite orbits a planet in a circle of radius 2.2×10^6 m. Relative to zero at infinity, the gravitational potential energy of the satellite is -6.0×10^9 J. What is the mass of the planet?

2. Ganymede, one of Jupiter's moons, is larger than the planet Mercury. Its mass is 1.54×10^{23} kg, and its radius is 2.64×10^6 m.
   (a) What is the gravitational field strength, *g*, on Ganymede?

   (b) What is the escape velocity for a space vehicle trying to leave Ganymede?

4.3 Review Questions

$G = 6.67 \times 10^{-11}$ Nm^2/kg^2
$M_e = 5.98 \times 10^{24}$ kg
$R_e = 6.37 \times 10^6$ m

1. What is the force of gravity exerted on a 70.0 kg person on Jupiter (assuming the person could find a place to stand)? Jupiter has a mass of 1.90×10^{27} kg and a radius of 7.18×10^7 m.

2. What is the gravitational field strength of Earth at a distance equal to the Moon's orbital radius of 3.84×10^8 m? Compare this with the centripetal acceleration of the Moon, calculated earlier in the chapter.

3. Calculate the orbital speed of the Moon around Earth, using the Moon's orbital radius and the value of Earth's gravitational field strength at that distance.

4. Both G and *g* are constants. Why is G a universal constant and not *g*? Under what conditions is *g* a constant?

5. Calculate the value of *g* at each of the locations in the table below. Express each answer as a multiple or a decimal fraction of Earth's *g*. Would the force of gravity on you be greatest on the Moon, on Ganymede (*one of Jupiter's Moons), or on Mercury?

	Mass	Radius
(a) On the Moon	7.34×10^{22} kg	1.74×10^6 m
(b) On planet Mercury	3.28×10^{23} kg	2.57×10^6 m
(c) On Ganymede*	1.54×10^{23} kg	2.64×10^6 m
(d) On the surface of the Sun	1.98×10^{30} kg	6.95×10^8 m

6. Use Newton's law of universal gravitation and the formula for centripetal force to show that you can calculate the mass of Earth knowing only the orbital radius and the period of an Earth satellite. Then calculate Earth's mass using the Moon's period (2.36×10^6 s) and orbital radius (3.84×10^8 m).

7. Calculate the gravitational force between the Sun and the planetoid Pluto. The mass of the Sun is 2×10^{30} kg, and the mass of Pluto is 6×10^{23} kg. Pluto is 6×10^{12} m away from the Sun.

8. An acrobat does a complete loop at the end of a rope attached to a horizontal bar. The distance from the support to the acrobat's centre of gravity is 3.0 m. How fast must she move at the top of her loop to feel "weightless" at that point?

9. A motocross rider travelling 20.0 m/s feels "weightless" as his bike rides over the peak of a mound. What is the radius of curvature of the mound?

10. Substitute values for G, M_e, and R_e in the formula for escape velocity and calculate the escape velocity for planet Earth. Does the mass of the space vehicle make a difference? Explain.

11. Calculate escape velocities for the Sun, the Moon, and Mars, given the following information.

	Mass	Radius
Sun	2.0×10^{30} kg	7.0×10^{8} m
Moon	7.4×10^{22} kg	1.7×10^{6} m
Mars	6.4×10^{23} kg	3.4×10^{6} m

12. Travelling to other planets involves not only Earth's gravitational field but also that of the Sun and the other planets. Would it be easier to travel to Venus or to Mars? (Which would require the lower escape speed?)

Chapter 4 Review Questions

$G = 6.67 \times 10^{-11}\ Nm^2/kg^2$

1. How much centripetal force is needed to keep a 43 kg object revolving with a frequency of 0.20 Hz in an orbit of radius 4.8 m?

2. What centripetal force must be exerted by the ice on a hockey player of mass 72 kg who cuts a curve of radius 3.0 m while travelling 5.0 m/s?

3. A 1.25 kg steel puck is swung in a circle of radius 3.6 m at the end of a cord of negligible mass, on a frictionless ice surface. The period of one revolution is 1.6 s. Calculate:
   (a) the speed of the puck.

   (b) the centripetal acceleration of the puck.

   (c) the centripetal force on the puck.

4. A satellite is orbiting Earth 1.00×10^2 km above the surface. At this altitude, $g = 9.5\ m/s^2$. If Earth's radius is 6.4×10^3 km, what is the period of revolution of the satellite?

5. How much centripetal force is needed to keep a 10.0 kg object revolving with a frequency of 1.5 Hz in an orbit of radius 2.0 m?

6. A 45 kg ape swings through the bottom of his arc on a swinging vine, with a speed of 3.0 m/s. If the distance from the supporting tree branch to his centre of gravity is 4.0 m, calculate the total tension in the vine.

7. A 1440 N football player, who missed a tackle in a very important high school game, is sent by his coach on a spaceship to a distance of four Earth radii from the centre of Earth. What will the force of gravity on him be at that altitude?

8. Earth's elliptical orbit around the Sun brings it closest to the Sun in January of each year and farthest in July. During what month would Earth's (a) speed and (b) centripetal acceleration be greatest?

9. What is the force of gravity on a 70.0 kg woman (a) here on Earth? (b) on an asteroid of mass 1.0×10^9 kg and radius 4.5×10^4 m?

10. What is the force of gravity on a 52 kg astronaut orbiting Earth 25 600 km above Earth's surface?

11. What is the altitude above Earth's surface of a satellite with an orbital speed of 6.5 km/s?

12. How far must you travel from Earth's surface before g is reduced to one-half its value at Earth's surface?

13. (a) At what speed must a satellite be travelling to complete a circular orbit just grazing Earth's surface?

(b) How does Earth's escape velocity compare with the speed needed to simply orbit Earth at the lowest possible altitude?

14. The "bump" on a motocross track is part of a circle with a radius of 50.0 m. What is the maximum speed at which a motorbike can travel over the highest point of the bump without leaving the ground?

15. At what distance from Earth, on a line between Earth's centre and the Moon's centre, will a spacecraft experience zero net gravitational force? (Earth's mass = 6.0×10^{24} kg; Moon's mass = 7.4×10^{22} kg; distance from Earth's centre to Moon's centre = 3.8×10^{8} m)

16. The acceleration due to gravity at the surface of a planet of radius 3.5×10^{6} m is 3.2 m/s^2. What is the mass of the planet?

17. A Snowbird jet travelling 600.0 km/h pulls out of a dive. If the centripetal acceleration of the plane is 6 *g's*, what is the radius of the arc in which the plane is moving?

18. Draw a vector diagram showing the forces acting on a car rounding a curve on a frictionless road that is banked at angle θ. Prove that the correct angle of banking (θ) that is appropriate for speed v and radius R is given by: $\tan\theta = \frac{v^2}{gR}$.

19. For a spherical planet of uniform density, show that $g = \frac{4}{3}r\ GR$, where ρ is the density of the planet and R is the radius of the planet.

Chapter 4 Extra Practice

1. If an object is in uniform circular motion, what can be said of the *magnitudes* of the object's velocity (v), acceleration (a), and centripetal force (F)?

2. (a) A 1.2×10^3 kg car rounds a curve of radius 75 m travelling 25 m/s. How much centripetal force is needed to take the car around this curve safely?
   (b) If the road is not banked, what is the minimum coefficient of kinetic friction needed?

3. If the gravitational force of attraction between a boy and a girl 1.00 m apart is F, what will it be when they move closer so they are only 0.25 m apart?

4. Observations of a satellite in orbit can be used to calculate the mass of the planet around which the satellite is revolving. The satellite has mass m, is at a distance R from the centre of the planet, and has an orbital period T. The universal gravitation constant is G. What is the *minimum information* you need to make the calculation of the planet's mass M?

5. In what units might gravitational field strength be measured?

6. On the Moon's surface, the force of gravity exerted by the Moon on a certain camera is 2.4 N. What will the force of gravity exerted by the Moon on the same camera be when the camera is placed in orbit with an orbital radius equal to twice the Moon's radius?

7. According to the equal-arm balance below, a gold sample has a mass of 60 g on Earth. If the same sample and balance are transported to the Moon, where g is only 1.6 m/s^2, what will the balance read for the mass of the gold sample there?

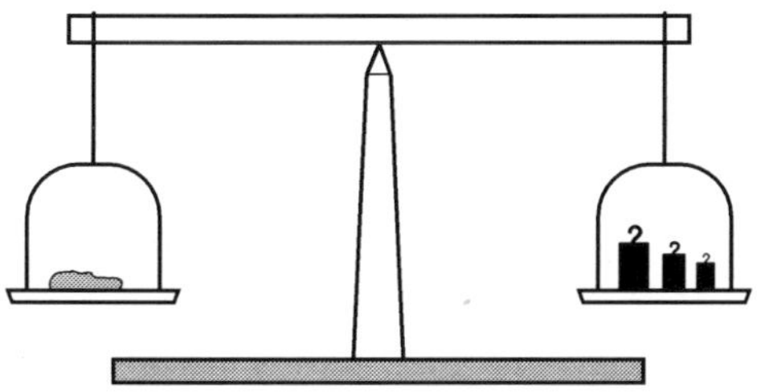

8. In the diagram below, a 0.20 kg air puck on the end of a string is moving in a horizontal circular path of radius 0.80 m.
   (a) If the tension in the string is 25 N, what is the period of revolution of the air puck?
   (b) If the period of the revolving air puck is reduced by one half, and the radius is kept the same, what will the tension be in the string?

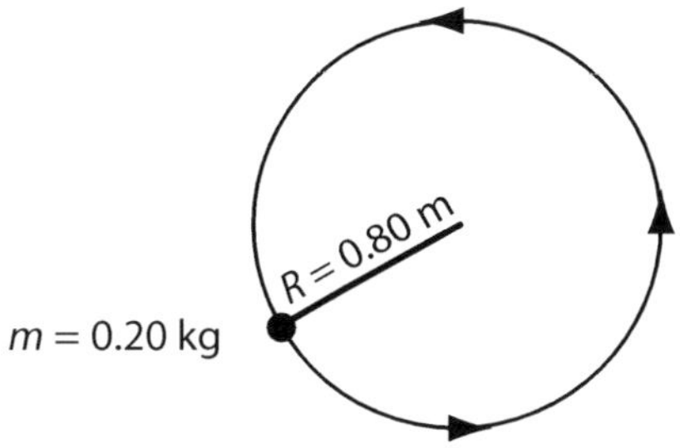

9. Jess has a mass of 45 kg. She is riding on a ferris wheel, so her seat travels in uniform circular motion. The centripetal force on Jess is 75 N. What is the upward force exerted by the seat on Jess (a) when she is at the top of the wheel? and (b) when she is at the bottom of the wheel?

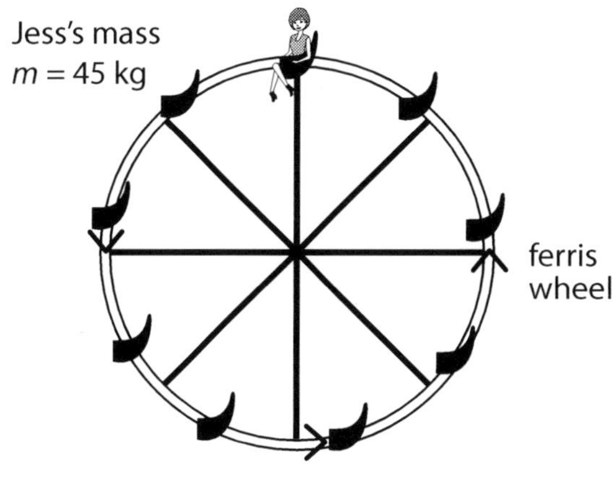

10. Why does an astronaut *feel* "weightless" in an orbiting space shuttle?

11. What is the acceleration of a satellite orbiting Earth in a circle of radius 7.30×10^6 m?

12. An Earth satellite orbits Earth in a circular orbit at a distance of 1.5×10^4 km from Earth's centre.
    (a) What is the speed of the satellite?
    (b) What is the gravitational field strength of Earth at this altitude?
    (c) If the satellite's mass is increased from *m* to 10*m*, how will this affect the answers to (a) and (b)?

13. A certain space station is shaped like a large bicycle wheel, and the occupants live out in the "tube" of the wheel, at a radius of 96 m. The "wheel" is rotated so that the centripetal acceleration simulates a gravitational field of 6.0 m/s^2. What is the period of rotation required to accomplish this?

14. With what speed does Earth orbit the Sun? The mass of the Sun is 2.0×10^{30} kg and Earth's orbital radius is 1.5×10^{11} m.

15. If a satellite requires 2.5 h to orbit a planet with an orbital radius of 2.6×10^5 m, what is the mass of the planet?

16. Calculate the mass of the Sun using Kepler's constant $K = 3.35 \times 10^{18}$ m^3/s^2, and $G = 6.67 \times 10^{-11}$ m^3/kg·s^2.

5 Electrostatics

By the end of this chapter, you should be able to do the following:

- Apply Coulomb's law to analyse electric forces
- Analyse electric fields and their effects on charged objects
- Calculate electric potential energy and change in electric potential energy
- Apply the concepts of electric potential to analyse situations involving point charges
- Apply the principles of electrostatics to a variety of situations

---

By the end of this chapter, you should know the meaning of these **key terms**:

- attract
- cathode ray tube
- conduction
- conductors
- Coulomb's law
- electric charge
- electric field
- electric field lines
- electric field strength
- electric force
- electric potential
- electric potential difference
- electric potential energy
- electron
- electron volt
- electrostatics
- elementary charge
- induction
- insulators
- law of conservation of charges
- point charge
- proton
- repel
- static electricity
- voltage

By the end of the chapter, you should be able to use and know when to use the following formulae:

$$F = k\frac{Q_1Q_2}{r^2} \qquad E = \frac{F}{Q} \qquad E = k\frac{Q}{r^2}$$

$$\Delta V = \frac{\Delta E_p}{Q} \qquad E = \frac{\Delta V}{d} \qquad E_p = k\frac{Q_1Q_2}{r}$$

$$V = k\frac{Q}{r}$$

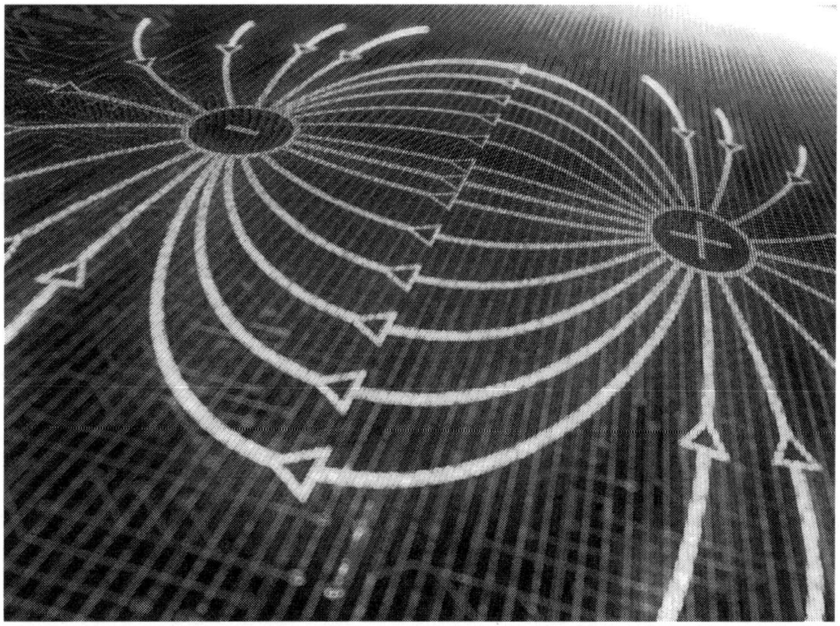

In this chapter, you will investigate electrostatic principles, like the electric field interactions modelled in this image.

5.1 Static Electric Charges

Warm Up

Place a metre stick on a watch glass. Rub an inflated balloon on your hair and bring it close to the metre stick. Observe the result. Describe and provide a reason for what you observe.

____

____

____

Attraction and Repulsion Forces

If your hair is dry and you comb it briskly, your comb will attract not only your hair but also bits of dust, paper, or thread. The comb is probably made of plastic, but many kinds of material will produce the same effect. As long ago as 600 B.C., the Greeks observed the "attracting power" of amber when it was rubbed with cloth. Amber is a fossilized resin from trees that the Greeks used for decoration and trade. Of course, magnets also have an "attracting power," but they only attract certain metallic elements such as iron, nickel, and cobalt, and some of their alloys. Amber, if rubbed with cloth, will attract small bits of just about anything.

In the late 1500s, the Englishman Dr. William Gilbert was curious about this interesting property of amber, and he did many experiments with it and other materials. Gilbert discovered that many materials, if rubbed with certain fabrics, could be electrified. Words like *electrified, electricity, electron*, and *electronics* come from the Greek word for *amber,* which was *elektron*.

In the early 1700s, Charles du Fay, a French scientist, was probably the first person to figure out that there were two kinds of electricity. He observed that if two glass rods were rubbed with silk and brought near each other, they would **repel** one another. "Repel" means to push away. Two amber rods rubbed with fur would also repel one another. If, however, an "electrified" amber rod was brought close to an "electrified" glass rod, the two rods would **attract** each other. Du Fay correctly deduced that there must be two kinds of electricity. Later in the 1700s, Benjamin Franklin called these "positive electricity" and "negative electricity."

By convention, a glass rod rubbed with silk is said to have a **positive charge**. An amber rod rubbed with wool or fur has a **negative charge.**

In classroom experiments, a good way to get a positive charge is to rub an acetate plastic strip with cotton. A negative charge is easily obtained by rubbing a vinyl plastic strip with wool or fur (Figure 5.1.1).

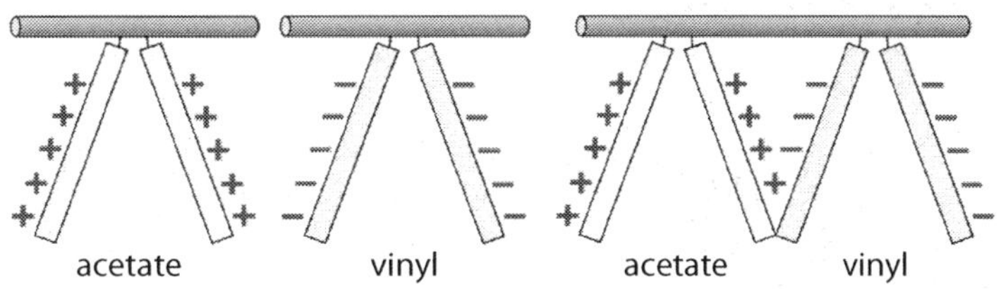

Figure 5.1.1 *Two charged acetate plastic strips (+), hanging freely from a supporting rod, repel each other. Two charged vinyl strips (–) also repel each other. However, a charged acetate strip will attract a charged vinyl strip.*

Since the electric charges on "electrified" objects are not moving, they are referred to as **static charges** or **static electricity**. "Static" means stationary or unmoving.

A charged object will attract any **neutral** body. A neutral body is one without any charge. It will also attract an oppositely charged body, but it will repel another body carrying the same charge.

> Bodies with the same charge repel each other.
> Bodies with opposite charges attract one another.
> A neutral body is attracted to either a positively charged body or a negatively charged body.

Elementary Atomic Structure

John Dalton's famous atomic theory assumed that all matter was made up of indivisible particles. A very important experiment by Ernest Rutherford showed that the atom actually had some internal structure to it. He was able to show that the atom had a **nucleus**, in which positive charge was concentrated. Since the atom as a whole is neutral, there must be negatively charged matter somehow distributed around the nucleus. Negatively charged particles were first identified by English physicist J. J. Thomson. These were later called **electrons**.

A simplified view of the atom as pictured in Rutherford's "planetary" model shows the nucleus of the atom with its positive charge, surrounded by negatively charged electrons. The positively charged particles in the nucleus are **protons**. Figure 5.1.2 also shows **neutrons**, but these were not discovered until 1932. An English physicist named James Chadwick, a contemporary of Rutherford, added this particle to the list of subatomic particles. Neutrons carry no electric charge, and their mass is just slightly greater than that of protons. Electrons are far less massive than protons or neutrons. The mass of a proton is 1.67×10^{-27} kg, which is 1836 times the mass of an electron.

The smallest atom is that of hydrogen. It has the simplest possible nucleus — one proton. The radius of the nucleus is approximately 10^{-15} m, compared with the radius of the hydrogen atom as a whole, which is approximately 10^{-10} m. Rutherford thought that the hydrogen nucleus might be the fundamental unit of positive charge. He was first to use the label proton for the hydrogen nucleus.

The normal state of an atom is neutral. However, atoms can gain or lose electrons, in which case they become electrically charged atoms called **ions.** Since protons are safely locked away in the nucleus of an atom, only electrons are transferred from one body to another during the "electrification" of normal objects.

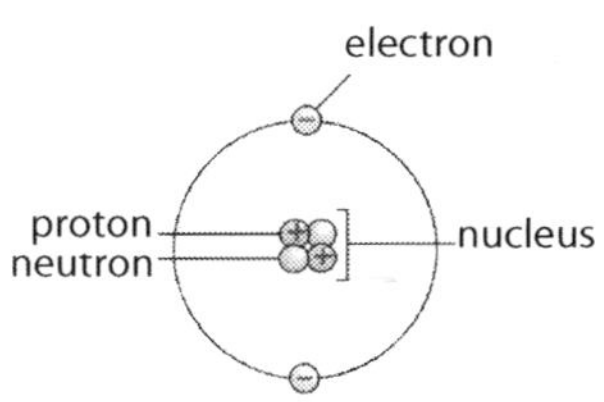

Figure 5.1.2 *The simple "planetary" model of the atom*

Electrification of Objects

Figure 5.1.3 shows what happens when a vinyl plastic strip is rubbed on wool. Vinyl has a stronger affinity for electrons than wool. When vinyl contacts wool, some electrons leave the wool and go to the surface of the vinyl. This leaves the vinyl with an excess of electrons, so it has a negative charge. The wool, having lost electrons, has a positive charge.

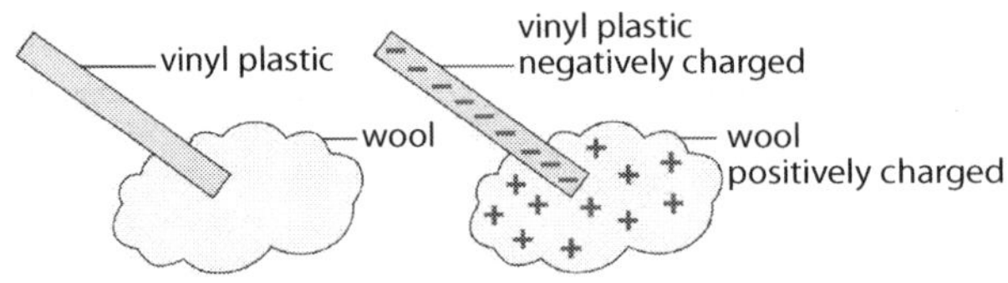

Figure 5.1.3 *Charging a vinyl rod with wool: the vinyl becomes negatively charged and the wool becomes positively charged.*

Similarly, if acetate plastic is rubbed with cotton, the cotton gains electrons from the acetate. The acetate becomes positively charged while the cotton becomes negatively charged.

All experiments show that there is no "creation" or "destruction" of electric charge during electrification. All that happens is a transfer of electrons from one body to another.

> According to the **law of conservation of charge**, electric charge is never created and never destroyed. Electric charge, like momentum and total energy, is a conserved quantity.

The Electrostatic or Triboelectric Series

Whether an object loses or gains electrons when rubbed with another object depends on how tightly the object holds onto its electrons. The electrostatic or triboelectric series lists various objects according to how tightly they hold onto their electrons (Figure 5.1.4). The higher up on the list the object is, the stronger its hold is on its electrons. The lower down on the list the object is, the weaker its hold is on its electrons. This means if we rub wool and amber together, electrons will be transferred from the wool to the amber. This results in the wool being positively charged and the amber being negatively charged.

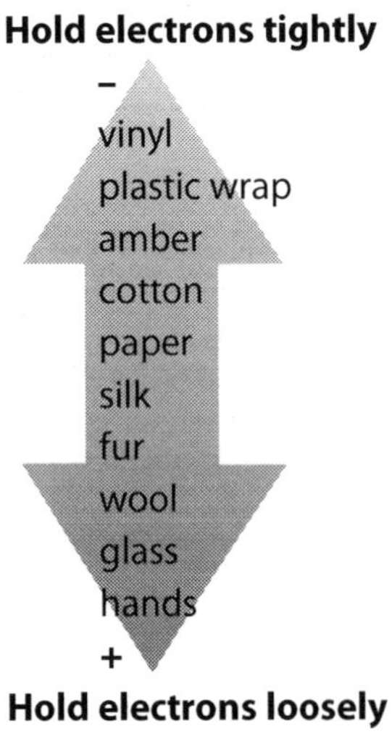

Figure 5.1.4 *The electrostatic or triboelectric series*

Conductors and Insulators

Conductors are materials that allow charged particles to pass through them easily. Metals such as silver, copper, and aluminum are excellent conductors of electricity, but all metals conduct to some extent. Atoms of metals have one or more outer electrons that are very loosely bound to their nuclei — so loosely attached that they are called "free" electrons.

In Figure 5.1.5, a metal rod is supported by a plastic cup. Plastic does not conduct electricity. A negatively charged vinyl strip is allowed to touch one end of the metal rod. When the vinyl touches the metal, a few excess electrons are conducted to the rod, so it becomes negatively charged as well. The negatively charged strip repels excess electrons to the far end of the metal rod. An initially neutral metal sphere, hanging from a silk string, is attracted to the charged rod. When the sphere touches the negatively charged rod, some of the excess electrons are conducted onto the sphere. Since the sphere is now the same charge as the rod, it is repelled from the rod.

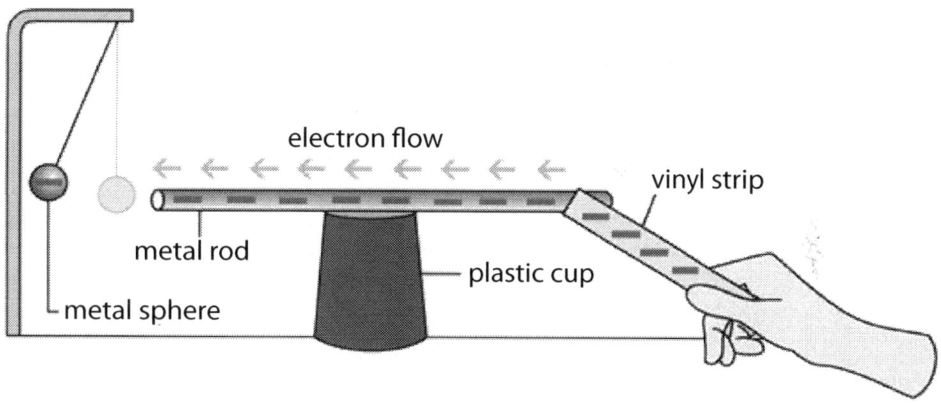

Figure 5.1.5 *Electrons transfer from the vinyl strip to the metal rod and onto the sphere.*

Now both the rod and the sphere have an excess of electrons. If the vinyl strip is taken away, the rod and the sphere will retain their negative charge and the sphere will remain in its "repelled" position. On a dry day, it may stay there for many hours.

If the metal rod is replaced with a glass or plastic rod of similar dimensions, the metal sphere does not move. This is because glass and plastic are **insulators**. Insulators are materials that resist the flow of charged particles through them. Plastics, rubber, amber, porcelain, various textiles, mica, sulphur, and asbestos are examples of good insulators. Carbon in the form of diamond is an excellent but very expensive insulator. Carbon in the form of graphite is a good conductor.

Non-metals such as silicon and selenium find many uses in transistors and computer chips because of their "semiconductor" behaviour.

It is easy to place a static charge on an insulator, because electrons are transferred only where the two objects come in contact. When an excess of charge builds up at a point on an insulator, the charge will not flow away — it remains static.

Charging by Conduction

An **electroscope** is a device designed to detect excess electric charge. In Figure 5.1.6, a positively charged acetate strip is brought close enough to touch the neutral, metal-coated sphere of an electroscope. When they touch, the free electrons on the surface of the conducting sphere will be attracted to the positively charged acetate plastic. The acetate will gain a few electrons, but its overall charge will remain overwhelmingly positive. The sphere, however, now has a positive charge, so it is repelled by the acetate strip. We say the sphere has been charged by contact or by **conduction**. You could just as easily charge the sphere negatively by touching it with a charged vinyl strip.

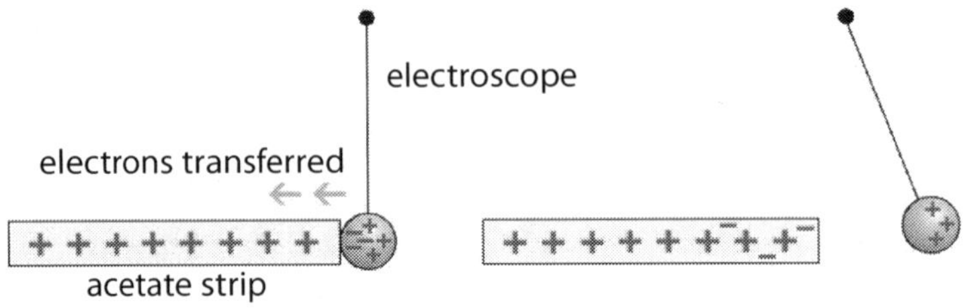

Figure 5.1.6 *Charging by conduction*

Charging by Induction

Objects can be charged without being touched at all, in which case we call it **charging by induction**. There are many ways to do this. Figure 5.1.7 shows one way. Two metal spheres are on insulated stands and are touching each other. A positively charged acetate strip is brought near the two spheres, but it does not touch them. Free electrons from the right sphere are attracted toward the left sphere by the positive acetate strip. Now the right sphere is pushed away using the insulated support stand. Tests with an electroscope will show that the right sphere has been charged **positively** by **induction**. The left sphere is charged **negatively** by **induction**.

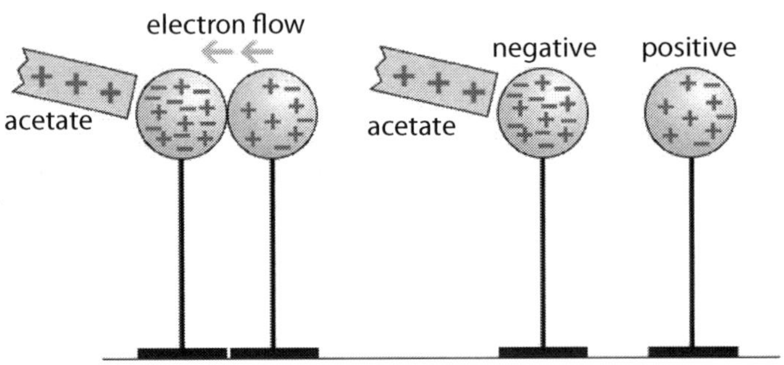

Figure 5.1.7 *Charging by induction*

Note that charge has not been "created" during this procedure. All that has happened is this: a few electrons have been transferred from the right sphere to the left sphere. The total charge is still the same as it was before the charging by induction was attempted. The net charge is still zero.

Investigation 5.1.1 Charging by Conduction and Induction

Purpose

To experiment with two different ways of placing a charge on an object

Part 1 Charging by Conduction

When you charge an object by touching it with another charged object, the electrons are conducted directly to it. In this process, you are charging by conduction.

Figure 5.1.8 *Styrofoam acts as an insulator.*

Procedure

1. Set two aluminum pop cans on or in Styrofoam cups as shown in Figure 5.1.8. Styrofoam is an excellent insulator, so it will keep any static charge you place on the cans from escaping to the bench.
2. Place a negative charge on one of the cans as follows:
   (a) Rub a vinyl strip with wool or fur. You may hear a crackling sound when the vinyl is being charged. The vinyl will have a negative charge on it.
   (b) Rub the charged vinyl strip over one of the insulated pop cans. Excess electrons from the vinyl will flow onto the can, giving the can a negative charge.
   (c) Repeat the process several times to make sure there is a lot of excess negative charge on the can.
3. Place a positive charge on the other can as follows:
   (a) Rub an acetate strip with cotton or paper. This will make the acetate positively charged, since electrons flow from the acetate to the cotton.
   (b) Rub the acetate strip onto the second can. The positively charged acetate strip will attract electrons from the second metal pop can, making the can positively charged.
   (c) Repeat this process several times to make sure the second can has lots of positive charge.
4. Do not touch the metal cans. Touching only their insulated Styrofoam bases, move the cans toward each other until they are about 3 cm apart.
5. Lower a graphite or pith ball between the two oppositely charged cans. Write down what you see happening.

Concluding Questions

1. What charge was on
   (a) the first can at the start?
   (b) the second can at the start?
   (c) the graphite ball before it was lowered between the cans?
2. Explain what happened to the graphite or pith ball during the experiment. Describe what happened to the electrons going to and from the three objects involved
3. Why does the action eventually stop?

Part 2 Charging by Induction

Imagine you have only a negatively charged strip, but you wish to place a positive charge on another object. If you touch the other object with a negatively charged strip, you will charge it negatively by conduction. However, if you use the induction method, you can give it a charge that is opposite to the charge on the charging body.

Procedure

1. Place a pop can on or in a Styrofoam cup.
2. Charge a vinyl strip negatively.
3. Bring the charged vinyl strip near and parallel to the pop can but do not let the vinyl strip touch the can.
4. Briefly touch the can with your finger, and then remove it and the vinyl strip completely. What do you think the charge is on the can? Repeat steps 2 to 4 until you can produce the same result three times in a row.
5. Work out a procedure to test for yourself whether the charge on the can is positive, negative, or neutral.

Concluding Questions

1. Before you brought your finger near the can,
   (a) what charge was on the vinyl strip?
   (b) what charge was on the side of the can near the vinyl strip?
   (c) what charge was on the other side of the can?
2. Your finger can conduct electrons to or from your body. In this experiment, were electrons conducted to the can from your body or from the can to your body?
3. (a) What was the final charge on the can?
   (b) Was this charge "conducted" from the vinyl strip?
   (c) How did the can obtain this charge?

5.1 Review Questions

1. What are the similarities and differences between the properties of an electron and a proton?

2. Describe the difference between a positive charge and a negative charge in terms of electrons.

3. Draw a diagram to show how an object can take on a negative charge using only a negatively charged vinyl strip.

4. Draw a series of diagrams to show how an object can take on a positive charge using only a negatively charged vinyl strip.

5. Why do clothes sometimes have static on them as soon as they come out of the clothes dryer?

6. What will be the charge on a silk scarf if it is rubbed with glass? With plastic wrap?

7. A charged rod is brought near a pile of tiny plastic spheres. The spheres are attracted to the charged rod and are then fly off the rod. Why does this happen?

8. What would happen if the vinyl strip in Figure 5.1.5 was replaced with a positively charged acetate strip? Why?

9. Outline a method by which you could determine, with certainty, whether the charge on your comb after you comb your hair is positive or negative.

5.2 The Electric Force

Warm Up

You have a charged acetate strip and some confetti. How could you use these two pieces of equipment to demonstrate which force is stronger — gravitational force or electric force?

____

____

____

Charles Coulomb

When you observe two objects being attracted or repelled due to electrostatic charge, you are observing non-contact forces in action. The two objects are exerting forces on each other without touching. The force exerted by one charged body on another can be measured. The force was initially measured by French scientist Charles Coulomb (1736–1806). He used an apparatus much like the Henry Cavendish's gravitational force apparatus to work out the relationship among these variables: force, distance, and quantity of charge. Figure 5.2.1 shows a setup similar to the one Coulomb used.

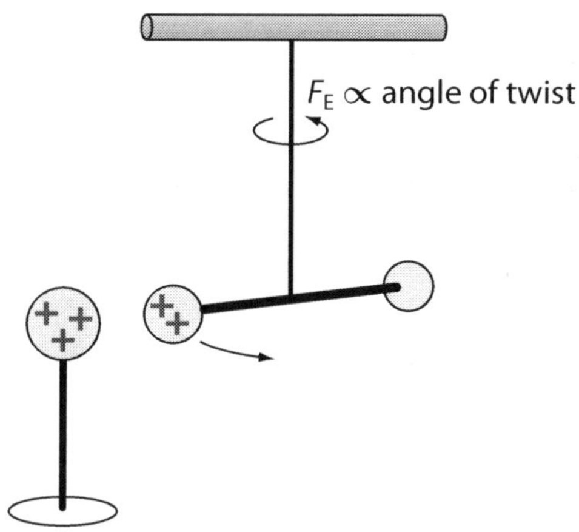

Figure 5.2.1 *Coulomb used an apparatus similar to this to study the relationship among the variables force, distance, and quantity of charge.*

In Coulomb's apparatus, a torque caused by the repulsion of two similarly charged spheres caused a length of vertical wire to twist through an angle. The amount of twist was used to calculate the force of repulsion between the two charged spheres. The apparatus is called a **torsion balance**.

Coulomb's Law

Coulomb was unable to measure the charges on the spheres directly. However, he found you can change the *relative* amount of charge in the following way: One sphere has an unknown charge Q on it, and the other identical sphere has zero charge. If you touch the two spheres together, both spheres will have the charge $\frac{1}{2}Q$. This assumes that the excess charge on the original sphere will be shared equally with the second, identical sphere. This sharing of excess charge can be repeated several times to obtain spheres with charges of $\frac{1}{4}Q$, $\frac{1}{8}Q$, and so on.

Experiments by Coulomb and others led to the conclusion that the force of attraction or repulsion between two point charges depends directly on the product of the excess charges on the bodies and inversely on the square of the distance between the two point charges. This is known as **Coulomb's law**, and is written symbolically like this:

$$F = \text{constant} \cdot \frac{Q_1 Q_2}{r^2} \text{, or}$$

$$F = k\frac{Q_1 Q_2}{r^2}$$

The magnitude of the proportionality constant k depends on the units used to measure the excess charge. If the measuring unit is the **elementary charge** (as on one electron or one proton), then Q would be measured in elementary charges, and the constant k in $F = k\frac{Q_1 Q_2}{r^2}$ has a magnitude of

$$\mathbf{k = 2.306 \times 10^{-28} \quad N{\bullet}m^2/(elem.\ charge)^2}$$

If the measuring unit for excess charge is the **coulomb** (named after Charles Coulomb), then Q would be measured in coulombs (**C**) and the constant k becomes

$$\mathbf{k = 8.988 \times 10^9\ N{\bullet}m^2/C^2}$$

The value of k was worked out after Coulomb's time. At the time he did his experiments, there was not yet a unit for "quantity of charge." When scientists decided on an appropriate measuring unit for charge, they named it after Coulomb.

The wording of Coulomb's law mentions "point charges." Coulomb's law applies to very small charged bodies. If the charged bodies are large relative to the distance between them, it is difficult to know what value of r to use. If the bodies are uniform spheres over which the charge is evenly spread, then you can use the distance between their centres. If two large, conducting spheres approach each other, forces between the charges will cause excess charges to rearrange themselves on the spheres in such a way that the "centres of charge" may not coincide with the "centres of mass."

The Coulomb and the Elementary Charge

It is now known that a coulomb of charge is equivalent to the amount of charge on 6.2422×10^{18} electrons (if the charge is negative) or on the same number of protons (if the charge is positive). The charge on one electron or one proton, called the elementary charge, is

$$\mathbf{1\ elementary\ charge\ (e) = \frac{1}{6.2422 \times 10^{18}\ /C} = 1.602 \times 10^{-19}\ C}$$

Sample Problem 5.2.1 — Coulomb's Law

What force would be exerted by a 1.00 C positive charge on a 1.00 C negative charge that is 1.00 m away?

What to Think About	How to Do It
1. Two charges are separated by a distance. This is a Coulomb's law question.	$F = k\frac{Q_1Q_2}{r^2}$
2. Find each charge and distance and remember to keep track of the sign.	$F = \frac{(8.988 \times 10^9\ Nm^2/C^2)(1.00\ C)(-1.00\ C)}{(1.00\ m)^2}$
3. Solve.	
4. As you can see, a +1.00 C charge would attract a −1.00 C charge 1 m away with a force of nearly 10 billion newtons! The coulomb is actually a *very* large amount of charge.	$F = -8.99 \times 10^9\ N$

Practice Problems 5.2.1 — Coulomb's Law

1. A small metal sphere with a charge of 3.00 μC (microcoloumbs) is brought near another metal sphere of charge 2.10 μC. The distance between the two spheres is 3.7 cm. Find the magnitude of the force of one charge acting on the other. Is it a force of attraction or repulsion?

2. What is the distance between two charges of 8.0×10^{-5} C and 3.0×10^{-5} C that experience a force of 2.4×10^2 N?

3. The force of repulsion between two identically charged small spheres is 4.00 N when they are 0.25 m apart. What amount of charge is on each sphere? Express your answer in microcoulombs (μC). (1 μC = 10^{-6} C) Use $k = 9.00 \times 10^9\ Nm^2/C^2$.

Electric Force Due to Multiple Point Charges

When more than two charges are in the same area, the force on any one of charges can be calculated by vector adding the forces exerted on it by each of the others. Remember, the electric force is a vector and adding vectors means considering both magnitude and direction.

Sample Problem 5.2.2(a) — Three Collinear Charges

Three tiny spheres are lined up in a row as shown in Figure 5.2.2. The first and third spheres are 4.00 cm apart and have the charges $Q_A = 2.00 \times 10^{-6}$ C and $Q_C = 1.50 \times 10^{-6}$ C. A negatively charged sphere is placed in the middle between the two positive charges. The charge on this sphere is $Q_B = -2.20 \times 10^{-6}$ C. What is the net force on the negatively charged sphere?

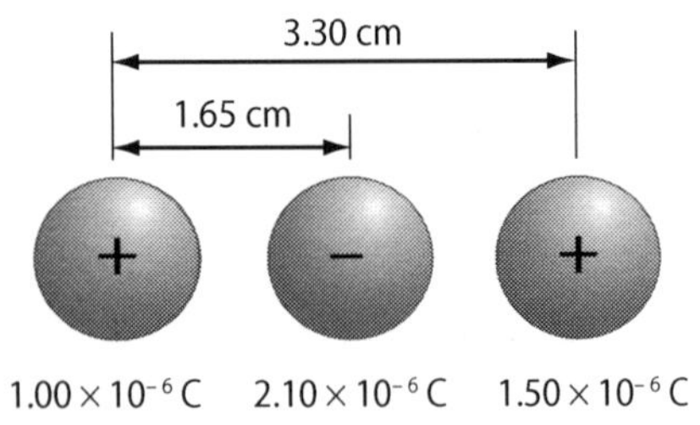

Figure 5.2.2 *Three collinear charges*

What to Think About	How to Do It
1. The charge on sphere B is negative and the charge on sphere A is positive. This means the force between the two charges is attractive. The same for the force between sphere B and C. For this problem, right will be positive.	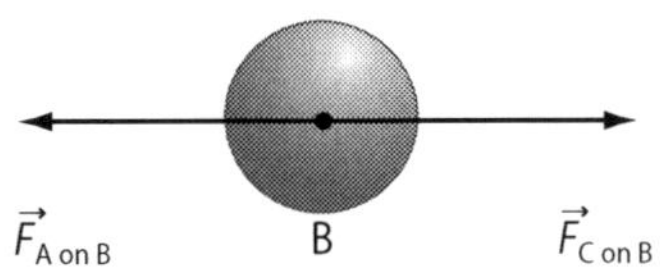 **Figure 5.2.3**
2. Determine the net force on sphere B by adding the two force vectors.	$F_{net} = F_{C\ on\ B} + F_{A\ on\ B}$ $F = k\frac{Q_C Q_B}{r^2} + k\frac{Q_A Q_B}{r^2}$ $F = \frac{9.00 \times 10^9\ Nm^2/C^2\ (2.20 \times 10^{-6}\ C)(1.50 \times 10^{-6}\ C)}{(0.20\ m)(0.20\ m)}$ $+ - \frac{9.00 \times 10^9\ Nm^2/C^2\ (2.20 \times 10^{-6}\ C)(2.00 \times 10^{-6}\ C)}{(0.20\ m)(0.20\ m)}$
3. The net force on sphere B is 0.25 N to the right.	$F = 0.742\ N + (-0.99\ N) = 0.25\ N$

Sample Problem 5.2.2(b) — Three Charges in a Triangle

Three tiny spheres with identical charges of +5.0 μC are situated at the corners of an equilateral triangle with sides 0.20 m long. What is the net force on any one of the charged spheres?

What to Think About

1. The net force on one of the charges will be the vector sum of the two repulsive forces exerted by the other two identical charges.

   Let the three charges be A, B, and C. Figure 5.2.4 shows their locations on the triangle, and vectors representing forces exerted on A by charges B and C.

2. First, calculate the magnitude of the force exerted by charge C on charge A.

   Note: The value of Coulomb's constant k is rounded off to 9.0×10^9 Nm²/C² for this problem.

3. The magnitudes of $F_{\text{C on A}}$ and $F_{\text{B on A}}$ are the same, but their directions are not. The two forces are vectors, and their resultant can be found by using vector addition, as in Figure 5.2.4.

   $$F_{\text{net}} = F_{\text{C on A}} + F_{\text{B on A}}$$

   You can solve for the net force several ways. You could use a scale diagram. You cannot use Pythagoras's theorem directly because the vector triangle is not a right-angled triangle. You could break it up into two right-angled triangles by drawing a line bisecting the 120° angle. The easiest solution is to use the sine law on the force triangle in Figure 5.2.4.

How to Do It

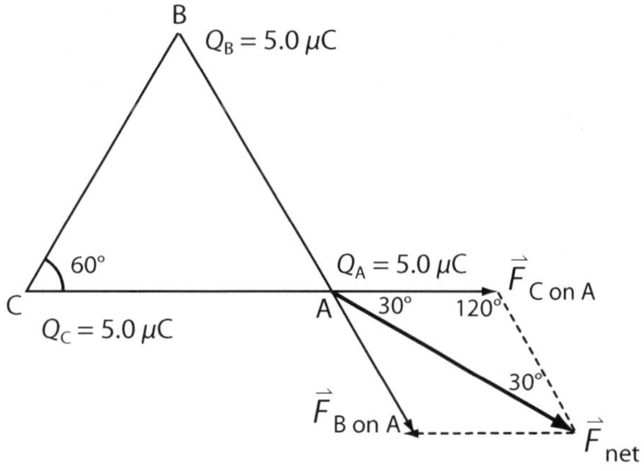

Figure 5.2.4

$$F = k\frac{Q_C Q_A}{r^2}$$

$$F = \frac{9.0 \times 10^9\ \text{Nm}^2/\text{C}^2 (5.0 \times 10^{-6}\ \text{C})(5.0 \times 10^{-6}\ \text{C})}{(0.20\ \text{m})(0.20\ \text{m})}$$

$$F = 5.63\ \text{N}$$

$$\frac{F_{\text{net}}}{\sin 120°} = \frac{F_{\text{C on A}}}{\sin 30°}$$

$$F_{\text{net}} = \sin 120° \bullet \frac{F_{\text{C on A}}}{\sin 30°} = \frac{(0.866)(5.63\ \text{N})}{(0.500)} = 9.80\ \text{N}$$

The direction of the net force is on a line bisecting angle A as shown in Figure 5.2.4.

Practice Problem 5.2.2 — Three Charges in a Triangle

1. A small metal sphere A with a negative charge of 3.30×10^{-6} C is 3.00 cm to the right of another similar sphere B with a positive charge of 2.0×10^{-6} C. A third sphere with a positive charge of 2.20×10^{-6} C is 1.50 cm directly above the second charge as illustrated in Figure 5.2.5.

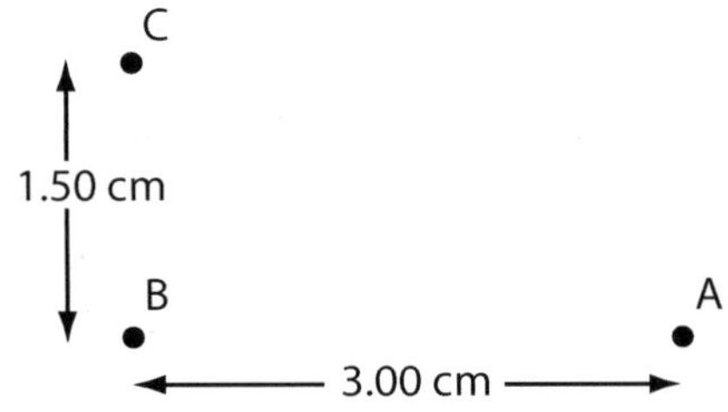

Figure 5.2.5

(a) Calculate the net force on sphere A.

(b) Calculate the net force on sphere B

(c) Calculate the net force on sphere C

Investigation 5.2.1 Coulomb's Law

Purpose

To investigate how the force between two electrically charged spheres varies with the distance between the centres of the two spheres

Introduction

Direct measurement of the force exerted by two charged spheres on each other is difficult, but an indirect method can be used to compare forces at different distances. **Figure 5.2.6(a)** shows a small graphite-coated sphere, mounted on an insulating stand. This sphere is given a charge by touching it with a charged acetate strip. A movable suspended sphere is also charged by the acetate strip. The charges placed on the spheres (Q_A and Q_B) should remain constant throughout the experiment.

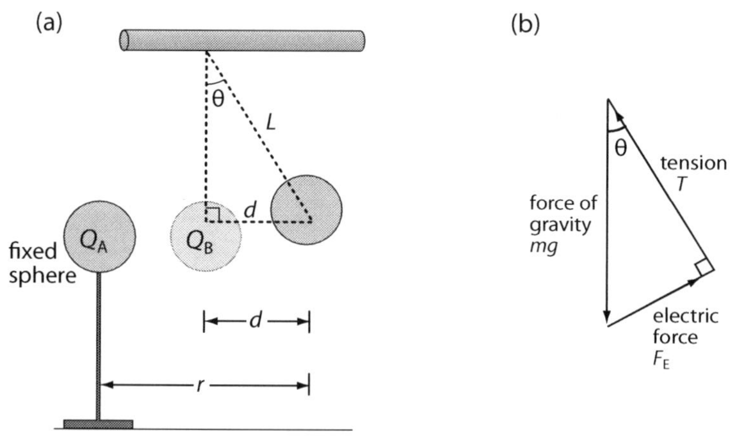

Figure 5.2.6

In Figure 5.2.6(a), *r* is the distance between the centres of the spheres, and *d* is the displacement of the movable ball from its starting position.
Figure 5.2.6(b) shows the three forces acting on the movable sphere when it is repelled by the similarly charged fixed sphere. Vectors representing the force of gravity, the electric force, and the tension in the string form a right-angled triangle. Note that this force triangle is *similar* to the displacement triangle in Figure 5.2.6(a). Since the triangles are similar,

$$\frac{F_E}{d} = \frac{mg}{L}$$

Therefore,

$$F_E = \frac{mg}{L}d$$

Since *m, g,* and *L* are constant during the experiment, we can write that

$$F_E = \text{constant} \cdot d$$

or

$$F_E \propto d$$

Since F_E is proportional to *d,* we can use *d* as a measure of the **electric force** between the two charged spheres at different distances *r.*

Procedure

1. Set up the apparatus for this experiment on the stage of an overhead projector. Project images of both spheres on a screen or a blackboard. Mark the position of the suspended ball before charging the spheres.
2. Charge both spheres by contact with a charged acetate strip. Do several practice runs, bringing the mounted sphere closer to the movable sphere and recording *r* and *d* at the same time. (If a graph grid is projected on the screen, measurements can be made in arbitrary units from the grid.) Practice is important. You must take your measurements very quickly, especially if humidity is high, since the charge may leak from the spheres to the air. Note: On the screen, the values of *r* and *d* will be larger than the true values, but both quantities are magnified by the same amount by the projector.
3. When you have mastered the technique of doing the measurements of *r* and *d* quickly, carry out the experiment and record your data in a table. Try to obtain at least five readings.
4. Plot a graph of *d* versus *r*. Examine its shape and make a reasonable guess at the nature of the relationship that exists between *d* and *r*. Plot a second graph of *d* versus r^n, where *n* is the exponent you think is most likely to produce a straight-line graph.

Concluding Questions

1. What relationship does your graph suggest might exist between the electric force F_E (which is proportional to *d*) and the separation distance *r*?
2. Careful experiments by Charles Coulomb led to his conclusion that the electric force between two point charges (very tiny charged bodies) varied as the inverse of the square of the separation between the point charges. In the ideal case, a graph of F_E (or *d*) versus r^{-2} would be straight. Discuss sources of error in your experiment, which might account for deviations from the "ideal" result.

5.2 Review Questions

Use the following numbers when calculating your answers:
$k = 9.00 \times 10^9$ Nm^2/C^2
1 elementary charge = 1.60×10^{-19} C
1 C = 6.24×10^{18} elementary charges

1. What will happen to the magnitude of the force between two charges Q_1 and Q_2 separated by a distance r if:
   (a) one of the charges is doubled?

   (b) both charges are doubled?

   (c) separation distance is doubled?

   (d) separation distance is tripled?

   (e) both charges are doubled and separation distance is doubled?

   (f) both charges are doubled and separation distance is halved?

2. What force would be exerted on a 1.00 μC positive charge by a 1.00 μC negative charge that is 1.00 m away from it?

3. What is the force of repulsion between two bodies carrying 6.0 μC of charge and separated by 1.0 μm?

4. What is the force of attraction between a proton and an electron in a hydrogen atom, if they are 5.00×10^{-11} m apart?

5. One electron has a mass of 9.1×10^{-31} kg. How many coulombs of charge would there be in 1 kg of electrons? How much force would this charge exert on another 1 kg of electrons 1.0 km away? (This is strictly an imaginary situation!)

6. Two small spheres are located 0.50 m apart. Both have the same charge on them. If the repulsive force is 5.0 N, what charge is on the spheres, in μC?

7. Three charged objects are located at the "corners" of an equilateral triangle with sides 1.0 m long. Two of the objects carry a charge of 5.0 μC each. The third object carries a charge of –5.0 μC. What is the resultant force acting on the –5.0 μC object? Assume all three objects are very small.

8. Imagine you could place 1 g of electrons 1.0 m away from another 1 g of electrons.
   (a) Calculate
      (i) the electric force of repulsion between the two charge collections.
      (ii) the gravitational force of attraction between them.
      (iii) the *ratio* of the electric force to the gravitational force.
   (b) Discuss the practical aspects of this imaginary situation.

9. Discuss whether you think gravity would play a major part in holding atoms together. Refer to your results in question 8. Calculate the gravitational force between a proton and an electron 5.00×10^{-11} m apart. Compare this force with the electric force calculated in question 4.

10. Two protons repel each other with a force of 1.0 piconewton (10^{-12} N). How far apart are the protons?

5.3 Electric Field Strength

Warm Up

A lit match is brought near a Van de Graaff generator. When the match gets close to the charged dome, it goes out. Why do you think this happens?

____

____

____

What Is a Field?

Scientists use scientific models to describe naturally occurring situations that are difficult to observe. One of the first models you probably encountered in school was the solar system. Planets were represented by scale and order from the Sun. While not exactly correct, it gave you a framework to understand the structure and general workings of the solar system. A force field is a model that gives a framework for understanding how forces are transmitted from one object to another across empty space. In physics, a **field** is a region of space in which a certain quantity has a definite value at every point.

Gravity is an example of a force field. Recall that the gravitational field strength, $\vec{g}$, due to a massive body like Earth is defined by $\vec{g} = \frac{\vec{F}}{m}$, where both $\vec{g}$ and $\vec{F}$ are vectors. The value of g changes as you move the "test mass" m away from Earth. In fact, $\vec{g}$ varies inversely as the square of the distance between m and Earth's centre of mass.

Representing Electric Fields

An **electric field** is a region of space in which a charged object is acted on by a force. To visualize an electric field, we use lines of force to create a field vector diagram. In a field vector diagram, vectors are drawn showing the direction of the field and its magnitude at various distances from a fixed charge. The direction of the vectors is the direction that the force would tend to move a positive **test charge** in that region of the field. A test charge is a charge so small that it does not affect a source charge and change its electric field. Figure 5.3.1 shows the field near a fixed positive charge.

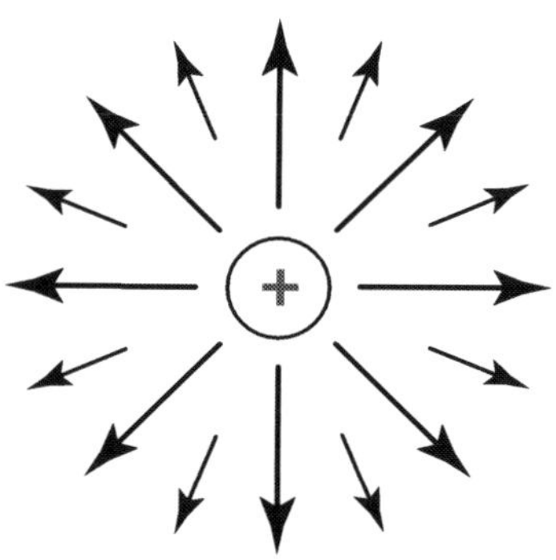

Figure 5.3.1 *Field around a positive test charge*

The idea of the electric field originated with Michael Faraday (1791–1867), but he used a different way of representing the field. He used lines of force, which showed the direction in which a positive test charge would tend to move if placed anywhere in the field. Figure 5.3.2 shows the lines of force around:

(a) a fixed positive charge and
(b) a fixed negative charge.

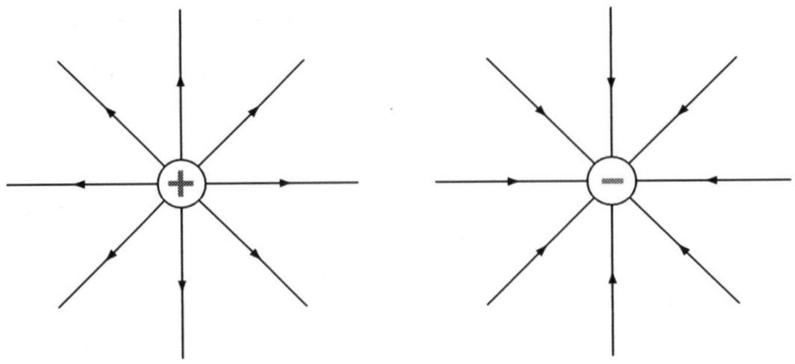

(a) (b)

Figure 5.3.2 *Lines of force around (a) a fixed positive charge and (b) a fixed negative charge*

Figure 5.3.3 shows the lines of force near
(a) two oppositely charged bodies and
(b) two similarly charged bodies (both positive).

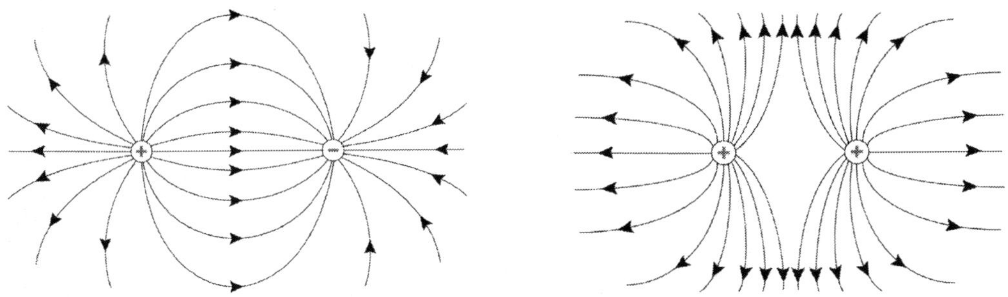

(a) (b)

Figure 5.3.3 *Lines of force around (a) two oppositely charged bodies and (b) two similarly charged bodies*

If two parallel metal plates are oppositely charged by a power supply a uniform electric field is created between the plates as shown in Figure 5.3.4.

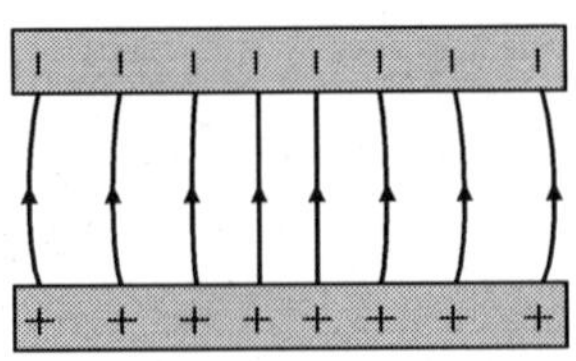

Figure 5.3.4 *A uniform electric field*

Properties of Electric Field Lines

To summarize, the properties of electric field lines are:

1. Field lines indicate the direction of the electric field.
2. Field lines are drawn so that the magnitude of the electric field is proportional to the number of lines drawn. The closer the lines are, the stronger the field.
3. Electric field lines start on positive charges and end at negative charges. The greater the magnitude of charge the greater the number of lines coming from or going to the charge.

Electric Field Patterns Formed by Celery Seeds

Figure 5.3.5 shows photographs of electric field patterns in a number of situations. An insulating liquid was placed in the dish with the various charged objects, and celery seed was dispersed in the liquid. The celery seeds line themselves up in the electric field in such a way that they give a visual representation of the shape of the electric field. Notice that the lines of force originate on the positively charged objects and terminate on negatively charged objects. The lines do not cross each other, and they always meet the surfaces of the objects at right angles. If the lines are spreading out, this means the field is getting weaker. The "line density" indicates relative strength of the field in different regions of the field.

(a) Lines of force around a single charged rod

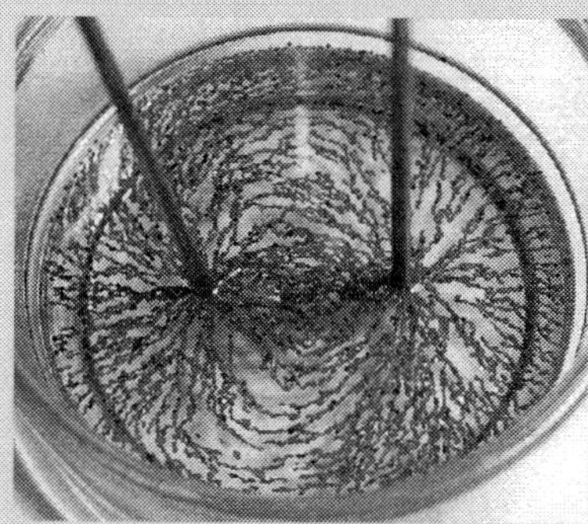

(b) Lines of force around two oppositely charged rods

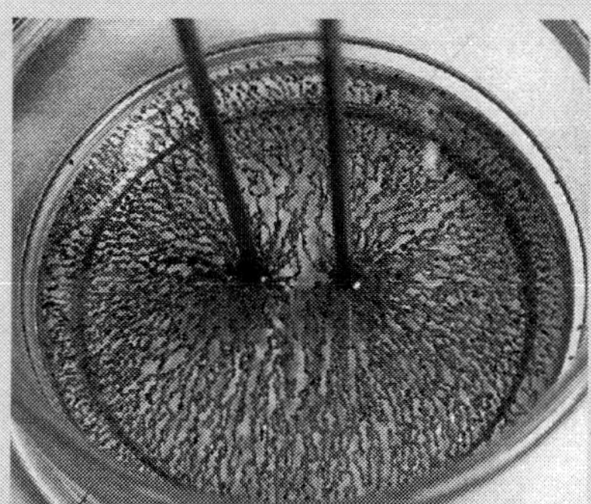

(c) Lines of force between two like-charged rods

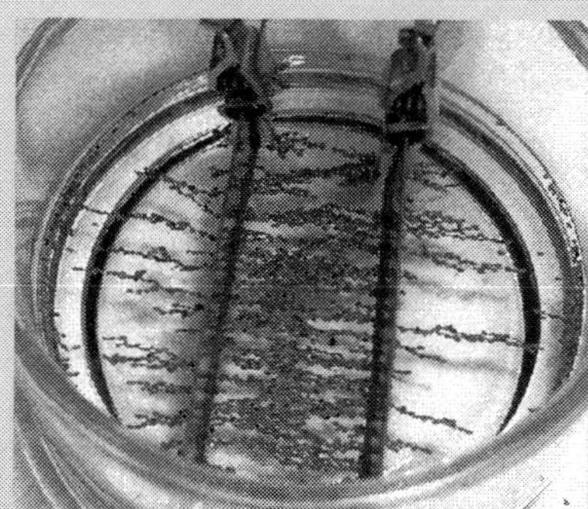

(d) Lines of force between two oppositely charged plates

Figure 5.3.5 *Lines of force illustrated using celery seeds in a liquid*

Quick Check

1. Draw and lable a sketch of each field represented by the celery seeds in Figure 5.3.5. Assume the wire on the right is positive.

   (a) (b)

   (c) (d)

2. Draw the electric field and show the direction between two positively charged objects.

3. A strip of vinyl is rubbed with fur and a strip of glass is rubbed with wool. Draw the electric field that occurs when the two charged objects are brought close together and parallel to each other.

Defining an Electric Field

We started this section discussing gravitational fields. Then we discovered there are electric fields around charges just as there is a gravitational field around masses. These fields and their interactions can be represented using electric field lines. We can also quantitatively calculate the strength of these fields.

While gravitational field strength is the force per unit mass, **electric field strength $\vec{E}$** is the force per unit charge. An electric field is a force field that exists wherever an electric force acts on a charge. Remember that $\vec{F}$ represents the force acting on a test charge in an electric field.

Electric field strength $$\vec{E} = \frac{\vec{F}}{Q}$$

Electric field strength is measured in newtons per coulomb (N/C).

Sample Problem 5.3.1 — Electric Field Strength

A positive test charge of magnitude 2.20×10^{-8} C experiences a force of 1.4×10^{-3} N toward the west. What is the electric field at the position of the test charge?

What to Think About	How to Do It
1. Determine what you know: a positive charge is in an electric field. You know the magnitude of the charge and the force the charge experiences.	Charge (Q) $= 2.20 \times 10^{-8}$ C Force (F) $= 1.4 \times 10^{-3}$ N
2. Identify the correct formula: you are looking for electric field.	$E = \frac{F}{Q}$
3. Plug in known values and solve	$E = \frac{1.4 \times 10^{-3} \text{ N}}{2.20 \times 10^{-8} \text{ C}} = 6.38 \times 10^{4} \frac{\text{N}}{\text{C}}$

Practice Problems 5.3.1 — Electric Field Strength

1. What charge exists on a test charge that experiences a force of 1.80×10^{-8} N at a point where the electric field intensity is 4.00×10^{-4} N/C?

2. A positive test charge of 1.00×10^{-5} C experiences a force of 0.45 N. What is the electric field intensity at that point?

3. What force is exerted on a charge of 5.00×10^{-6} C when it is placed in an electric field of strength 60.0 N/C?

Magnitude of the Electric Field Around a Source Charge

The magnitude of an electric field around a source charge at a particular point can also be determined if Coulomb's law is combined with electric field strength. Notice that it is important to remember which charge is the source charge (Q_1) and which is the test charge (Q_2) as in Figure 5.3.6.

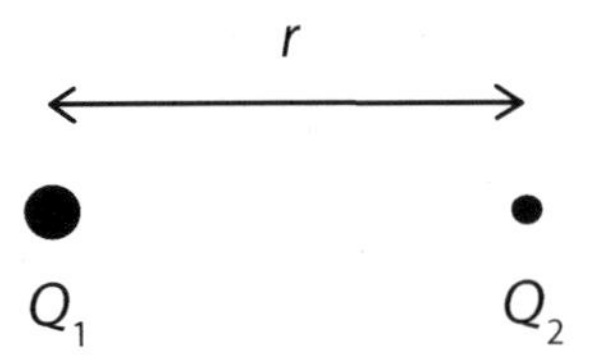

Figure 5.3.6 *The source charge is Q_1 and the test charge is Q_2.*

$$\vec{E} = \frac{\vec{F}}{Q_2} \text{ and } \vec{F} = \frac{kQ_1Q_2}{r^2} \text{ then}$$

$$\vec{E} = \frac{\frac{kQ_1Q_2}{r^2}}{Q_2}$$

$$\vec{E} = \frac{kQ_1}{r^2}$$

The test charge Q_2 cancels out so only the source charge Q_1 is considered.

Quick Check

1. What is the electric field strength at a distance of 0.75 m away from a 90 μC charge?

2. A proton has a charge of 1.60×10^{-19} C. At what distance from the proton would the magnitude of the electric field be 4.45×10^{11} N/C?

3. A charge is producing a 35.0 N/C electric field at a point 3.00 cm away from it. What is the magnitude of this charge?

Multiple Charges Creating Electric Fields

There are times when more than one charge creates an electric field. As electric fields are vector quantities, the net field at any point is the vector sum of the fields from all the charges contributing to the field. The following example illustrates how to vector addition to determine a net electric field.

Sample Problem 5.3.2 — Multiple Charges and Electric Fields

Two negatively charged spheres, A and B, are 30 cm apart and have the following charges of 3.0×10^{-6} C and 1.5×10^{-6} C as in Figure 5.3.7. What is the net electric field at a point P, which is exactly in the middle between the two charges?

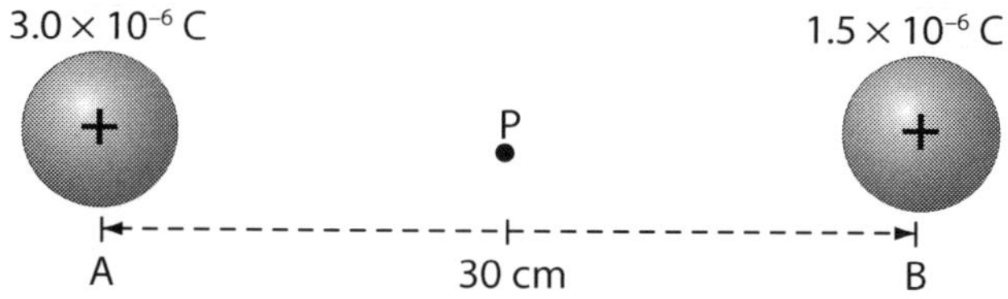

Figure 5.3.7

What to Think About

1. Determine what you know: both charges have an electric field. Electric field Q_A is directed to the right at point P. Electric field Q_B is to the left. Since Q_A is double the charge, the net field will be the right. Make the right positive.

How to Do It

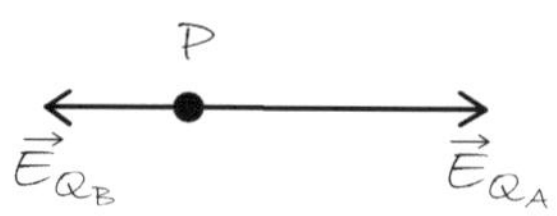

Figure 5.3.8

2. Find the electric field at point P created by Q_A and then do the same for Q_B

$$\vec{E}_{Q_A} = k\frac{Q_A}{r^2} = \frac{(9.0 \times 10^9 \frac{N \cdot m^2}{C^2})(3.0 \times 10^{-6} C)}{(0.15 m)^2}$$

$$= 1.2 \times 10^6 N/C$$

$$\vec{E}_{Q_B} = k\frac{Q_B}{r^2} = \frac{(9.0 \times 10^9 \frac{N \cdot m^2}{C^2})(-1.5 \times 10^{-6} C)}{(0.15 m)^2}$$

$$= -6.0 \times 10^5 N/C$$

3. Electric fields are vector quantities, so use vector addition to add the two electric fields at point P.

$$\vec{E}_{\text{Net at P}} = \vec{E}_{Q_A} + \vec{E}_{Q_B}$$

$$= -1.2 \times 10^6 N/C + -6.0 \times 10^5 N/C$$
$$= 6.0 \times 10^5 N/C$$

4. Summarize.

The net electric field is 6.0×10^5 N/C to the right.

Practice Problems 5.3.2 — Multiple Charges and Electric Fields

1. Figure 5.3.9 shows a positive charge located near a smaller (in magnitude) negative charge. Circle the roman numeral that represents the region where the electric field due to the two charges is equal to zero. Draw field lines to support your answer.

Figure 5.3.9

2. What is the net electric field at point P between the two oppositely charge spheres in Figure 5.3.10?

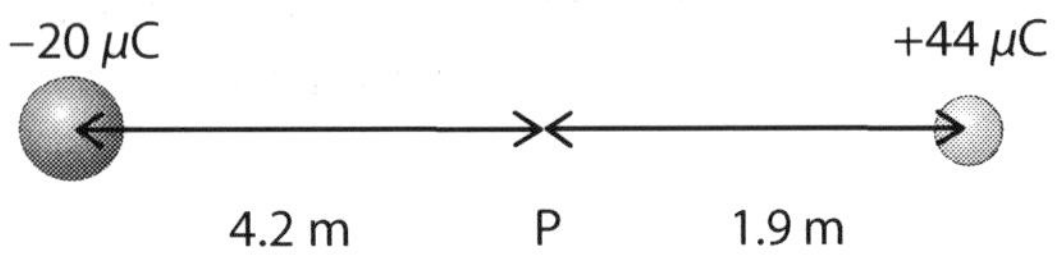

Figure 5.3.10

3. What is the magnitude and direction of the electric field at point P in Figure 5.3.11?

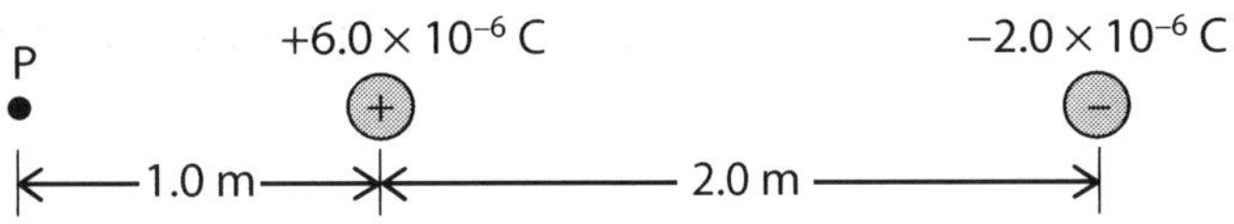

Figure 5.3.11

5.3 Review Questions

1. An electron carries a charge of -1.6×10^{-19} C. If a force of 3.2×10^{-17} N causes the electron to move upward, what is the magnitude and direction of the electric field?

2. A proton has a charge of $+1.6 \times 10^{-19}$ C. If it is in an electric field of strength 9.00×10^{2} N/C, what force acts on the proton?

3. A positively charged sphere weighing 3.5×10^{-14} N is held in place by a vertical electric field as shown in the diagram below. If the electric field strength is 7.5×10^{4} N/C, what is the charge on the sphere?

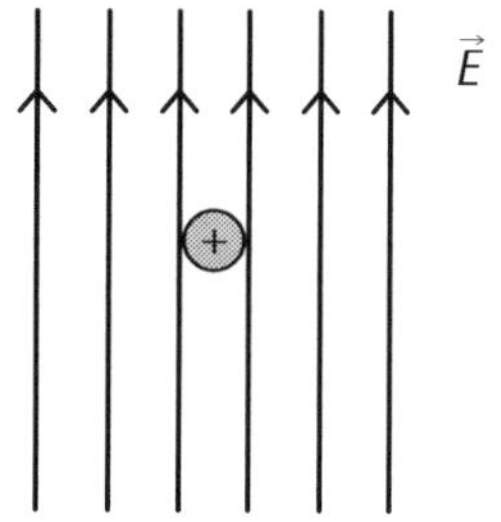

4. The atomic nucleus of iron contains 26 protons. What is the direction and magnitude of the electric field 4.50×10^{-10} m from the nucleus?

5. A proton passing between parallel plates 0.040 m apart experiences an upward electric force of 9.4×10^{-15} N as shown below. What is the magnitude of the electric field between the plates?

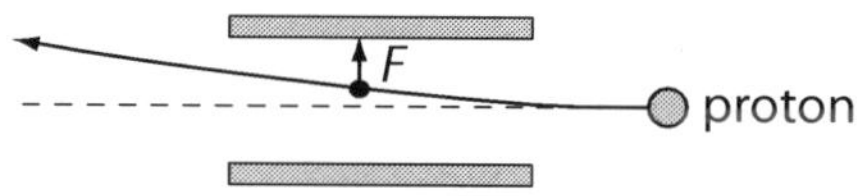

6. What is the magnitude and direction of the electric field at a distance of 0.180 m from a fixed charge of 3.60×10^{-2} C?

7. A $+36\ \mu$C charge is 0.80 m away from a $+108\ \mu$C charge. What is the magnitude and direction of the electric field at a point midway between the two charges?

8. What is the magnitude of the electric field at point P in the diagram below?

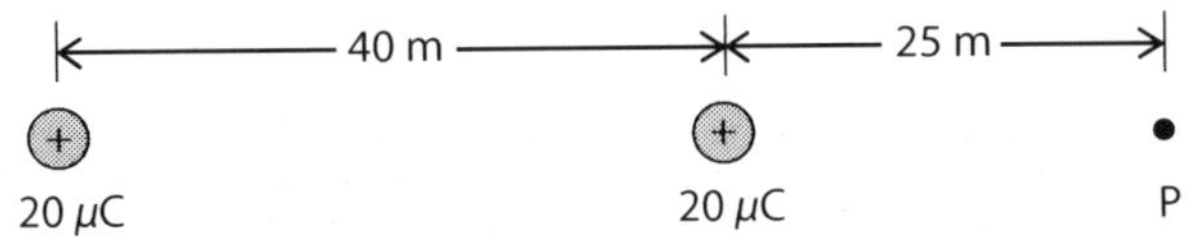

9. What is the resultant electric field strength E at point A in the diagram below? Give both the magnitude and the direction.

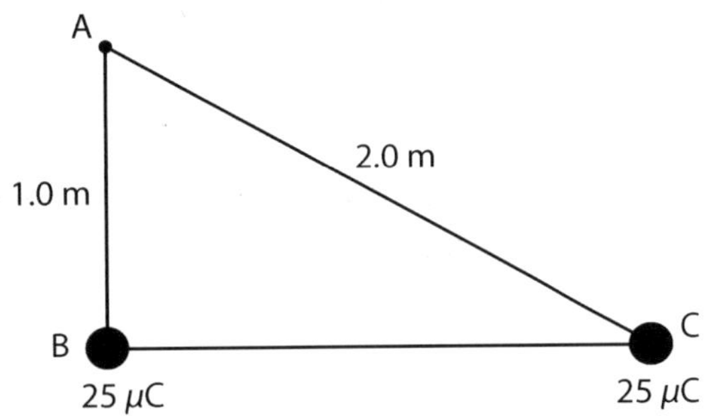

10. The magnitude of the net electric field at P in the diagram below is 4.0×10^4 N/C. What is the magnitude of charge Q_2?

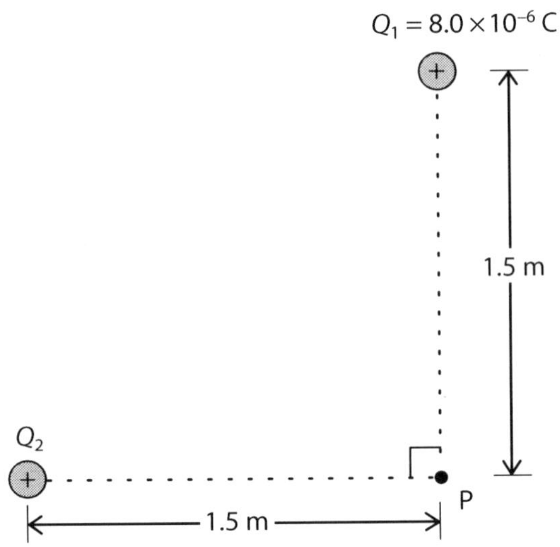

11. A proton has a mass of 1.67×10^{-27} kg. At what rate will it accelerate in an electric field of strength 1.0×10^3 N/C?

5.4 Electric Potential Energy, Electric Potential, and Electric Potential Difference

Warm Up

A household electrical outlet normally has a voltage around 110 V. A Van de Graaff generator can have a charge of thousands of volts. Why does a shock from the generator not injure a person, but a shock from the 110-V household outlet does?

____

____

____

Electric Potential Energy in Uniform Fields

In earlier science classes, you studied the work-energy theorem. The theorem states that the work done on an object is equal to the change in the object's energy. A common example of this is when you lift an object against gravity, like lifting a book from the floor to your desk. The book gains gravitational potential energy when you lift it or, expressed another way, when you do work on it. The work-energy theorem is written as:

$$W = \Delta E_p$$

We can use the gravitational potential energy example as an analogy to explain what happens to the potential energy of a charge in a uniform electric field.

Table 5.4.1 *Using Gravity to Explain the Potential Energy of a Charge*

<table>
<tr><th></th><th>Gravity</th><th>Electric Charge</th></tr>
<tr><td>1. A gravitational field near Earth's surface and the electric field between two charged plates are uniform.</td><td>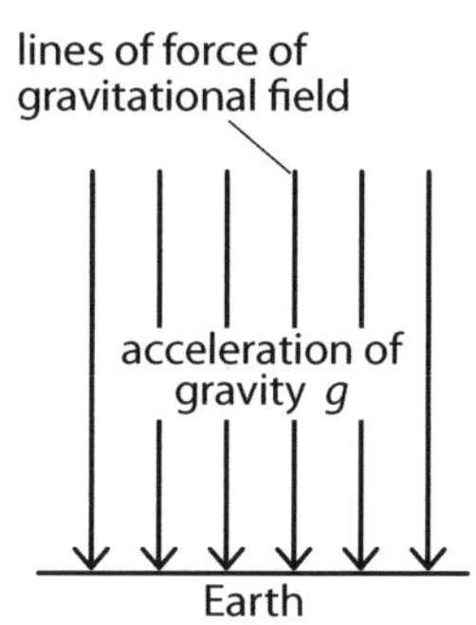
</td><td>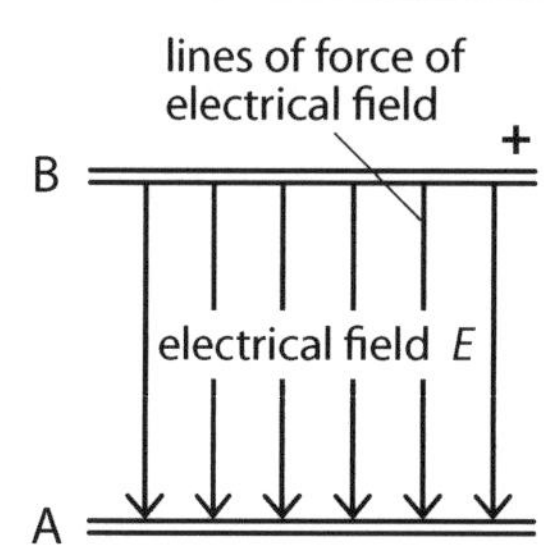
</td></tr>
</table>

Table 5.4.1 *Using Gravity to Explain the Potential Energy of a Charge (Continued)*

	Gravity	Electric Charge
2. A mass in a gravitational field experiences a force equal to *mg*. A positively charged particle experiences a force of *QE*.	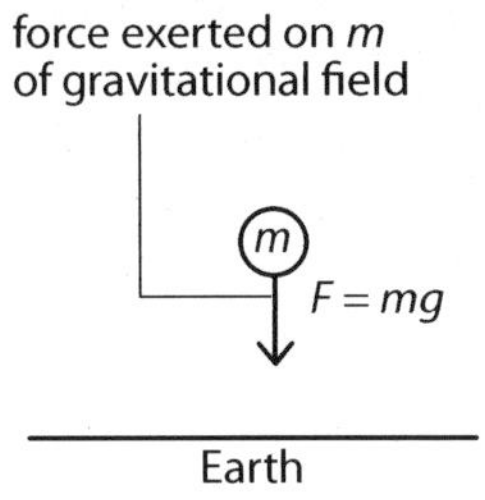	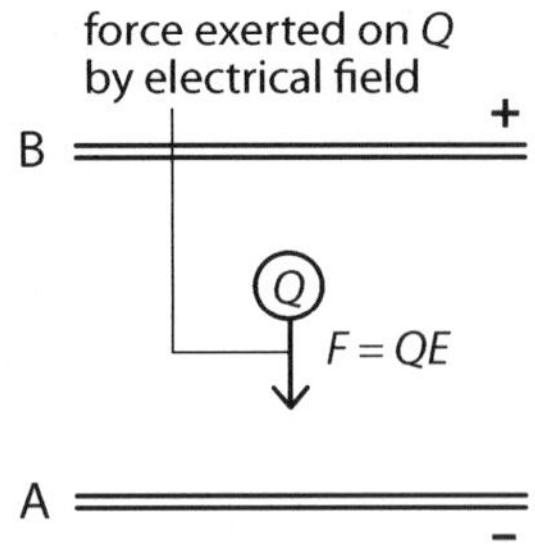
3. The work done on the object in moving it a distance *h* is equal to the change in potential energy. If the charge is moved from plate A to plate B, the work done is *QEd* relative to plate A. This is the electric potential energy in the charge when at plate B with respect to plate A.	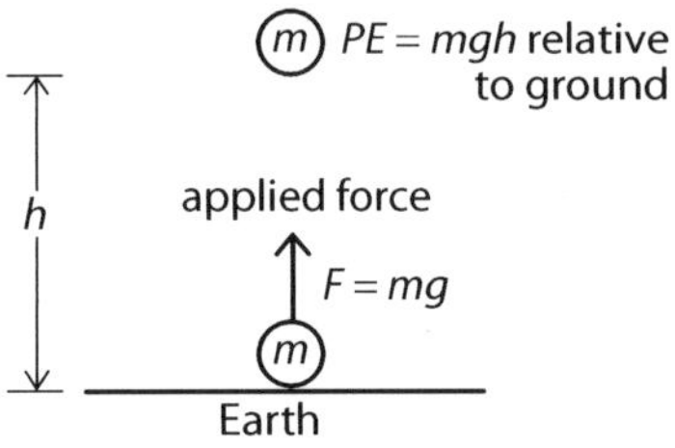	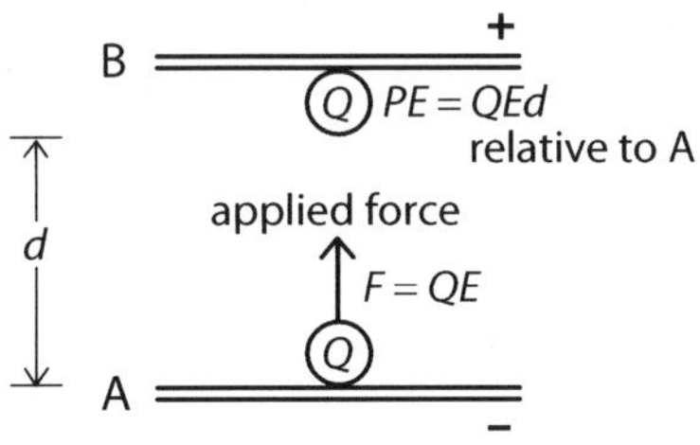
4. Letting go of the mass causes it to fall to the ground and all the potential energy has been converted to kinetic energy when it reaches the ground. Letting go of the charge means it will be attracted to plate A. All the electric potential energy will be converted to kinetic energy when it reaches plate A.	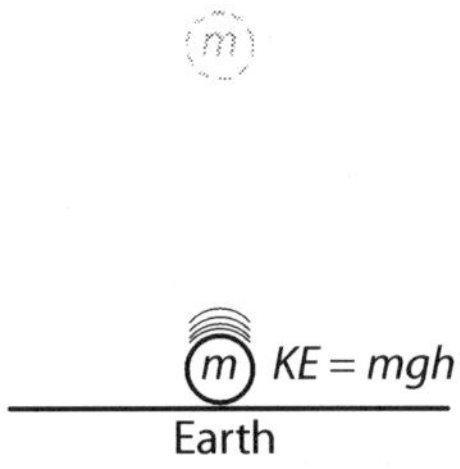	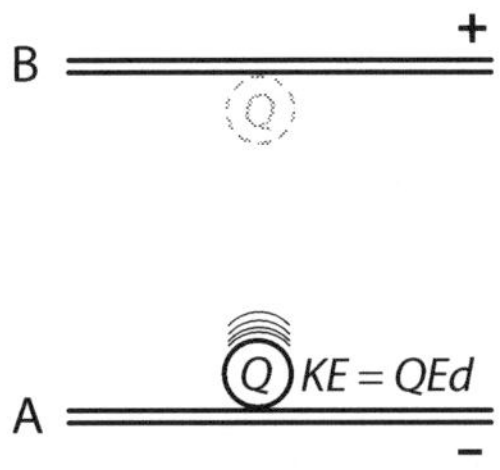

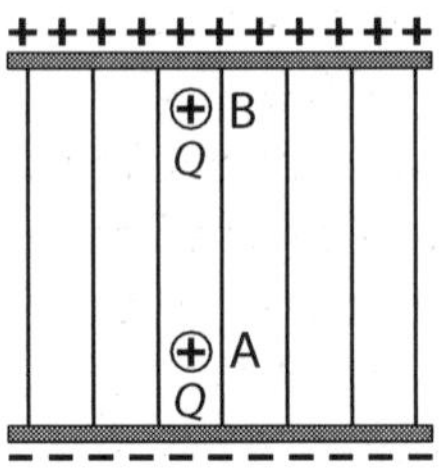

Figure 5.4.1 *At position B, the charge positive charge has more potential energy than at position A.*

The positive test charge *Q* in Figure 5.4.1 has electric potential energy E_{pA} at position A. It will have more electric potential energy if it is moved toward the positive plate to position B. This is because work must be done to move the positive charge against the repulsive force that exists between two like-charged bodies. At position B, the electric potential energy is E_{pB}.

Quick Check

1. Explain the changes in energy that an electron undergoes as it is moved toward a negatively charged plate and is then released.

2. Using Figure 5.4.2 below, explain, in terms of potential and kinetic energy, how accelerating a charge through an electric field is like a mass rolling down a hill.

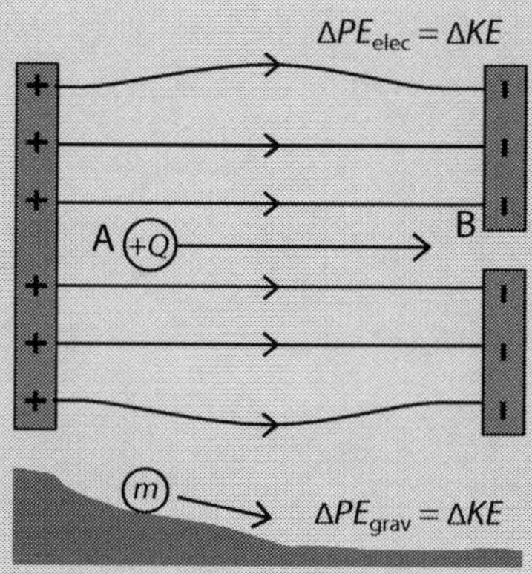

Figure 5.4.2

3. If the electric field in question 2 were doubled, how would the slope of the hill change? What if the electric field was halved?

Electric Potential Energy of Multiple Charges — Non-Uniform Field

Many electrostatic situations are not in a uniform field. Consider the situation where a small positive test charge (Q_2) is in the field of larger positive charge (Q_1). This is an example of a two-charge system with a non-uniform field. Q_1 is located a distance *r* from the test charge Q_2. The test charge has electric potential energy because there is a force exerted on it by the electric field of Q_1. When Q_1 and Q_2 have the same sign, the force is repulsive. When the charges have the opposite signs, the force is attractive. When Q_2 is released, it moves away from the positive Q_1. In energy terms this means it will begin to move and acquire kinetic energy at the expense of its original potential energy. And, to return it to its original position would require work to be done on the charge, which would increase its potential energy.

Potential energy of any kind must be specified relative to a reference location. When we calculated gravitational potential energy in Table 5.4.1, we used Earth's surface as zero potential energy. In the case of electric charges interacting with one another, the reference point is taken to be infinity, since the electric field of a charge falls to zero an infinite distance away.

This allows us to calculate the electric potential energy of a system of two charges relative to infinity. This gives the equation:

$$E_p = k\frac{Q_1Q_2}{r}$$

If the charges have the same sign, their potential energy is positive. This means a positive potential energy represents a repulsive force. If the charges have opposite signs, the potential energy is negative. This means a negative potential energy represents an attractive force.

The potential energy of a charge decreases as it moves away from another charge of the same sign (Figure 5.4.3) and increases as it moves away from another charge of opposite sign.

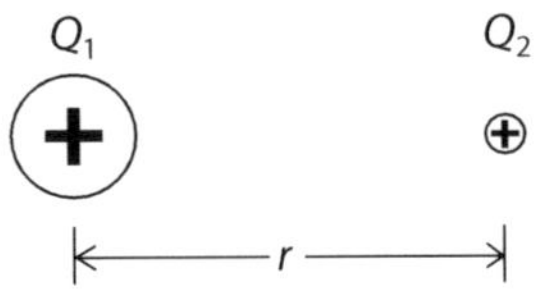

At rest, Q_2 has *PE* only.

When released, Q_2 gains *KE* at the expense of its original *PE*. Returning the charge to its original position will require work done on the charge. This increases its *PE*.

Figure 5.4.3 *Changes in potential energy*

Sample Problem 5.4.1 — Calculating Electric Potential Energy

What is the electric potential energy, relative to infinity, of an electron in a hydrogen atom if the electron is 5.0×10^{-11} m from the proton?

What to Think About	How to Do It
1. Determine what you know. One charge is the electron; the other is the proton in a hydrogen atom.	$Q_1 = +1.6 \times 10^{-19}$ C $Q_2 = -1.6 \times 10^{-19}$ C $r = 5.0 \times 10^{-11}$ m $k = 9.0 \times 10^9$ Nm^2/C^2 $E_p = ?$
2. Select the correct equation.	$E_p = k\frac{Q_1 Q_2}{r}$
3. Determine the nature of the question: it is a "plug in" type question, so you can solve it with known values.	$E_p = \frac{(9.0 \times 10^9 \text{ Nm}^2/\text{C}^2)(+1.6 \times 10^{19} \text{ C})(1.6 \times 10^{19} \text{ C})}{5.0 \times 10^{11} \text{ m}}$ $E_p = -4.6 \times 10^{-18}$ J
4. Summarize.	The potential energy is *negative* because of the attractive force between the electron and the proton. If you wanted to ionize the hydrogen atom (remove its electron 'to infinity') you would need $+4.6 \times 10^{-18}$ J of energy to do it.

Practice Problems 5.4.1 — Calculating Electric Potential Energy

1. How much work is needed to bring a point charge of 1.0×10^{-6} C from infinity to a point that is 3.0 m away from a positive point charge of 1.0×10^{-4} C?

2. In Figure 5.4.4 below, there are two charges. If there is twice as much charge on one charge compared to the other, is the electric potential energy of both charges the same or different? Explain your answer.

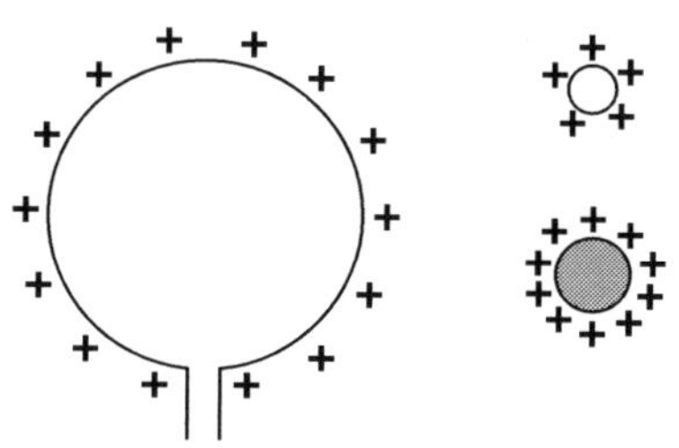

Figure 5.4.4

Practice Problems 5.4.1 — Calculating Electric Potential Energy (Continued)

3. How far apart are two electrons if the potential energy to bring one of the electrons from infinity is 9.45×10^{-20} J?

Summary

In summary, when two charged objects interact, we can explain the interaction by describing the forces on each object in the system using Coulomb's law (see section 5.2) or we can describe the potential energy associated with the interaction. Electric potential energy depends on the amount of electric charge and the distance from the source charge.

When two charges are separated by a distance, the electric potential energy associated with the interaction is:

$$E_p = k\frac{Q_1Q_2}{r}$$

We define infinity as the point at which the potential energy for one charge is zero.

Quick Check

For each of the following situations, explain what will happen to the potential energy in the test charge.

1. A positive test charge is moved from A to B.

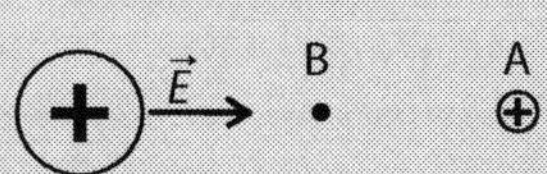

2. A positive test charge is moved from B to A.

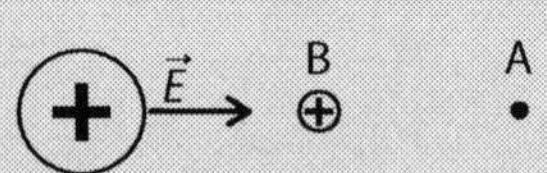

3. A positive test charge is moved from A to B.

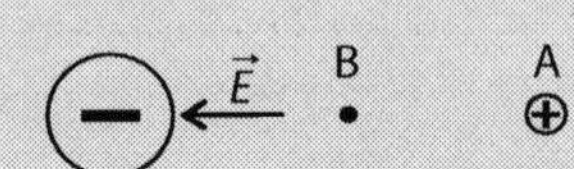

4. A positive test charge if moved from B to A.

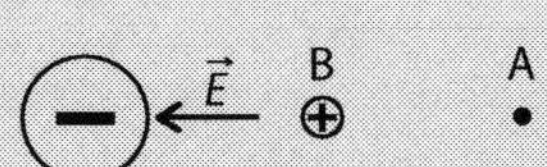

Electric Potential — It's All About Location, Location, Location

Consider two negative charges being pushed toward a negatively charge plate. One charge has twice the number of coulombs as the other. This means that at any given point, the larger charge will require twice as much work done on it, and will have twice as much potential energy as the smaller charge as it moves towards the plate. You could calculate the total energy required to move both charges in the system.

Sometimes it will be more useful to determine the electric potential energy per unit charge at a location rather the electric potential energy in one or more charges. The electric potential energy stored per unit charge is the amount of work required to move a unit charge to a point in the electric field. This is also called **electric potential** or **voltage**. While electric potential energy depends on the charge of the object experiencing the electric field, electric potential is location dependent. It is written as:

$$V = \frac{E_p}{Q}$$

where V is electric potential or voltage measured in volts, E_p is the electric potential energy measured in joules, and Q is the charge measured in coulombs. So,

$$1 \text{ volt} = \frac{1 \text{ joule}}{1 \text{ coulomb}}$$

Electric potential is used to express the effect of a source's electric field in terms of location within the electric field. For example, look at the three charges shown in Figure 5.4.5. The three charges are in an electric field at the same location so that their electric potential is 20 J/C. The 2 C test charge has twice as much charge as the 1 C charge and four times as much charge as the 0.5 C charge. The larger charge would possess two times and four times the potential energy at a given location when compared to the 1 C and 0.5 C charges. But the electric potential at that location would be the same for all three charges.

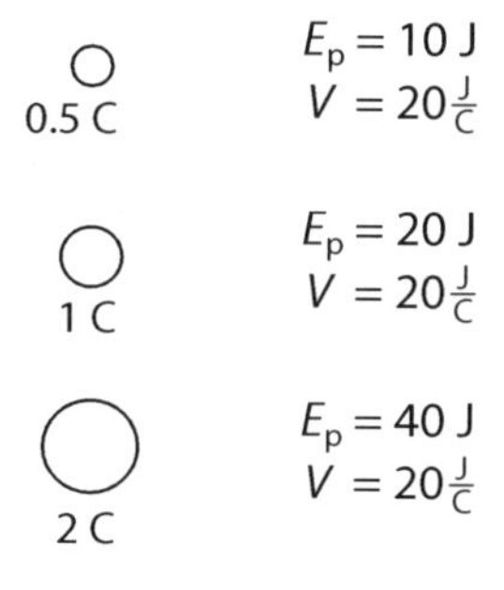

Figure 5.4.5 *Electric potential of three different charges in the same location*

Because location, not amount of charge, is key, a negative test charge would be at a high electric potential when held close to a negative source charge and at a lower electric potential when held farther away. In this way, electric potential is a property of the location of the charge within an electric field, not of the amount of charge.

Quick Check

1. A charge of 4.00×10^{-3} C is moved between two charged parallel plates. This increases the potential energy in the charge by 7.3×10^{-15} J. What is the electric potential between the two plates?

2. How much energy does an electron have if it has an electric potential of 50.0 V?

3. What is the charge on an small sphere that has 1.00×10^{3} J of potential energy while suspended between two charged parallel plates that have an electric potential of 200 V?

Electric Potential of Single Point Charges

We know that the force between two point charges Q_1 and Q_2 is given by Coulomb's law:

$$\vec{F} = k\frac{Q_1Q_2}{r^2}$$

We also know that the potential energy of charge Q_2 at a distance r from Q_1 is found by taking the area under the F vs. r graph between r and infinity. The result is:

$$E_p = k\frac{Q_1Q_2}{r}$$

We can combine these two concepts with the definition for electric potential of a single point charge rather than a uniform electric field. The electric potential V, which is the potential energy per unit charge relative to infinity, is then

$$V = \frac{E_p}{Q_2} = k\frac{Q_1}{r}$$

Remember that both electric potential energy and electric potential are taken to be zero at infinity.

Quick Check

1. Two charges are separated by a distance *d*. If the distance between them is doubled, how does the electric potential between them change?

2. What is the electric potential relative to infinity at a distance of 0.90 m from a point charge of
   (a) +50 μC?

   (b) –50 μC?

Electric Potential Difference

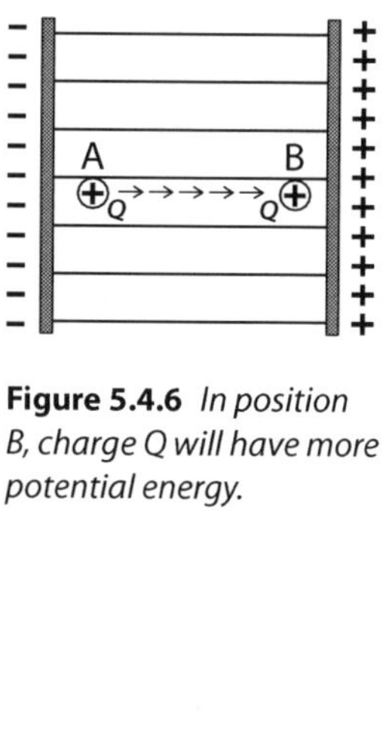

Figure 5.4.6 *In position B, charge Q will have more potential energy.*

Recall that a positive test charge Q has electric potential energy E_{pA} at position A (Figure 5.4.6). It will have more electric potential energy if it is moved toward the positive plate to position B, because work must be done to move the positive charge against the repulsive force that exists between two like-charged bodies. At position B, the electric potential energy is E_{pB}.

For the charge Q at A, $V_A = \frac{E_{pA}}{Q}$

When the charge Q is moved to B, $V_B = \frac{E_{pB}}{Q}$

The difference in potential energy per unit charge between two points A and B is called the potential difference, V_{AB} or just ΔV.

$$V_{AB} = \Delta V = V_B - V_A$$

In Figure 5.4.6, the potential difference between points A and B is equal to the work done moving charge Q from A to B. Potential difference could be measured in joules per coulomb (J/C), but usually this unit is called a volt (V).

$$V_{AB} = \frac{W_{AB}}{Q} = \frac{E_{pB} - E_{pA}}{Q} = \frac{W_{AB}}{Q}$$

Or, in the general form

$$\Delta V = \frac{\Delta E_p}{Q}$$

Potential difference is usually called **voltage** and ΔV is measured in volts, ΔE_p in joules, and Q in coulombs.

The **potential difference (*V*)** between two points is defined as the amount of work required to move a unit of positive charge from the point that is at a lower potential to the point that is at the higher potential, relative to an arbitrary reference point (such as the positive plate in Figure 5.4.6).

Sample Problem 5.4.2 — Working with Potential Difference

How much work is needed to move 1.00×10^{-6} C of positive charge between two points where the potential difference is 12.0 V?

What to Think About	How to Do It
1. Determine what you know.	$W = \Delta E$ $\Delta V = 12.0$ V $Q = 1.00 \times 10^{-6}$ C
2. Select the correct equation.	$\Delta V = \frac{\Delta E}{Q} = \frac{W}{Q}$ Therefore, $W = VQ$
3. Solve with known values to find the amount of work done to move the charge.	$W = (12.0\ V)(1.00 \times 10^{-6}\ C)$ $W = 1.2 \times 10^{-5}$ J

Practice Problems 5.4.2 — Working with Potential Difference

1. A small charge of 6.4×10^{-19} C is moved between two parallel plates from an electric potential of 1.5×10^{2} V to another position of 3.0×10^{2} V. What is the potential difference between these two positions?

2. What is the energy stored in a 9.0 V battery if the total charge transferred from one set of electrodes to the other is 4.0×10^{5} C?

3. A 1.00×10^{-10} C charge is between two charged plates that are 2 cm apart. The charge experiences a force of 3.00×10^{-5} N. What is the potential difference between the plates?

Electron Volt

On an atomic scale, the joule is a very, very large amount of energy. A smaller unit of energy, the **electron volt (eV)** is used when solving problems about electric potential in situations on the atomic or nuclear scale. One electron volt is defined as the amount of energy gained by one electron when it moves through a potential difference of 1.0 V. Since the charge on one electron is only 1.6×10^{-19} C, and $W = VQ$, one electron volt is only 1.6×10^{-19} J.

$$\mathbf{1\ eV = 1.6 \times 10^{-19}\ J}$$

Sample Problem 5.4.3— Working with Electron Volts

If a 750 V cathode ray tube (CRT) is used to accelerate electrons, how much kinetic energy will the electrons gain?

What to Think About	How to Do It
1. Determine the assumptions in the question.	Assume all the work done by the electric field is converted to kinetic energy of the electrons. This means $W = VQ$ and $E_K = W$, where E_K is kinetic energy.
2. List the information you know.	$V = 750$ V $Q = 1$ e
3. Select the correct equation.	$E_K = W = VQ$
4. Determine the type of question: this is a "plug in" type question, so you can solve it with known values to find the how much kinetic energy the electrons gain. Remember to find your answer in joules.	$E_K = W = (750 \text{ V})(1 \text{ e}) = 750 \text{ eV}$ To convert this to joules: $750 \text{ eV} = (750 \text{ eV})(1.6 \times 10^{-19} \text{ J/eV})$ $750 \text{ eV} = 1.2 \times 10^{-16} \text{ J}$

Practice Problems 5.4.3— Working with Electron Volts

1. At room temperature, a molecule has 0.04 eV of energy. What is this in joules?

2. An electron hitting a screen in a CRT display has approximately 20 000 eV. What is the potential difference the electron is accelerated through?

5.4 Review Questions

1. A system of two charges has a positive potential energy. What does this mean in terms the charge on the two charges?

2. A tiny plastic sphere is midway between two metal plates, which are 0.050 m apart. When a battery is connected to the plates, the sphere experiences an electric force of 1.200×10^{-3} N. How much work is needed to move the charged sphere from one plate to the other?

3. What is the change in potential energy of a particle of charge $+Q$ that is brought from a distance of $4r$ to a distance of $2r$ by a particle of charge $-Q$?

4. How much work is needed to bring a +5.0 μC point charge from infinity to a point 2.0 m away from a +25 μC charge?

5. What is the electric potential energy of an electron (relative to infinity) when it is 7.5×10^{-11} m away from a proton?

6. As shown below, a 4.5×10^{-7} C charge is initially located 7.0 m from a fixed 6.0×10^{-6} C charge. What is the minimum amount of work required to move the 4.5×10^{-7} C charge 1.5 m closer?

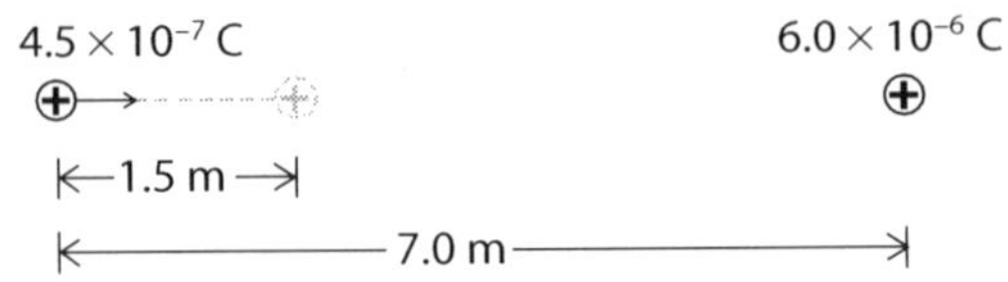

7. How much potential energy would an electron in a hydrogen atom lose if it fell toward the nucleus from a distance of 7.5×10^{-11} m to a distance of 5.0×10^{-11} m?

8. How much work is done moving a proton from infinity to a distance of 1.0×10^{-11} m from another proton?

9. A proton is pushed into an electric field where it has a 5.0 V electric potential. If three electrons are pushed the same distance into the same field, what is the electric potential of these three electrons?

10. The following diagrams show an electric field with two points, 1 and 2, positioned within the field. Point 1 is a positive test charge. For each diagram, indicate:
    (i) If work is done on the charge when it moves from position 1 to position 2;
    (ii) Where is electric potential energy the greatest – position 1 or position 2;
    (iii) Where is electric potential the greatest – position 1 or position 2

(a)

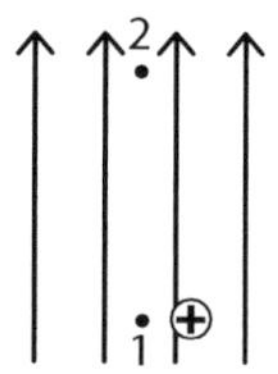

(b)

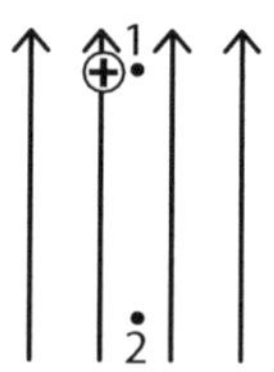

(c)

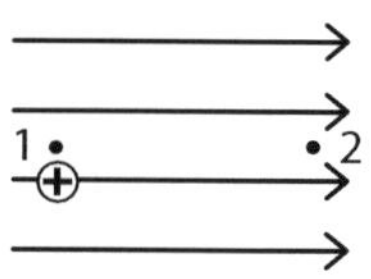

(d)

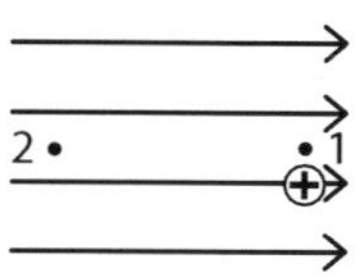

11. What is the difference between electric potential energy and electric potential difference?

12. Two parallel plates are separated by 0.024 m and have a potential difference between them of 120 V, as shown below. Point P is located midway between the plates. What is the potential difference between point P and one of the plates?

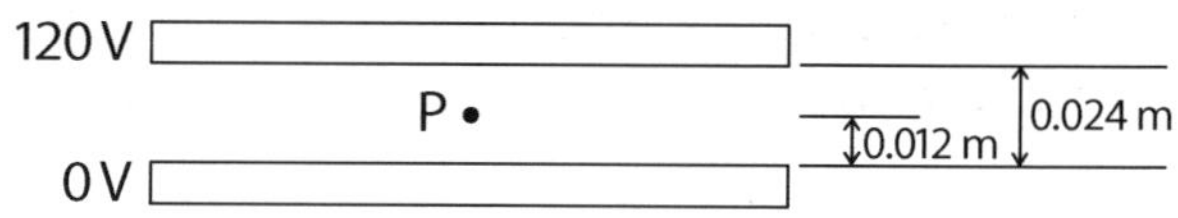

13. An electron has a velocity of 2.0×10^7 m/s. What is the energy of the electron in eV?

5.5 Electric Field and Voltage — Uniform field

Warm Up

In your own words, describe the difference between the electric potential and electric potential difference of a charge in a uniform field.

____

____

____

Electric Field and Voltage — Uniform Fields

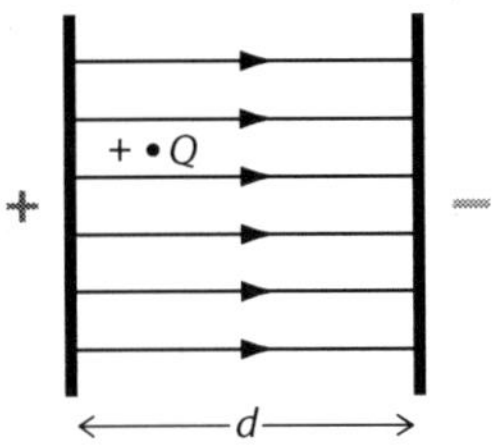

Figure 5.5.1 *No matter where the test charge is between the two plates, it will experience the same electric force.*

Consider a test charge Q located between two oppositely charged plates a distance d apart (Figure 5.5.1). This test charge will experience the same electric force $\vec{F}$ anywhere between the two plates, because the electric field $\vec{E}$ is the same anywhere between the plates. The Big Idea Physics Question on the next page provides a proof of this.

You know that when the positive test charge Q is moved from the negatively charged plate to the positively charged plate, through distance d, an amount of work W will be done, given by $W = \vec{F}d$. The charge Q will gain electric potential energy E_p equal to $\vec{F}d$.

We also know from section 5.4 that the change in potential energy per unit of charge as it moves between two points is called the potential difference or voltage between the two points. The symbol for potential difference or voltage is V.

Since $V = \dfrac{\vec{F}d}{Q}$ and $\vec{E} = \dfrac{\vec{F}}{Q}$, then $V = \dfrac{\vec{F}}{Q}d = \vec{E}d$.

Therefore, the electric field strength can be calculated if we know the potential difference and the distance between two charged plates. It is calculated as follows:

$$\vec{E} = \frac{V}{d}$$

Since potential difference (voltage) has the dimensions of "energy per unit charge," it could be measured in J/C. However, the volt (V) is the standard unit for measuring voltage. This means that electric field strength can be expressed in volts per metre (V/m) as well as in newtons per coulomb (N/C). Dimensionally, they are the same thing.

$$1\,\frac{\text{V}}{\text{m}} = 1\,\frac{\text{J/C}}{\text{m}} = 1\,\frac{\text{Nm/C}}{\text{m}} = 1\,\frac{\text{N}}{\text{C}}$$

Big Idea Physics Question

Is the force field near a large, uniformly charged flat surface constant?

Here is the proof to answer the Big Idea Physics Question for electrostatics.
Consider a small test charge q, which is a distance d from a large, flat plate, over which a charge is uniformly distributed. Looking toward the large plate from q through an imaginary rectangular "cone," we can "see" an area of the large plane, with an amount of charge Q on it (Figure 5.5.2). The test charge q is now moved twice as far away to distance $2d$. What happens to the electric force on the test charge?

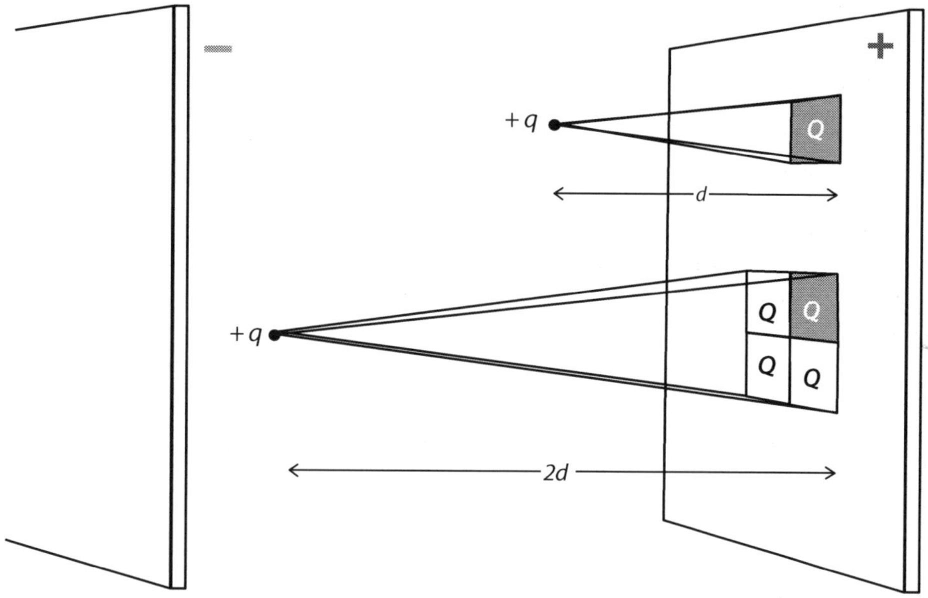

Figure 5.5.2

Looking at the plane again from twice the distance through the same imaginary "cone," we would "see" four times the area on the plane, and therefore four times the charge (4Q).

In the first instance, the force on q was $F = k\dfrac{Qq}{d^2}$ (*Coulomb's law*).

At the new position twice as far away, $F = k\dfrac{(4Q)q}{(2d)^2} = k\dfrac{Qq}{d^2}$

Since the force on test charge q has not changed, neither has the electric field strength F/q. It can be shown that the electric field strength between two large parallel plane surfaces is *uniform anywhere between the plates.* (The field near the edges is not uniform.)

Sample Problem 5.5.1 — Working with Electric Field Calculations

A piece of scientific equipment has two metal electrodes that form parallel plates. If the voltage between the plates is 4.50×10^3 V and the distance between the plates is 5.00 mm, what is the electric field?

What to Think About	How to Do It
1. State what you know and what you are looking for.	$\Delta V = 4.50 \times 10^3$ V $d = 5.00$ mm $= 5.0 \times 10^{-3}$ m $\vec{E} = ?$
2. Choose the equation.	$\vec{E} = \dfrac{V}{d}$
3. Solve for *E*.	$\vec{E} = \dfrac{4.50 \times 10^3 \text{ V}}{5.00 \times 10^{-3} \text{ m}}$ $\vec{E} = 9.00 \times 10^5$ V/m

Practice Problems 5.5.1 — Working with Electric Field Calculations

1. An inkjet printer sprays charged ink droplets onto paper to form images. If the charged ink droplets passed between two plates that have a potential difference of 5.00×10^3 V and the electric field is 2.10×10^6 V/m, what is the distance between the plates?

2. Two oppositely charged plates are separated by a distance of 2.45 mm. What voltage must be applied to them to create an electric field of 2.00×10^4 N/C?

3. Show that N/C is the same unit as V/m.

Application of Uniform Electric Fields — The Cathode Ray Tube

A cathode ray tube (CRT) is a special kind of vacuum tube in which a beam of electrons is produced, accelerated, focused, deflected, and displayed on a fluorescent screen. CRTs are used in oscilloscopes, radar, and older television sets and computer monitors. In Investigation 5.5.1, you will use a miniature oscilloscope to observe the effect of electric fields on beams of electrons.

How the Beam of Electrons Is Obtained

A small alternating voltage is applied to the filament in the "electron gun" in Figure 5.5.3, and the resulting current heats the filament to incandescence. When the filament is incandescent, electrons "boil off" and form a charge cloud around it.

In front of the filament is an electrode called the **grid.** The grid is negatively charged, so electrons are repelled by it. The grid makes electrons converge to a focus point as they pass through a hole in the grid. This crossover point acts as a point source of electrons. Electrons stream from the point source outward accelerated by an electric field applied between the grid and the **anode**. The anode is a positively charged electrode.

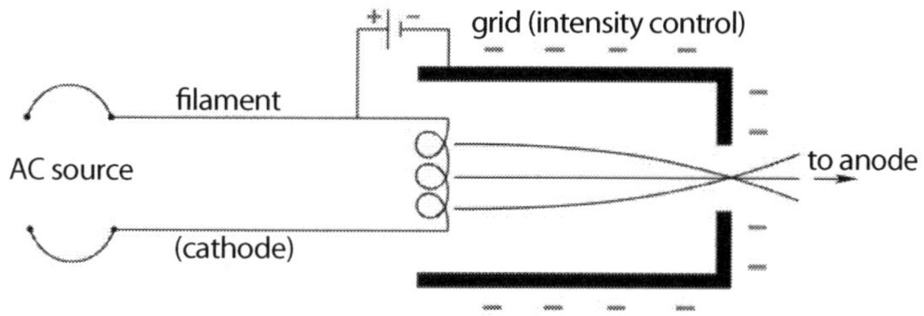

Figure 5.5.3 *How a beam of electrons is created using an "electron gun"*

The voltage applied to the grid can be changed, allowing more or fewer electrons through the opening. Since this will vary the intensity of the beam, which determines the brightness of the beam as seen on the CRT screen, the grid control is called the **intensity control.**

How the Beam Is Focused and Accelerated

Electrons leaving the grid opening are diverging. A **focusing anode** (A_1) acts as an electronic "lens," shaping the beam so that when it reaches the screen it will appear as a tiny spot. The **accelerating anode** (A_2) accelerates the electrons horizontally (Figure 5.5.4). The potential difference (voltage) between the filament and the accelerating anode is quite high — typically 500 V, 750 V or 1000 V in a classroom model. The high voltage between the filament of the electron gun and the accelerating anode creates the electric field that accelerates the electrons.

Because of the electric field *E*, work is done on the electrons, and their electric potential energy is changed into kinetic energy E_k. The accelerating voltage V_a is a measure of the change in electric potential energy per unit charge. If the potential energy is changed into kinetic energy of the electrons, then

$$V_a = \frac{E_k}{Q} = \frac{\frac{1}{2}mv^2}{Q}$$

where V_a is the accelerating voltage (between A_2 and the filament);
m is the mass of one electron (9.11×10^{-31} kg);
v is the maximum speed reached by each electron; and
Q is the charge on one electron (1.60×10^{-19} C).

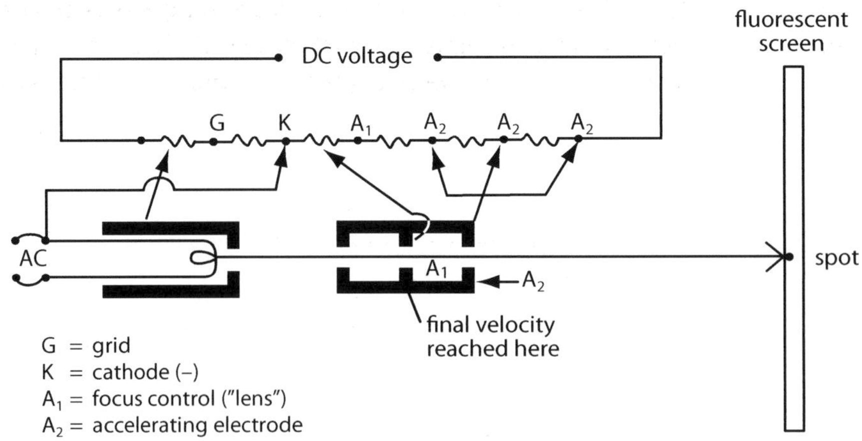

Figure 5.5.4 *Focusing the electron beam*

How the Beam Is Deflected

Once the beam is accelerated by V_a and up to speed v, it is made to pass between two mutually perpendicular pairs of deflecting plates (Figure 5.5.5). One pair is arranged to deflect the beam in the *y* direction. This pair of plates is labeled Y_1 and Y_2. The other pair of plates is arranged to deflect the electron beam in the *x* direction. These plates are labeled X_1 and X_2.

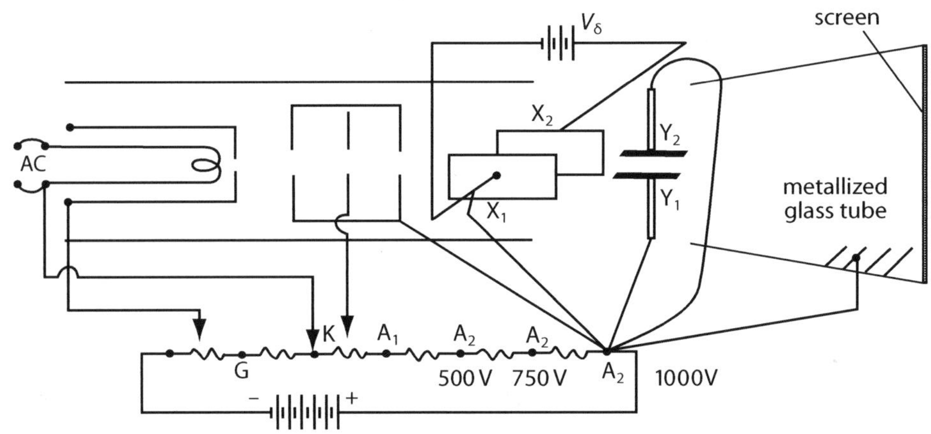

Figure 5.5.5 *Cathode ray tube (CRT) with power supply (simplified)*

Notice that plates X_1 and X_2 have a small DC voltage V_δ applied to them. Both Y_1 and Y_2 are connected to A_2, but only one of the X-plates is connected to A_2. This means that both Y plates are at the same voltage as A_2, so an electron beam passing through the Y-plates "sees" no difference in potential and will not be deflected by the Y-plates. However, one of the X-plates does have a slightly different potential than the other X-plate because of the **deflecting voltage** V_δ applied to the X-plates. (δ is the Greek letter delta.)

How Does the Amount of Deflection Depend on E?

Figure 5.5.6 shows a beam of electrons moving with speed v through a pair of parallel deflecting plates. Remember that the electric field between parallel plates is constant anywhere between the plates; therefore, the electric force is also constant.

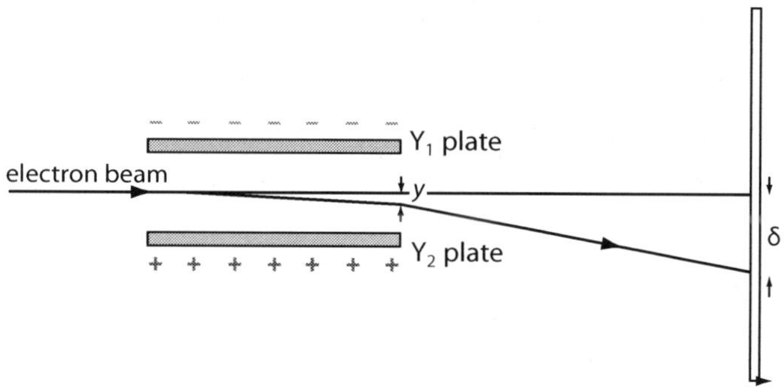

Figure 5.5.6 *An electron beam moving between two parallel plate*

Experiencing a constant unbalanced force, the electrons will accelerate at a rate, a, (downward in Figure 5.5.6). While passing through the plates in time t, the downward acceleration makes the beam fall through displacement y. The displacement of the electron beam while it is between the plates is given by

$$y = \frac{1}{2}at^2$$

but since, $a = \dfrac{F}{m}$

therefore $y = \dfrac{1}{2}\dfrac{F}{m}t^2$

Since the electric field $E = \dfrac{F}{Q}$, therefore $F = EQ$ and so

$$y = \frac{1}{2}\frac{EQ}{m}t^2$$

For a given beam of electrons accelerated by a given accelerating voltage, $\frac{1}{2}$, Q, m, and t will remain *constant*, and it can be assumed that $y = constant \cdot E$, or that $y \propto E$.

Also, since $E = V_\delta/d$ where d is the distance between the deflecting plates and V_δ is the deflecting voltage, therefore the deflection y is proportional to the deflecting voltage V_δ.

$$y \propto V_\delta$$

Note: The deflection that you measure on the screen is *not y*. Once the beam leaves the deflecting plates, the electrons travel in a straight line to the fluorescent screen. On the screen, you see the deflection δ. Fortunately, it can be shown that the **screen deflection** δ *is directly proportional to* the **true deflection** y within the plates.*

Since δ is proportional to y, and y is proportional to V_δ, therefore

$$\delta \propto V_d$$

This means that the deflection of the beam, as measured on the screen, is a measure of the voltage applied to the deflecting plates. The cathode ray tube (CRT) can therefore be used as a voltmeter.

Showing that δ Is Proportional to *Y

Consider an electron entering the deflecting plates with horizontal speed v_x (Figure 5.5.7). The electron travels a distance $x = \ell$, in a time *t*. Time is related to distance and speed as follows: $t = x/v_x$, therefore the time the electron spends between the two plates is ℓ/v_x.

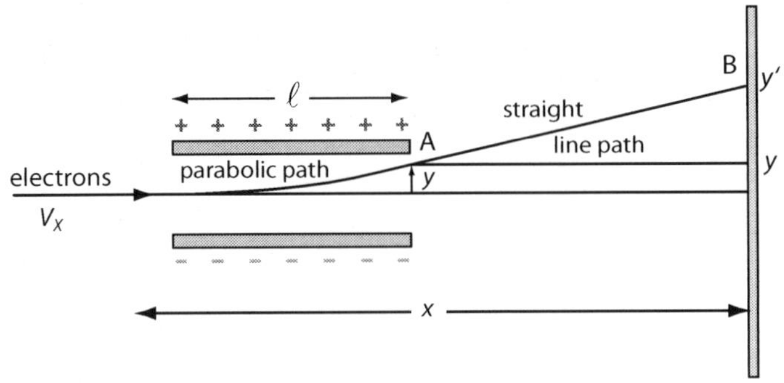

Figure 5.5.7 *Deflection of an electron beam passing between two plates*

Now consider the vertical deflection of the electron as it passes through the deflecting plates. Since the electric field and therefore the force on the electron is uniform, the acceleration is uniform, and $y = ½at^2 = ½a\,[x^2/v_x^{\;2}]$. This is the equation for a *parabola*. To find the *slope* of the parabola at the instant the electron reaches A (where the deflecting plates end), we must use calculus:

$$\frac{dy}{dx} = 2(\frac{1}{2}a)\frac{x}{v_x^2} = \frac{ax}{v_x^2} = \frac{a\ell}{v_x^2}$$

Once the electron leaves A, it travels in a straight line to B, so the slope of its path remains the same as it was at A. For AB, the slope is

$$\frac{y' - \frac{1}{2}a\ell^2/v_x^2}{x - \ell} = \frac{a\ell}{v_x^2}$$

So, $y' - ½a\ell^2/v_x^{\;2} = a\ell\,(x - \ell)/v_x^{\;2}$

Now, when $y' = 0$, $-½\ell = (x - \ell)$ and $x = ½\ell$.

This means that the straight-line path of the electron after it leaves the plates at A can be extrapolated back to the exact centre of the plates. This creates two similar triangles, with heights *y* and *y*′. The deflection you actually see on the screen is *y*′, and $y' = \delta$. In Figure 5.5.7, the deflection within the plates is *y*. Similar triangles tell us that $\delta \propto y$!

Quick Check

1. In a CRT, a voltage of 1.0×10^3 V accelerates electrons from rest to a high speed. Assuming all the work done by the electric field is used to give the electrons kinetic energy, $\frac{1}{2}mv^2$, what speed do the electrons reach? (The charge on an electron is 1.6×10^{-19} C and the mass of one electron is 9.1×10^{-31} kg.) What fraction of the speed of light ($c = 3.0 \times 10^8$ m/s) is this?

2. If an accelerating voltage of 1.0×10^3 V were used to accelerate protons, what speed would they reach? ($m_{proton} = 1.67 \times 10^{-27}$ kg)

3. A CRT is used with an accelerating voltage of 750 V to accelerate electrons before they pass through deflecting plates, to which a deflecting voltage of 50.0 V is applied.
   (a) What speed do the electrons reach?

   (b) When the electrons travel through the deflecting plates, which are separated by a distance of 2.0 cm, what is the electric field strength between the plates?

   (c) What is the force that will deflect electrons as they pass through the plates?

   (d) At what rate will the electrons accelerate as they pass through the plates?

   (e) The plates have a length of 5.0 cm. For what length of time will the electrons be between the plates?

   (f) What is the deflection in a *y*-direction of the electrons as they pass through the plates?

   (g) If the screen is 0.20 m beyond the end of the deflecting plates, what deflection (δ) will you see on the screen?

Investigation 5.5.1 Deflecting a Beam of Electrons Using an Electric Field

Part 1

Purpose

How does the deflection of a beam of electrons of given speed depend on the *deflecting voltage* applied to the deflecting plates between which the beam passes?

Procedure

1. Figure 5.5.8 is a schematic diagram of a CRT device similar to one you will use in this activity. A varying deflection voltage, V_δ, will be applied to the X-plates. Connect X_1, Y_1, and Y_2 to the common binding post at A_2. Use an accelerating voltage V_a of 500 V throughout all of Part 1.

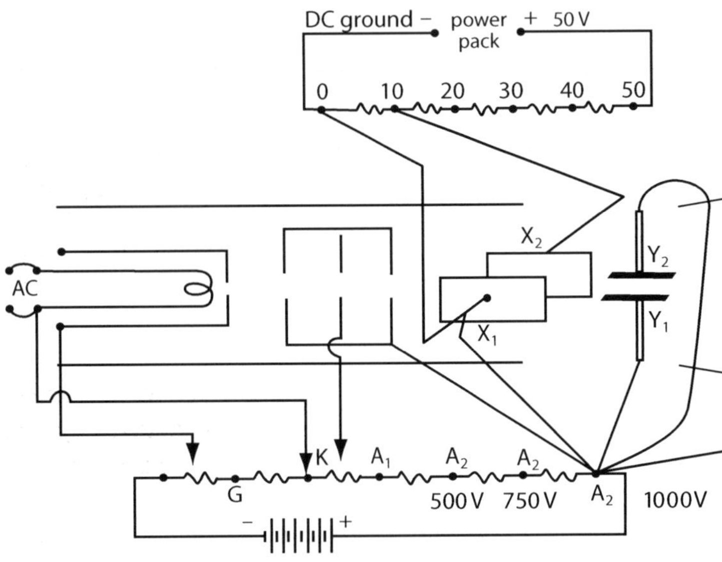

Figure 5.5.8

2. To vary the deflecting voltage V_δ, make the following apparatus using your high voltage DC power supply (Figure 5.5.9):
   (a) Connect a wire lead from the DC ground binding post to one end of a string of five identical 10 kΩ resistors.
   (b) Connect a second wire lead from the +50 V binding post of the power supply to the other end of the string of resistors.
   (c) Connect a lead from X_1 to the common ground (0 V) side of the resistors. The lead from X_2 can now be connected to any point in the string of resistors, so that you can obtain voltages of 0 V, 10 V, 20 V, 30 V, 40 V, or 50 V.
   (d) Use a voltmeter to check the exact values obtained at each of the terminals (resistor junctions), and to confirm that this arrangement does give a series of voltages which are multiples of one another.

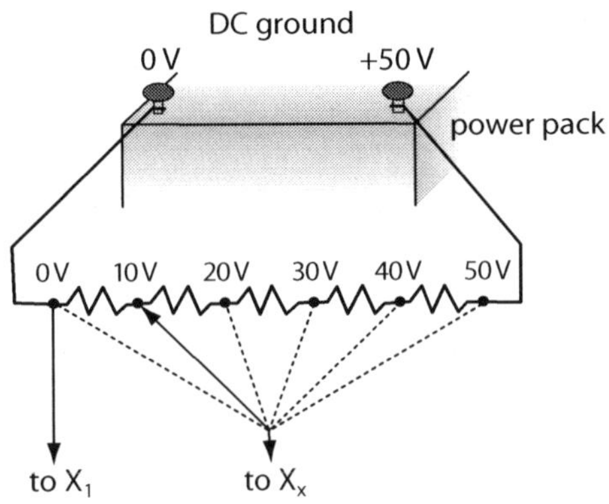

Figure 5.5.9

3. Put a piece of masking tape on the screen of the CRT so that you can mark the position of the beam when different deflecting voltages are applied. Mark the location of the beam for each of the voltages you use (0 V, 10 V, 20 V, 30 V, 40 V, and 50 V if the power supply voltage is "true").
4. Measure the deflection δ in mm and enter the values of V_δ and δ in a data table.
5. Prepare a graph of δ vs. V_δ.

Concluding Questions

1. How does the deflection δ of the electron beam depend on the deflecting voltage V_δ? Write an equation for your graph, including the slope in appropriate units.
2. How does the deflection depend on the electric field strength between the plates? How does your answer follow from the results of this experiment? (Remember how E and V_δ are related.)

Part 2

Purpose

How does the deflection of the beam of electrons depend on accelerating voltage, if a constant deflecting voltage is used?

> **Instructor Note:** See your CRT manual if these instructions for varying V_a do not apply to the model your students have.

Procedure

1. Locate the "zero" position of the beam as you did in Part 1, and mark it on a fresh piece of masking tape attached to the screen. In Part 1, you used an accelerating voltage V_a of 500 V and varied the deflecting voltage. This time, leave the deflecting voltage at a set value such as 50 V throughout all of Part 2. (You will use zero deflecting voltage to locate the "zero" position, of course.)
2. Mark the position of the electron beam on the screen when the accelerating voltage is 500 V. ***Turn off the power supply.*** Reset the accelerating voltage at 750 V. Turn on the CRT again, refocus if necessary, and measure the new deflection when $V_a = 750$ V.
3. ***Turn off the power supply.*** Change V_a to 1000 V. Turn on the CRT again, refocus and measure δ.
4. Before analyzing your results, use a voltmeter to check the actual voltages at the three A_2 terminals. Measure the voltage between the filament and each of the A_2 terminals. These are more reliable values to use for V_a than what you read on the apparatus. The labeled values are only approximate voltages.
5. Tabulate your results, then plot a graph of deflection δ (y-axis) vs. accelerating voltage V_a (x-axis).
6. Make an educated guess at the power law relationship that exists between δ and V_a, and plot a graph that will tell you what the value of n is in $\delta = k \cdot V_a^n$.
7. Derive an expression for the deflection within the plates in terms of V_a. Keep in mind that y is proportional to δ. Start with the fact that the deflection within the plates is $y = \frac{1}{2}at^2$.

   Use the fact that the time spent within the plates will be $\frac{\ell}{v_x}$.

   The acceleration of the electrons is $a = \frac{F}{m} = \frac{Eq}{m}$.

   Also, the accelerating voltage $V_a = \frac{1}{2}\frac{mv_x^2}{q}$.

   According to your derivation, how does y (and therefore δ) vary with V_a?

Concluding Questions

1. Write a simple equation relating deflection (δ) and accelerating voltage (V_a). Include a numerical value for the constant of proportionality (slope).

2. If V_a were doubled and V_δ were kept the same, what would happen to δ?

3. If V_δ were doubled and V_a remained the same, what would happen to δ?

4. If ***both*** V_a and V_δ were doubled, what would happen to δ?

Challenge

1. (a) What happens if you apply a low (6.3 V) alternating voltage to the X-plates of your CRT?
   (b) What if you apply AC voltage to the Y-plates and the X-plates simultaneously?
   (c) Read up on Lissajous curves in an electronics book. Use a full-size oscilloscope to display them.

5.5 Review Questions

1. Two parallel plates have a potential difference of 120 V. The separation between the two plates is 10 cm. Calculate the electric field between them.

2. Two electrodes on spark plugs have an electric field between them of 500 V/m and are separated by 0.020 m. What is the voltage between the two plates?

3. What is the distance between two plates that have a voltage of 800 V and an electric field of 1.4×10^3 N/C?

4. A nichrome wire 30.0 cm long is connected to the terminals of a 1.5 V dry cell. What is the magnitude and direction (relative to the terminals) of the electric field inside the wire?

5. Two parallel deflecting plates in an oscilloscope have a voltage of 120 V applied to them. They are separated by a distance of 2.4 mm.
   (a) What is the strength of the electric field between the plates?

   (b) At what rate will an electron (mass 9.1×10^{-31} kg) accelerate at the instant it enters the space between the plates? (The electron is initially moving in a direction perpendicular to the field lines.)

6. A tiny plastic sphere of mass 1.0×10^{-15} kg is held suspended between two charged plates by balancing the downward gravitational force with an upward electrical force of equal magnitude.
   (a) What is the magnitude of the electrical force acting on the sphere?

   (b) If the voltage applied to the plates is 30.0 V, and the plates are separated by a distance of 1.47 mm, what is the amount of excess charge on the sphere?

   (c) If the top plate is positively charged, is the charge on the sphere positive or negative?

   (d) What type of elementary charged particles are on the sphere, and how many of these excess elementary charged particles are there on the sphere?

7. Two parallel plate have a potential difference of 2000 V between them and are 2.0×10^{-2} m apart. A proton is released from the positive plate at the same time as an electron is released from the negative plate. Compare and describe their speed and kinetic energy as they strike the opposite plate.

8. A subatomic, charged particle of 8.4×10^{-5} C is accelerated from rest through a voltage of 2.4×10^{4} V. If the final speed of the particle is 7.2×10^{3} m/s, what is the mass of the particle?

9. A proton at rest is accelerated between two parallel plates with a potential difference of 600 V as shown below. What is the maximum speed of the proton?

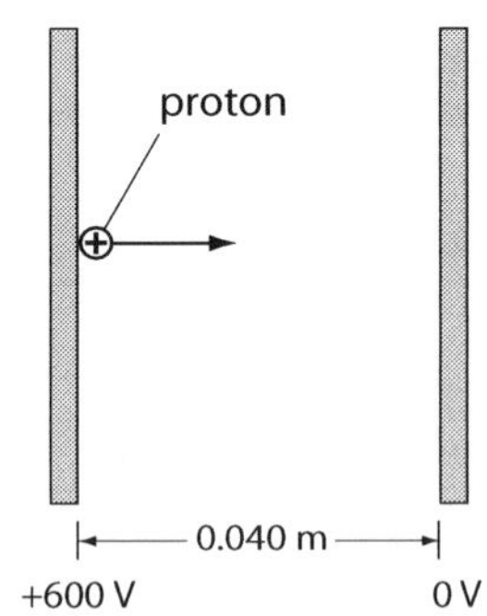

10. In the diagram below, a charged sphere of 2.0×10^{-16} C and a mass of 5.0×10^{-15} kg is held in the middle of two charged plates and balanced by the gravitational and electric forces. What is the voltage V applied to these plates?

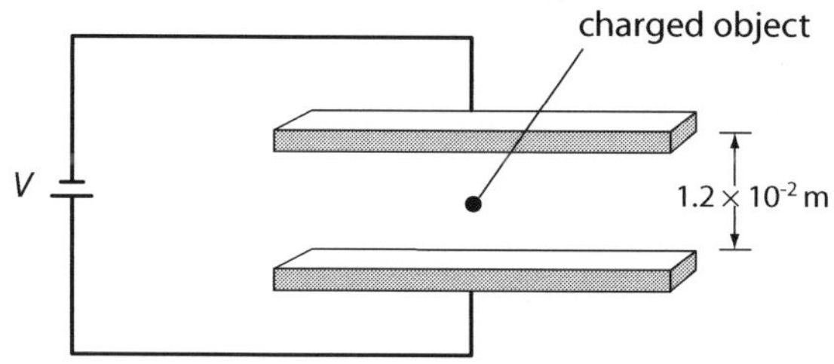

11. In a CRT, the deflection on the screen is 2.4 cm when the accelerating voltage is 480 V and the deflecting voltage is 36 V. What deflection (δ) will you see on the screen if the accelerating voltage is 960 V and the deflecting voltage is 18 V?

Chapter 5 Review Questions

1. Two equal charges Q are separated by a distance r. The repulsive force between them is F.
   (a) What will the force be if both charges are doubled?

   (b) What will the force be if the charges remain Q but the distance between them is reduced to $\frac{1}{2}r$?

   (c) What will the force be if charges are both increased to $4Q$ and the distance between them is reduced to $\frac{1}{4}r$?

2. A negatively charged rod is brought near a suspended metal sphere. The sphere is "grounded" by touching it with a finger. The finger and the rod are now removed. What charge will be on the sphere, positive or negative? Describe what has happened.

3. (a) A tiny plastic sphere is midway between two metal plates, which are 0.050 m apart. When a battery is connected to the plates, the sphere experiences an electric force of 1.2×10^{-3} N. How much work is needed to move the charged sphere from one plate to the other?

   (b) If the charge on the sphere is 0.20 μC, what is the battery voltage?

4. What is the repulsive force between two alpha particles that are 1.0 mm apart? (An alpha particle is a helium ion, He^{2+}, so it carries an excess of two elementary positive charges.)

5. How far apart are two protons if they repel each other with a force of 1.0 mN?

6. If a body with a charge of 1.0×10^{-3} C experiences a force of 1.0 N in an electric field, what is the electric field strength?

7. A proton is placed in an electric field of strength 5.0×10^3 N/C. At what rate will it accelerate? (Proton mass = 1.67×10^{-27} kg; proton charge = 1.6×10^{-19} C)

8. What is the magnitude and direction of the electric field strength midway between a 75 μC charge and a −25 μC charge, if the charges are 2.0 m apart?

9. The electric field strength between two plates that are 3.0 cm apart is 3.0×10^3 N/C. What is the voltage between the plates?

10. The deflecting voltage applied to the plates in a CRT is 50.0 V. The plates are 1.2 cm apart.
    (a) What is the electric field strength between the plates?

    (b) What force will the field exert on an electron passing between the plates?

    (c) At what rate and in what direction will the electron accelerate? (Electron mass = 9.1×10^{-31} kg)

11. An accelerating voltage of 750 V produces a screen deflection of 4.2 cm on a CRT. If the deflecting voltage is kept constant but the accelerating voltage is increased to 1000 V, what will the deflection become?

12. When the accelerating voltage in a CRT is 500 V and the deflecting voltage is 15 V, the beam deflection is 1.2 cm on the screen. If the accelerating voltage is changed to 750 V and the deflecting voltage is changed to 45 V, what will the deflection be?

13. How much work must be done to move a positive charge of $+2.0\ \mu C$ from infinity to a point 1.2 m away from a positive point charge of $+3.0 \times 10^3\ \mu C$?

14. What is the electric potential relative to infinity at a distance of 10^{-11} m from a proton?

15. Two point charges of $+ 8.0\ \mu C$ are separated by a distance of 1.0 m. If the force between them is F, what will the force be if $4.0\ \mu C$ are removed from one point charge and transferred to the other point charge?

16. Two very small spheres each have a charge of $3.0\ \mu C$. They are 4.0 cm apart. What is the potential relative to infinity at point P? P is 3.0 cm from both of the charged spheres, as shown below.

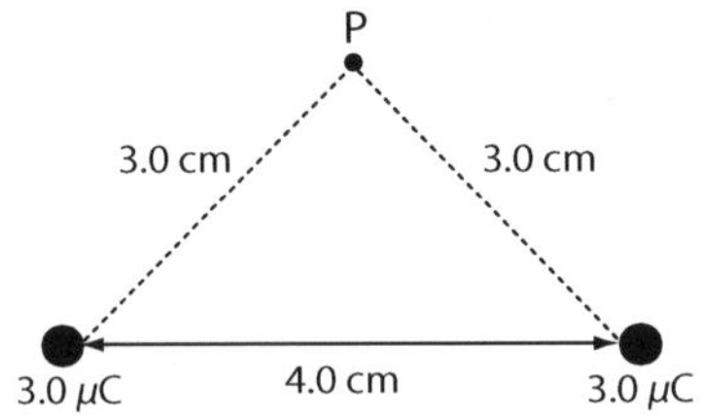

17. Protons are accelerated through a potential difference of 6.0 MV (megavolts) and then make head-on collisions with atomic nuclei with a charge of + 82 elementary charges. What is the closest distance of approach between the protons and the nuclei? Assume the nuclei are stationary.

18. How much work must be done to bring three protons from infinity to a distance of 1.0×10^{-11} m from one another?

Chapter 5 Extra Practice

Answer questions 1 and 2 using the diagram below.

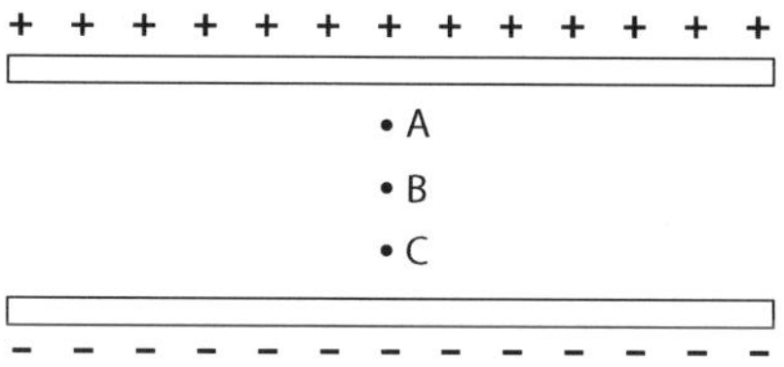

1. What is the direction of the electric field at **B**, which is located between a pair of oppositely charged plates?

2. Where is the electric field strength between the plates the strongest and the weakest?

3. What is the direction of the electric field at **P** due to point charges Q_1 and Q_2 in the diagram below?

4. Which of the following units is a measure of electric field strength?
   (a) N/A
   (b) J/C
   (c) N/A•m
   (d) N/kg
   (e) V/m

5. The electric field strength at a distance of 1.0 m from a point charge is 4.0×10^4 N/C. What will the electric field strength be at a distance of 2.0 m from the same point charge?

6. A beam of electrons in a cathode ray tube is accelerated toward the anode by an accelerating voltage of 100 V. After passing through the anode, the electrons are deflected as they pass between two oppositely charged parallel deflecting plates. On the screen, the observed deflection is δ. If the accelerating voltage is increased to 400 V, what deflection will be observed on the screen?

7. An atom carrying an excess charge of 1.60×10^{-19} C is accelerated from rest by a potential difference of 750 V. It reaches a peak speed of 8.50×10^4 m/s. What is the mass of the atom?

8. What increase in electric potential energy occurs when an alpha particle with a charge of 3.2×10^{-19} C is brought from infinity to a distance of 5.0×10^{-10} m of a stationary charge of 7.5×10^{-18} C?

9. Calculate the electrostatic force of attraction between a positive charge of 8.0×10^{-6} C and a negative charge of 5.0×10^{-6} C, when they are 0.30 m apart.

10. When a charged object is accelerated through a potential difference of 500 V, its kinetic energy increases from 2.0×10^{-5} J to 6.0×10^{-5} J. What is the magnitude of the charge on the object?

11. How fast will an electron be moving if it is accelerated from rest, in a vacuum, through a potential difference of 200 V?

12. Two parallel plates are 4.0 mm apart. If the potential difference between them is 200 V, what is the magnitude of the electric field strength between the plates?

13. An electron enters the space between two oppositely charged parallel plates, as shown below. What is the magnitude and direction of the electrostatic force that acts on the electron when it is between the two plates?

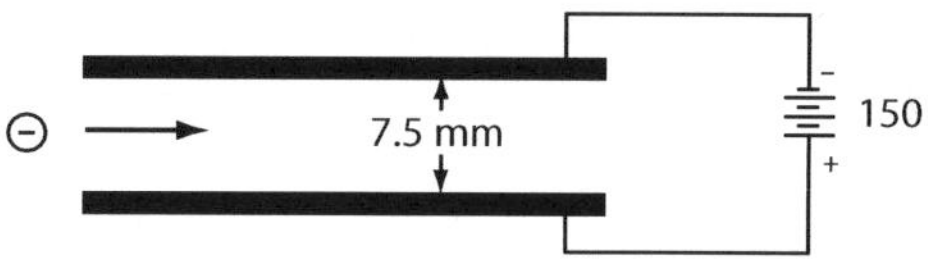

14. The 3.0×10^{-6} C charge q in the diagram below experiences opposing forces exerted by Q_1 and Q_2 of 5.0 N and 11.0 N respectively. What is the magnitude and direction of the electric field strength at the location of q?

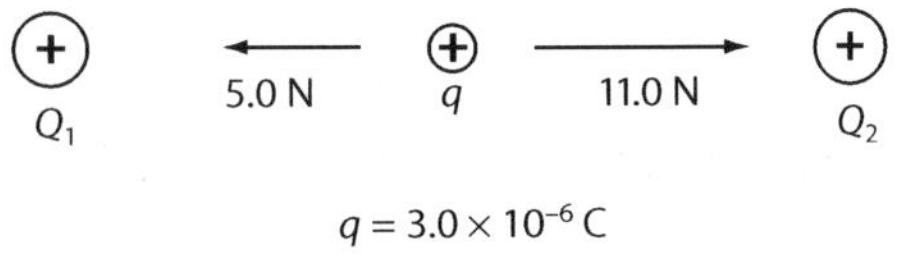

15. How much work must be done to move charge $Q_2 = 2.0 \times 10^{-6}$ C from A to B, as shown in the diagram below? The other charged object has a charge $Q_1 = 8.0 \times 10^{-6}$ C.

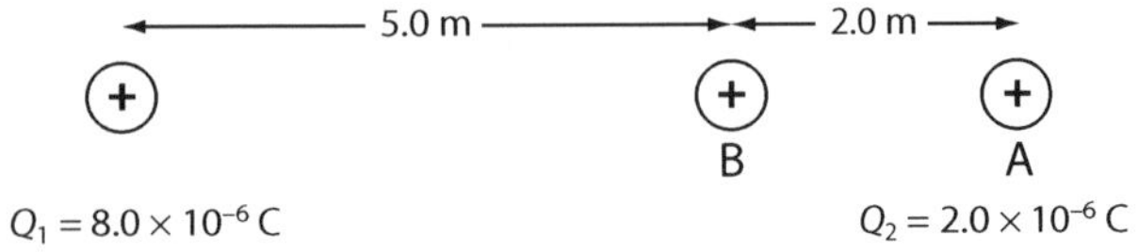

16. What is the electric potential, relative to infinity, of an electron that is 5.3×10^{-11} m from the proton in a hydrogen atom?

17. What is the electric potential at **P** due to charges Q_1 and Q_2?

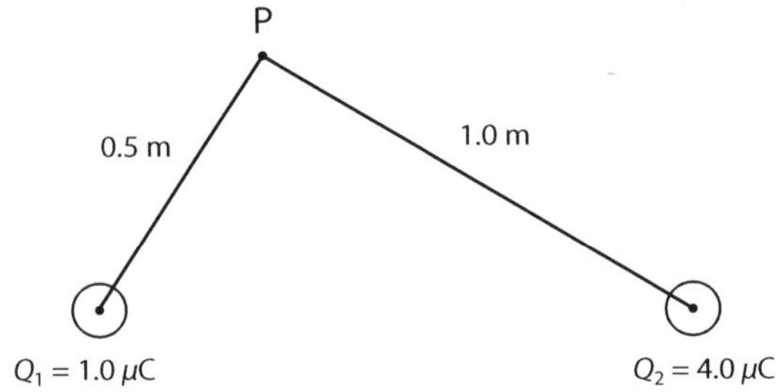

6 Electric Circuits

By the end of this chapter, you should be able to do the following:

- Apply Ohm's law to a variety of direct current circuits
- Apply Kirchhoff's laws to a variety of direct current circuits
- Correctly use ammeters and voltmeters
- Solve a range of problems involving current, resistance, electric potential difference, electric power, and efficiency

By the end of this chapter, you should know the meaning of these **key terms**:

- ammeter
- ampere
- conventional electric current
- electric current
- electric power
- electromotive force (emf)
- equivalent resistance
- internal resistance
- parallel circuit
- resistance
- series circuit
- terminal voltage
- voltmeter

By the end of this chapter, you should be able to use and know when to use the following formulae:

$I = \frac{\Delta Q}{t}$ $V = IR$ $P = IV$ $V_{terminal} = \mathcal{E} \pm Ir$

These high voltage transmission lines have an important role in transporting electrical energy to your home and school where the energy is used to power a range of electrical devices including hybrid vehicles.

6.1 Current Events in History

Warm Up

Your teacher will give you a light source, energy source, and wire. How many different ways can you arrange these three items so that the light source goes on? Draw each circuit.

Galvani's and Volta's Experiments

Until 200 years ago, the idea of producing a steady current of electricity and putting it to use was nonexistent. The discovery of a way to produce a flow of electric charges was, in fact, accidental. In the year 1780, at the University of Bologna, Italian professor of anatomy Luigi Galvani (1737–1798) was dissecting a frog. First, he noticed that when a nearby static electricity generator made a spark while a metal knife was touching the frog's nerves, the frog's legs would jump as its muscles contracted! Galvani proceeded to look for the conditions that caused this behaviour. In the course of his investigations, Galvani discovered that if two different metal objects (such as a brass hook and an iron support) touched each other, while also touching the frog's exposed flesh, the same contractions of the frog's legs occurred. Galvani thought that the source of the electricity was in the frog itself, and he called the phenomenon "animal electricity."

Another Italian scientist, physics professor Alessandro Volta (1745–1827), of the University of Pavia, set about to test Galvani's "animal electricity" theory for himself. Before long, Volta discovered that the source of the electricity was in the contact of two different metals. The animal (frog) was incidental. If any two different metals are immersed in a conducting solution of acid, base, or salt, they will produce an electric current. Volta was able to show that some pairs of metals worked better than other pairs. Of course, no ammeters or voltmeters were available in those days to compare currents and voltages. One way that Volta compared currents was to observe the response of the muscle tissue of dead frogs.

Neither Galvani nor Volta could explain their observations. (There is no truth to the rumour that the frog's leg jumped because 1780 was a leap year.) Many years later, it was learned that radio waves generated by the sparking generator induced a current in the metal scalpel that was penetrating the frog, even though the scalpel was some distance from the generator!

Volta eventually invented the first practical electric battery. Zinc and silver disks, separated by paper pads soaked with salt water, acted as electric cells. Stacked one on top of another, these cells became a "battery" that yielded more current than a single cell.

Cells and Batteries

There are many types of electric cells in existence today. Usually when you purchase a "battery" in a store, you are actually buying a single **cell.** Strictly speaking, a battery consists of two or more cells connected together. Nine-volt batteries used in portable radios, tape recorders, calculators, and smoke alarms are true batteries. If you open up a discarded 9 V battery, you will see six small 1.5 V cells connected together, one after the other in what is called "a series."

Figure 6.1.1 shows one type of **voltaic cell** (named after Volta). The two rods, called **electrodes**, are made of carbon and zinc, as in the traditional **dry cell**, but they are immersed in a solution of ammonium chloride (NH_4Cl). In a real dry cell, a paste containing NH_4Cl, sawdust, and other ingredients is used. The chemistry of voltaic cells will be left to your chemistry courses. The reaction that occurs, however, has the effect of *removing electrons* from the carbon electrode (making it *positive*) and adding them to the zinc (making the zinc *negative*). In a real dry cell, the outer casing of the cell is made of zinc. The zinc is dissolved away as the cell is used, and may eventually leak its contents.

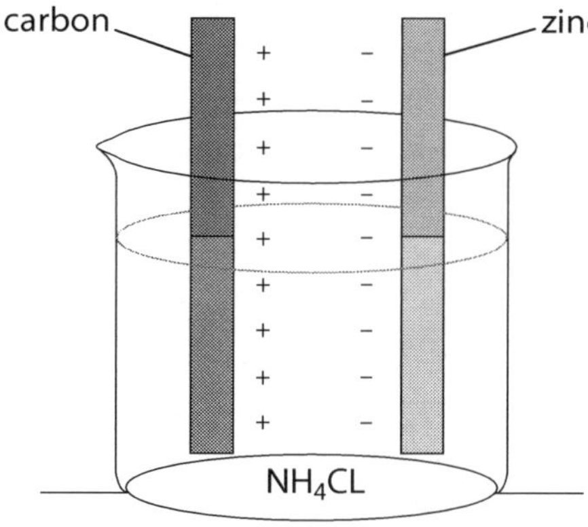

Figure 6.1.1 *A voltaic cell*

There are many kinds of cells and batteries. Rechargeable "batteries" may use nickel and cadmium, or molybdenum and lithium, or lead and lead oxide (as in the standard car battery). There are many kinds of cells on the market today, but they all produce electric current when connected to a conducting path.

Electromotive Force

In a carbon-zinc dry cell, forces resulting from the chemical reaction within the cell drive charges to the terminals, doing work to overcome the repulsive forces. The work done on the charges increases their potential energy. The difference in potential energy between the terminals amounts to 1.5 J for every coulomb of charge separated. We say the **potential difference** is 1.5 J/C, or 1.5 V. For a cell or battery that is not supplying current, the potential difference is at its peak value, which is called the **electromotive force (emf)**. It is given the symbol $\mathcal{E}$.

For a dry cell, the emf is 1.5 V. A nickel-cadmium cell is usually labelled 1.2 V or 1.25 V, but a freshly charged nickel-cadmium battery will have an even higher emf than its labelled rating. The cells in a lead storage battery have emfs of 2 V each. Six of these cells connected in series within the battery give a total emf of 12 V.

Electric Current

When electric charges *flow*, we say a current exists. A current will exist as long as a continuous conducting path is created for charges to flow from and back to a source of emf, as shown in Figure 6.1.2.

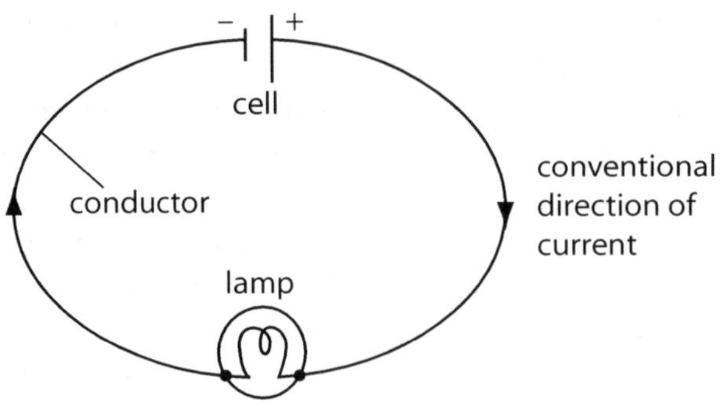

Figure 6.1.2 *Electric charges flow as a current through a conductor as long as there is no break in the path.*

Electric current is defined as the amount of electric charge that passes a point in a circuit in one second. If an amount of charge Q passes a point in a circuit in a time t, then the average current I through that point is $I = \frac{Q}{t}$.

Current could quite logically be measured in coulombs per second (C/s), but this unit is called the **ampere (A)** after André Ampère (1775–1836), a French physicist.

1 A = 1 C/s

One ampere is the sort of current that exists in a 100 W light bulb in a lamp in your home. (A 100 W lamp in a 110 V circuit would draw approximately 0.9 A.) In terms of electrons,

$$1\ \text{A} = 6.24 \times 10^{18}\ \text{electrons/s}$$

Current Direction

The direction of current was defined arbitrarily by André Ampère to be the direction that positive charges would move between two points where there is a difference of potential energy. In many simple circuits, we now know it is negative charges (electrons) that actually move. In solid conductors, the positive charges are locked in the nuclei of atoms, which are fixed in their location in the crystal. Loosely attached electrons can move through the conductor from atom to atom. In liquids and gases, however, the flow of charges may consist of positively charged ions as well as negatively charged ions and electrons.

Throughout this book, we shall use conventional current direction: the direction that positive charges would move between two points where there is a potential difference between the points.

Drift Velocity

How fast do electrons move in a wire carrying a current of, for example, 1 A? When a switch is closed in a circuit, the effect of the current can be detected immediately throughout the entire circuit. This might lead you to conclude that the electric charges (usually electrons) travel at very high velocity through the circuit. In fact, this is not so! The average **drift velocity** of electrons in a given set of circumstances can be calculated.

Within a length of metal wire, there are many, many loosely attached electrons (sometimes called "free electrons"). These electrons move about much like the molecules in a container of gas might move.

Let's consider the movement of electrons in a silver wire. Silver is an excellent conductor. Let's assume there is one free electron for every silver atom in a piece of wire. When the wire is connected to a source of emf, the potential difference (voltage) will cause electrons to move from the negative terminal of the source of emf toward the positive terminal. This movement is *superimposed* on the random motion of the electrons that is going on all the time with or without a source of emf.

The trip the electrons make from the negative to the positive terminal is not a smooth one (as it is, for example, in the vacuum of a CRT). Electrons in the metal wire collide with positive silver ions on the way, and transfer some of their kinetic energy to the silver ions. The increased thermal energy of the silver ions will show up as an increase in temperature of the silver conductor.

Assume the current in the silver wire in Figure 6.1.3 is 1.0 A. Then there are 6.24×10^{18} electrons passing the observer each second. This is because

$$\mathbf{1.0\ A = 1.0\ C/s = 6.24 \times 10^{18}\ e/s}$$

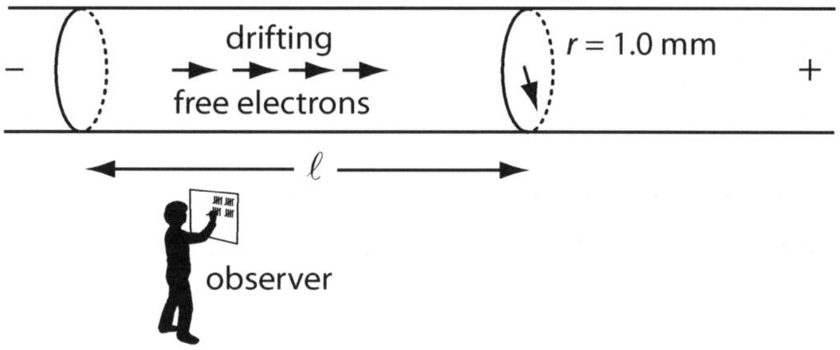

Figure 6.1.3 *Calculating the average drift velocity of electrons through a silver wire*

To calculate the average drift velocity of the electrons, we start by again assuming that there is *one free electron for every silver atom,* a reasonable assumption, since chemists tell us that silver usually forms ions with a charge of +1.

All we need to know is what length of the silver wire in Figure 6.1.3 would contain 6.24×10^{18} silver atoms (and therefore 6.24×10^{18} free electrons). We can find this out in three steps, as follows:

1. The mass of silver needed to have 6.24×10^{18} free electrons is

$$\text{mass} = \frac{6.24 \times 10^{18}\ \text{atoms}}{6.02 \times 10^{23}\ \text{atoms/mole}} \times 108\ \text{g/mole} = 1.12 \times 10^{-3}\ \text{g}$$

2. The volume of silver wire needed to have 6.24×10^{18} free electrons is

$$\text{volume} = \frac{\text{mass}}{\text{density}} = \frac{1.12 \times 10^{-3}\ \text{g}}{10.5\ \text{g/cm}^3} = 1.07 \times 10^{-4}\,\text{cm}$$

3. The radius of the silver wire in Figure 6.1.3 is 1.0 mm, or 1.0×10^{-1} cm. Its cross-sectional area is πr^2, so the length, ℓ, can be found as follows:

$$\text{length}, \ell = \frac{\text{volume}}{\text{area}} = \frac{1.07 \times 10^{-4}\ \text{cm}^3}{\pi(1.0 \times 10^{-1}\ \text{cm})^2} = 3.4 \times 10^{-3}\ \text{cm}$$

Since a length of 3.4×10^{-3} cm contains 6.24×10^{18} electrons, and this many electrons pass the observer in 1 s, the average drift velocity of the conducting electrons is 3.4×10^{-3} cm/s, or 0.034 mm/s! This is true only for the stated conditions, of course. If the amount of current, the nature of the material in the conductor, or the dimensions of the conductor change, then the drift velocity will also change.

When you turn on a switch to light a lamp using a battery, the change in the electric field may travel at the speed of light, but the electrons themselves drift ever so slowly through the wire, under the influence of the electric field.

Representing Electric Circuits

Figure 6.1.4 shows a simple electric circuit. There is an energy source or battery, a device to use the electrical energy (such as a lamp), a switch or control, and wires to carry the energy.

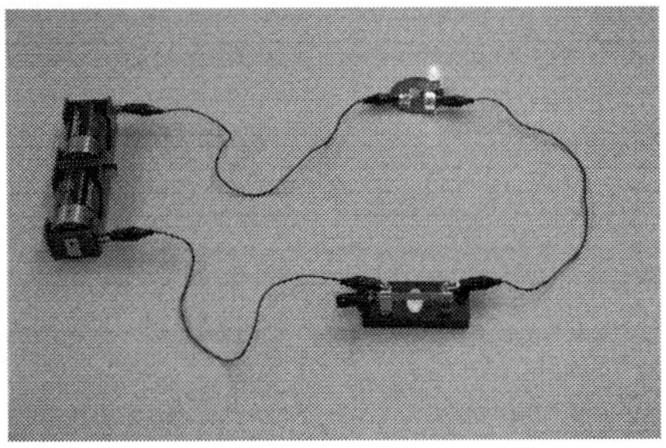

Figure 6.1.4 *A simple electric circuit*

Any circuit can be represented with a schematic diagram using a set of common symbols. Table 6.1.1 lists some of the more common symbols used for drawing electrical circuits. You will need to know each of these symbols so you can draw electrical circuits.

Table 6.1.1 *Common Symbols Used in Circuit Diagrams*

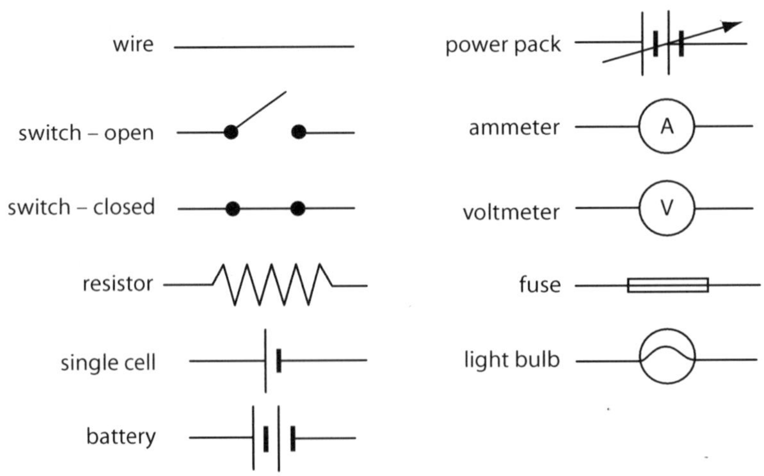

The circuit in Figure 6.1.4 can be represented as shown in Figure 6.1.5.

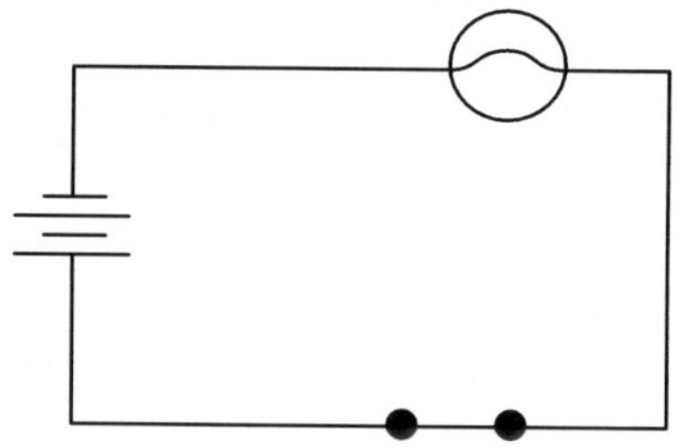

Figure 6.1.5 *A schematic drawing of the circuit shown in Figure 6.1.4*

Quick Check

1. Draw a circuit that has two light bulbs, a battery, a fuse, and closed switch.

2. Design a circuit that has a switch that can turn off two light bulbs at the same time.

3. Design a circuit that has two light bulbs and one switch that can turn one light bulb on and off while keeping the other light bulb on.

How to Read the Scale on an Ammeter

Figure 6.1.5 shows the face of a typical milliammeter. There are three scales printed on the face, but there are eight different ranges for this meter. When you connect the meter into a circuit, the terminal post labeled "C" is always connected to the negative terminal of the power source or to a part of the circuit that eventually leads to the negative terminal.

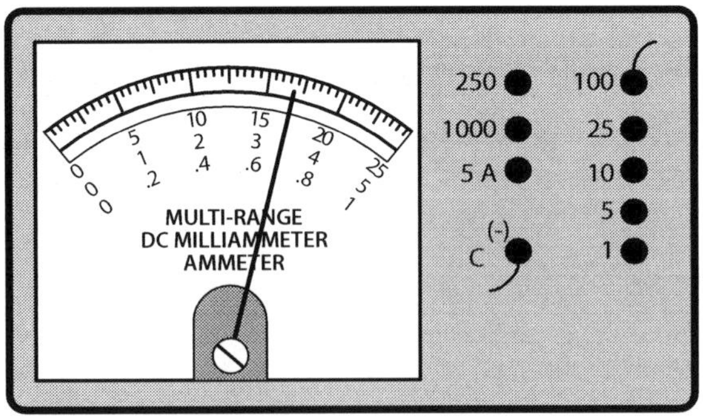

Figure 6.1.6 *An ammeter*

You must choose a suitable range for the current you have to measure. If you are not sure what range to use, try the red 5A terminal post first. This is the least sensitive range for the meter, so it can handle the most current safely. On this range, the milliammeter can handle up to 5 A.

What do the numbers on the terminal posts mean?

If you connect to the 5 A range, the meter reads anywhere from 0 A up to a maximum of 5 A. Read the middle scale of your meter. The markings mean exactly what they say: 0 A, 1 A, 2 A, 3 A, 4 A, and 5 A. On this range, the needle in Figure 6.1.6 is at 3.3 A.

If you connect to the 1000 range, the meter reads anywhere between 0 mA and 1000 mA. Read the bottom scale, but read the 1 on the scale as 1000 mA. Read 0.2 as 200 mA, 0.4 as 400 mA, 0.6 as 600 mA, and 0.8 as 800 mA. On this range, the needle in Figure 6.1.6 reads 660 mA.

If you connect to the 250 range, the meter reads anywhere from 0 mA up to 250 mA. Use the top scale but 25 reads as 250 mA. Read 5 as 50 mA, 10 as 100 mA, 15 as 150 mA, and 20 as 200 mA. On this range, the needle in Figure 6.1.6 reads 170 mA.

Quick Check

1. Look at the 100 scale on the meter in Figure 6.1.6.
   (a) What is the highest reading the scale will measure?

   (b) What is the needle reading in Figure 6.1.6?

2. What is the needle reading in Figure 6.1.6 for each of the following scales?

   (a) the 25 mA scale

   (b) the 10 mA scale

   (c) the 5 mA scale

   (d) the 1 mA scale

Investigation 6.1.1 Measuring Current Using Electroplating

Purpose

To measure current by counting copper atoms deposited on a carbon rod in a measured amount of time

Introduction

A solution of copper II sulfate contains two kinds of ions: Cu^{2+} ions, which give the solution its blue colour, and SO_4^{2-} ions, which are colourless (Figure 6.1.7). Two electrodes are immersed in the copper II sulfate solution and connected to a source of emf. The electrode connected to the positive terminal of the cell will attract SO_4^{2-} ions, and the electrode connected to the negative terminal of the cell will attract Cu^{2+} ions.

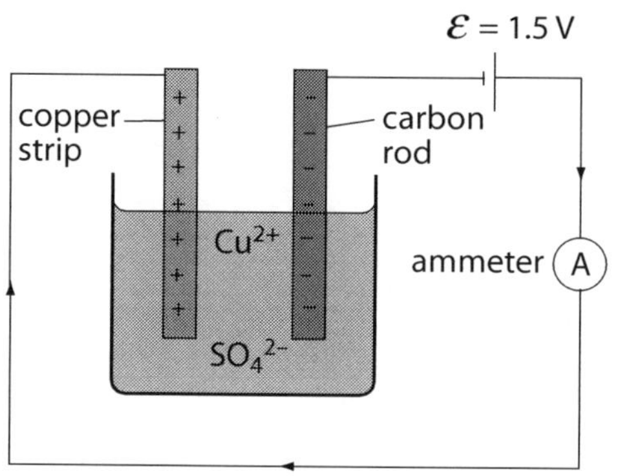

Figure 6.1.7

Cu^{2+} ions attracted to the negative electrode pick up two electrons, and deposit themselves on the negative electrode as copper atoms, Cu^0.

$$Cu^{2+} + 2e^- \rightarrow Cu^0$$

Meanwhile, at the positive electrode, which is made of copper, copper atoms *lose* two electrons and become copper ions, thus replenishing the Cu^{2+} ions in the solution.

$$Cu^0 \rightarrow Cu^{2+} + 2e^-$$

The two electrons return to the source of emf, the cell.

In this experiment, you allow the copper atoms to plate onto a negatively charged carbon electrode. If you measure the increase in mass of the carbon electrode after, say, 20 min of copper plating, you can calculate the mass of copper plated. This will give you the number of copper atoms plated, and from this, the number of electrons that were transferred in the 20 min. Finally you can calculate the current in amperes. You can also compare your calculated current with the current measured with an ammeter placed in the same circuit.

Procedure

1. Measure the mass of a dry, clean carbon rod as precisely as you can.
2. Set up the circuit shown in Figure 6.1.7. Make sure the carbon rod is connected to the negative terminal of the dry cell or other DC power source. The red binding post of the ammeter should be connected to the positive terminal of the cell, and an appropriate current range chosen as quickly as possible when the current is turned on. *Let the current run for a carefully measured time, such as 20 min.* Record current frequently, and *average* it.
3. As soon as the current is turned off, carefully remove the carbon electrode. Dip it in a beaker of methyl hydrate, and allow it time to dry. A heat lamp can be used to speed drying.

Caution! Methyl hydrate is both highly toxic and flammable!

4. Measure the mass of the plated carbon rod precisely, and calculate the amount of copper that has plated on its surface. Record the mass of copper.
5. To remove the copper, set up the circuit once more, but *reverse the connections* to the cell so that the copper plates back onto the copper strip.

Concluding Questions

1. One mole of copper atoms (63.5 g) contains 6.02×10^{23} atoms. Using this information and the mass of copper plated on the carbon rod, calculate
   (a) the number of copper atoms plated
   (b) the number of electrons transferred
   (c) the number of coulombs transferred in 20 min
2. If 1 A = 1 C/s, what was the current in amperes?
3. Compare your calculated current with the measured current by calculating the percent difference between the two currents.

6.1 Review Questions

1. If the current in a wire is 5.0 A, how many coulombs of charge pass a point in the wire in 1 min?

2. What is the current if 6.0×10^3 C pass a point in a circuit in 10.0 min?

3. If the current in a circuit is 12 A, how many electrons pass a point in 1 h?

4. The drift speed of electrons in a copper wire running from a battery to a light bulb and back is approximately 0.020 mm/s. The battery is at the front of a classroom and wires run around the perimeter of the room to the light bulb. The total length of wire is 40.0 m. How long would it take a single electron to drift from the negative terminal of the battery back to the positive terminal? Express your answer in days.

5. How much copper would be plated by a current of 1.5 A in a time of 1.0 h?

6. How much silver is deposited by a current of 1.000 A in 1.000 h? The mass of one mole of silver atoms is 107.9 g.

$$Ag^+ + 1e^- \rightarrow Ag^0$$

7. Draw a circuit with three light bulbs and two switches, and show the different combinations where one, two, and three light bulbs are lit.

8. What is the reading of the milliammeter below?

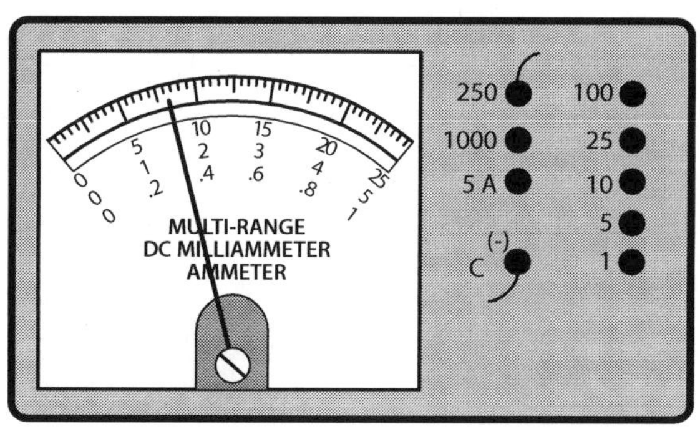

6.2 Ohm's Law

Warm Up

If you draw a line with a graphite pencil, it will conduct electricity. Why does more current go through a 5.0 cm line of graphite than a 10.0 cm line?

____

____

____

Resistance

Georg Simon Ohm (1787–1854) experimented with current in wires using variations in voltage to produce different currents. He found that for metal conductors at a given temperature, the current was directly proportional to the voltage between the ends of the wire.

$$I \propto V$$

$$\text{Therefore, } \frac{V}{I} = \text{constant.}$$

For example, the potential difference (voltage) between the ends of a wire is 1.50 V and the current is 2.00 A. If the potential difference is increased to 3.00 V, the current will also double to 4.00 A.

The constant of proportionality is called the **resistance (*R*)** of the length of wire. The relationship among current, voltage, and resistance is written:

$$\frac{V}{I} = R$$

where *R* is the resistance, in **ohms** (Ω)**.** This is called **Ohm's law.** Ohm's law can be written in two other forms, but all three forms are equivalent.

$$\frac{V}{I} = R \qquad V = IR \qquad \frac{V}{R} = I$$

Sample Problem 6.2.1 — Ohm's Law

The current in a portable stove's heating element is 12.0 A when the potential difference between the ends of the element is 120 V. What is the resistance of the stove element?

What to Think About	How to Do It
1. Determine what you know from the problem.	$I = 12.0\ A$ $V = 120\ V$
2. Determine the appropriate formula.	$R = \frac{V}{I}$
3. Solve.	$R = \frac{120\ V}{12.0\ A} = 1.0 \times 10^1\ \Omega$

Practice Problems 6.2.1 — Ohm's Law

1. A resistor allows 1.0 mA to exist within it when a potential difference of 1.5 V is applied to its ends. What is the resistance of the resistor, in kilohms? ($1 k\Omega = 10^3 \Omega$)

2. If a 10.0 Ω kettle element is plugged into a 120 V outlet, how much current will it draw?

3. A current of 1.25 mA exists in a 20.0 kΩ resistor. What is the potential difference between the ends of the resistor?

Resistors

Under normal circumstances, every conductor of electricity offers some resistance to the flow of electric charges and is therefore a **resistor**. However, when we use the term "resistors," we are usually referring to devices manufactured specifically to control the amount of current in a circuit.

There are two main kinds of resistor: (1) wire-wound resistors, made of a coil of insulated, tightly wound fine wire and (2) carbon resistor (Figure 6.2.1). Carbon resistors consist of a cylinder of carbon, with impurities added to control the amount of resistance. Metal wire leads are attached to each end of the carbon cylinder, and the whole assembly is enclosed in an insulating capsule.

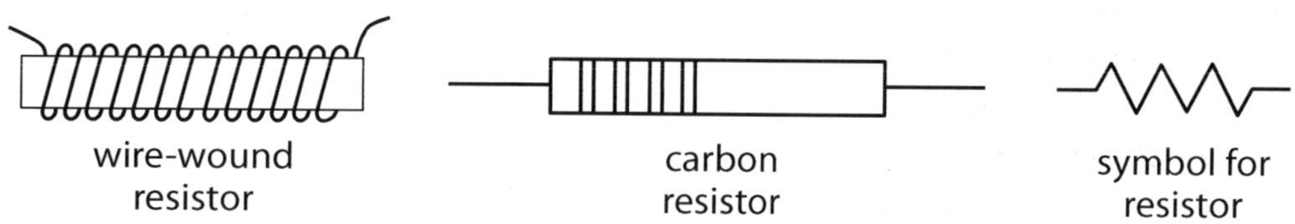

Figure 6.2.1 *Types of resistors and the symbol for resistors used in circuit diagrams*

In any resistor, electrical energy is transformed into thermal energy. There are some materials which, if cooled to temperatures approaching 0 K, offer no resistance to the flow of charges. These materials are called **superconductors**.

Resistor Colour Code

Resistors are either labelled with their resistance or colour-coded with four coloured bands, each of which has significance. The first coloured band gives the *first digit*. The second coloured band gives the *second digit*. The third coloured band gives the *power-of-10 multiplier (the number of zeros following the first two digits)*. Table 6.2.1 lists the colours and their codes. If there is no fourth coloured band, the manufacturer's tolerance is 20%. If the fourth band is gold, the tolerance is 5%. If the fourth band is silver, the tolerance is 10%. Think of tolerance as a range for the value of the resistor. No resistor is exactly the value indicated — the value is plus or minus the tolerance percentage given.

Table 6.2.1 *Resistor Colour Codes*

Band Colour	Number	Multiplier	Tolerance
black	0	10^0	
brown	1	10^1	
red	2	10^2	
orange	3	10^3	
yellow	4	10^4	
green	5	10^5	
blue	6	10^6	
violet	7	10^7	
gray	8	10^8	
white	9	10^9	
gold			5%
silver			10%
(no colour)			20%

Sample Problem 6.2.2 — Resistor Colour Codes

What is the value of a resistor that has the colours gray, blue, red, and silver?

What to Think About	How to Do It
1. Use Table 6.2.1 to interpret the colour code.	First colour: gray = 8 Second colour: blue = 6 Third colour: red = 2 Resistor rating: 8600 Ω
2. Determine the tolerance of the resistor.	Tolerance: silver (10%) 10% of 8600 Ω ± 860 Ω
3. Summarize the result.	Resistor's value is 8600 Ω ± 860 Ω.

Practice Problems 6.2.2 — Resistor Colour Codes

Use Table 6.2.1 to figure out the resistance rating of the following colour-coded resistors:

1. Red, red, red, silver
2. Brown, black, orange, gold
3. Brown, green, green, silver
4. Yellow, violet, yellow

Limitations of Ohm's Law

Ohm's law applies to metal resistors and metal-like resistors such as those made of compressed carbon. The ratio of potential difference to current, which is resistance, is constant for this class of material, providing that the temperature of the material remains constant.

Ohm's law only applies to metallic or metal-like conductors at a specific temperature. It does *not* apply to just any conductor in a circuit. For example, Ohm's law would not apply to a conducting solution or to a gas discharge tube.

Joule's Law

The English physicist James Prescott Joule (1818–1889) did experiments to measure the amount of heat released by various resistors under different conditions. He found that, for a particular resistor, the amount of thermal energy released in a unit of time by a resistor is proportional to the square of the current. The rate at which energy is released with respect to time is called **power**, so Joule's results can be expressed as follows:

$$P \propto I^2$$

$$\text{or } P = \text{constant}\cdot I^2$$

The constant in this equation will have units with the dimensions W/A^2, since constant = P/I^2. Consider the following simplification of these measuring units (W/A^2):

$$1\frac{W}{A^2} = 1\frac{\frac{J}{s}}{\frac{C^2}{s^2}} = 1\frac{\frac{J}{C}}{\frac{C}{s}} = 1\frac{V}{A} = 1\,\Omega$$

The ohm (Ω) is the unit for resistance. In fact, the constant of proportionality in the relationship discovered by Joule is the same constant of proportionality that is in Ohm's law. The ratio P/I^2 is the resistance of the resistor.

Joule's law can be written as follows: $P = RI^2$. By combining Joule's law with Ohm's law for resistors, other expressions for electrical power can be derived:

$$P = RI^2 = \frac{V}{I}I^2 = VI$$

$$\text{And } P = VI = V \times \frac{V}{R} = \frac{V^2}{R}$$

In summary, $$P = RI^2 = VI = \frac{V^2}{R}$$

Quick Check

1. What is the resistance of a 60.0 W lamp, if the current in it is 0.50 A?

2. A 600 W coffee percolator is operated at 120 V.
   (a) What is the resistance of the heating element of the percolator?

   (b) How much thermal energy does it produce in 6.0 min?

3. How much thermal energy is released by a 1500 W kettle in 5.0 min?

EMF, Terminal Voltage, and Internal Resistance

In Figure 6.2.2, the dry cell has a rated emf of 1.50 V. Assume you are using a high quality voltmeter to measure the potential difference between the terminals A and B of the cell, when essentially no current is being drawn from the cell other than a tiny amount going through the voltmeter itself. In that case, the voltage between the terminals will be nearly equal to the ideal value of the emf. That is, with no current, the terminal voltage of the battery, V_{AB}, will equal the emf, $\mathcal{E}$.

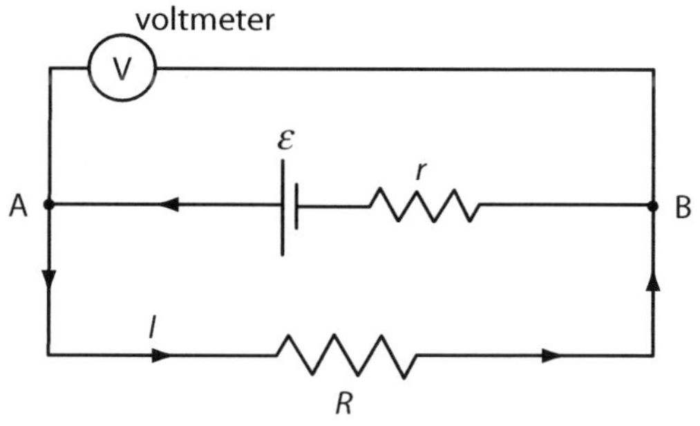

Figure 6.2.2 *The dry cell in this circuit has a rated emf of 1.50 V.*

If, however, the cell is connected to a resistor R so that a current I exists in the simple circuit including in the cell itself, then the terminal voltage is *less than* the cell emf.

$$V_{AB} < \mathcal{E}$$

This is because the cell itself has an internal resistance of its own, symbolized by r. According to Ohm's law, the loss of potential energy per coulomb between the terminals is Ir. The measured terminal voltage of the cell will be less than the ideal emf by an amount equal to Ir.

$$V_{AB} = \mathcal{E} - Ir$$

Sample Problem 6.2.3 — Terminal Voltage and Internal Resistance

A dry cell with an emf of 1.50 V has an internal resistance of 0.050 Ω. What is the terminal voltage of the cell when it is connected to a 2.00 Ω resistor?

What to Think About	How to Do It
1. Determine what you know from the problem.	$\mathcal{E} = 1.50$ V $R = 2.00\ \Omega$ $r = 0.050\ \Omega$
2. To solve, apply Ohm's law to the circuit as a whole, and consider the internal resistance r to be in series with the external resistance R. This means you will solve for the current in the circuit.	$I = \frac{\mathcal{E}}{R + r} = \frac{1.50\text{ V}}{2.05\ \Omega} = 0.732\text{ A}$
3. Now find the terminal voltage.	$V_{AB} = \mathcal{E} - Ir$ $V_{AB} = 1.50\text{ V} - (0.732\text{ A})(0.050\ \Omega)$ $V_{AB} = 1.50\text{ V} - 0.037\text{ V}$ $V_{AB} = 1.46\text{ V}$

Practice Problems 6.2.3 — Terminal Voltage and Internal Resistance

1. A dry cell with an emf of 1.50 V and an internal resistance of 0.050 Ω Is "shorted out" with a piece of wire with a resistance of only 0.20 Ω. What will a voltmeter read if it is connected to the terminals of the dry cell at this time?

2. A battery has an emf of 12.50 V. When a current of 35 A is drawn from it, its terminal voltage is 11.45 V. What is the internal resistance of the battery?

Investigation 6.2.1 Ohm's Law

Purpose

To investigate the relationship between the voltage applied to a resistor and the current in the resistor

Procedure

1. Set up the circuit shown in Figure 6.2.3. Start with one cell, an ammeter, and a carbon resistor. These are all in series as they form one path. A voltmeter is connected in parallel with the resistor, as there are two paths for the current to travel.

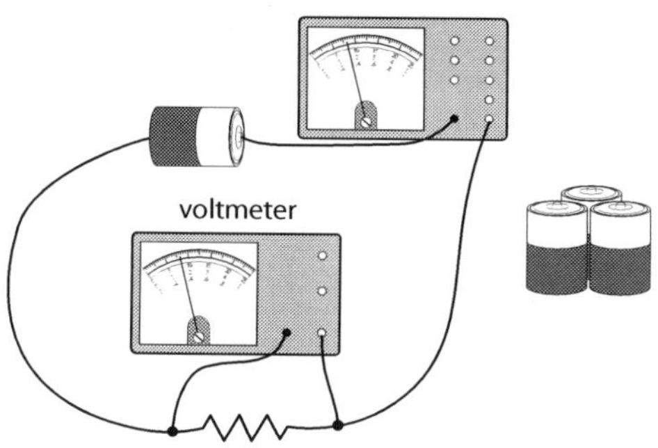

Figure 6.2.3

2. Prepare a copy of Table 6.2.2.

Table 6.2.2 Data Table

Number of Cells Used	Voltage across Resistor (V)	Current in Resistor (A)	Calculated Resistance (Ω)
1			
2			
3			
4			

Resistor rating: ______________________

3. With one cell in the circuit, measure the current in milliamperes (mA) and the voltage in volts (V). Convert the current from mA to A by dividing by l000. (Move the decimal three places to the left. For example, 2.4 mA is equal to 0.0024 A.) Enter the current and voltage in your copy of Table 6.2.2.
4. Add a second cell in series with the first cell. Record the current and the voltage in your copy of Table 6.2.2.
5. Repeat with three cells, then with four cells. Enter your results in your copy of Table 6.2.2.
6. Complete the final column of your copy of Table 6.2.2. Divide voltage (*V*) by current (*I*) for each trial. This ratio, *V*/*I*, is the resistance (*R*) of the resistor, measured in ohms.
7. Replace the resistor with one of a different colour and repeat Procedure steps 1 to 6.

Concluding Questions

1. What happens to the voltage across a resistor when the number of cells in series with it is
   (a) doubled? (b) tripled? (c) quadrupled?
2. What happens to the current across a resistor when the number of cells in series with it is
   (a) doubled? (b) tripled? (c) quadrupled?
3. What happens to the resistance ($R = V/I$) across a resistor when the number of cells in series with it is
   (a) doubled? (b) tripled? (c) quadrupled?
4. What is the resistance in ohms (Ω) of (a) the first resistor you used? (b) the second resistor you used?
5. Consult Table 6.2.1 to see the manufacturer's rating of your resistors. Record these resistances in your notes. Why is the measured value different from the manufacturer's rating?

6.2 Review Questions

1. A current of 1.2 mA exists in a resistor when a potential difference of 4.8 V is applied to its ends. What is the resistance of the resistor? Express your answer in kilohms (1 kΩ = 1000 Ω).

2. A current of 3.0 mA exists in a 2.0 kΩ resistor. What is the voltage between the ends of the resistor?

3. What current will exist in a 30 Ω resistor if a 120 V voltage is applied to its ends?

4. A 3.0 V battery is connected to a carbon resistor.
   (a) If the current is 3.0 mA, what is the resistance of the resistor?

   (b) If a 6.0 V battery is connected to the same resistor, what will the current be?

   (c) What is the resistance of the resistor when the 6.0 V battery replaces the 3.0 V battery?

5. A 12 V battery sends a current of 2.0 A through a car's circuit to the headlights. What is the resistance of the filament in a headlight?

6. What voltage is needed to send 0.5 A through a 220 Ω light bulb filament?

7. What current exists in a 120 V coffee percolator, if the resistance of its heating element is 24 Ω?

8. A resistor has the following coloured bands: brown, black, red, gold. What is the manufacturer's rating of this resistor (see Table 6.2.1)?

9. Use Table 6.2.1 to figure out the resistance rating of the following colour-coded resistors:
   (a) Orange, red, brown, silver

   (b) Red, black, black, gold

   (c) Gray, green, blue, silver

   (d) White, violet, red

10. What colour code would you find on the following resistors?
    (a) 500 Ω ± 20%

    (b) 37 000 Ω ± 5%

    (c) 10 Ω ± 10%

    (d) 8600 Ω ± 20%

11. What is the resistance of the element of a 1500 W kettle if it draws 12.5 A?

12. A 1500 W kettle is connected to a 110 V source. What is the resistance of the kettle element?

13. When you pay your electricity bill, you are charged not for power but for the energy used. The unit for measuring the energy used is the kilowatt•hour (kW•h).
    (a) How many joules are there in one kW•h?

    (b) How much energy, in kW•h, does a 400-W TV set use in a month (30 days), if it is used an average of 6.0 h each day?

    (c) If electrical energy costs \$0.06/kW•h, what will it cost you to operate the TV set for one month?

14. How many kW•h of energy does a 900 W toaster use in 3.0 min?

15. A 1.0 kΩ resistor is rated ½ W. This rating means the resistor will be destroyed if more than than ½ W passes through it. What is the maximum voltage you can apply to this resistor without risking damage to it?

16. A battery with an emf of 6.00 V has an internal resistance of 0.20 Ω. What current does the battery deliver when the terminal voltage reads only 5.00 V?

6.3 Kirchhoff's Laws

Warm Up

What will happen to the brightness of the remaining six light bulbs in a parallel circuit if the seventh bulb in the circuit is unhooked?

___

___

___

Resistors in Series

In Figure 6.3.1, four resistors are connected end-to-end so that there is one continuous conducting path for electrons coming from the source of emf, through the resistors, and back to the source. Electrons move through the resistors, one after the other. The same current exists in each resistor. Resistors arranged like this are said to be "in **series**" with each other. Figure 6.3.1 shows a typical series circuit.

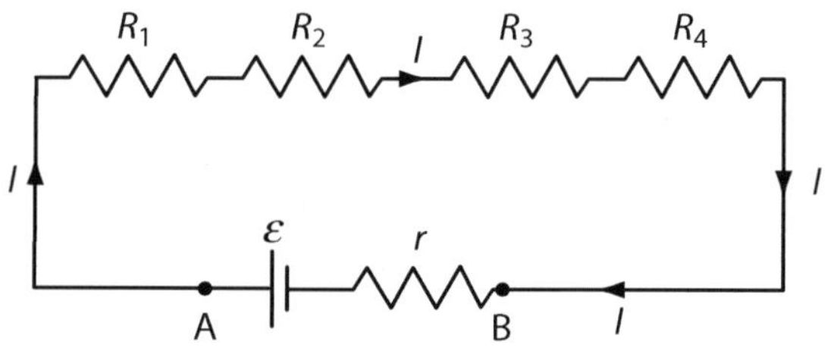

Figure 6.3.1 *A series circuit*

Within the cell, the gain in potential energy per unit charge is equal to the emf, $\mathcal{E}$. When a current I exists, energy will be lost in resistors R_1, R_2, R_3, R_4, and r. The loss of potential energy per unit charge in each resistor is the voltage V across that resistor. From Ohm's law, we know that $V = IR$. The law of conservation of energy requires that the total gain in energy in the cell(s) must equal the total loss of energy in the resistors in the circuit. It follows that the total gain in energy per unit charge (E) must equal the total loss of energy per unit charge in the circuit.

$$E = Ir + IR_1 + IR_2 + IR_3 + IR_4$$

$$\therefore\ E - Ir = IR_1 + IR_2 + IR_3 + IR_4$$

Recalling that terminal voltage $V_{AB} = E - Ir$,

$$V_{AB} = IR_1 + IR_2 + IR_3 + IR_4 = V_S$$

where V_S is the sum of voltages across the resistors in the external part of the circuit.

Another way of writing this is: $V_{AB} = V_1 + V_2 + V_3 + V_4 = V_S$

Equivalent Resistance

What is the total resistance of a series circuit like the one in Figure 6.3.1? In other words, what single resistance, called the **equivalent resistance** R_S, could be used to replace R_1, R_2, R_3, and R_4 without changing current I?

If $V_S = IR_S$ and $V_S = IR_1 + IR_2 + IR_3 + IR_4$, then

$$IR_S = IR_1 + IR_2 + IR_3 + IR_4$$

$$\therefore R_S = R_1 + R_2 + R_3 + R_4$$

Summary: For a Series Circuit

1. Current (I) is the same everywhere throughout the circuit.
2. The net gain in potential energy per coulomb in the circuit equals the net loss of potential energy per coulomb in the circuit. That is, for a circuit like the one in Figure 6.3.1, with a single source of emf,
$$V_{AB} = V_1 + V_2 + V_3 + V_4 + ... + V_n$$
3. The equivalent resistance of all the resistors in series with each other is equal to the sum of all their resistances.
$$R_S = R_1 + R_2 + R_3 + R_4 + ... + R_n$$

Resistors in Parallel

The resistors in Figure 6.3.2 are connected in **parallel**. The current divides into three branches. Electrons coming from the cell take one of three paths, which meet at a junction where the electrons all converge to one path again and return to the battery.

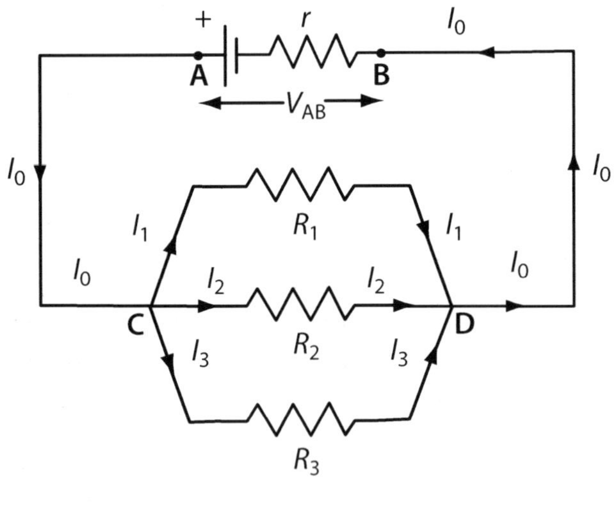

Figure 6.3.2 *Resistors R_1, R_2, and R_3 are placed in parallel in this circuit.*

Electric charge is a conserved quantity. The electrons are not "created" or "lost" during their journey through the parallel network of resistors. The number of electrons entering a junction (such as D) per second will equal the number of electrons leaving that junction per second. Likewise, the number of electrons entering junction C per second will equal the number of electrons leaving C per second. (The actual direction of electron flow is opposite to the conventional current direction shown in Figure 6.3.2.) If we express current in C/s or in A, as is normally the case,

$$I_0 = I_1 + I_2 + I_3$$

The net gain in potential energy per unit charge in the cell, which is V_{AB}, is equal to the loss in potential energy per unit charge between C and D. If you think of C as an extension of terminal A and D as an extension of terminal B of the cell, you can see that the difference in potential between C and D is the same no matter which of the three paths the electrons take to get from one terminal to the other. In fact,

$$V_{AB} = V_1 = V_2 = V_3$$

where V_{AB} is the terminal voltage of the cell, and V_1, V_2, and V_3 are the voltages across resistors R_1, R_2, and R_3 respectively.

Since the voltages are the same in each branch, we shall use the label V_p for the voltage in *any* branch of the parallel network.

Equivalent Resistance

What single resistance could be used in place of the parallel network of resistors, and draw the same total current? Call this the **equivalent resistance** R_p.

If the voltage across the parallel network is V_p, and the equivalent single resistance is R_p, we can apply Ohm's law as follows to find the total current I_0 entering the network:

$$I_0 = \frac{V_p}{R_p}$$

However, $I_0 = I_1 + I_2 + I_3$

Using Ohm's law again: $$\frac{V_p}{R_p} = \frac{V_p}{R_1} + \frac{V_p}{R_2} + \frac{V_p}{R_3}$$

Eliminating V_p: $$\frac{1}{R_p} = \frac{1}{R_1} + \frac{1}{R_2} + \frac{1}{R_3}$$

Summary: For a Parallel Circuit Network

1. Voltage is the same between the ends of each branch of a parallel network.
2. The total current entering a junction of a parallel network is equal to the total current leaving the same junction. As a result, the total current entering a parallel network of resistors or leaving the same network is equal to the sum of the currents in the branches.
3. The reciprocal of the single equivalent resistance that will replace all the resistance in a parallel network, and draw the same current, is equal to the sum of the reciprocals of the resistances in the branches.

$$\frac{1}{R_p} = \frac{1}{R_1} + \frac{1}{R_2} + \frac{1}{R_3} + \ldots + \frac{1}{R_n}$$

Combined Series and Parallel Circuits

Figure 6.3.3 shows a combined **series-parallel circuit.** The rules you have learned for series and parallel circuits can be applied to this problem. A logical approach for finding the equivalent resistance and current for the circuit in Figure 6.3.3 is to first reduce the parallel network to a single equivalent resistance, then treat the circuit as a series circuit.

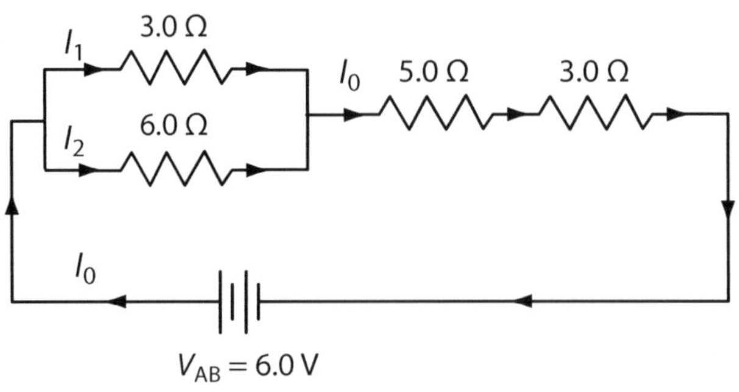

Figure 6.3.3 *A combined series-parallel circuit*

Sample Problem 6.3.1 — Resistors in Parallel

(a) What is the equivalent resistance of the circuit in Figure 6.3.3?
(b) What is the voltage across the 6.0 Ω resistor?

What to Think About	How to Do It
(a)	
1. First, reduce the parallel network to an equivalent single resistance.	$\frac{1}{R_p} = \frac{1}{3.0\ \Omega} + \frac{1}{6.0\ \Omega} = \frac{2+1}{6.0\ \Omega} = \frac{3}{6.0\ \Omega} = \frac{1}{2.0\ \Omega}$ $R_p = 2.0\ \Omega$
2. Next, add the three resistances that are in series with one another.	$R_s = 2.0\ \Omega + 5.0\ \Omega + 3.0\ \Omega = 10.0\ \Omega$
3. Then, find the current using Ohm's law with the total equivalent resistance and the battery terminal voltage.	$I_0 = \frac{V_{AB}}{R_S} = \frac{6.0\ V}{10.0\ \Omega} = 0.60\ A$
(b)	
1. Find the voltage across the parallel network by using Ohm's law on the parallel network by itself.	$V_p = I_0 R_p = (0.60\ A)(2.0\ \Omega) = 1.2\ V$

Practice Problems 6.3.1 — Resistors in Parallel

1. (a) Draw a circuit showing a 6.0 V battery with an internal resistance of 0.50 Ω connected to a parallel network consisting of a 25.0 Ω resistor in parallel with a 6.25 Ω resistor.

   (b) Calculate the current in the battery.

2. Calculate the equivalent resistance of each of the networks of resistors in Figure 6.3.4.

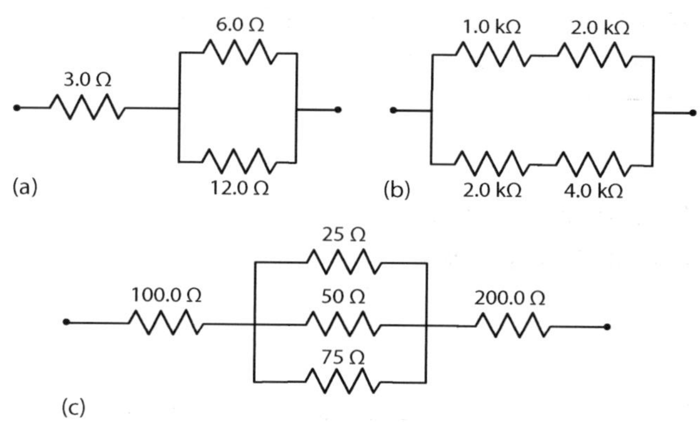

Figure 6.3.4

   (a)

   (b)

   (c)

Kirchhoff's Laws for Electric Circuits

So far, we have looked at series and parallel circuits from the points of view of (a) conservation of energy, (b) conservation of charge, and (c) Ohm's law. Most simple circuits can be analyzed using the rules worked out for series and parallel circuits in this section. For more complicated circuits, a pair of rules called **Kirchhoff's rules** or **Kirchhoff's laws** can be applied.

Kirchhoff's Current Rule
At any junction in a circuit, the sum of all the currents entering that junction equals the sum of all the currents leaving that junction.

Kirchhoff's current rule follows from the law of conservation of electric charge. Charged particles are not "lost" or "created" in a circuit. The number of charged particles (usually electrons) that enter a junction point equals the number that leave that junction point.

Kirchhoff's Voltage Rule
The algebraic sum of all the changes in potential around a closed path in a circuit is zero.

Kirchhoff's voltage rule is really a restatement of the law of conservation of energy. In Investigation 6.3.1, you will examine several circuits from the point of view of Kirchhoff's laws.

Quick Check

1. Calculate the current in the cell in the circuit in Figure 6.3.5.

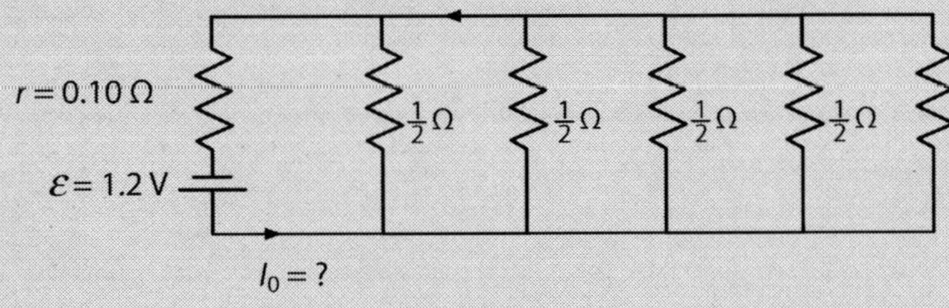

Figure 6.3.5

Quick Check continues

2. A wire has length ℓ and resistance R. It is cut into four identical pieces, and these pieces are arranged in parallel. What will be the resistance of this parallel network?

3. Four identical resistors are connected in parallel, as shown in Figure 6.3.6. The current is 2.0 A with all four resistors in the circuit. What will be the current if the wire at X is cut?

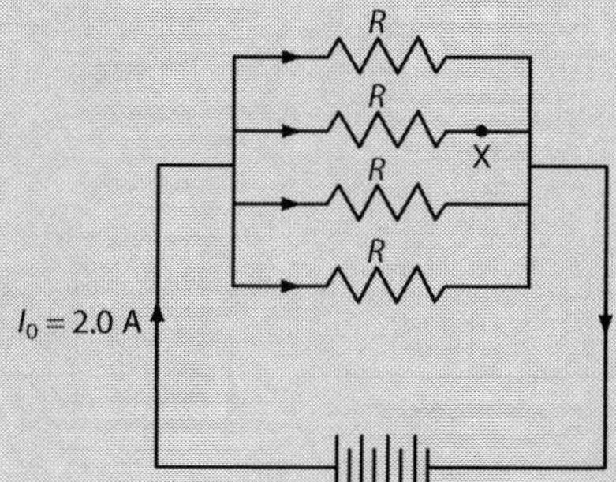

Figure 6.3.6

4. (a) What is the equivalent resistance of the network of resistors in Figure 6.3.7?

   (b) What current exists in the 3.0 Ω resistor?

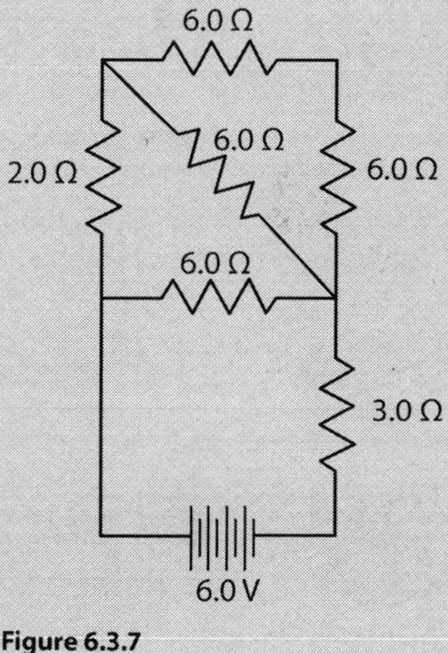

Figure 6.3.7

Investigation 6.3.1 Kirchhoff's Laws for Circuits

Purpose

To examine several circuits from the point of view of Kirchhoff's laws

Part 1 — A Series Circuit

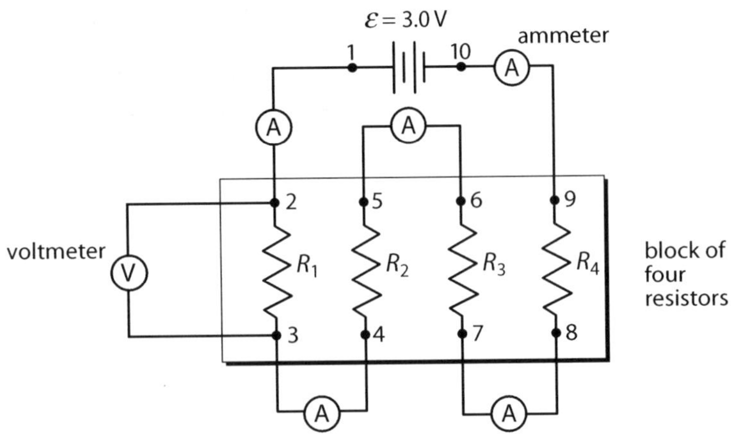

Figure 6.3.8

Procedure

1. To check Kirchhoff's current law, wire a series circuit like the one in Figure 6.3.8, and insert your ammeter in *each* of the locations, in turn, where the symbol A for ammeter is shown in the diagram. Record each current in your notebook (possibly on a diagram like Figure 6.3.8).

   I_{1-2} = ______ I_{3-4} = ______ I_{5-6} = ______ I_{7-8} = ______ I_{9-10} = ______

2. To check Kirchhoff's voltage law, measure the terminal voltage of the battery or power supply, V_{1-10}. Then measure the voltages between the ends of each resistor. Remember that the voltmeter is not in the same conducting path as the circuit. An example is shown in Figure 6.3.8, where the voltmeter is connected correctly across the ends of resistor R_1. The symbol for the voltmeter is V. Record all the voltages in your notebook.

   V_{1-10} = ______ V_{2-3} = ______ V_{4-5} = ______ V_{6-7} = ______ V_{8-9} = ______

Concluding Questions

1. Do your current readings support Kirchhoff's current law? How would you describe the current at various junctions in your series circuit?
2. Compare the potential gain in the battery (terminal voltage) with the potential drop in the resistors in the circuit. Do your results suggest that $\sum V = 0$?
3. What are some sources of error in this investigation? For example, how might the ammeter itself affect the results for current, and how might the voltmeter affect the results for voltage?
4. Calculate the resistance of each resistor using Ohm's law and the current and voltage readings for each individual resistor. Compare your calculated resistances with the manufacturer's ratings. (See Table 6.2.1 for resistor colour codes.) Organize your results in a table like Table 6.3.1 below.

Table 6.3.1 *Data Table*

	R_1	R_2	R_3	R_4
Measured Voltage, V	V	V	V	V
Measured Current, I	A	A	A	A
Calculated Resistance, R	Ω	Ω	Ω	Ω
Colour Code Rating, R	Ω	Ω	Ω	Ω

5. Calculate the equivalent resistance R_S of the whole series circuit by using Ohm's law and dividing the terminal voltage of the battery or power supply by the current in the battery. Compare this value with the sum of the individual calculated resistances.
6. What is the percent difference between R_S and $\sum [R_1 + R_2 + R_3 + R_4]$?

Part 2 — A Parallel Circuit

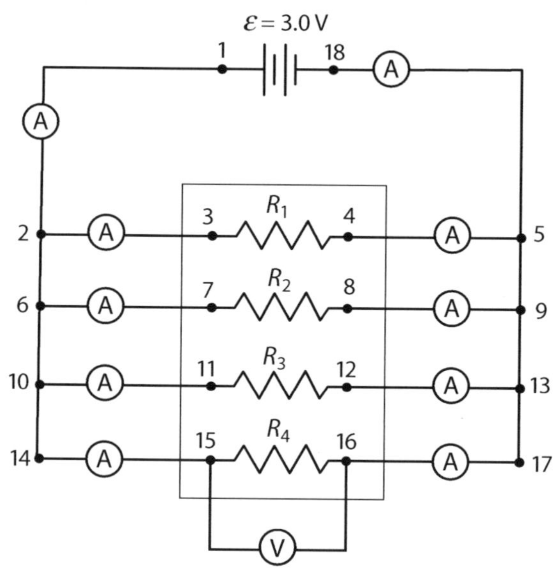

Figure 6.3.9

Procedure

1. Set up the circuit shown in Figure 6.3.9. To simplify recording your data, copy the diagram into your notebook. When you measure the current at each point labeled A, record the current right on the diagram in the ammeter circle.
2. Measure the voltage of the battery (V_{1-18}) and also the voltage across each resistor. Record the voltages in your notebook.

V_{1-18} = ______ V_{3-4} = ______ V_{7-8} = ______ V_{11-12} = ______ V_{15-16} = ______

Concluding Questions

1. Examine the currents at each of the eight junctions of the parallel network of resistors. Do your results confirm Kirchhoff's current law?
2. Compare the potential gain in the battery (terminal voltage) with the potential drop across each branch of the circuit, in turn. Do your measurements seem to confirm Kirchhoff's voltage law?

3. What are some sources of error in this experiment?
4. Use the measured voltage across each resistor, and the measured current in each resistor, to calculate R_1, R_2, R_3, and R_4. Calculate the resistance of the parallel network:

$$\frac{1}{R_p} = \frac{1}{R_1} + \frac{1}{R_2} + \frac{1}{R_3} + \frac{1}{R_4}$$

Organize your data in a table like Table 6.3.2 below.

Table 6.3.2 *Data Table*

	R_1	R_2	R_3	R_4
Measured Voltage, V	V	V	V	V
Measured Current, I	A	A	A	A
Calculated Resistance, R	Ω	Ω	Ω	Ω

(a) R_p calculated in Concluding Question 4 =	Ω
(b) R_p calculated from $\frac{V_{1-18}}{I_0}$ =	Ω
Percent difference between (a) and (b) =	%

5. Calculate the equivalent resistance of the parallel network by dividing the terminal voltage of the battery by the current in the battery. What is the percent difference between this R_p and the result from Procedure step 4?

Challenge

1. Set up a series-parallel circuit like the one in Figure 6.3.10. Test Kirchhoff's two laws for this circuit.

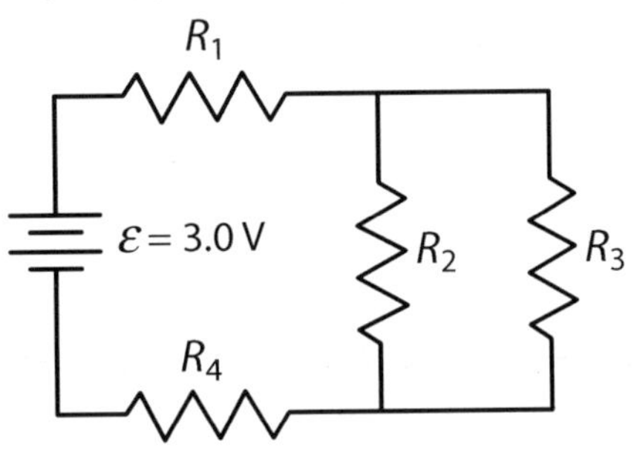

Figure 6.3.10

6.3 Review Questions

1. The current through A is 0.50 A when the switch S is open. What will the current be through A when the switch S is closed?

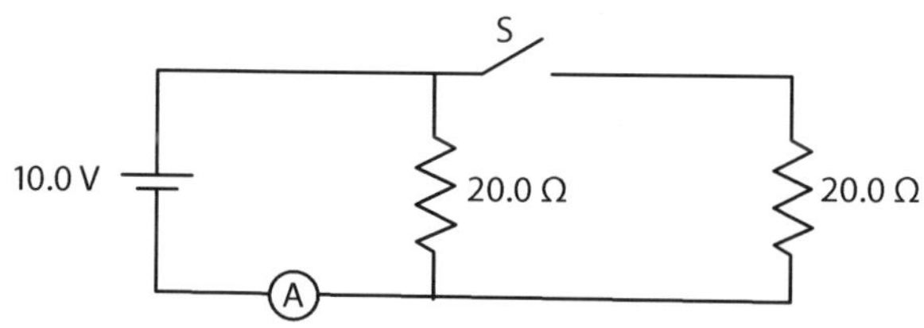

2. Which one of the following arrangements of four identical resistors will have the least resistance?

(a)

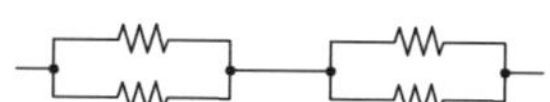

(b)

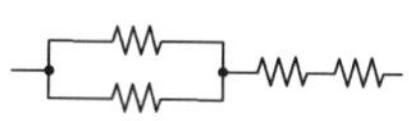

(c)

(d)

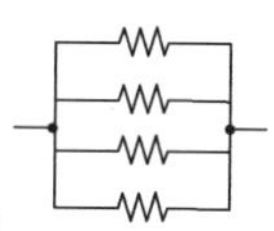

3. Use this circuit diagram to answer the questions below.

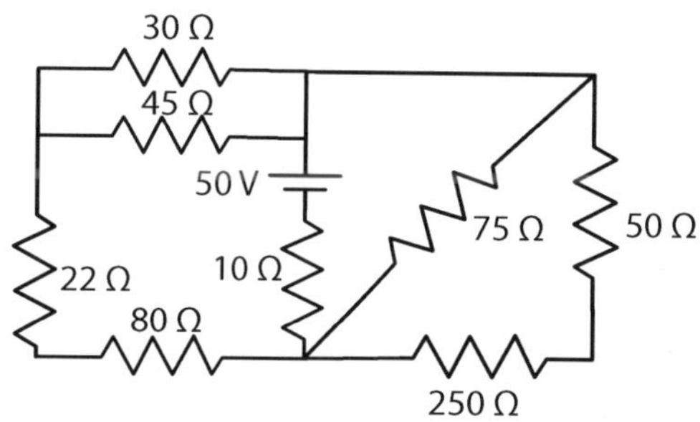

(a) What is the equivalent resistance of the entire circuit?

(b) What current is drawn from the battery?

(c) What is the current in the 50 Ω resistor?

(d) What is the voltage across the 22 Ω resistor?

4. What is the current in the ammeter A in this circuit?

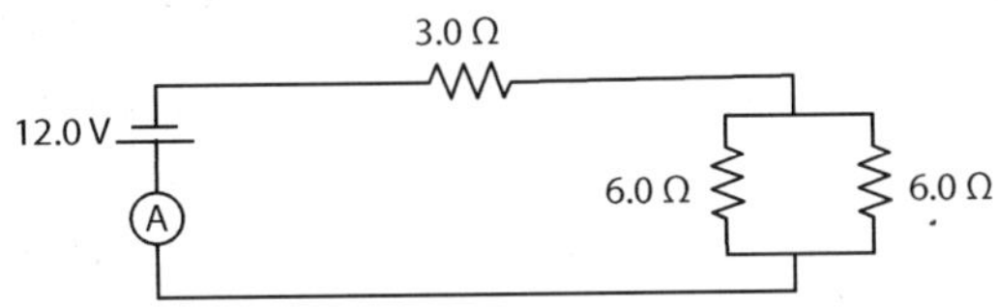

5. What is the emf of the battery if the current in A is 1.2 A and the internal resistance of the battery is 0.0833 Ω in this circuit?

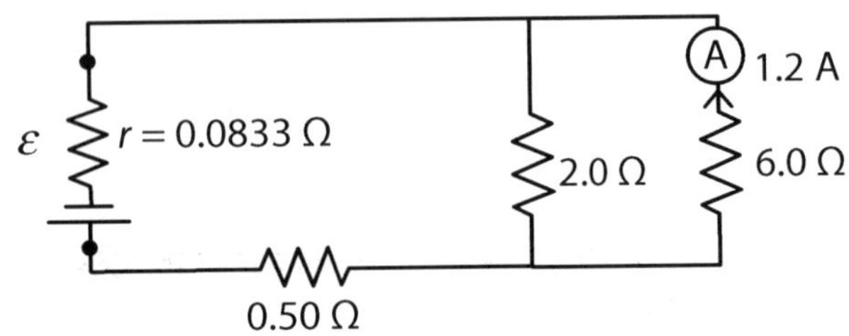

6. What is the voltage V of the power supply in the circuit below?

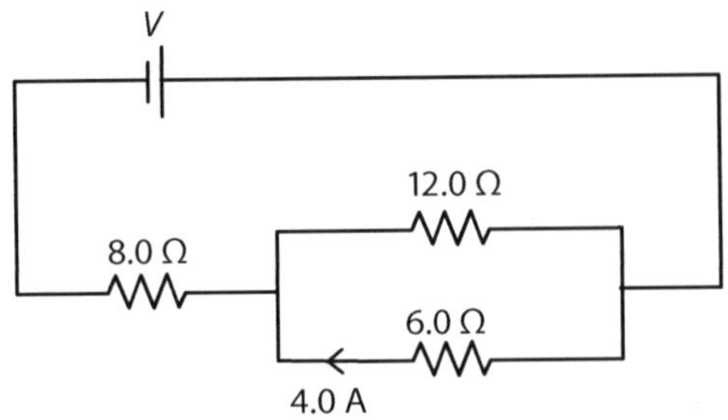

7. What is the internal resistance of the battery shown here?

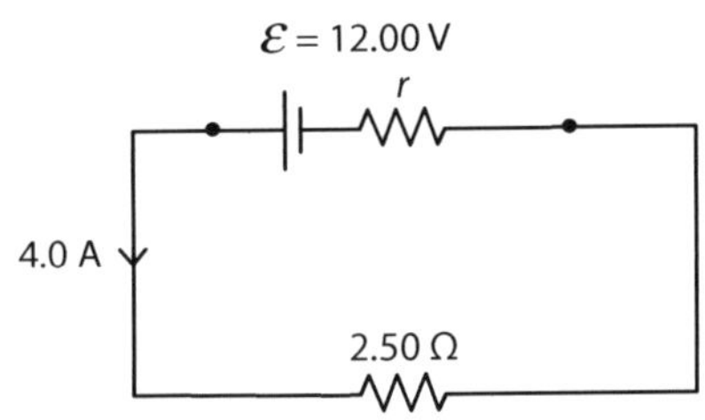

8. Use this circuit diagram to answer the questions below.

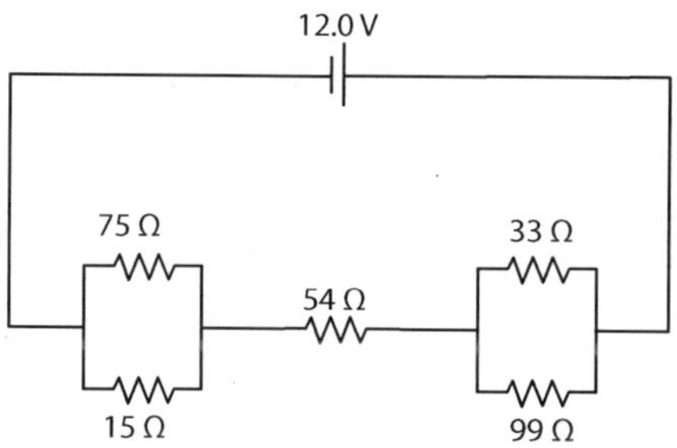

(a) What is the equivalent resistance of this circuit?

(b) What is the current through the 54 Ω resistor?

(c) How much power is dissipated in the 54 Ω resistor?

9. Use this circuit diagram to answer the questions below.

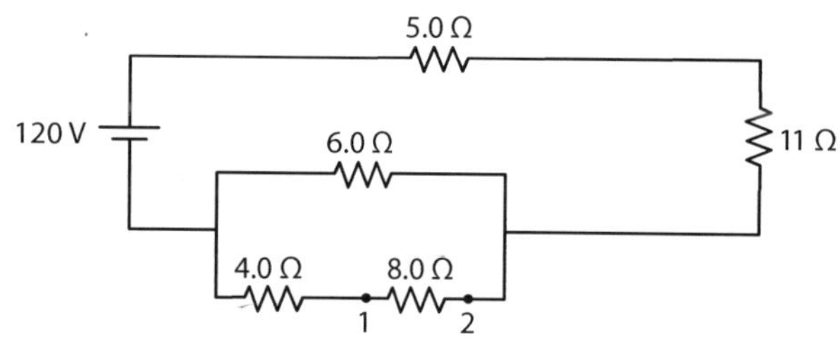

(a) What is the voltage across the 8.0 Ω resistor (between 1 and 2)?

(b) How much power is dissipated in the 5.0 Ω resistor?

Chapter 6 Review Questions

1. What is the difference between the terminal voltage of a battery and its emf?

2. What current exists in a wire if 2.4×10^3 C of charge pass through a point in the wire in a time of 6.0×10^1 s?

3. The current through an ammeter is 5.0 A. In one day, how many electrons will pass through the ammeter?

4. How much silver will be electroplated by a current of 0.255 A in one day?

5. A mercury cell has an emf of 1.35 V and an internal resistance of 0.041 Ω. If it is used in a circuit that draws 1.50 A, what will its terminal voltage be?

6. A set of eight decorative light bulbs is plugged into a 120 V wall receptacle. What is the potential difference across each light bulb filament, if the eight light bulbs are connected:

   (a) in series?

   (b) in parallel?

7. What is the resistance of a resistor if a potential difference of 36 V between its ends results in a current of 1.20 mA?

8. What is the potential difference (voltage) between the ends of a resistor if 24.0 J of work must be done to drive 0.30 C of charge through the resistor?

9. A resistor has the following coloured bands: brown, black, yellow, and gold. What is the manufacturer's rating of the resistance of this resistor?

10. You need a 4.7 MΩ resistor from a box of miscellaneous resistors. What coloured bands should you look for in your collection?

11. A 2.2 kΩ resistor is rated at ½ W. What is the highest voltage you could safely apply to the resistor without risking damage to it from overheating?

12. What current will a 1500 W kettle draw from a 120 V source?

13. A toaster draws 8.0 A on a 120 V circuit. What is its power rating?

14. A 60.0 W light bulb and a 40.0 W light bulb are connected in parallel in a 120 V circuit. What is the equivalent resistance of the two light bulbs?

15. A circuit in your house has the following appliances plugged into it: a 1500 W kettle, a 150 W light, and a 900 W toaster. The circuit is protected by a 20 A circuit breaker. If the house voltage is 120 V, will the circuit breaker be activated? Explain your answer.

16. How many kW•h of energy will a 400 W television set use in one month, if it is turned on for an average of 5.0 h per day? What will it cost you at $0.06/kW•h?

17. The cell in the diagram below is short-circuited with a wire of resistance 0.10 Ω. What is the terminal voltage under these conditions?

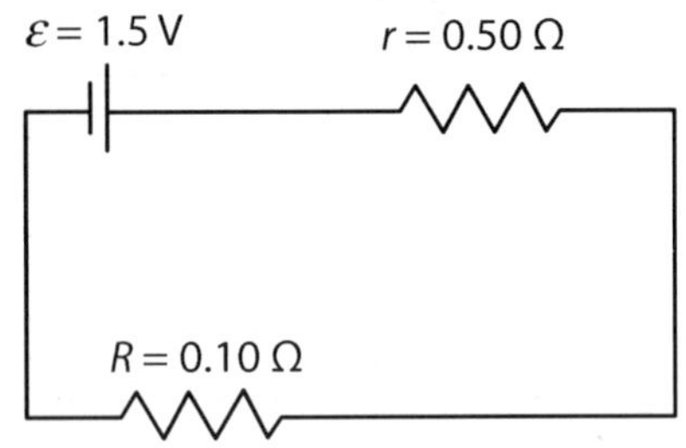

18. A storage battery has an emf of 12.0 V. What is the terminal voltage if a current of 150 A is drawn just as the starter motor is turned on? The internal resistance is 0.030 Ω.

19. What is the equivalent resistance of resistors of 8.0 Ω, 12.0 Ω, and 24.0 Ω if they are connected

(a) in series?

(b) in parallel?

20. A resistor is intended to have a resistance of 60.00 Ω, but when checked it is found to be 60.07 Ω. What resistance might you put in parallel with it to obtain an equivalent resistance of 60.00 Ω?

21. A 12.0 Ω resistor and a 6.0 Ω resistor are connected in series with a 9.0 V battery. What is the voltage across the 6.0 Ω resistor?

22. What is the resistance R in diagram below, if the current through the battery is 5.0 A?

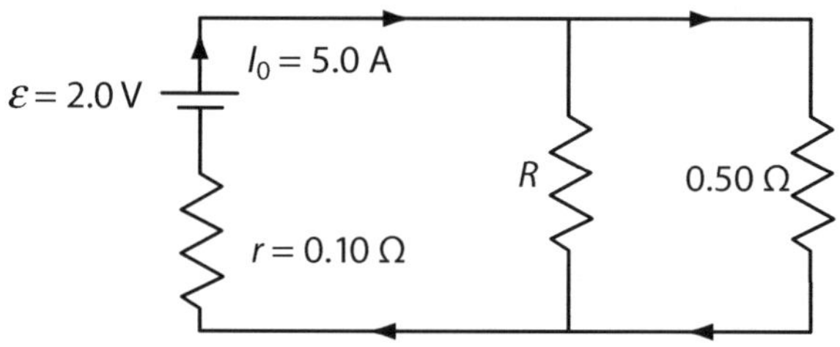

23. You have three 6.0 kΩ resistors. By combining these three resistors in different combinations, how many different equivalent resistances can you obtain with them? (All three must be used.)

24. For each circuit, find
(i) the equivalent resistance of the entire circuit, and
(ii) the current at the point marked I.

(a)

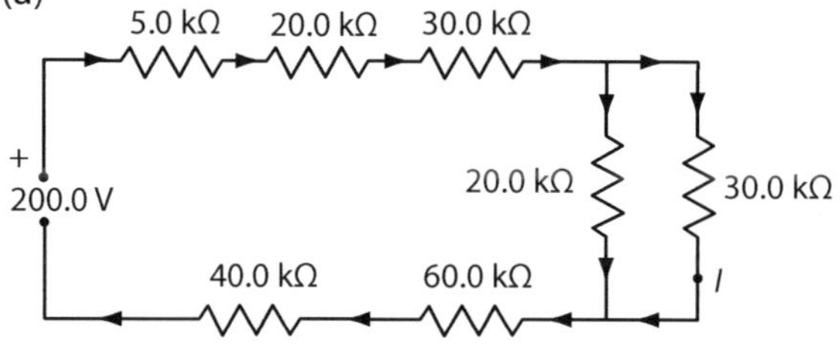

(b)

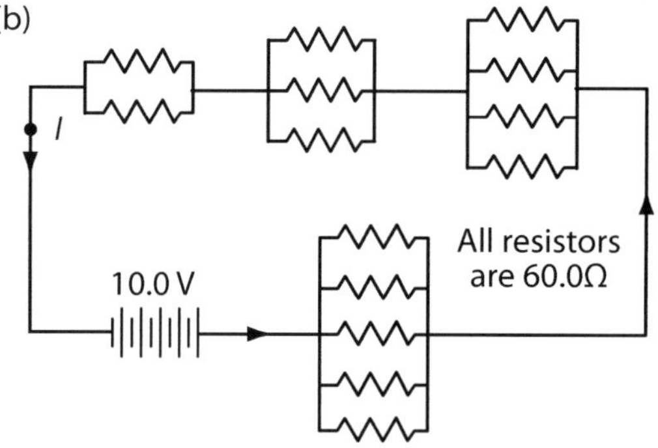

(c)

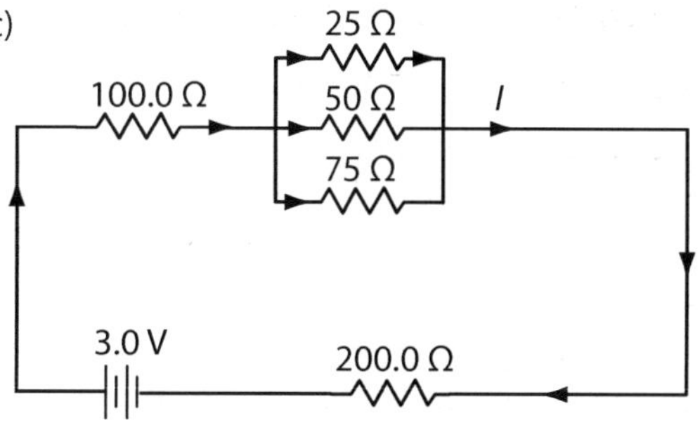

25. What is the voltage across the 6.0 Ω resistor in the diagram below?

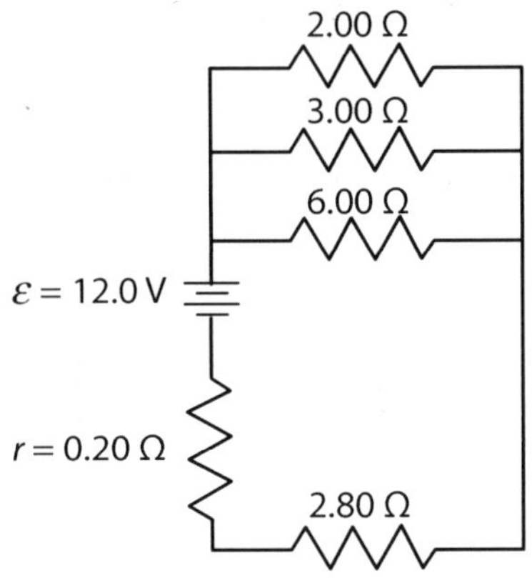

26. Twelve identical pieces of resistance wire, each of resistance 1.0 Ω, are formed into a cubical resistance network, shown in the diagram below. If a current of 12 A enters one corner of the cube and leaves at the other corner, what is the equivalent resistance of the cube between the opposite corners? Use Kirchhoff's laws.

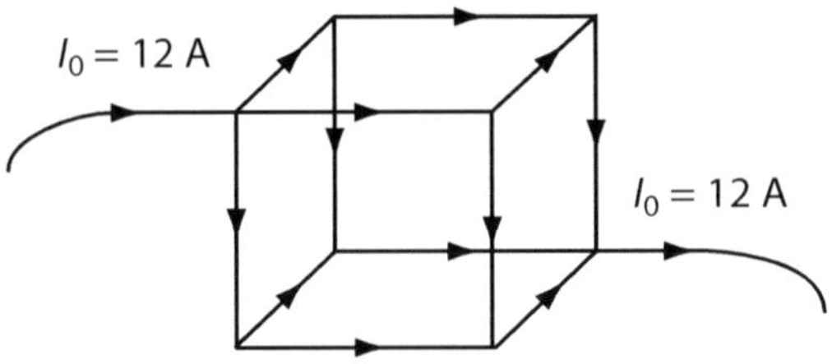

Chapter 6 Extra Practice

1. What are appropriate units for current?

2. How do the readings on voltmeters 1 and 2 change when the resistor R is added to the circuit as shown in circuit 2?

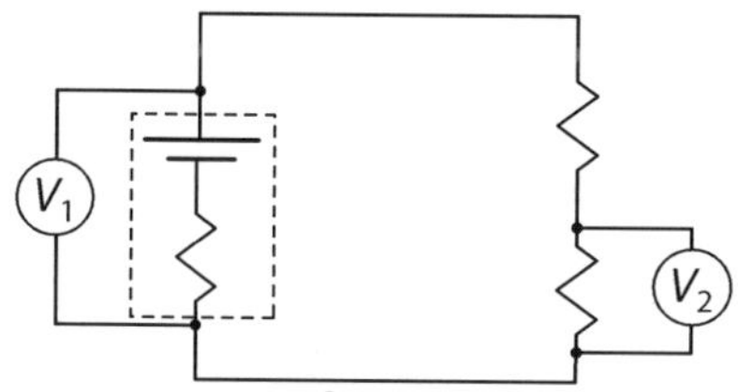

Circuit 1

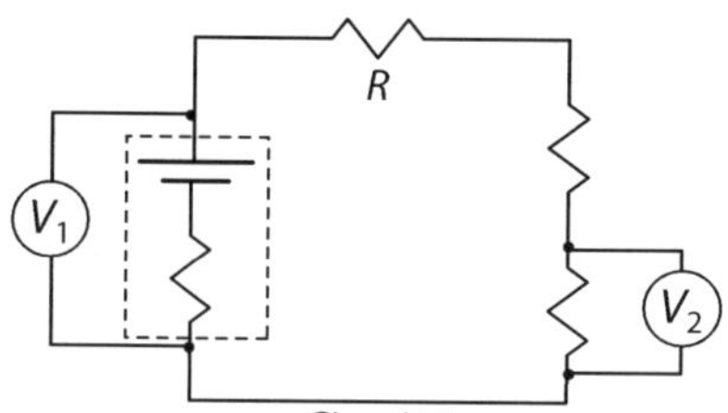

Circuit 2

3. What is the total resistance of this circuit?

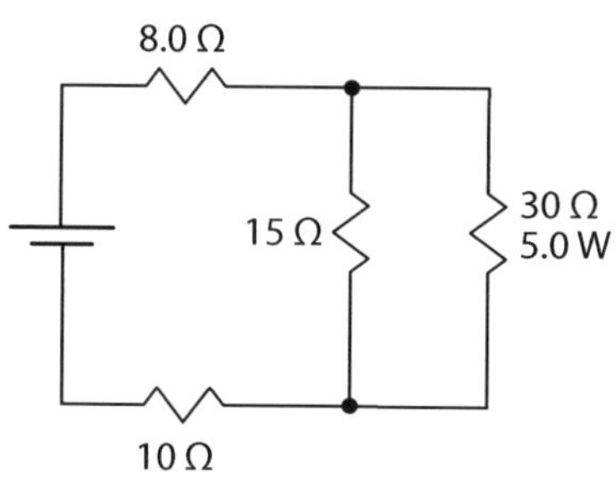

4. What is the current through the 20 Ω resistor?

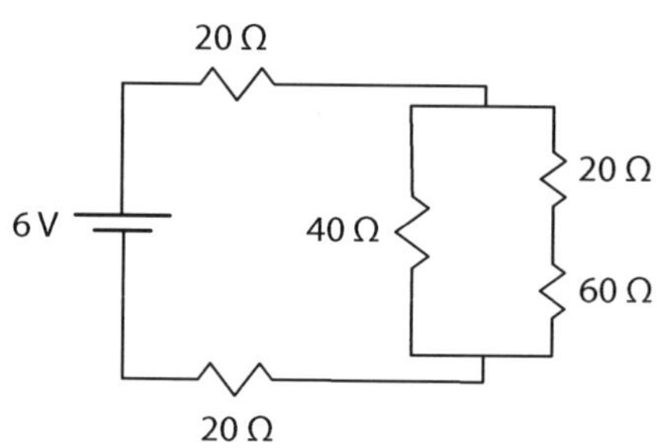

5. What is the current through R_2?

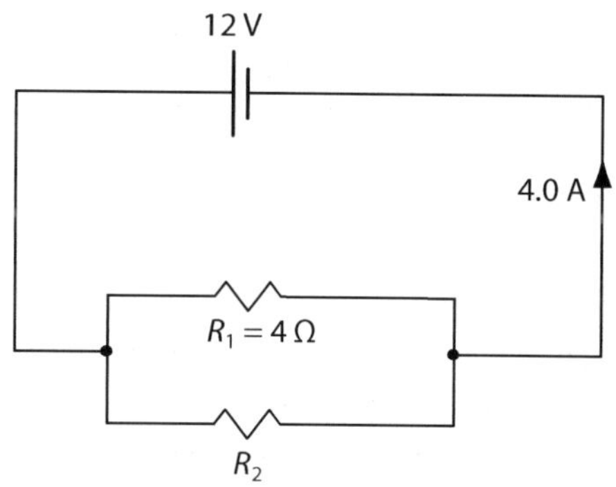

6. In what combination and how many 160 Ω resistors can be connected to draw a current of 6.0 A from a 120 V source? (Use the fewest number of resistors possible.)

7. A 12.0 Ω resistor is connected to a 24 V battery. What is the total charge that flows through the resistor in 1 min?

8. Given that the potential difference across the 5.0 Ω resistor is 2.0 V, find the current through the battery.

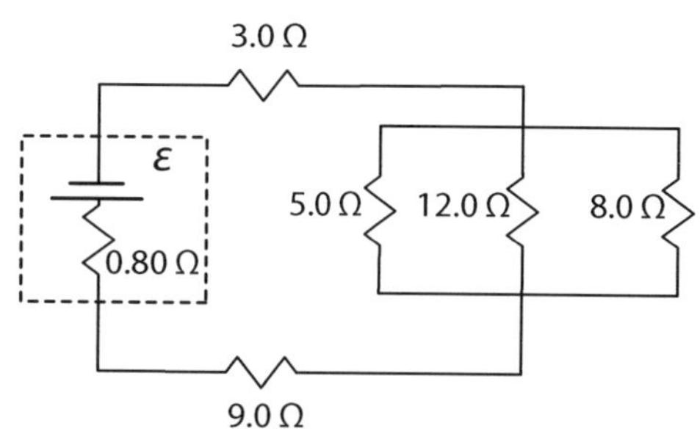

9. Given that the current through the battery is 1.2 A, what is the value of the unknown resistor R?

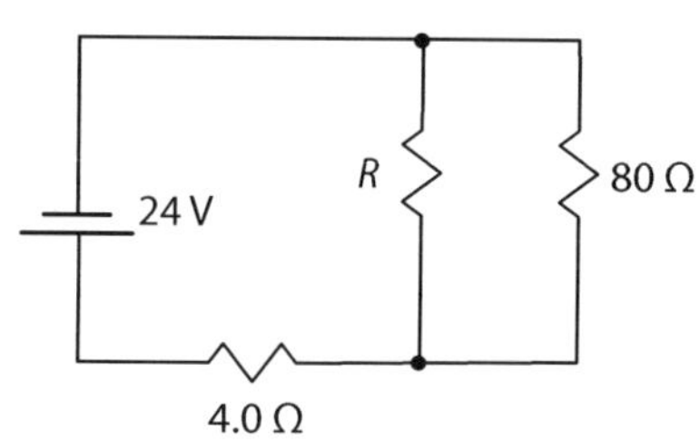

10. What happens to the terminal voltage of the cell when the switch is changed from closed (as shown) to open?

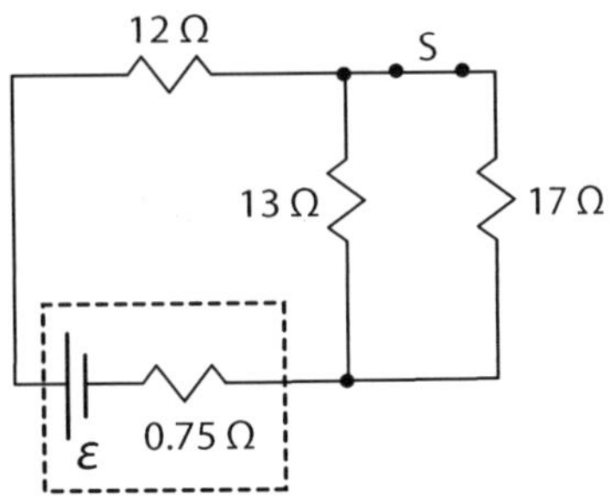

11. Where is the current in this circuit the lowest magnitude?

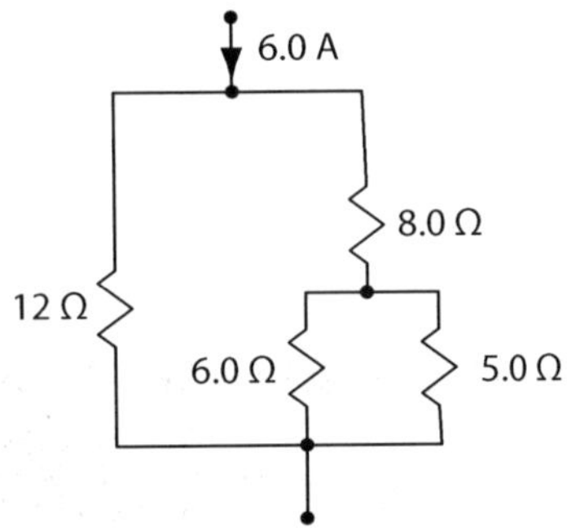

12. Where should you place a voltmeter(s) to calculate the potential difference of the voltage source?

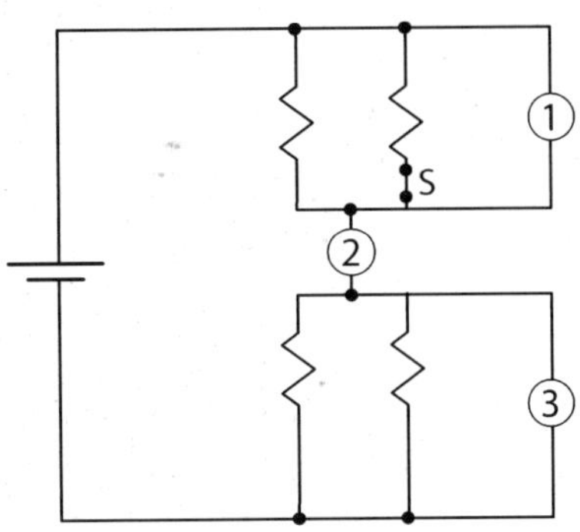

13. A battery has an internal resistance of 0.50 Ω. A voltmeter is hooked up to the terminals of the battery and reads 9.0 V when there is no current. What does the voltmeter read when there is a current of 1.2 A flowing through the battery?

14. What is the potential difference across the 15 Ω resistor?

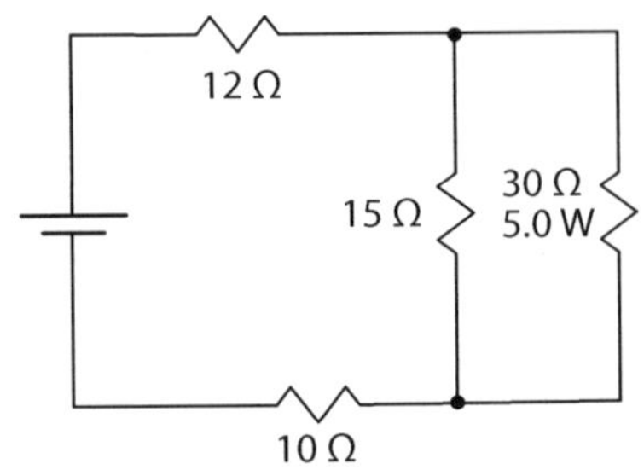

15. What is the power dissipated in this entire circuit?

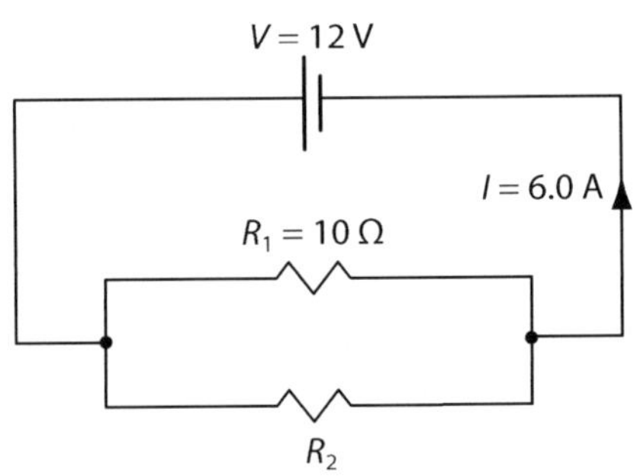

7 Magnetic Forces

By the end of this chapter, you should be able to do the following:

- Analyze electromagnetism, with reference to magnetic fields and their effects on moving charges

By the end of this chapter, you should know the meaning of these **key terms**:

- Ampère's law for solenoids
- Ampère's rule
- bar magnet
- electromagnet
- magnetic field line
- magnetic force
- magnetic pole
- mass spectrometer
- right hand motor rule
- solenoid
- split-ring commutator
- tesla

By the end of this chapter, you should be able to use and know when to use the following formulae:

$F = BQv$

$B = \mu_0 nI = \mu_0 \dfrac{N}{\ell} I$

$F = BI\ell$

Charged particles giving off light energy as the particles move through Earth's magnetic field create a light show called the northern lights or aurora borealis.

7.1 Basic Ideas about Magnets

Warm Up

Recall your previous experiences with magnets. Are the magnetic poles of magnets similar to electric charges or are they different? Explain your thinking.

____

____

____

Permanent Magnets

If a magnet is suspended from a string or supported at its centre of gravity so that it is free to rotate, it will turn until one end of it points toward the north. The end that points north is called the *north-seeking* or **north pole**. The opposite end is the *south-seeking* or **south pole**. This property of magnets has been used in compasses for many centuries.

Two magnets placed close together will exert a force on each other. If two *like* poles are near each other, they will *repel* each other. Two *unlike* poles will *attract* each other (Figure 7.1.1).

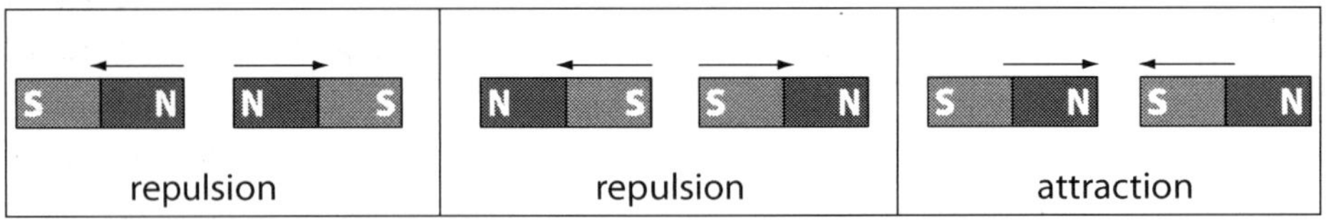

Figure 7.1.1 *If two north poles or two south poles are nearby, they will repel each other. If a north pole and a south pole are nearby will attract each other.*

Like poles repel each other. Opposite poles attract each other.

Bar magnets are examples of *permanent* magnets, because they stay magnetized (if handled carefully) for a long time. **Electromagnets** are magnetized only while there is electric current in them.

Permanent magnets found in school laboratories are usually made of some kind of steel alloy. **Alnico** magnets are especially strong. They are made from an alloy that contains cobalt, nickel, iron, and the non-magnetic element aluminum.

Only a few elements are strongly magnetic. The three best-known magnetic elements are iron, nickel, and cobalt. These are called **ferromagnetic** elements (after the Latin *ferrum*, which means iron). Less well-known ferromagnetic elements include the rare-earth elements neodymium and gadolinium.

The naturally occurring mineral **magnetite**, also called **lodestone** (an iron oxide with the formula Fe_3O_4), is strongly magnetic. Its magnetic properties have been known since ancient times.

Magnetic Fields and Lines of Force

Just as there is a gravitational field around any massive body and an electrical field around a charged body, there is a magnetic field around any magnet. Figure 7.1.2 depicts the **magnetic field** around a bar magnet. A series of **lines of force** show the direction of the field at any point. The direction of a magnetic line of force is taken to be the direction that an isolated north pole (if one existed) would tend to move in that region of the field. The direction of the field at any point can be determined by using a small compass needle. Its north end will point in the direction of the field at that point.

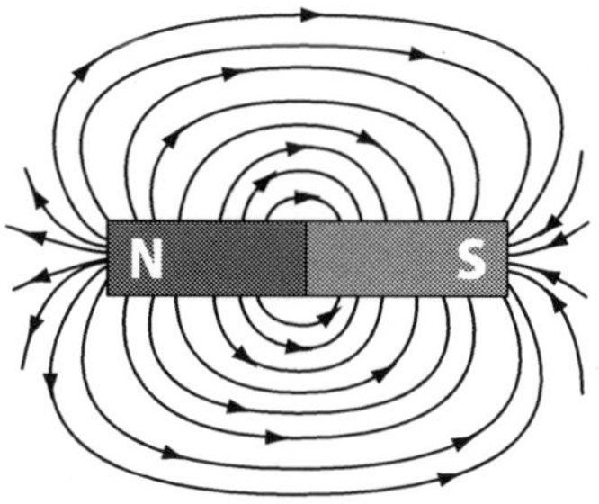

Figure 7.1.2 *Magnetic field lines around a bar magnet*

If fine iron filings are sprinkled on a piece of white cardboard that sits on top of a magnet, the overall shape of the field can be seen. The tiny iron filings become magnets themselves in the field of the permanent magnet. Figure 7.1.3 shows the shape of the field around (a) a single bar magnet, (b) two bar magnets with like poles facing each other, and (c) two bar magnets with opposite poles facing each other.

Notice that the lines of force are closest together near the poles, and farthest apart at distances well away from the poles. Iron filings tend to bunch up near the poles, suggesting that the field is strongest near the poles. Another observation you might make from the diagrams is that the lines of force do not cross each other.

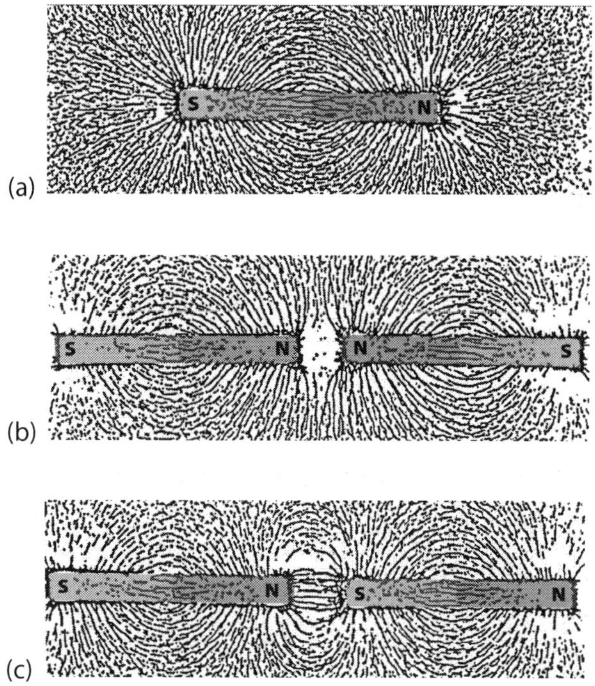

Figure 7.1.3 *Magnetic field lines around bar magnets*

Electromagnets

In 1820, a Danish physicist named Hans Christian Oersted (1777–1851) made a chance observation, which turned out to be one of the most important discoveries ever made by a scientist. He was using a simple electric circuit, consisting of a wire connected to a battery. He happened to notice that a compass needle nearby was deflected from its normal north-south alignment when current existed in the wire. (Figure 7.1.4). When the battery was disconnected, the compass needle returned to its normal position.

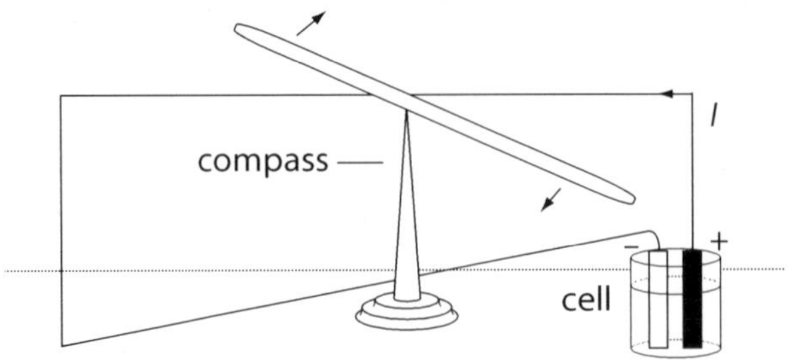

Figure 7.1.4 *A compass needle deflected by a current in a wire*

If the needle deflected in one direction when it was held *above* the conducting wire, it would reverse direction when held *below* the wire. Experiments showed that the magnetic field around the conductor appeared to be *circular* and only existed if there was current in the wire.

André Ampère (1775–1836), a French physicist, quickly followed up on Oersted's discovery by investigating magnetic fields caused by electric currents in conductors of various shapes and sizes. Some of his conclusions will be outlined later in this chapter.

In Figure 7.1.5, a piece of heavy gauge copper wire has been poked through a white file card, which sits on a paper cup for support. A high current from a rechargeable battery was passed through the wire, and iron filings were sprinkled on the card. The diagram shows the circular shape of the lines of force in the magnetic field around the wire. Since the filings are most crowded near the wire, and spread out farther away from the wire, it appears that the strength of the field falls off with distance from the wire. Ampère showed that the magnetic field strength near a long straight piece of wire is inversely proportional to the distance from the wire.

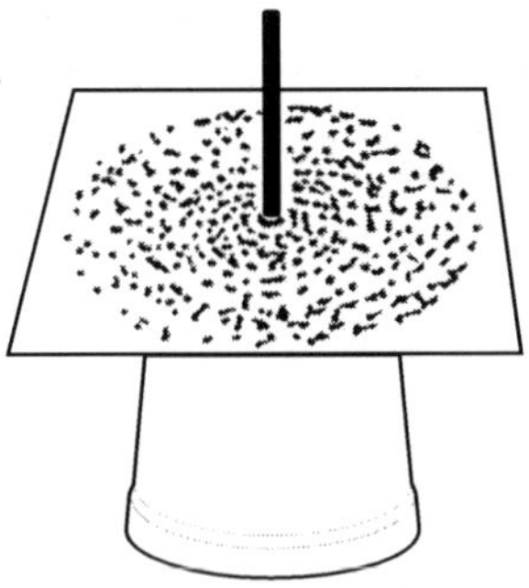

Figure 7.1.5 *Magnetic field lines around a copper wire carrying a current*

If a wire is formed into a single turn, the magnetic field looks like Figure 7.1.6 (a). When a long coil with many turns is constructed, the coil is called a **solenoid**. Figure 7.1.6 (b) shows the shape of the magnetic field around and inside a solenoid. Notice the strong similarity to the field around a bar magnet (Figure 7.1.3). Inside the solenoid, the lines of force run parallel with each other. The magnetic field inside a solenoid is uniform for the entire length of the solenoid.

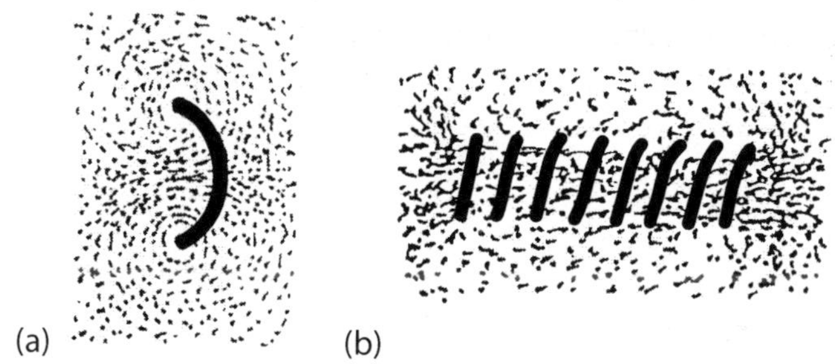

Figure 7.1.6 *(a) Magnetic field lines around a curved wire. (b) Magnetic field lines around and through a solenoid*

While iron filings show the shape of the field nicely, they do not indicate its direction. A small compass needle can be used for that purpose. When the direction of the lines of force around a conductor is established using a compass needle, a definite pattern can be seen, which is best expressed by **Ampère's rule**, sometimes called the **right hand rule.** Figure 7.1.7 illustrates the right hand rule for a straight conductor.

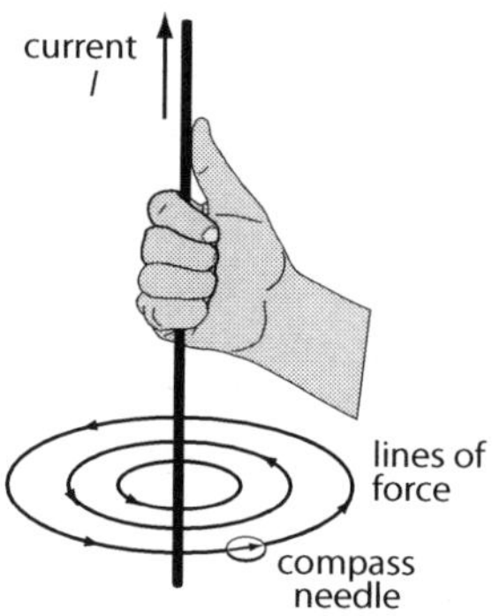

Figure 7.1.7 *Ampère's rule or the right hand rule: your thumb points in the direction of the current and your fingers curving around the wire show the direction of the magnetic field.*

This can also be demonstrated by a compass placed on top of and under a current-carrying conductor (Figure 7.1.8). The magnetic field formed around the current in the conductor caused the north-pointing needle of the compass to align in the direction of the magnetic field.

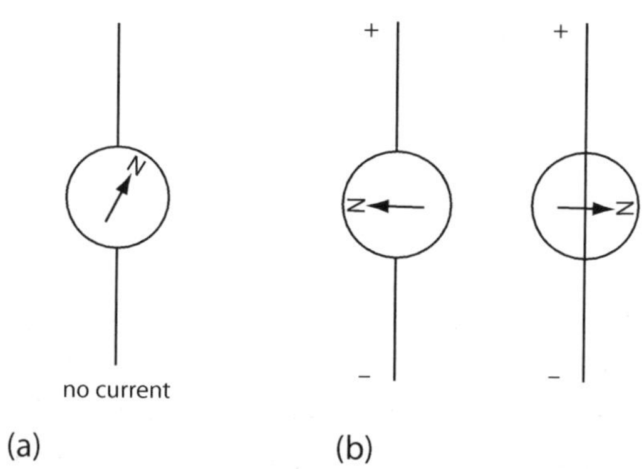

Figure 7.1.8 *A compass placed on top of a wire will align with the direction of the magnetic field that occurs when a current is passing through the wire.*

Right Hand Rule for Straight Conductors
Imagine you are holding the conductor in your right hand, with your thumb pointing in the direction of conventional current (the direction that positive charges would like to move). Then your fingers will curl in the same direction as the magnetic lines of force.

Ampère's right hand rule for a straight conductor will work with a single loop of wire (Figure 7.1.9(a)) or with a single turn of a solenoid (Figure 7.1.9(b)). Notice that inside the solenoid, the lines of force go from south to north. Outside the solenoid, the lines go from north to south, as you observed with a bar magnet.

With either a single loop or a solenoid, there is a north pole and a south pole, as with a bar magnet. It is assumed that within a bar magnet the iron atoms obtain their magnetism from the motion of electrons within them.

The movement of electrons around the nucleus produces a magnetic effect in any atom, but the overall effect of the motions is small. There are as many electrons orbiting in one direction as in the other, so that magnetic effects tend to cancel. In most atoms, the spins of the electrons, which also produce a magnetic effect, tend to cancel each other's effects as well. In ferromagnetic elements, however, there appears to be an imbalance in the spins that produces a strong magnetic field in their atoms. Ferromagnetism is a complicated subject, which must be left for more advanced courses.

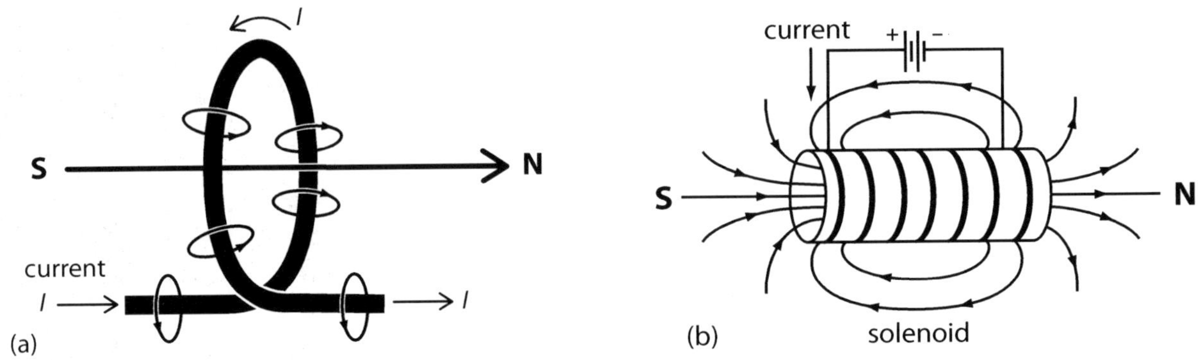

Figure 7.1.9 *Ampère's rule or the right hand rule will work for either a single loop of wire or a solenoid.*

If an iron core is placed inside a solenoid, the iron core itself becomes magnetized. When the atoms of iron add their magnetic strength to that of the solenoid, the magnetic field strength of the combination far exceeds that of the solenoid itself. The combination of a solenoid and an iron core is called an **electromagnet.**

Electromagnets have many, many uses. Every transformer, motor, generator, doorbell, loudspeaker, and junkyard magnet has an electromagnet inside it. Since Oersted's discovery in 1820, scientists and engineers have found countless ways of using electromagnetism!

Quick Check

1. In Figure 7.1.10, the conductor on the left carries current "into the page." The conductor on the right carries current "out of the page."

Figure 7.1.10

(a) Draw sample lines of force around each conductor, showing their direction.

(b) Would these conductors attract each other or repel each other? Explain your answer. (**Hint:** If you place two bar magnets side by side so that the lines of force of their magnetic fields are in the same direction, how do the magnets affect each other?)

2. Which end of the solenoid (A or B) in Figure 7.1.11 will be north?

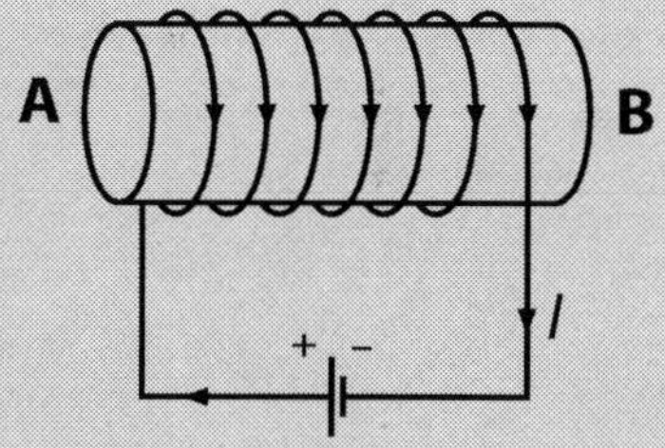

Figure 7.1.11

How Magnetic Fields Affect Moving Charged Particles

Consider a solitary charged particle, perhaps a single electron or proton. In an electric field, there will be a force on that charged particle, and it will accelerate because of the electric force on it. The charged particle will be affected by an electric field whether the charged particle is initially stationary or already moving.

Curiously, a magnetic field has no apparent effect on a stationary charged particle. Once a charged particle is moving, however, it may experience a force in the presence of a magnetic field. What determines whether there will be a force on a moving charged particle and what the direction and strength of the force will be? Investigation 7.1.1 will look at some of the factors involved. First, we'll consider the direction of the force on a moving electron.

Magnetic Force on a Beam of Electrons

Figure 7.1.12 shows a simple cathode ray tube (CRT), which allows a narrow beam of electrons to pass through a slit (visible on the left) and strike a fluorescent screen, so that the path of the electrons can easily be seen on the screen. In Figure 7.1.12, the lines of magnetic force due to the bar magnet are directed out of the page into the south pole of the bar magnet. As you can see, the electrons are pushed upward. The moving charges are *not* attracted to the poles of the magnet, but are deflected in a direction perpendicular to the magnetic field.

In the situation in Figure 7.1.12, the velocity, the field, and the force are all mutually perpendicular.

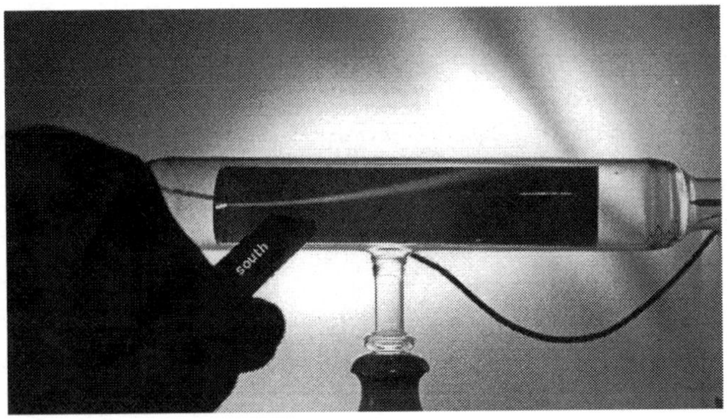

Figure 7.1.12 *The cathode rays curve upward in this photo of a CRT.*

Another Rule of Thumb: The Right Hand Motor Rule

If you experimented with the apparatus in Figure 7.1.12, varying the alignment of the bar magnet in every way you can, you would find that the direction of the deflection of the electron beam is predictable.

There is a convenient rule of thumb for predicting the direction in which a beam of charged particles will be deflected by a magnetic field. It is called the **right hand motor rule** (for reasons you will understand better when you look closely at how an electric motor works). To predict the direction of the magnetic force on moving charged particles:

(1) Point your thumb in the direction that positively charged particles would move (the direction of conventional current).

(2) Point your fingers in the direction of the magnetic field (from north to south).

(3) Your palm now faces in the direction that the positive charges would be pushed by the magnetic field. See Figure 7.1.13.

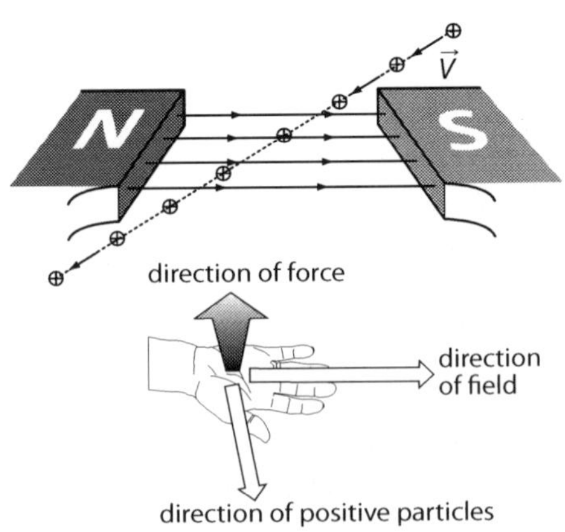

Figure 7.1.13 *The right hand motor rule*

In Figure 7.1.12, electrons (negatively charged) move from left to right, therefore the direction of conventional current is from right to left. The magnetic field in Figure 7.1.12 is "out of the page." Use the right hand rule for the situation in Figure 7.1.12, and it should predict a force upward, as is the case in the figure.

Investigation 7.1.1 Deflecting a Beam of Electrons Using a Magnetic Field

Purpose

To investigate the deflection of electron beams by magnetic fields, using a laboratory cathode ray tube

Introduction

In Investigation 5.2.1 in Chapter 5, you observed that the deflection y of an electron moving in an electric field was proportional to the electric field strength $\vec{E}$. The experiment actually showed that y was proportional to the deflecting voltage V_δ, which produces the electric field.

$$\text{Since } \vec{E} = V_\delta / d \text{ and } d \text{ is constant, then } y \propto \vec{E}.$$

In this Investigation, you will use a solenoid carrying known currents to produce a magnetic field. This magnetic field will be used to deflect electrons moving through a cathode ray tube (CRT). You will also vary the *accelerating voltage* of the CRT to see how changing the speed of the electrons affects the deflection.

Comparing Forces

For any body acted on by a constant, unbalanced force F, there is an acceleration a causing a displacement y in time t.

$$y = \frac{1}{2}at^2$$

For an electron travelling through a field exerting a constant force F, if the electron is travelling at speed v and the length of the field region is ℓ, and the mass of the electron is m, then

$$y = \frac{1}{2}\frac{F}{m} \bullet \frac{\ell^2}{v^2}$$

If the same accelerating voltage V_a is used throughout an experiment, then speed v will be constant. Since m and are also constant, this means that

$$y = \text{constant} \cdot F$$

$$\text{or } y \propto F$$

If the accelerating voltage is kept constant, you can use the deflection of the beam as a means of comparing magnetic forces.

Strictly speaking, the magnetic force on an electron moving through a magnetic field *cannot* be constant (except in magnitude) because the direction of the force is continually changing! If, however, the beam deflection is kept *small*, you can assume that the force is essentially constant throughout the field, and assume with little error that $y \propto F$.

General Information

In this investigation, the X and Y deflecting plates are not used at all.

All four plates (X_1, X_2, Y_1, and Y_2) should be connected to the second anode A_2 so that they are at the same potential as A_2 and cause no deflection whatever.

To obtain a uniform field, arrange two solenoids in series, as shown in Figure 7.1.14, so that they can be left in exactly the same position around the base of the CRT throughout this entire experiment. Use a small compass to check that the coils are wired such that if pole A is north, pole B is south (or vice versa). The experiment requires that lines of force run approximately "straight" through the base of the CRT. Use books or other supporting material to ensure that the solenoids are at the same level as the base of the CRT.

A variable resistor (rheostat) is used to vary the current in the solenoids. The ammeter measures the current in the solenoids. The reversing switch allows you to reverse the direction of the current in the solenoids, which reverses the magnetic field direction and therefore the deflection direction. To measure deflection caused by a given current, pass that current through the solenoids and mark the position of the beam on the screen. Reverse the current and mark the new position. Measure the total change, divide by two, and you have a good measure of the average deflection caused by that particular current in the solenoids. Call this deflection δ.

Part 1

Problem

To determine how the deflection of an electron beam depends on the current in the solenoids whose magnetic field is causing the deflection

Procedure

1. Set up the apparatus as in Figure 7.1.14. Set the accelerating voltage V_a at 750 V, and leave it there throughout Part 1. Make sure that all deflecting plates are connected to A_2.
2. With a current of, for example, 1.0 A in the solenoids, mark the position of the beam. Reverse the current with the reversing switch. Mark the new position and measure the distance between the two marks. Divide this distance in two to get the average deflection caused by 1.0 A in the solenoids.
3. Repeat step 2 with at least four other currents in the solenoid.
4. Prepare a graph of deflection δ vs. solenoid current I.

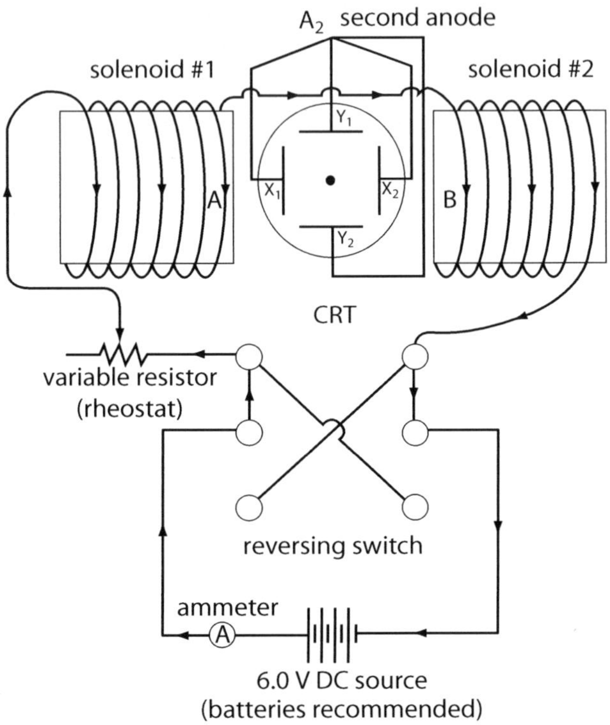

Figure 7.1.14

Concluding Questions

1. How does the deflection of the beam depend on solenoid current? Express your answer in an equation, complete with a numerical value for the slope, in appropriate units.
2. If $\delta \propto y$, and $y \propto F$, how does the magnetic force depend on the solenoid current?

Part 2

Problem

To determine how the deflection of the beam of electrons depends on the accelerating voltage, if the solenoid current is kept constant

Procedure

1. Set the solenoid current at a fixed value, such as 4.0 A. Do not vary this current throughout this part of the experiment.

> To vary the electron speed, you have to vary the accelerating voltage V_a. (Recall from Chapter 5 that V_a equals the gain in kinetic energy per unit charge of the accelerated electrons, so $V_a = ½mv^2/Q$.) Your CRT is labelled with accelerating voltages of, for example, 500 V, 750 V, and 1000 V. *These labelled values must be checked with a voltmeter, since they are only approximate.*

2. Measure the average deflection δ for at least three different accelerating voltages. (You will probably have to refocus the beam when you change accelerating voltages.)
3. Plot a graph of average deflection δ vs. accelerating voltage, V_a.
4. Make an educated guess at the power-law relation between δ and V_a, and plot a second graph that will give you a straight line.

Concluding Questions

1. Write an equation that describes how deflection varies with accelerating voltage, when an electron moves through a magnetic field. Include a numerical value for your slope, complete with proper units.
2. The accelerating voltage is $V_a = \frac{1}{2}\frac{mv^2}{Q}$. Work out a relationship between beam deflection and electron speed. In

   other words, how does δ vary with v?
3. In the Introduction it was shown that $y = \frac{1}{2}at^2 = \frac{1}{2}\frac{F}{m} \cdot \frac{\ell^2}{v^2}$. Since m and ℓ are constant in Part 2 (speed v is a variable this time), we can say that $y \propto \frac{F}{v^2}$, and since $y \propto \delta$, therefore $\delta \propto \frac{F}{v^2}$. How does the magnetic force vary with the electron speed?
4. What is a simple way to tell whether a deflection on a CRT screen is caused by an electric field or a magnetic field?
5. What are some sources of error in this experiment?

7.1 Review Questions

1. You are experimenting with two identical permanent magnets. One magnet is coloured blue, and the other is coloured red. If the blue magnet attracts the red magnet with a force of 75.0 N, what is the force of attraction between the red and the blue magnet?

2. Explain how you could determine the north and south poles of an unlabelled magnet.

3. If four compasses are arranged around a magnet as shown in the diagram below, in what direction will the north end of each compass needle point? Draw the needles in the diagram.

4. One magnet is suspended by a string and a second magnet is brought close to it, as shown below. Draw the magnetic field lines around both magnets when they interact, but do not touch.

5. What will happen to the suspended magnet as a second magnet is brought close?

6. Draw the direction the compass needle will point when the compass is placed on the current-carrying conductor in each diagram below.

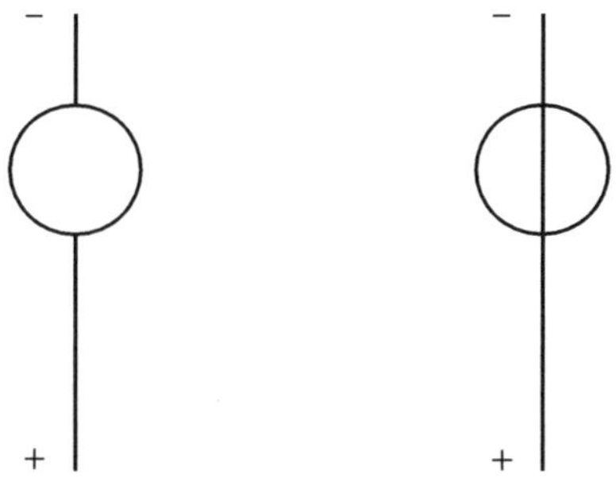

(a) (b)

7. Draw the direction of the magnetic field inside the loops and outside the loops in the figure below.

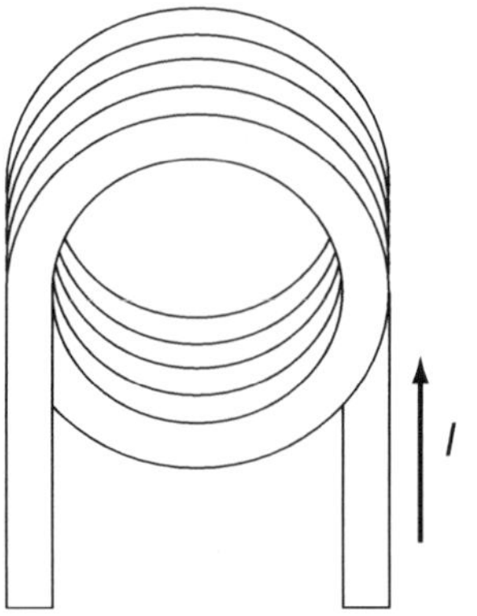

8. In which direction will the force be directed when a current is passed through the conductor positioned between two magnets as shown in the diagram below?

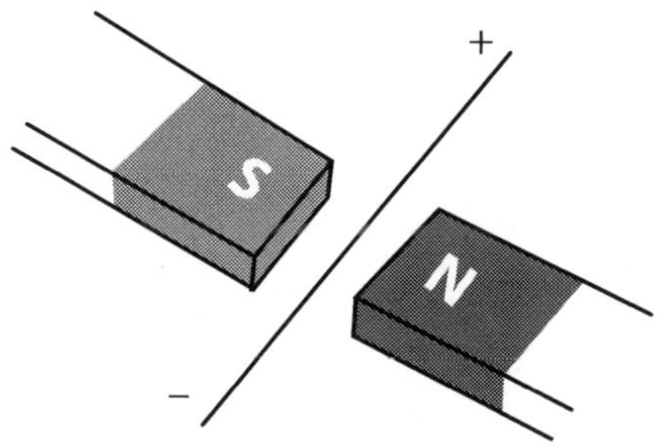

9. When the solenoid current in the arrangement used in Investigation 7.1.1 is 2.2 A, the beam in the CRT is deflected 1.2 cm. What will the deflection be if the solenoid current is increased to 3.6 A?

10. The deflection on a CRT screen is 1.4 cm when the accelerating voltage is 500 V. If the solenoid current is kept constant, what will happen to the magnetic deflection in the following cases?
    (a) The accelerating voltage is increased to four times its original value.

    (b) The electron speed is increased four times.

11. The deflection on a CRT screen is 1.2 cm when the solenoid current is 1.5 A and the accelerating voltage is 500. V. If the solenoid current is changed to 3.0 A, what accelerating voltage is needed to maintain the same deflection?

12. While holding a magnet in one hand you suspend five nails in a row from the south pole of the magnet. What is the induced pole on the last nail hanging at the bottom of the five nails?

7.2 Magnetic Field Strength, B

Warm Up

When you move a magnetic through a solenoid, a current is produced. Set up a circuit with a solenoid and galvanometer. Using one or more magnets, find and record at least two ways to create a larger current through the solenoid.

____

____

____

Calculating Magnetic Field Strength

Investigation 7.1.1 suggests, in a roundabout way, that the magnetic force that a charged particle experiences while travelling through a magnetic field depends directly on the speed of the particle. It is a curious fact that the faster a charged particle travels, the greater the force exerted on it by a magnetic field.

$$F \propto v$$

Other experiments show that the magnetic force on a charged particle moving through a magnetic field depends directly on the amount of charge on the particle. That is, $F \propto Q$.

If $F \propto v$ and $F \propto Q$, then $\qquad F \propto Qv$

Therefore, $\qquad \dfrac{F}{Qv} = \text{constant}$

The constant ratio $\left(\dfrac{F}{Qv}\right)$ can be used as a measure of the **magnetic field strength** ($\vec{B}$) at the point in the magnetic field where the moving charge is passing. The dimensions of the units for magnetic field strength are

$$1\,\frac{\text{N}}{\text{C}\frac{\text{m}}{\text{s}}} = 1\,\frac{\text{N}}{\text{A}\cdot\text{m}} = 1\ \text{T}$$

This unit is called the **tesla (T)** after Nicola Tesla (1856–1943). (1 T = 1 N/A·m)

The relationship among magnetic force, magnetic field strength, charge, and velocity can be written as

$$\vec{F} = \vec{B}Q\vec{v}$$

In Investigation 7.1.1, the charged particles (electrons) were moving in a direction perpendicular to the direction of the magnetic field. Sometimes charges do not move perpendicular to the magnetic field. If that is the case, then you must use the component of $\vec{B}$ that is perpendicular to v.

In Figure 7.2.1, a particle carrying charge Q is moving through a magnetic field of strength $\vec{B}$, making an angle θ with the lines of force of the field. Since the component of the magnetic field in a direction perpendicular to the direction of motion is $\vec{B}\sin\theta$, the force on the moving charge is $\vec{F} = \vec{B}Qv\sin\theta$.

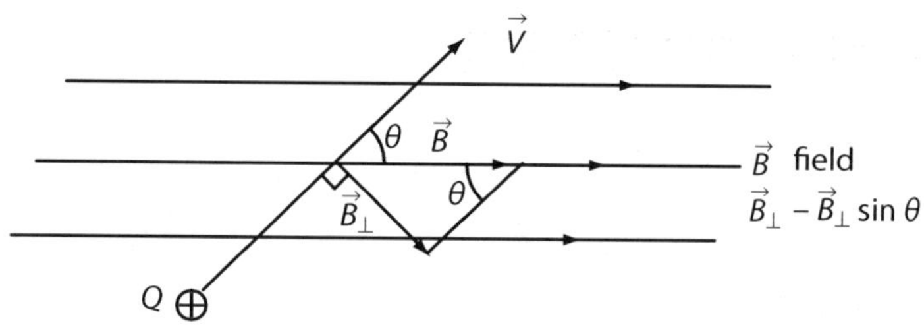

Figure 7.2.1 *When a charge moves perpendicular to the magnetic field, you must use $B_{\perp}$.*

If the charged particles move in a direction *parallel* with the magnetic field, so that $\theta = 0°$, then $\sin\theta = 0$ and $\vec{F} = \vec{B}Qv(0) = 0$. The particles experience no force if they move parallel with the lines of force!

If the charged particles move in a direction *perpendicular* to the magnetic field, so that $\theta = 90°$, then $\sin\theta = 1.000$, and $\vec{F} = \vec{B}Qv(1.000) = \vec{B}Qv$.

The maximum force is experienced when the particles move in a direction that is perpendicular to the magnetic field. In most situations you will encounter in this course, the formula reduces to

$$\vec{F} = \vec{B}Q\vec{v}$$

Quick Check

1. An electron travelling with a speed of 2.0×10^6 m/s moves in a direction perpendicular to a magnetic field of strength 2.5×10^{-2} T.
   (a) What is the force acting on the electron?

   (b) What is the magnitude and the direction of the acceleration?

2. A proton travelling at a speed of 3.0×10^6 m/s travels through a magnetic field of strength 3.0×10^{-3} T, making an angle of 45° with the magnetic lines of force. What force acts on the proton?

Quick Check continues

3. (a) A beam of alpha particles (He^{2+}) is travelling between the magnetic poles in Figure 7.2.2. In what direction will the alpha particles be deflected?

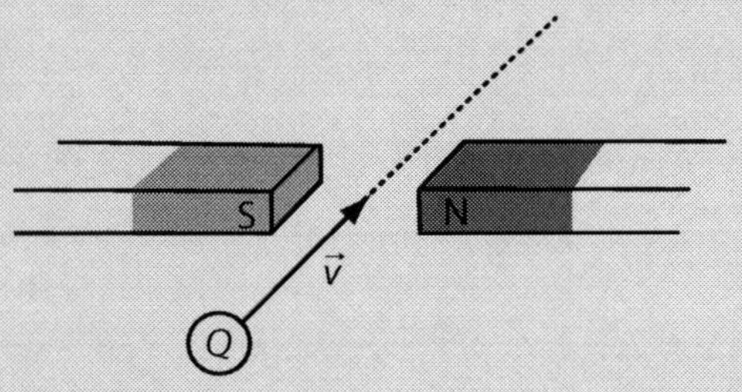

Figure 7.2.2

(b) If the magnetic field strength is 6.4 T and the alpha particles move with a speed of 6.0×10^7 m/s, what will be the magnetic force on the alpha particles?

The Magnetic Field Strength of a Solenoid

André Ampère thoroughly investigated the magnetic fields associated with solenoids. He observed that the magnetic field inside a long solenoid is uniform, with straight lines of force running parallel with the axis of the solenoid (Figure 7.2.3(a)). Figure 7.2.3(b) shows a cross-section of this solenoid and the magnetic field around it when a current is passed through the wire.

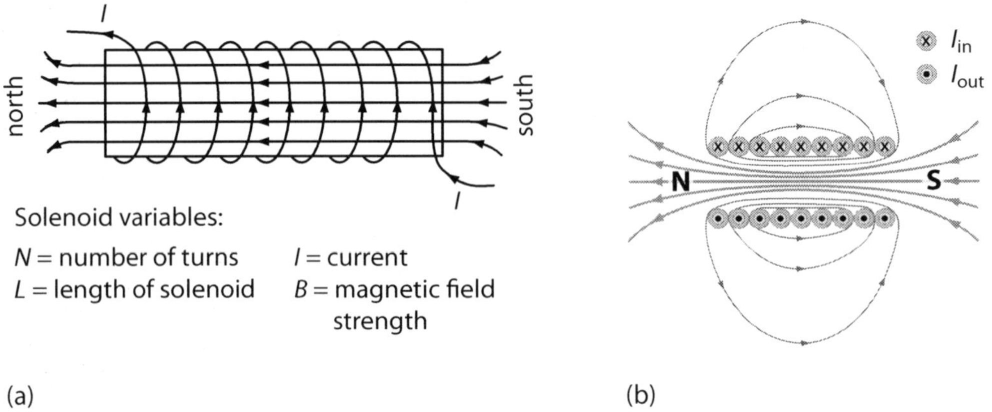

Figure 7.2.3 *(a) The lines of force run straight through the solenoid, parallel to its axis. (b) Cross-section of the solenoid, showing the magnetic field*

The strength, B, of the magnetic field inside a solenoid depends primarily on two factors:

(1) The number of turns of wire N per unit length of solenoid L and
(2) The current in the solenoid I.

In symbols,

$$B \propto \frac{NI}{L} \text{ or}$$

$$B = \text{constant} \cdot \frac{NI}{L}$$

The constant of proportionality is given the impressive title of the **permeability of free space**. The symbol used for the permeability of free space is μ_0, where

$$\mu_0 = 4\pi \times 10^{-7} \text{ Tm/A}$$

Ampère's law for solenoids is written in either of two forms:

$$B = \mu_0 \frac{NI}{L} \text{ or}$$

$$\boldsymbol{B = \mu_0 nI}$$

where n is the number of turns per unit of length (m^{-1}) of the solenoid.

Ampère's law for solenoids will be used to calculate the magnetic field of the solenoids you used in Investigation 7.1.1 and will use again in Investigation 7.2.1.

Quick Check

1. A solenoid is 15.0 cm long and has 250 turns. What is the magnetic field strength inside the solenoid if the current in the coils is 3.8 A?

2. A solenoid is to be wound on a cardboard form 30.0 cm long. How many turns of wire are needed to produce a magnetic field of 6.28×10^{-3} T, if the maximum allowable current is 5.0 A?

3. A solenoid 40.0 cm long has a magnetic field of 5.0×10^{-3} T when the current in it is 10.0 A. How many turns of wire does it have?

Magnetic Force on a Current in a Wire

Since a wire carrying a current has a magnetic field around it, you would expect such a wire to experience a force when placed in the field of an external magnet. A wire carrying a current is a wire carrying moving charges, which you already know will experience a magnetic force if they move through a magnetic field at an angle greater than 0° with the direction of the field lines.

In Figure 7.2.4, a straight piece of wire is placed between the poles of a large U-magnet. Current is going "into the page." The wire segment between the poles of the magnet will experience an upward force just as individual positive charges would.

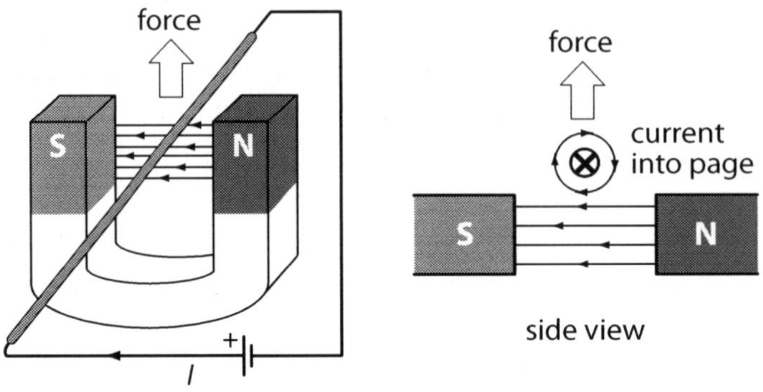

Figure 7.2.4 *The wire between the magnet's poles experiences an upward force.*

The right hand motor rule can be applied here as well as with individual positive charges. Point your right thumb in the direction of conventional current. Point your fingers straight out in the direction of the magnetic lines of force. The palm of your hand will now be "pushing" in the direction of the force on the wire segment carrying the current. Again, the magnetic field, the current, and the magnetic force are mutually perpendicular.

Figure 7.2.5 shows a short segment of wire of length ℓ through which an amount of charge Q travels in time t. Since the segment is perpendicular to the magnetic field lines, you would expect that the force on the charges moving through the wire would be $\vec{F} = \vec{B}Qv$, where v is the speed of the charges moving in the wire. Now $v = \frac{\ell}{t}$, so $\vec{F} = \vec{B}Q\frac{\ell}{t}$.

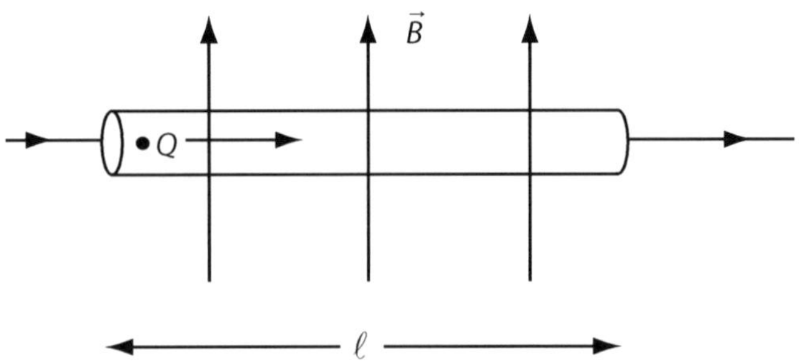

Figure 7.2.5 A *charge experiences a force over the length of wire when passing through a perpendicular magnetic field.*

Now the current in the segment, which we'll call I_S, is equal to $\frac{Q}{t}$. Therefore, the magnetic force on a segment of wire of length ℓ carrying current I_S would be given by the equation below.

$$\vec{F} = \vec{B}I\ell$$

If the wire segment is not perpendicular to the lines of magnetic force, then the component of B perpendicular to the wire segment must be used. The situation is very much the same as for isolated charges moving through a magnetic field (Figure 7.2.1). In Figure 7.2.6 the wire segment makes an angle θ with the lines of force.

$$\vec{F} = \vec{B}I_s\ell\sin\theta$$

If the segment is perpendicular to the field lines, this reduces to $F = BI_s\ell$ In Investigation 7.2.1 you will check whether the force is proportional to I_S.

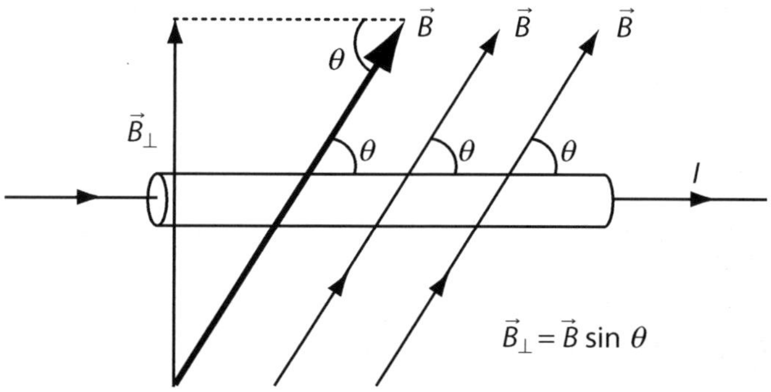

Figure 7.2.6 *Isolated charges moving through a magnetic field*

Investigation 7.2.1 The Current Balance

Purpose

To measure the magnetic field strength of a solenoid for different solenoid currents using a current balance

Introduction

Figure 7.2.7 shows the essential components of a current balance. A source of emf (6.0 V DC) is connected to the large solenoid, with a variable resistor and an ammeter in the solenoid circuit.

A plastic "teeter totter" is balanced at the opening at one end of the solenoid. A current is passed through a conducting strip that runs around one end of the teeter-totter. The magnetic field of the solenoid exerts a net force on the portion of the strip that runs perpendicular with the solenoid's lines of force — the segment ℓ on the diagram.

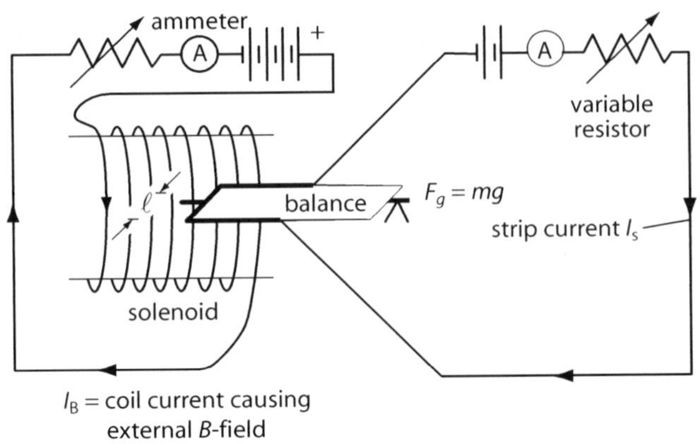

Figure 7.2.7

Current direction in the strip is chosen so that the end of the balance arm (teeter-totter) *inside* the solenoid is pushed *downward*. To measure the downward magnetic force on the strip, you simply balance it by using the force of gravity on known masses added at the other end of the balance.

Procedure

1. Set the current through the solenoid at 4.0 A or as close to this value as possible. This is current I_B. *Do not change I_B during the first part of the experiment.*
2. With the balance in position on its pivot, send a small current through the strip and check that the magnetic force is pushing *down* inside the solenoid.

Turn off the current while doing step 3.

3. You will need at least five different masses to add to the end of the current balance. Use 10 mg standard masses, if they are available. If they are not available, prepare a set of standard masses as follows: Measure the mass of a 10 m length of fine transformer wire. Calculate the length of wire needed to have a mass of 10 mg. Cut at least five pieces of wire this length. Calculate the force of gravity on each standard mass by multiplying the mass (10 mg = 1.0×10^{-5} kg) by 9.8 N/kg.
4. Place a standard mass on the free end of the current balance. ***Make sure that the standard masses are placed in a position such that they are the same distance from the pivot of the teeter totter as the conducting strip at the other end of the teeter-totter.*** (Why is this so important?)

   The free end of the balance arm should now move downward. Turn on the solenoid current I_B and the strip current I_s. Adjust the current in the strip until the magnetic force on the strip just equals the force of gravity on the other end of the balance, and the balance arm remains horizontal. Record the strip current (I_s) and the force of gravity needed to balance the magnetic force.
5. Repeat step 4 with at least four different masses. Prepare a data table and record the strip currents and forces of gravity used in each situation.
6. Plot a graph of magnetic force (F) vs. strip current I_s. The magnetic force equals the force of gravity needed each time to balance the balance arm. Why? Calculate the slope of your graph and record this slope in appropriate units.

7. Measure precisely the length of the conducting strip, ℓ, in metres.
8. The slope of your graph of F vs. I_s will be $\Delta F/\Delta I_s$. If the graph is a straight line going through (0,0), then $\Delta F/\Delta I_s = F/I_s$. In the theoretical discussion before this investigation, it was predicted that $F = BI_s\ell$, where B is the magnetic field strength of the solenoid. Calculate a predicted value for B using $B = \frac{F}{I_s\ell}$.
9. You will now keep the *strip current* constant and vary the solenoid current, I_B. Set the strip current I_s at 2.0 A and leave it there for the remainder of the experiment. **Turn off the solenoid current.** Place a 10 mg mass on the free end of the balance. Turn on the solenoid current and gradually increase I_B until the balance arm remains horizontal. Record I_B and the force of gravity on the 10 mg mass.
10. Repeat step 9 with at least four other masses. Record all currents and balancing forces as before.
11. Plot a graph of magnetic force F vs. solenoid current I_B. Find the slope and express it in appropriate units.

Concluding Questions

1. How does the magnetic force on the strip vary with the current in the strip, if the solenoid current is kept constant?
2. When the solenoid current was 4.0 A, what was the magnetic field strength due to the solenoid current?
3. When the solenoid current is varied and the strip current is kept constant, how does the magnetic force depend on the solenoid current?
4. For Investigation 7.3.1 you need to know what the magnetic field strength of your solenoid is for any current in the solenoid. Calculate its magnetic field strength per ampere of solenoid current as follows:
In general, the force on a segment of conductor is $F = BI_s\ell$. When you kept I_s constant and varied I_B, your graph probably indicated that

$$F = (\text{constant})\cdot I_B$$

Since the "constant" equals the graph's slope,

$$F = (\text{slope})\cdot I_B$$

Since

$$BI_s\ell = (\text{slope})\cdot I_B$$

$$\therefore \frac{B}{I_B} = \frac{\text{slope}}{I_s\ell}$$

> Record this important ratio for future reference. It permits you to calculate magnetic field strength of your solenoid for any current you put through it.

5. According to Ampère's law for solenoids, the magnetic field strength of a solenoid can be calculated as follows: $B = \mu_0 \frac{N}{L} I_B$, where N is the number of turns in the coil, L is the length of the solenoid, I_B is the current in the solenoid, and μ_0 is the magnetic permeability of free space.

$$\mu_0 = 4\pi \times 10^{-7}\ \text{Tm/A}$$

Measure L carefully and find out what N is for your solenoid.* Calculate the ratio, B/I_B, using Ampere's law. Calculate the percent difference between the ratio you obtained this way and the ratio you obtained from data in Procedure step 4.

> * If data is not available, and you do not wish to dismantle a solenoid, use $N = 525$ turns if the solenoid is the standard PSSC model.

6. Discuss the major sources of error in this experiment.

7.2 Review Questions

1. A particle carrying a charge of 0.50 μC enters a magnetic field of strength 0.045 T, with a velocity of 350 m/s. The velocity is perpendicular to the magnetic field. What is the magnetic force acting on the charged particle?

2. A segment of conducting wire 5.0 cm long carrying 5.0 A of current is perpendicular to a magnetic field of 12 T. What magnetic force acts on the segment?

3. A wire that is 0.75 m long carries a current of 10.0 A is at a right angle to a uniform magnetic field. The force on the wire is 0.50 N. What is the strength of the magnetic field?

4. What is the magnitude of force on a wire that is 30 cm long and positioned at a right angle to a 0.40 T uniform magnetic field? The current through the wire is 5.0 A.

5. A half-kilometre length of wire is positioned perpendicular to a 0.40 T magnetic field. What is the current carried in the wire if a force of 2.0 N acts on the wire?

6. What magnetic field strength is needed to exert a force of 1.0×10^{-15} N on an electron travelling 2.0×10^{7} m/s?

7. (a) A 5.0 cm segment of wire carrying 2.5 A is perpendicular to a magnetic field of 25 T inside a solenoid. What is the magnetic force on the segment?

   (b) If the current inside the solenoid is increased to five times its original value, what will the new magnetic field strength be?

8. A solenoid 0.20 m long has 600 turns of wire. What current must be passed through the solenoid to produce a magnetic field of 2.0×10^{-2} T?

9. A magnetic resonance imaging machine (MRI) is used to take medical diagnostic images of the body. To create these images, a large solenoid is used and the person is placed in the centre of the solenoid. A current of 1500 A is carried through a 2.00 m long solenoid that has 2500 loops. What is the magnetic field strength inside the solenoid?

10. A 61 mg mass just balances the balance arm of a current balance when the strip current is 3.0 A. If the strip is 2.2 cm long, what is the magnetic field strength inside the solenoid in which the current balance is located?

7.3 Magnetic Fields and the Electron

Warm Up

In the first two sections of this chapter, you have observed how a magnetic field can deflect a beam of electrons. Why can't the field do work on the electrons to speed them up?

____

____

____

Electron Behaviour

J. J. Thomson (1856–1940) was not the first to observe cathode rays, which we now know are made up of electrons. He is credited with the discovery of electrons because he was the first to make a significant measurement of a property of the cathode rays. What he measured was the *ratio of the charge to the mass* of the particles in the cathode rays. Thomson used a combination of magnetic and electric fields to do this.

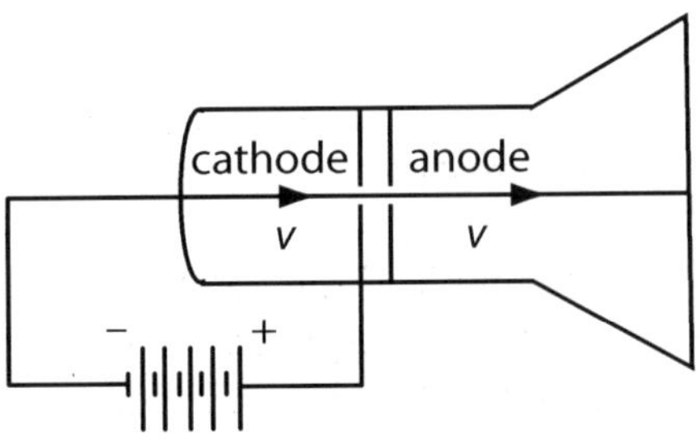

Figure 7.3.1 *The cathode rays, made up of electrons, form a spot on the screen of the tube at C.*

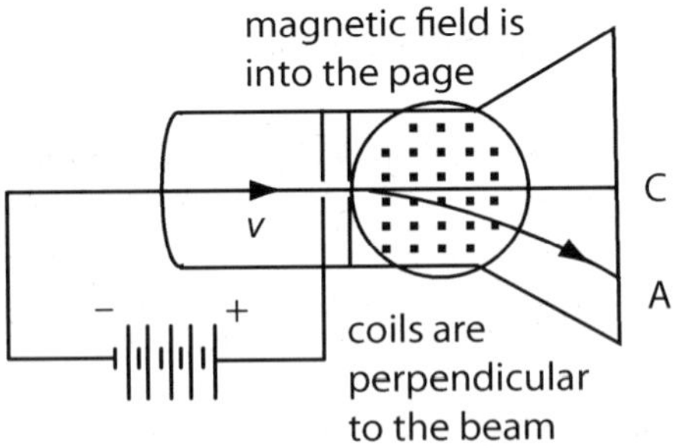

Figure 7.3.2 *A magnetic field in the direction indicated deflects the electron beam downward.*

Figure 7.3.1 shows a simple cathode ray tube (CRT), where electrons (once called cathode rays) are accelerated by a high voltage toward an anode. Electrons passing through the holes in the anode travel at a speed v to a fluorescent screen, where they form a spot on the screen at C.

If a magnetic field B is applied perpendicular to the path of the electrons, as in Figure 7.3.2, the beam of negative electrons will be deflected downward (right hand motor rule) and form a spot on the screen at A.

The magnetic field pushes electrons downward with a force $F = BQv = Bev$, where e is the charge on one electron.

The magnetic force is always perpendicular to the velocity of the electron, so it acts as a centripetal force. It produces acceleration toward the centre of a circular path. Therefore,

$$F = Bev = \frac{mv^2}{R}$$

From these equations, the ratio of charge to mass can be determined to be

$$\frac{e}{m} = \frac{v}{BR}$$

Both B and R are measurable. Thomson eliminated the need to know v by using a clever technique. If an electric field $\vec{E}$ is applied to the same beam of electrons and adjusted so that the electric force on the electrons ($F = EQ = Ee$) is just equal to the magnetic force, then $Bev = Ee$ (Figure 7.3.3).

When these conditions are fulfilled, then

$$v = \frac{E}{B}$$

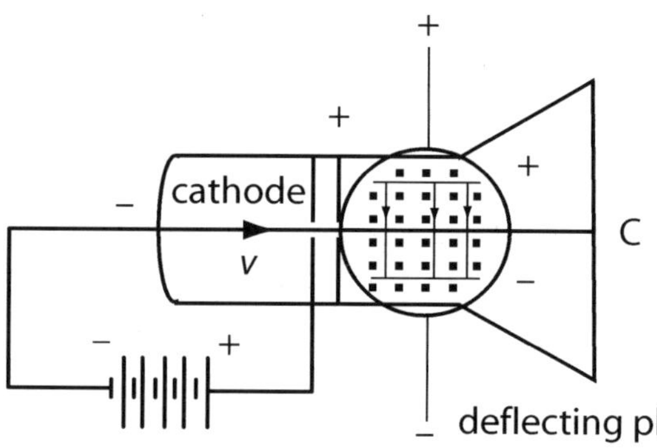

B-field is into the page
B-field pushes electrons DOWN
E-field is "down"
E-field pushes electrons UP

E and B are adjusted so that electric force = magnetic force, and deflection = 0.

Figure 7.3.3 *A cathode ray tube has both magnetic fields and electric fields to deflect the electrons as they pass through the field. Adjusting the field strength will vary the amount of deflection.*

The speed of the electrons is equal to the ratio of the electric field strength to the magnetic field strength, when the electric force just balances the magnetic force to produce zero deflection. When this condition is met, we can substitute this value for speed in the equation for charge-to-mass ratio, and we get

$$\frac{e}{m} = \frac{v}{BR} = \frac{\frac{E}{B}}{BR} = \frac{E}{B^2R}$$

Using this equation, Thomson determined the charge-to-mass ratio.

The modern value of the charge-to-mass ratio is

$$\frac{e}{m} = 1.76 \times 10^{11} \text{ C/kg}$$

J. J. Thomson was certain that electrons were subatomic particles and not just a type of atom. Later on, Robert A. Millikan (1868–1953) successfully measured the charge on one electron. He did this with an extremely intricate experiment in which electrically charged oil drops were suspended between parallel charged plates. Electrical forces were used to balance the gravitational forces on the tiny drops. He was able to calculate the charge on the drops and found that the charge was always a multiple of 1.6×10^{-19} C. No charge smaller than this was ever found in his experiment, so he assumed that this was the **elementary charge,** the smallest charge in nature.

Knowing that $e = 1.6 \times 10^{-19}$ C, and that $\frac{e}{m} = 1.76 \times 10^{11}$ C/kg, the mass of one electron could now be calculated.

$$m_{electron} = \frac{1.6 \times 10^{-19}\ \text{C}}{1.76 \times 10^{11}\ \text{C/kg}} = 9.1 \times 10^{-31}\ \text{kg}$$

This tiny mass of the electron confirmed Thomson's view that the electron was a subatomic particle.

Quick Check

1. A magnetic field of strength 4.34×10^{-3} T deflected electrons into a circular path of radius 1.1×10^{-2} m. The accelerating voltage used to get the electrons up to maximum speed was 200.0 V. If the charge on an electron is 1.6×10^{-19} C, what is the mass of an electron?

2. A beam of protons passes through a magnetic field of strength 4.0×10^{-3} T and is deflected into a curved path of radius 1.14 m. If the accelerating voltage was 1.0×10^{3} V, what is the mass of a proton?

The Mass Spectrometer

The **mass spectrometer** was developed as a tool for measuring the masses of charged atoms. Electric current or heat is used to ionize atoms at source S. Ions pass through a slit into the **velocity selector,** where those with a chosen velocity, $v = \frac{E}{B}$ get through the crossed electric and magnetic fields and through the slit that lets them enter a different magnetic field region. In this region, the ions are forced into a circular path ending on a photographic film (Figure 7.3.4).

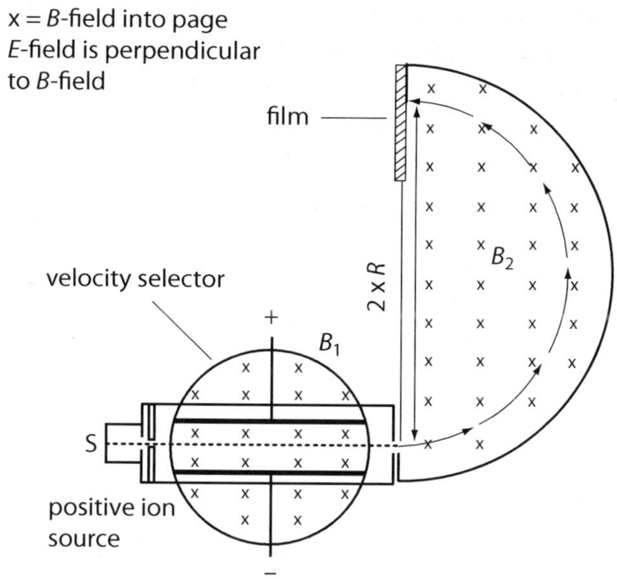

Figure 7.3.4 *How a mass spectrometer works*

Two different magnetic fields are used in the mass spectrometer. In the velocity selector portion, the field is B_1. The velocity of the charged particles that emerge from the velocity selector will be $v = \frac{E}{B_1}$.

The charged particles entering the larger magnetic field region will experience only a magnetic force, and this will accelerate them into a circular path. Since

$$F = B_2Qv = \frac{mv^2}{R}$$

$$\therefore m = \frac{B_2QR}{v} = \frac{B_2QR}{E/B_1} = \frac{B_1B_2QR}{E}$$

Since all the quantities on the right side of the equation are measurable, the mass of an ion can be calculated from this result. You can see that for an atom of a given charge, the radius traced out in its circular path through the second magnetic field is proportional to its mass. Isotopes of the same element can be separated in a beautifully simple way using the spectrometer! The mass spectrometer can be used to separate the elements in a mixture or the isotopes in an element. It can also be used to measure the mass of charged molecules.

Quick Check

1. Two isotopes of hydrogen are present in a particle beam issuing through the final slit into the magnetic field outside the velocity selector of a mass spectrometer. Protons and deuterons, both with a charge of +1, are subjected to the same magnetic field strength. Both go into a circular path. If the proton path radius is R, what will the deuteron path radius be? (A deuteron is a deuterium nucleus, which consists of a proton and a neutron.)

2. What is the velocity of ions that pass successfully through a velocity selector, if the electric field has strength 1.5×10^5 N/C and the magnetic field in the velocity selector is 0.50 T? What will the radius of the path of these ions be, if the bending magnet has a field strength of 0.75 T? Assume the ions have a charge of +e, and an atomic mass of 20 u, where 1 u = 1.67×10^{-27} kg.

Electric Motors

Figure 7.3.5 shows a simple one-turn coil motor operated on direct current. The coil in a motor is called the **armature.** Of course, a real motor will have many turns of wire. The external or "field" magnet may also be an electromagnet rather than a permanent magnet. The external magnetic field exerts a torque on the armature, causing it to turn continuously.

Note the importance of the **split-ring commutator.** When the armature makes one-half turn, the split-ring commutator makes the current in the two halves of the coil *change direction* so that the magnetic force (and therefore the torque) is always "down" on the left side and "up" on the right side.

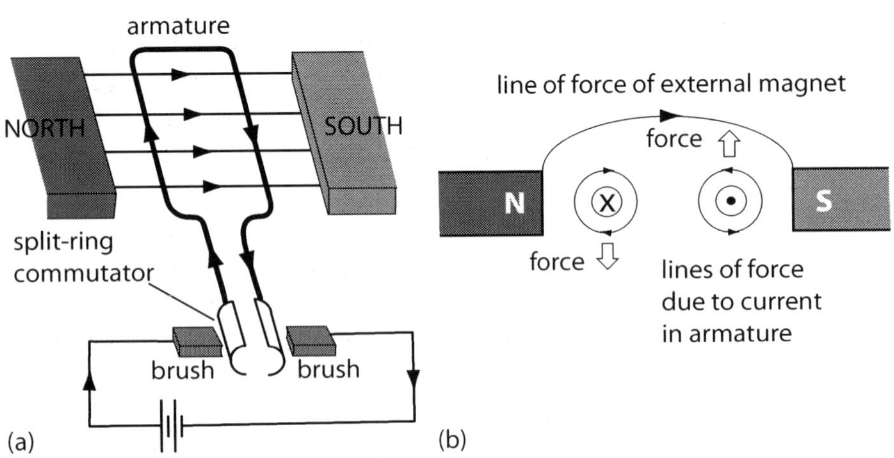

Figure 7.3.5 *(a) A simple motor is a coil of wire in a magnetic field. The wire turns by the force created when a current is passed through the coil. Note the arrows in the circuit and coil show the direction of the current. (b) A cross-section of the coil showing the magnetic force being generated as the current moves through the coil in a magnetic field.*

Figure 7.3.6 shows the construction of a typical laboratory demonstration motor called the **St. Louis motor**. Current enters the armature at A. The contact is called a **brush** and is made of copper. Commercial motors may use a graphite brush that is spring-loaded to keep it in firm contact with the armature.

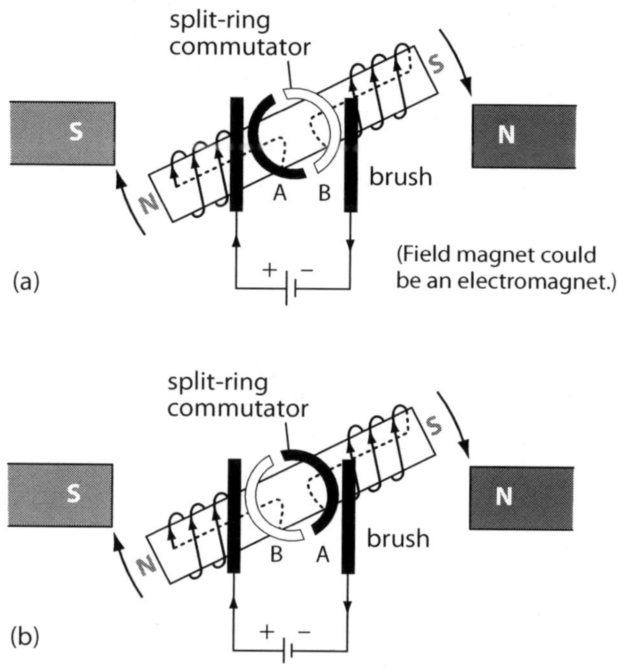

Figure 7.3.6 *A St. Louis motor in operation. The magnetic field is set up around the armature when the current passes through the wire. (a). Note the north and south poles of the armature. This creates an attraction to the permanent magnet. Inertia carries the armature past the permanent pole. (b) As the armature swings around the current switches due to the split ring commutator.*

The split metal cylinder on the armature is the split-ring commutator. Current direction is from the brush at A to the left half of the commutator, then to the coil of wire on the armature. Current direction is such that the left end of the armature is an N-pole and the right end is an S-pole. Current leaves the right side of the split-ring commutator at B and returns to the battery.

Since opposite poles attract, the external field magnets exert a torque on the armature. When the armature has made one-half a turn, current direction in the armature reverses because of the commutator. Current now enters at B and leaves at A. The external field magnets keep on turning the armature clockwise as before, because the left side is still an N-pole and the right side is still an S-pole.

Electric motors come in all sizes. Some are very tiny and drive toys; others are huge and drive trains or buses. You will find electric motors in toy trains, automobiles, clocks, wheelchairs, streetcars, can openers, cement mixers, furnace fans, robots and many other devices.

The motors described in Figures 7.3.5 and 7.3.6 operate only on direct current. Alternating current motors work on essentially the same principle, but do not use a split-ring commutator. Since the current is already "alternating," there is no need for a split-ring commutator to reverse the current every half-turn.

Investigation 7.3.1 Estimating the Mass of the Electron

Purpose

To measure the approximate mass of an electron, using a tuning-eye diode and a solenoid that was calibrated in Investigation 7.2.1

Introduction

When an electron moving at speed v passes through a magnetic field B, in a direction perpendicular to the magnetic lines of force, the electron is deflected into a circular path of radius R. The magnetic force, $F = Bev$, is therefore a centripetal force, and we can write the equation,

$$Bev = \frac{mv^2}{R} \quad (1)$$

Assume that the voltage between the cathode and the anode of a vacuum diode tube is V_a. Then V_a is the work done per unit charge to accelerate electrons from the cathode to the anode. The work shows up as the kinetic energy of the electrons, and it reaches a maximum just as the electrons reach the anode.

$$V_a = \frac{\frac{1}{2}mv^2}{e} \quad (2)$$

Equation (1) assumes that electrons are moving at a constant speed through a magnetic field. In equation (2), the speed is the maximum speed achieved by the accelerating electrons. In the tuning-eye diode tube that you use in this experiment, the design is such that the electrons, although they are accelerating, reach near maximum speed just before they enter the region outside the dark metal cap you see when you look down into the tube. While the electrons are in your field of view as they move toward the fluorescent anode is, their speed is, for all practical purposes, constant. This means that we can combine equations (1) and (2) to derive an expression for the mass of the electron.

From equation (1), $v = \frac{BeR}{m}$. Substituting for v in equation (2),

$$V_a = \frac{\frac{1}{2}m}{e} = \frac{B^2e^2R^2}{m^2}$$

Simplifying and solving for m,

$$m_{\text{electron}} = \frac{B^2eR^2}{2V_a}$$

Since all the variables on the right side of the equation are known or are measurable, the mass of the electron can be determined.

Inside the tuning-eye diode, electrons accelerate radially from the central cathode toward the fluorescent anode (Figures 7.3.7 and 7.3.8). Deflecting electrodes cause a fan-shaped shadow to form. With no magnetic field applied, the edges of the shadow are straight, indicating that the electrons are travelling in straight lines from cathode to anode.

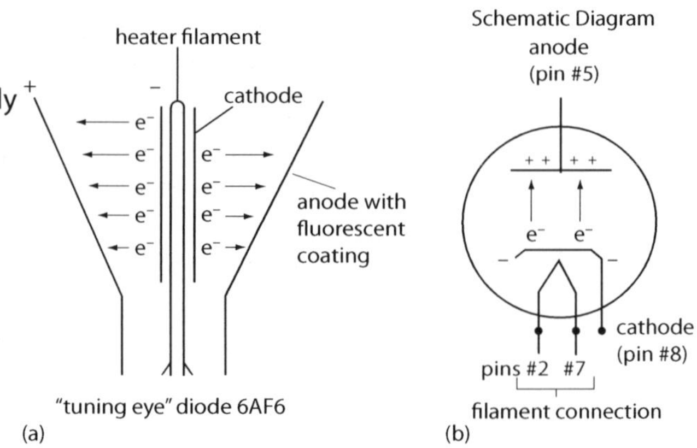

Figure 7.3.7

When a solenoid is lowered over the tube, so that its magnetic field is perpendicular to the flow of electrons, the electrons are sent into a curved path, which can be seen on the screen (Figure 7.3.8(b)).

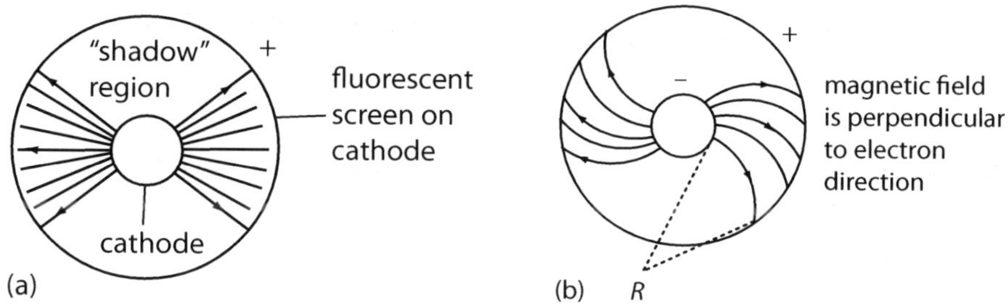

Figure 7.3.8

Procedure

1. Connect the apparatus as in Figure 7.3.9. Use an anode voltage of 100 V to start.

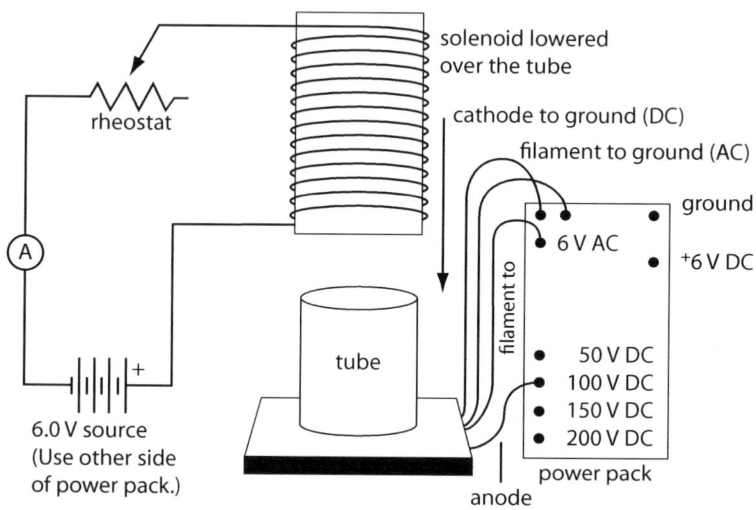

Figure 7.3.9

2. Place an air-cored solenoid (calibrated in Investigation 7.2.1) over the tube. A rheostat and ammeter are in series with the solenoid, which is connected to a 6.0 V DC source.
3. Vary the current in the solenoid until the curvature of the edge of the electron beam can be conveniently matched with that of a piece of wood dowelling or a non-magnetic brass cork borer, inserted down through the solenoid. If you now measure the diameter of the dowelling or cork borer, you can calculate the radius of curvature of the electron beam. Record this value of *R*. Also, record I_B.
4. Consult your data from Investigation 7.2.1 (The Current Balance) to see what the magnetic field strength of your solenoid would be for the solenoid current you just used to measure *R*. (Investigation 7.2.1 gave you a value for B/I_B. Multiply B/I_B by I_B to obtain *B*.)
5. Measure the voltage you are using for the anode voltage, V_a. The power supply label of 100 V may not be reliable.
6. You now know *B*, *R*, *e*, and V_a. Calculate the mass of an electron using $m_{electron} = \dfrac{B^2eR^2}{2V_a}$.

7. Do at least two more trials using different solenoid currents and possibly different accelerating voltages. Calculate the mass of the electron in each trial.

Concluding Questions

1. What is the mean value you obtained for the mass of the electron? The accepted value is 9.1×10^{-31} kg. What is the percent difference between your value and the accepted value?
2. This method of measuring the mass of an electron is quite crude, but you should be able to obtain a "ball park" figure for the mass of one electron. What are some of the 'assumptions' made in this experiment that might introduce sources of error?

7.3 Review Questions

1. Deuterium ions have twice the mass of a proton but carry the same charge. What would be the radius of curvature of magnetically deflected deuterium ions if the magnetic field strength were 4.0×10^{-3} T and the accelerating voltage were 1.0×10^3 V?

2. Protons are accelerated and made to pass through crossed fields where the electric field is perpendicular to the magnetic field. The protons are moving at such a speed that the magnetic force just equals the electric force but is in the opposite direction, so that there is no overall deflection of the beam. At what speed are the particles moving if $B = 0.50$ T and $E = 5.5 \times 10^4$ N/C? (Such a device was used by J. J. Thomson when he was measuring the charge-to-mass ratio of electrons. It is called a velocity selector.)

3. (a) A particle of mass m and charge Q is moving with speed v in a circular path of radius R in a uniform magnetic field B. How would you calculate the radius from the other information?

   (b) An alpha particle of mass 6.7×10^{-27} kg and charge 3.2×10^{-19} C is accelerated from rest by a voltage of 2.00×10^3 V. What will be the radius of curvature of its path in a uniform magnetic field of 0.070 T?

   (c) What is the momentum of the alpha particle?

4. Two solenoids are being used to deflect the same beam of electrons in a cathode ray tube. Use the following diagram to answer the questions below.

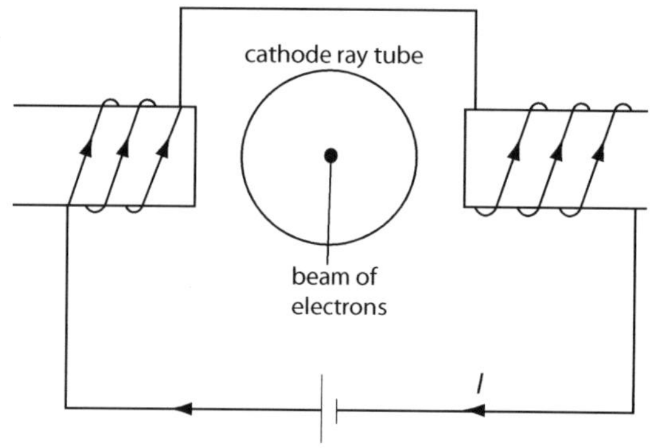

   (a) In what direction will the electron beam be deflected? Circle one of the following.

   A ← B ↑ C → D ↓

   (b) If the magnetic field strength B is doubled, what will be the deflection δ?

   (c) If the accelerating voltage V_a is doubled, how much will the deflection δ change?

Chapter 7 Review Questions

1. Name at least three ferromagnetic elements.

2. If you wanted to accelerate a stationary proton, would you use an electric field or a magnetic field? Explain.

3. Draw a diagram showing a conductor with conventional current moving into your page. Draw a few sample lines of magnetic force around the conductor, including their directions.

4. Describe the magnetic field inside a long solenoid.

5. Draw a solenoid with current moving in a direction of your choice. Label the north end of the solenoid.

6. When the switch is closed on this "magnetic swing," will it move "out" from the poles of the magnet or "in" toward the magnet? Use the right hand motor rule.

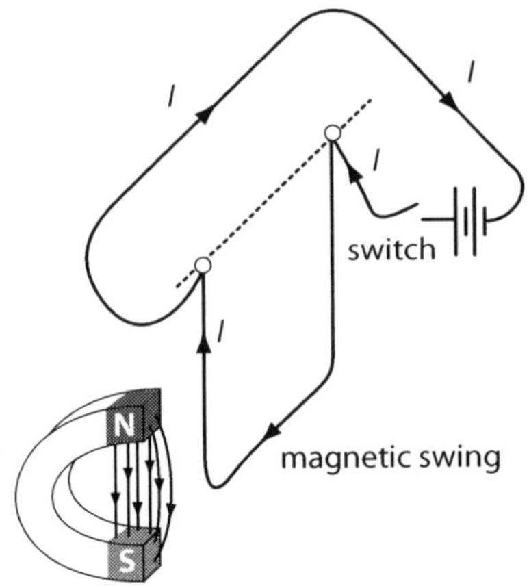

7. An electron moving with a speed of 0.10 c moves through a magnetic field of strength 0.60 T. What force acts on the electron? ($c = 3.0 \times 10^8$ m/s; $e = 1.6 \times 10^{-19}$ C)

8. A solenoid is wound with 100 turns per centimetre. What is the magnetic field strength inside the solenoid when it carries a current of 5.0 A? ($\mu_0 = 4\pi \times 10^{-7}$ T• m/A)

9. A magnetic field from a solenoid is used to deflect a beam of electrons 0.80 cm on the screen of a CRT. If the current in the solenoid is doubled, what will the deflection be then?

10. An electron beam in a CRT is deflected 0.64 cm when the accelerating voltage is 500.0 V. By how much will the beam be deflected if the magnetic field is kept constant but the accelerating voltage is increased to 2000.0 V?

11. A wire carries a current of 6.0 A. What is the magnetic force exerted on a 12 cm segment of this wire in a perpendicular magnetic field of strength 36 T?

12. If the force on a 5.0 cm piece of wire carrying 12 A is 1.0×10^{-3} N, what is the magnetic field strength of the perpendicular field through which the current passes?

13. A conducting wire 1.0 m long carries a current of 7.5 A. It is placed in a magnetic field of strength 5.0×10^{-5} T. If the wire makes an angle of 60° with the magnetic lines of force, what is the force acting on the wire?

14. A 75 mg mass just balances the strip in a current balance when the current in the strip is 2.5 A. If the strip is 2.0 cm long, what is the magnetic field strength inside the solenoid in which the current balance is located?

15. An alpha particle is accelerated by a voltage of 1.53×10^{3} V and is then deflected by a magnetic field of strength 0.020 T into a circular path of radius 0.40 m. If the alpha particles have a charge of 3.2×10^{-19} C, what is their mass?

16. Why does a DC motor need a split-ring commutator?

17. Two parallel wires carry currents in the same direction. Will the wires attract or repel each other? Explain with the help of a diagram.

18. In the velocity selector part of a mass spectrometer, a field of 0.65 T is used for magnetic deflection of a beam of protons travelling at a speed of 1.0×10^6 m/s. What electric field is needed to balance the force due to the magnetic field? If the distance between the plates of the electrical deflection apparatus is 0.50 cm, what voltage must be applied to the plates?

19. What speed must electrons in a beam of electrons going through a velocity selector have if the beam is undeflected by crossed electric and magnetic fields of strengths 6.0×10^3 V/m and 0.0030 T respectively? If the electric field were shut off, what would be the radius of the beam due to the unbalanced magnetic force?

Chapter 7 Extra Practice

1. At X, what is the direction of the magnetic field due to the bar magnet?

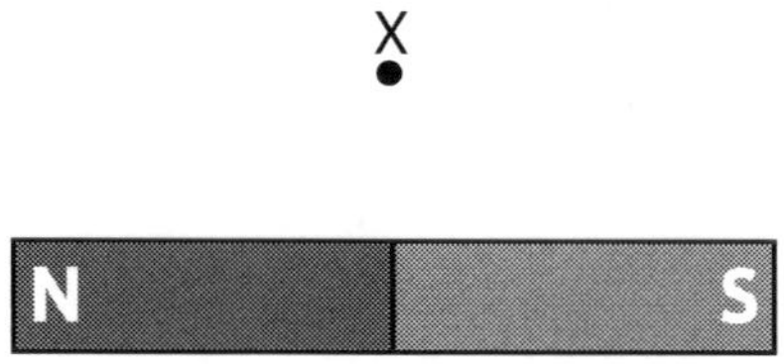

2. Identify the poles of the magnet in the diagram below.

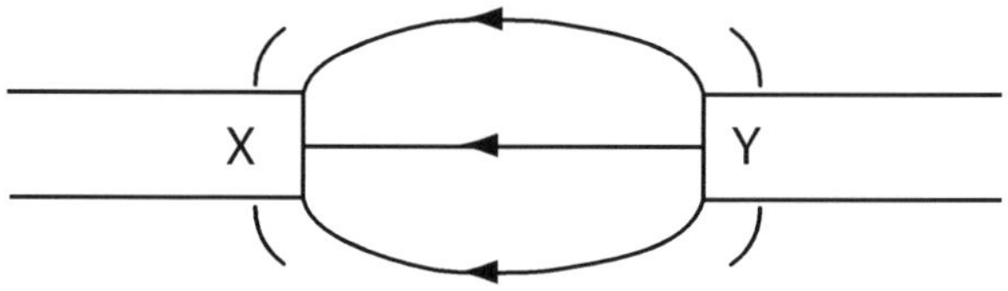

3. What is the direction of the magnetic force on the conductor in the diagram?

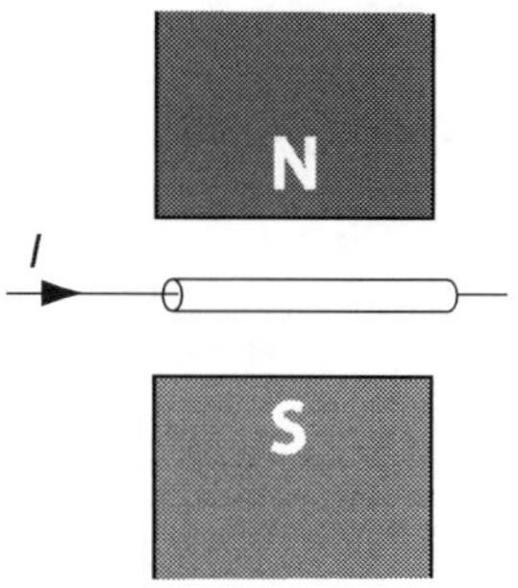

4. The conductor on the left is carrying conventional current into the page. In which direction will a compass needle point if the compass is placed at P?

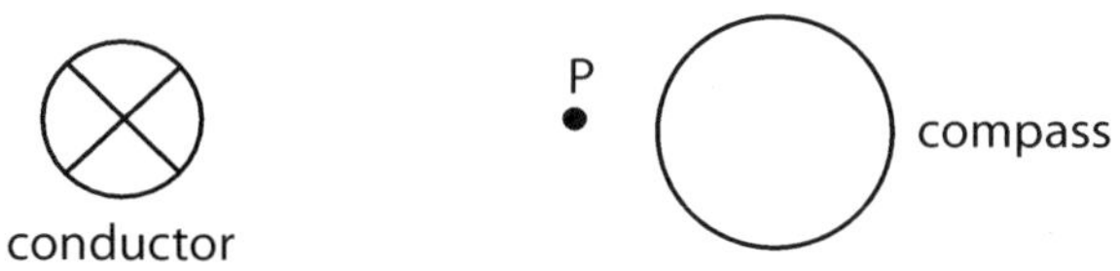

5. Two conducting wires, R and S, run parallel with each other, and both carry current into the page. Conductor R is fixed, but conductor S can move. In what direction will the magnetic fields due to currents in the wires tend to make conductor S move?

Use the diagram below to answer questions 6 to 8. Two solenoids are being used to deflect the same beam of electrons in a cathode ray tube.

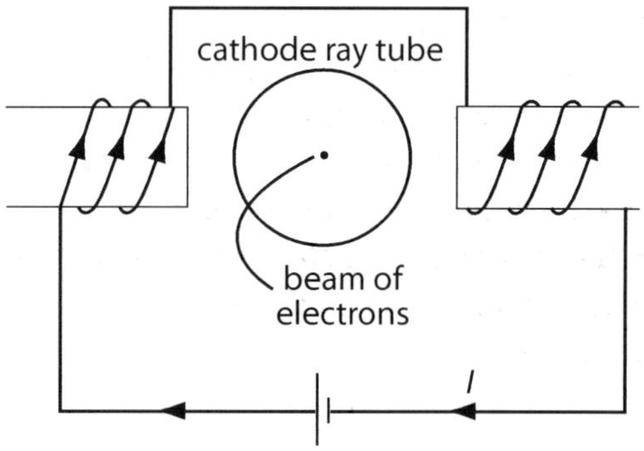

6. In what direction will the electron beam be deflected?

7. If the magnetic field strength B is doubled, the deflection will change from δ to what value?

8. If the accelerating voltage V_a is doubled, the deflection will change from δ to what value?

9. A conductor 25 cm long carries a current of 50.0 A. It is placed in a magnetic field of strength 49 T. What force is exerted on the conductor if it makes these angles with the magnetic lines of force: (a) 0°, (b) 45°, (c) 90°?

10. The magnetic field strength inside a certain solenoid is 0.025 T. If a 3.2 cm conducting strip, which is perpendicular to the magnetic field inside the solenoid, experiences a force of 5.9×10^{-4} N, what is the current in the conducting strip?

11. The force acting on a wire that is at right angles to a 0.90 T magnetic field is 3.6 N. The current in the wire is 5.5 A. How long is the wire?

12. A particle carrying a charge of 0.50 μC enters a magnetic field of strength 0.045 T, with a velocity of 350 m/s. The velocity is perpendicular to the magnetic field. What is the magnetic force acting on the charged particle?

13. A segment of conducting wire 5.0 cm long carrying 5.0 A of current is perpendicular to a magnetic field of 12 T. What magnetic force acts on the segment?

14. A solenoid 0.20 m long has 600 turns of wire. What current must be passed through the solenoid to produce a magnetic field of 2.0×10^{-2} T?

15. (a) A particle of mass m and charge Q is moving with speed v in a circular path of radius *R* in a uniform magnetic field *B*. How would you calculate the radius from the other information?

    (b) An alpha particle, of mass 6.7×10^{-27} kg and charge 3.2×10^{-19} C, is accelerated from rest by a voltage of 2.00×10^{3} V. What will be the radius of curvature of its path in a uniform magnetic field of 0.070 T?

    (c) What is the momentum of the alpha particle?

16. What is the magnetic field *B* inside the solenoid of this current balance, if the force of gravity on the 0.50 g mass provides just enough torque to balance the torque due to the magnetic force on the current balance?

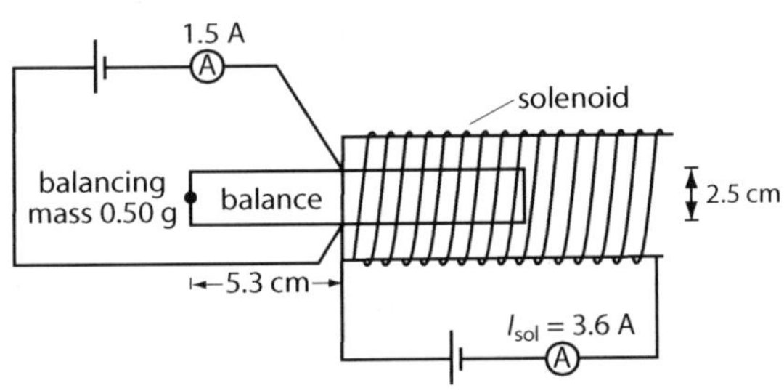

8 Electromagnetic Induction

By the end of this chapter, you should be able to do the following:

- Analyze the process of electromagnetic induction

By the end of this chapter, you should know the meaning of these **key terms**:

- alternating current
- back emf
- electromagnetic induction
- Faraday's law of induction
- Lenz's law
- magnetic flux
- primary coil
- secondary coil
- transformer
- weber

By the end of this chapter, you should be able to use and know when to use the following formulae:

$$\varepsilon = \frac{BQv\ell}{Q} = Bv\ell \qquad \phi = B_{\perp}A = BA\cos\theta \qquad \varepsilon = -N\frac{\Delta\Phi}{\Delta t} \qquad \varepsilon_B = V_{AB} - IR \qquad \frac{\varepsilon_S}{\varepsilon_P} = \frac{N_S}{N_P} \qquad \frac{\varepsilon_S}{\varepsilon_P} = \frac{I_P}{I_S}$$

The St. Louis motor is an example of an electric motor commonly found in science labs. It allows you to observe the working parts. In this chapter, you will study the physics concepts that explain the operation of a St. Louis motor and any other type of electric motor.

8.1 Induced Emf

Warm Up

You know that when electric charges move, they produce a magnetic field. In addition, a magnetic field will exert a force on moving charges. Consider the following question: If a current produces magnetism, could magnetism produce a current? Explain your answer.

____

____

____

Magnetism, EMF, and Electric Current

In the previous chapter, you learned that when electric charges move, they produce a magnetic field. In addition, a magnetic field will exert a force on moving charges. Early in the 19th century, scientists such as Michael Faraday (1791–1867) in England and Joseph Henry (1797–1878) in the United States were aware of these properties. Both asked the obvious question, "If a current produces magnetism, might magnetism produce a current?"

Both scientists discovered that magnetism could be used to induce an emf that would produce a current in a circuit. Faraday was the first to publish his discovery, and he studied electromagnetic induction in more detail.

In Investigation 8.1.1, you will observe a number of ways in which an emf can be induced using changing magnetic fields. The main purpose of Investigation 8.1.1 is to give you some concrete experience with magnetic induction devices, so that the more theoretical discussion of electromagnetic induction that follows will be more understandable.

Inducing an EMF in a Straight Piece of Wire

If a length of conducting wire (ℓ) is made to move through magnetic lines of force that are perpendicular to the conductor, an emf will develop between the ends of the conductor (Figure 8.1.1). If the conductor is part of a complete circuit, a current will exist in the circuit.

Consider a quantity of charge Q at one end of the segment of wire. The charge is free to move, since this is a conducting material. For simplicity in applying the right hand motor rule, let the charge be positive, although you know that in a metal, it is really negative electrons that move.

Let the wire be made to move straight down through the perpendicular lines of force in the direction of the arrow labeled v. This is the velocity of the wire and therefore is also the vertical velocity of the charge in the wire (Figure 8.1.1(a)).

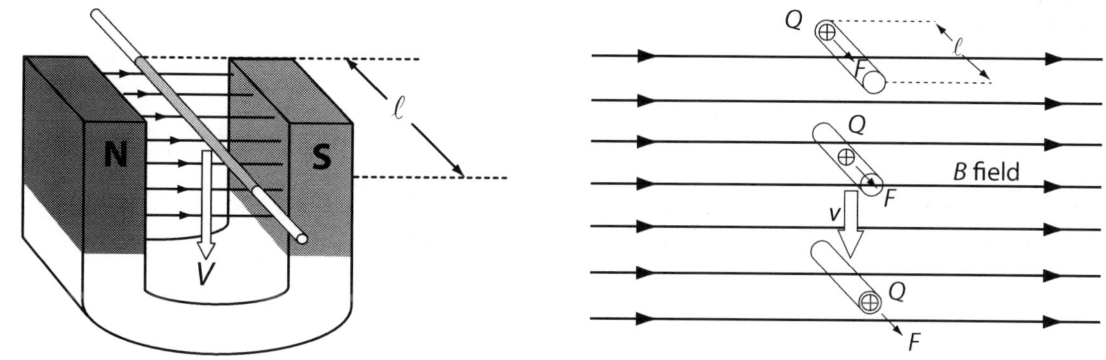

(a) (b)
Figure 8.1.1 *Using a magnet to induce an emf in a straight piece of wire*

Charges moving downward through the magnetic field will experience a force $F = BQv$, due to the external magnetic field. According to the right hand motor rule, the direction of this force will be out of the page, which means the charges will be forced to move along the length of the wire, which is also coming out of the page (Figure 8.1.1(b)).

When a charge Q is forced to move the length ℓ of the segment of wire in the magnetic field, the amount of work done on it will be

$$W = F \cdot d = BQv\ell$$

Because of the work done on them, the charges gained potential energy. The gain in potential energy per unit charge between the two ends of the segment of wire is the emf between the ends of the wire.

$$\text{Induced emf: } \mathcal{E} = \frac{BQv\ell}{Q} = Bv\ell$$

At first glance, it may seem unlikely that the units for emf in this formula could possibly be volts, so it is worth doing a unit check on this formula. The units of *Bvl* will be:

$$[\text{T}][\frac{\text{m}}{\text{s}}][\text{m}] = [\frac{\text{N}}{\text{Am}}][\frac{\text{m}}{\text{s}}][\text{m}] = \frac{\text{Nm}}{\text{As}} = \frac{\text{J}}{\text{C}} = \text{V}$$

Sample Problem 8.1.1 — Inducing EMF

How fast must a 25 cm piece of wire be made to move through the poles of a 0.50 T magnet in order to develop a potential difference of 1.0 V between its ends?

What to Think About	How to Do It
1. What do you know?	$\mathcal{E} = 1.00 \text{ V}$ $B = 0.50 \text{ T}$ $\ell = 0.25 \text{ m}$
2. Use $\mathcal{E} = Bv\ell$ and rearrange to solve for *v*.	$v = \dfrac{\mathcal{E}}{B\ell}$
3. Solve for *v*.	$v = \dfrac{1.00 \text{ V}}{(0.50 \text{ T})(0.25 \text{ m})} = 8.00 \text{ m/s}$

Practice Problems 8.1.1 — Inducing EMF

1. An aircraft with a wingspan of 30.0 m travelling 250 m/s dives perpendicular to the lines of force of Earth's magnetic field (5.0×10^{-5} T). What emf is induced between the two wing tips?

2. A 15 cm piece of wire is moved through the poles of a 0.40 T magnet with a speed of 5.0 m/s. What is the potential difference between the ends of the wire?

3. In Figure 8.1.1(b), in which direction would electrons tend to move along the segment of wire? (Into the page or out of the page?)

The Generator

Michael Faraday invented the generator. Figure 8.1.2 shows a simple, hand-operated generator with a coil consisting of only one turn (to simplify the explanation). When the coil is rotated, the two long sides of the coil cut across the lines of force of the magnet, and a varying emf is induced in these two segments.

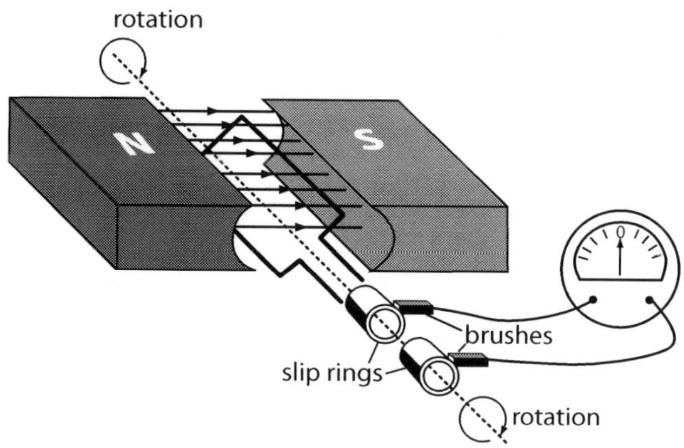

Figure 8.1.2 *A simple, hand-operated generator*

When the coil is vertical, as in Figure 8.1.3(a), the two segments of wire in which an emf can be induced are both moving parallel with the lines of force, and *no* emf is induced.

When the coil is horizontal, as in Figure 8.1.3(b), the segments in which an emf can be induced are perpendicular to the lines of force through which they are moving, and the induced emf is at its maximum or **peak voltage**.

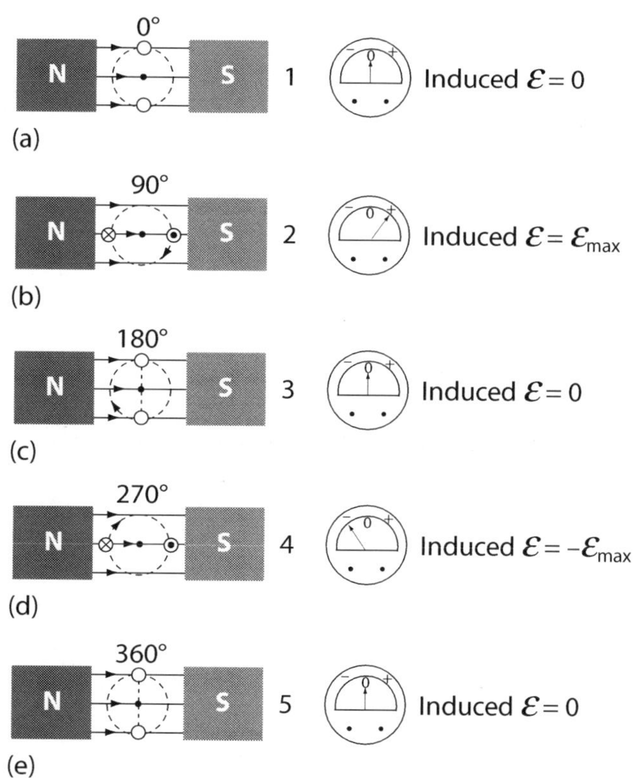

Figure 8.1.3 *As the coil turns in a magnetic field, it induces an emf. At 0°, 180°, and 360° the emf is zero. In each case, the coil is perpendicular to the lines of force. As the coil turns, the velocity vector is perpendicular to the magnetic field lines and an emf is induced. Maximum emf is achieved at 90° and 270°.*

Figure 8.1.3 begins with the coil of the generator perpendicular to the lines of force. Consider just the top segment of wire. Its length is ℓ and its speed is v. The strength of the magnetic field is B. The angle between the plane of the coil and the vertical position is $\theta = 0$.

At any position of the segment, the induced emf is $\mathcal{E} = B\ell v_{\perp}$, where $v_{\perp}$ is the component of v that is perpendicular to the magnetic field lines. When the segment is at the top position, $v_{\perp} = 0$. Therefore, when $\theta = 0$, $\mathcal{E} = 0$.

In Figure 8.1.3(b), the segment has made one-quarter of a rotation, and now $\theta = 90°$. In this position, the velocity vector is perpendicular to the magnetic field lines. At $\theta = 90°$, $v_{\perp} = v$, and the induced emf is at its maximum.

$$\mathcal{E} = \mathcal{E}_{max} = B\ell v$$

In Figure 8.1.3 (c), $v_{\perp} = 0$ again, so $\mathcal{E} = 0$ as well. In the fourth position (Figure 8.1.3 (d)) where $\theta = 270°$, the velocity vector has reversed its direction, so the induced emf also reverses. Therefore, at 270°, $\mathcal{E} = -\mathcal{E}_{max}$.

At any angle θ, $v_{\perp} = v\sin\theta$, and $\mathcal{E} = B\ell v\sin\theta$ (Figure 8.1.4). This is the emf induced in one segment. Since the coil has two segments whose emf's are additive, their combined emf is $2B\ell v\sin\theta$. For a more realistic generator coil with N turns in it,

$$\mathcal{E} = 2NB\ell v\sin\theta$$

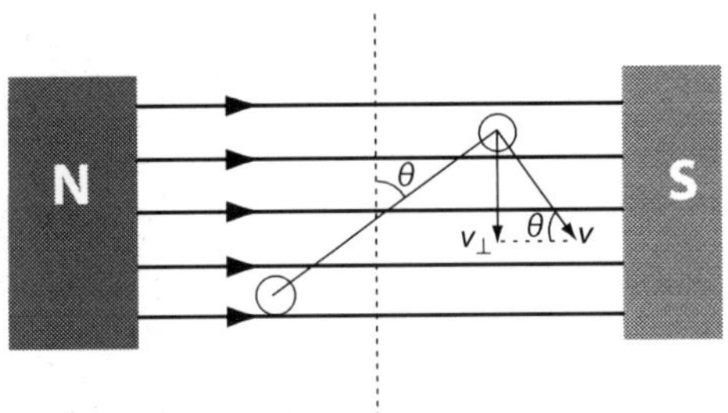

Figure 8.1.4 *At any angle θ, $v_{\perp} = v\sin\theta$, and $\mathcal{E} = B\ell v\sin\theta$.*

The maximum value of the induced emf is achieved when $\theta = 90°$, where $\sin\theta = 1$, and when $\theta = 270°$, where $\sin\theta = -1$.

Therefore, $\mathcal{E}_{max} = \pm 2NB\ell v$

And, in general:

$$\mathcal{E} = \mathcal{E}_{max}\sin\theta$$

Figure 8.1.5 is a graph showing how the induced emf varies with the angle through which the coil rotates. A graph of emf vs. time would have the same shape, since the coil will rotate with a constant frequency of rotation under normal circumstances.

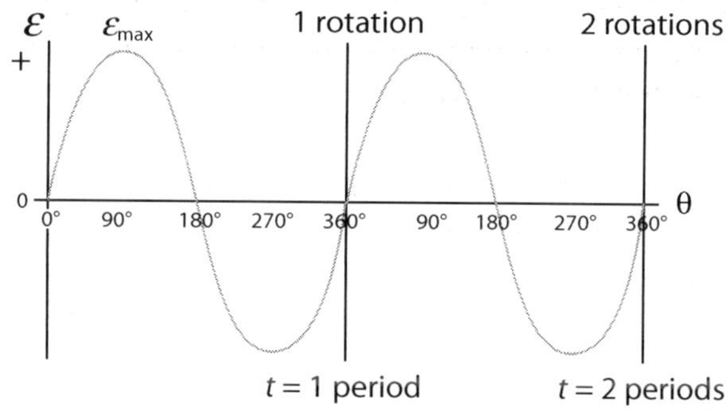

Figure 8.1.5 *Emf varies with the angle through which the coil rotates.*

The graph in Figure 8.1.5 is a typical *sinusoidal* graph since the emf varies as the sine of the angle. A graph of *current* vs. angle, or vs. time, is also sinusoidal because current is proportional to emf. The shape of this graph is the familiar shape of *alternating current*. Commercial generators in North America have a frequency of 60 Hz. This means they make one full cycle (360°) 60 times in one second.

Quick Check

1. (a) How might you convert the generator in Figure 8.1.2 so that instead of producing alternating emf and current, it will produce direct current? Would it be a steady DC?

   (b) Sketch a graph to show how the emf would vary with time.

2. Start with the formula for the induced emf of a generator: $\mathcal{E} = 2NB\ell v \sin\theta$. The speed of a segment of the coil can be calculated from $v = 2\pi R/T$, where R is the radius of the circle traced out by the rotating segment, and T is the period of the rotation. Write an equation for the emf induced by a generator in terms of the frequency (f) of rotation of the coil.

3. Assuming the coil in a generator is rectangular, its area would equal its length times its total width; that is, $A = 2\ell r$. Rewrite your equation from question 2 in terms of the *area* of the coil.

Investigation 8.1.1 Electromagnetic Induction

Purpose
To investigate some ways of inducing an emf

Part 1

Procedure

1. Attach the two ends of a 2.0 m length of wire to the terminals of a sensitive galvanometer, as shown in Figure 8.1.6.

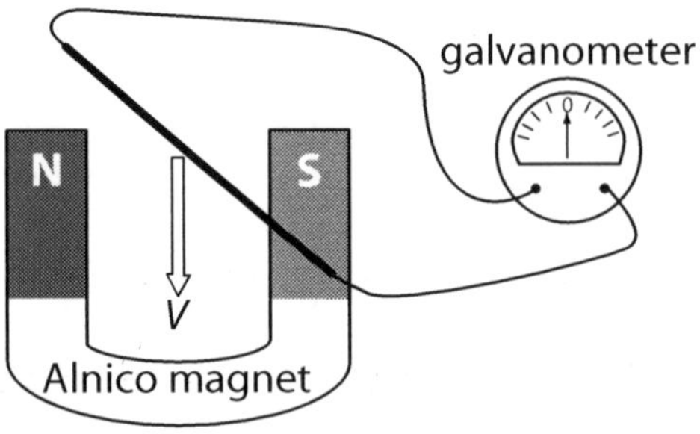

Figure 8.1.6

2. Move a section of the wire swiftly downward between the poles of a strong Alnico horseshoe magnet. Watch the galvanometer scale carefully for a very small deflection. Note the direction of the deflection. Move the section of wire swiftly upward in the opposite direction between the poles of the magnet. Observe the direction of the galvanometer deflection again.
3. Leave the wire stationary and move the magnet instead of the wire.
4. Try moving the wire in a direction parallel with the lines of force of the magnet.
5. Form a coil with *one* turn of the wire, and try moving the coil over one pole of the magnet, as shown in Figure 8.1.7.

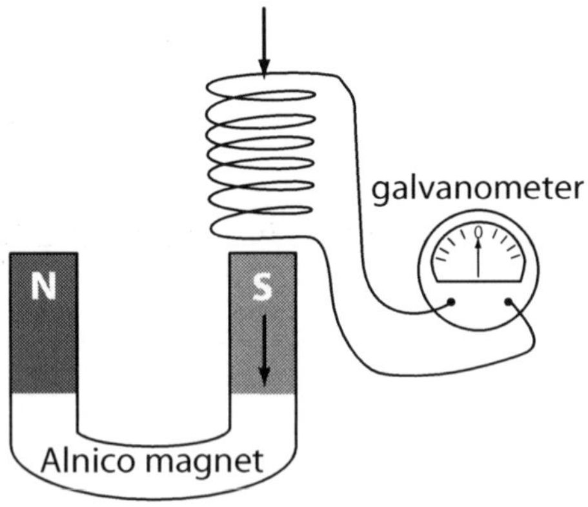

Figure 8.1.7

6. Experiment with more turns on the coil and with different speeds. Does it matter whether the coil moves or the magnet moves? Does the direction of the induced current depend on the direction of motion of the coil relative to the magnet?

7. Connect your galvanometer to a commercial solenoid like the one you used in the investigations in the last chapter (Figure 8.1.8). Insert the north pole of a bar magnet into the solenoid. Observe the direction of the induced current while the magnet's north pole is (a) entering and (b) leaving the solenoid.

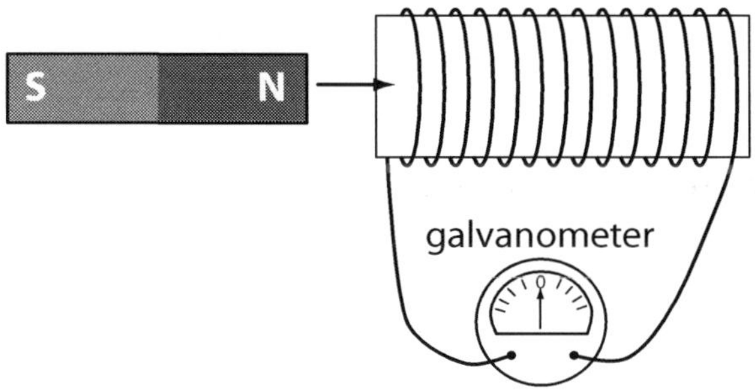

Figure 8.1.8

8. Try inserting the south pole of your bar magnet first. Again, observe the current direction while the magnet is (a) entering and (b) leaving the solenoid.
9. Try using two bar magnets held with like poles side by side. This will be approximately double the magnetic field strength.
10. Experiment until you are satisfied that you know what variables contribute to obtaining the highest possible induced current.
11. Draw a diagram showing a bar magnet being inserted north pole first into a solenoid. Show the direction of the induced current on the diagram. Now use Ampère's right hand rule to determine the magnetic polarity of the end of the solenoid that is nearest the north pole of the bar magnet.

Concluding Questions

1. Summarize the factors that contribute to a larger induced current when a magnet and a coil are used.
2. When a magnet is moved into or out of a solenoid, a current is induced in the solenoid. This in turn produces a magnetic field in the solenoid. Describe the polarity of the solenoid relative to the polarity of the permanent magnet being used to induce the emf in the solenoid (a) when the bar magnet enters the solenoid and (b) when the bar magnet leaves the solenoid.

Part 2

Procedure

1. Set up the arrangement shown in Figure 8.1.9. The battery is connected by way of a switch to the first coil, but not the second. A galvanometer is connected to the second coil.

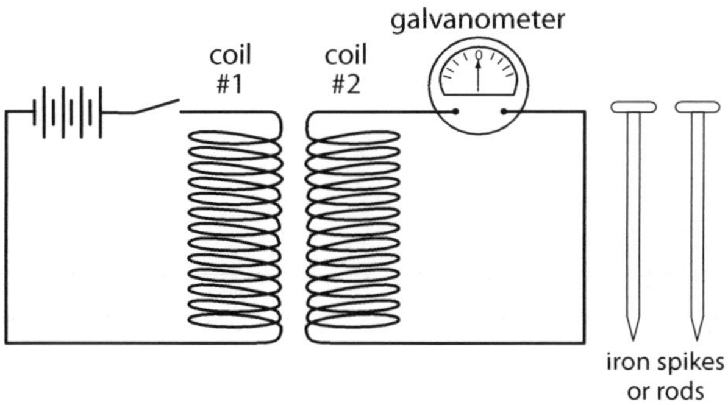

Figure 8.1.9

2. With the two coils very close but not touching, turn on the switch to send current through the first coil. Does the galvanometer indicate current in the second coil? Turn off the current. If you did not see anything happen, try it all again. Watch the galvanometer needle very closely while you are turning the switch on and while you are turning it off.
3. Place a soft iron core (perhaps a few large spikes) inside each of the coils, and repeat step 2.
4. If available, use a smaller solenoid as a second coil that will fit inside the first coil. Repeat step 2 with and without an iron core. Find out what the effect is of varying the number of turns in coil number 1, by inserting coil number 2 only a small fraction of the way inside the larger coil.
5. Examine a demonstration induction coil. How is "off" and "on" switching accomplished with this high voltage device?

Concluding Questions

1. Under what conditions is a current induced in the second coil by a current in the first coil? Why do you think there is no induced current when the current in the first coil is constant?
2. Describe the direction of the induced current while the current in the first coil is turned off, compared with the direction of the induced current when the current in the first coil is turned on.

Challenge

1. Examine a demonstration transformer. This is an excellent example of a device in which an emf is induced. Why does the transformer require no on-off switching mechanism?

Figure 8.1.10 *A demonstration transformer*

8.1 Review Questions

1. How can you move the wire in the diagram below to induce an emf in the wire XY?

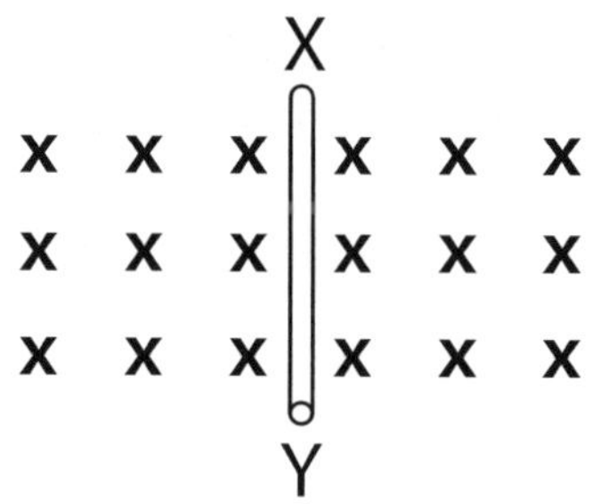

2. When the north end of the bar magnet is moved out of the solenoid as shown below, what is the direction of the induced current in the solenoid? What is the polarity of end B of the solenoid?

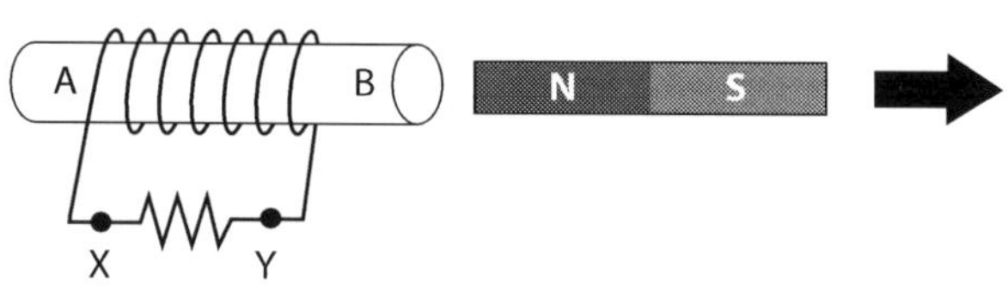

3. List four factors you could change to increase the emf produced by a generator. Describe how you would change them.

4. How fast would you have to move a 0.50 m wire perpendicular to Earth's magnetic field (5.0×10^{-5} T) to induce an emf of 1.5 V?

5. In what position will switch S need to be for the galvanometer G to indicate a small current in this circuit?

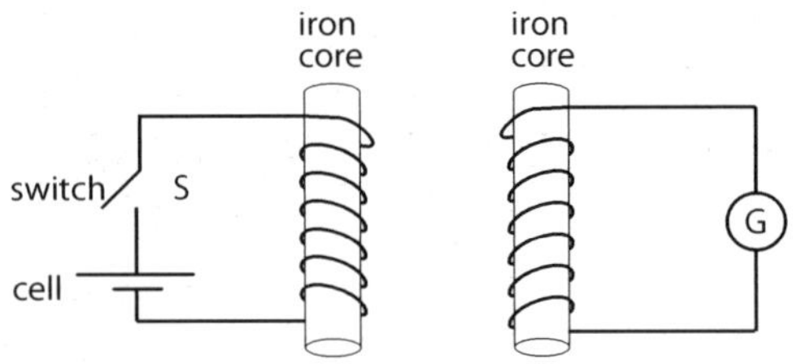

6. An airplane with a wingspan of 12.0 m travels at right angles through a magnetic field of strength 5.0×10^{-3} T. An emf of 1.5 V is induced between the ends of the wingtips. How fast was the airplane moving?

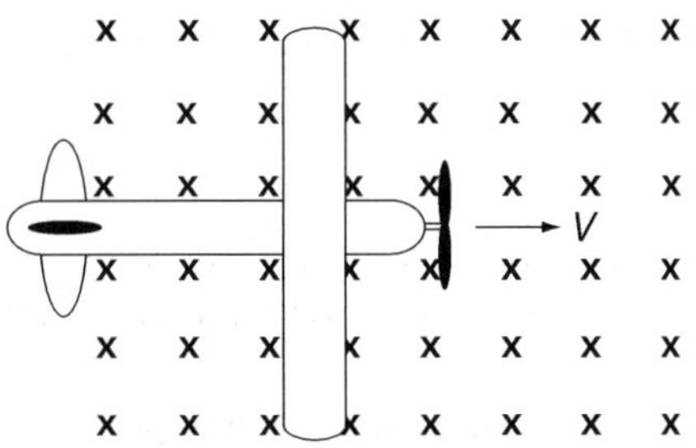

7. The armature of a 60 Hz AC generator rotates in a magnetic field of strength 0.48 T. If the area of the coil is 2.4×10^{-2} m^2 and it contains 120 loops, what will the peak emf be?

8. A generator coil has 170 turns. It has a cross-sectional area of 4.00×10^{-2} m^2. In a time of 0.20 s, the magnetic field changes from 1.20 T to 1.50 T. What is the average emf induced in the coil?

8.2 Magnetic Flux and Faraday's Law of Induction

Warm Up

Your teacher will drop a circular magnet through a copper tube or show you a video of this happening. Describe what you observe and suggest a possible explanation.

____

____

____

Magnetic Flux

Investigation 8.1.1 probably convinced you that an essential requirement for inducing an emf in a wire or a coil is a changing magnetic field. You obtained a changing field in two ways in that investigation:

(1) by moving a permanent magnet relative to a conductor or vice versa
(2) by turning a current on or off, causing the magnetic field to build up or collapse in the area of the conductor

You probably noticed that the faster you changed the field, the more induced current you observed on the galvanometer. Since the current was caused by the induced emf, it would appear that the induced emf is greater when the time duration of the change in the magnetic field is less.

$$\mathcal{E} \propto 1/\Delta t$$

Michael Faraday observed that the amount of induced emf depended not simply on the change in magnetic field strength (B), but on the change in **magnetic flux.** The symbol for magnetic flux is ϕ.

Magnetic flux ϕ is defined as the product of (a) the component of the magnetic field strength B that is perpendicular to the plane of the coil, and (b) the area A of the coil (Figure 8.2.1 and 8.2.2). If the angle between B and the axis of the coil is θ, then

$$\textit{Magnetic flux } \phi = B_{\perp}A = BA\cos\theta$$

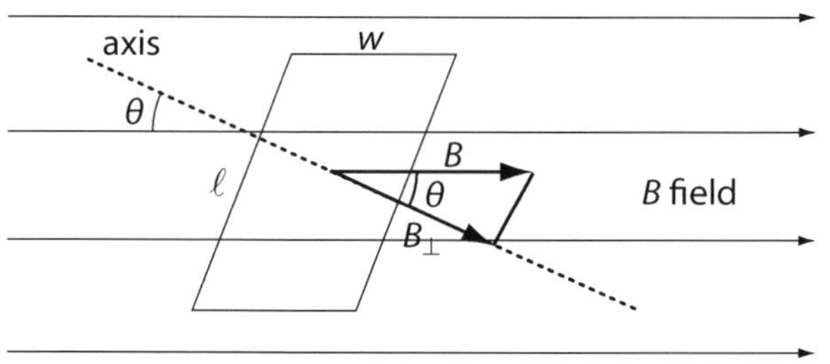

Figure 8.2.1 *Magnetic flux ϕ is defined as the product of (a) the component of the magnetic field strength B that is perpendicular to the plane of the coil, and (b) the area A of the coil.*

What Faraday found out was that the amount of induced emf depends on the rate at which the magnetic flux changes with respect to time.

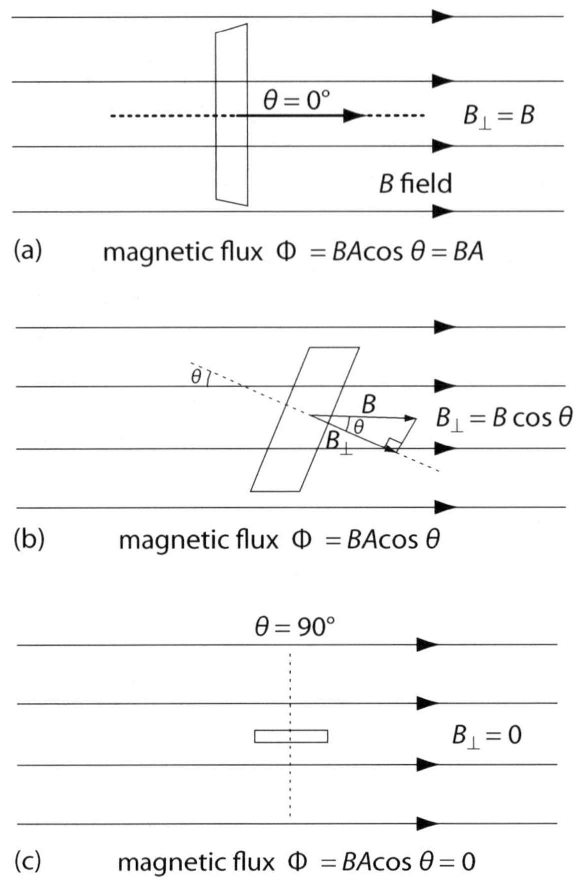

Figure 8.2.2 *Variations in magnetic flux*

For a wire loop of one turn (Figures 8.2.1 and 8.2.2), if the magnetic flux changes from ϕ_1 to ϕ_2, the change in magnetic flux will be $\Delta\phi = \phi_2 - \phi_1$ in a time interval of Δt. The induced emf will be

$$\mathcal{E} = -\frac{\Delta\Phi}{\Delta t}$$

For a wire loop with *N* turns, $\mathcal{E} = -N\frac{\Delta\Phi}{\Delta t}$

This general rule for magnetic induction is called **Faraday's law of induction.**

Units for Magnetic Flux

The measuring unit for magnetic flux ϕ could be T·m^2, since flux is the product of magnetic field and area, but for historical reasons this unit is called the **weber (Wb)**.

$$1 \text{ Wb} = 1 \text{ T·m}^2$$

It is worthwhile doing a unit check on the formula for Faraday's law.

$$\mathcal{E} = -N\frac{\Delta\Phi}{\Delta t} = -N\frac{\Delta(BA\cos\theta)}{\Delta t}$$

$$1\left[\frac{\text{Wb}}{\text{s}}\right] = 1\left[\frac{\text{Tm}^2}{\text{s}}\right] = 1\left[\frac{\frac{\text{N}}{\text{Am}}\text{m}^2}{\text{s}}\right] = 1\left[\frac{\text{Nm}}{\text{As}}\right] = 1\left[\frac{\text{J}}{\text{C}}\right] = 1\text{ V}$$

Since emf should be in volts, the units "check out."

Why the Minus Sign?

When a changing flux causes an emf to be induced, the induced emf in turn produces an induced current. The induced current causes a magnetic field to be induced around it. This induced magnetic field opposes the magnetic flux that produced the induced emf in the first place!

This observation is called Lenz's law, after Heinrich Lenz who first made it. Lenz's law is really a special case of the law of conservation of energy. To obtain energy from a generator, mechanical energy must be used to obtain the electrical energy. Work must be done to overcome the repulsive or attractive forces that exist between the permanent magnet's field and the induced magnetic field that results from the induced current.

Lenz's Law
The polarity of the induced emf will always be such that it will produce a current whose magnetic field opposes the changing flux that produced the emf.

Sample Problem 8.2.1 — Applying Faraday's Law of Induction

A circular loop of wire of radius 2.5 cm is in a magnetic field of 0.40 T. If the loop is removed from the field in a time of 0.050 s, what is the average induced emf? (The axis of the loop is parallel with the field.)

What to Think About	How to Do It
1. Identify what you know.	$N = 1$ $\Delta\Phi = \Delta[B_{\perp}A]$ $B_{\perp 1} = 0.40\text{ T}$ $B_{\perp 2} = 0.00\text{ T}$ $\Delta t = 0.050\text{ s}$ $A = \pi r^2 = \pi(0.025\text{ m})^2$
2. Find the change in magnetic field strength. Remember that area of a circle is πr^2. 3. Solve to find the average induced emf	$\mathcal{E} = -N\frac{\Delta\Phi}{\Delta t} = -N\frac{\Delta[B_{\perp}A]}{\Delta t} = -NA\frac{[B_{\perp 2} - B_{\perp 1}]}{\Delta t}$ $\mathcal{E} = \frac{-(1)(\pi)(2.5\times10^{-2}\text{ m})^2(0-0.40\text{ T})}{(0.050\text{ s})}$ $\mathcal{E} = 1.6\times10^{-2}\text{ V}$

Practice Problems 8.2.1 — Applying Faraday's Law of Induction

1. A square coil of wire 5.0 cm on a side has 100 turns. It lies between the poles of a magnet of field strength 0.020 T. If it is rotated through 90° in a time of 2.0×10^{-3} s, what is the average induced emf?

2. A square loop with sides 12 cm by 12 cm has 25 turns of wire and is in a magnetic field of strength 4.2×10^{-2} T, with its axis perpendicular to the direction of the field. If it is rotated in 0.15 s so that its axis is parallel to the field, what is the average induced emf during this quarter turn of the loop?

3. The magnetic flux in a coil of 50 turns changes from –0.56 Wb to +0.14 Wb in a time of 7.0 ms. What is the average induced emf?

Counter EMF ("Back EMF") in a Motor

An electric motor has essentially the same design as a generator. The generator changes mechanical energy into electrical energy, whereas the motor does the exact opposite. It changes electrical energy into mechanical energy. When current exists in the armature of a motor, the armature turns in the magnetic field of the motor. This causes the motor to produce an induced emf that *opposes* the voltage of the source making the motor turn!

The motor cannot help itself! It automatically becomes a generator as soon as its armature turns. Consistent with Lenz's law, the induced emf acts counter to the source emf, so it is called **counter emf** or **back emf**. The back emf increases when the motor armature frequency increases, as would be expected of a generator.

Kirchhoff's law applies in this situation. If the source emf is $\mathcal{E}_S$, then

$$\mathcal{E}_S = Ir + IR + \mathcal{E}_B$$

where I is the current, r is the internal resistance of the source, R is the resistance of the armature of the motor, and E_B is the back emf (Figure 8.2.3).

$$\mathcal{E}_B = \mathcal{E}_S - Ir - IR, \text{ or}$$

$$\varepsilon_B = V_{AB} - IR$$

where V_{AB} is the **terminal voltage** of the source.

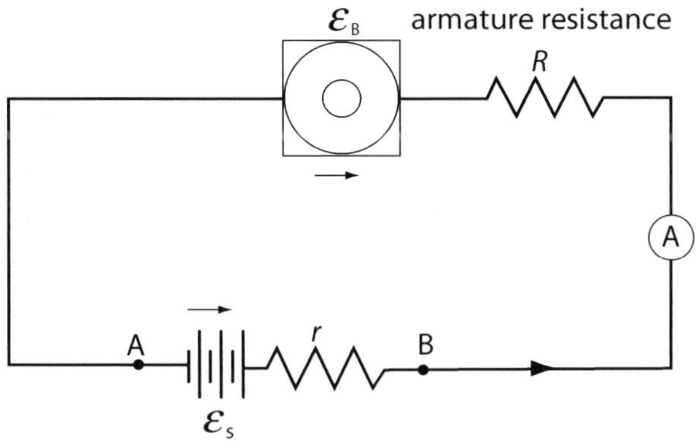

Figure 8.2.3 *When current exists in the armature of a motor, the armature turns in the magnetic field of the motor. This causes the motor to produce an induced emf that opposes the voltage of the source emf.*

Quick Check

1. An electric motor is operated from a 6.0 V supply. When the armature is held still, the current in it is 4.0 A. When the armature is allowed to turn freely, the current is 2.4 A.
   (a) What is the resistance of the armature?

   (b) What is the back emf of the motor at this frequency of rotation?

   (c) If the load on the motor is increased so that its frequency is reduced to three-quarters of what it was, what will the back emf be?

2. A motor has an armature resistance of 1.8 Ω. Running at full speed, it draws a current of 0.50 A when connected to a 12.0 V source. What is the back emf?

Transformers

A **transformer** is designed specifically to alter the voltage in an alternating current (AC) circuit. Electricity is transmitted over long distances at very high voltages, because it is more economical to do so. (The reasons for this will be discussed later.) The electricity delivered into your house is at a much lower voltage (120 V or 240 V). Your doorbell system might operate at approximately 18 V. A transformer can change a low voltage to a high voltage *or* a high voltage to a low voltage.

The transformer has two coils in it, called the **primary coil** and the **secondary coil**. In an iron-core transformer such as the one in Figure 8.2.4, the coils are linked magnetically by a laminated, soft iron core. A magnetic field produced by the primary coil will also engulf the secondary coil.

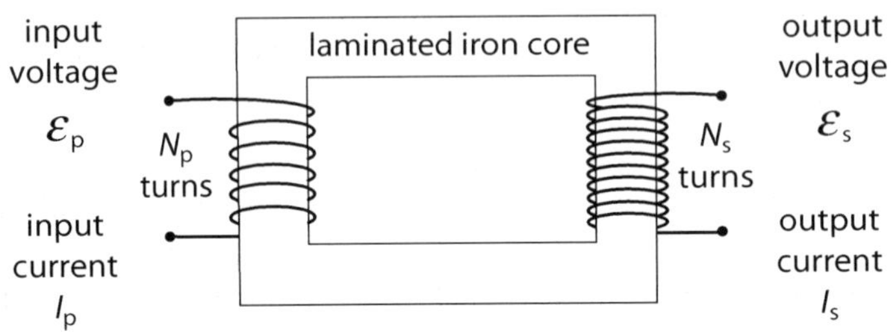

Figure 8.2.4 *A transformer with 6 turns on the primary coil and 11 turns on the secondary coil*

If an AC voltage $\mathcal{E}_p$ is applied to the primary coil of the transformer, the AC current in the primary coil will produce a changing magnetic field, and therefore a changing magnetic flux. If the rate of change of flux with respect to time is $\Delta\phi/\Delta t$, then the emf induced in the secondary coil will be of magnitude

$$\mathcal{E}_s = -N_s \frac{\Delta\phi}{\Delta t}$$

The changing flux simultaneously induces a counter-emf in the primary coil that (if resistance is negligible in the primary circuit) just equals the applied voltage. This is consistent with Kirchhoff's voltage law applied to the primary circuit.

$$\mathcal{E}_p = -N_p \frac{\Delta\phi}{\Delta t}$$

If the two equations are divided, then

$$\frac{\mathcal{E}_s}{\mathcal{E}_p} = \frac{N_s}{N_p}$$

This is a fundamental transformer equation. What it says is this:

- If you want to step up the voltage, use more turns in the secondary coil than in the primary coil. (This is what a step-up transformer does.)
- If you want to step down the voltage, use fewer turns in the secondary coil than in the primary coil. (This is what a step-down transformer does.)

Transformers can be very efficient. In other words, the power output at the secondary coil is very nearly equal to the power input at the primary coil. (An efficiency of 99% is common.) If we assume that

$$P_p = P_s$$

$$\text{then, } I_p\mathcal{E} = I_s\mathcal{E}_s$$

$$\frac{\mathcal{E}_s}{\mathcal{E}_p} = \frac{I_p}{I_s}$$

The ratio of the voltages in the coils is inversely proportional to the ratio of the corresponding currents.

Long-Distance Transmission of Electricity

Transformers are essential to long-distance transmission of power. In order to minimize power loss in transmission lines, the voltage produced at the generator is stepped up to higher voltages, typically 500 000 V, before transmitting the power. The step-up in voltage is accompanied by a step-down in current, since

$$\frac{I_s}{I_p} = \frac{\mathcal{E}_p}{\mathcal{E}_s}$$

An example will illustrate why it is more economical to deliver power at high voltage than it is at low voltage.

Example: A generator at city A delivers power at the rate of 1.00 MW to city B. The total resistance of the very low resistance cables between A and B is only 10.0 Ω.

Situation I Power is delivered at a low voltage of only 5000 V.	**Situation II** Power is delivered at a higher voltage of 500 000 V
1. The current in the cables would be: $I = \frac{P}{V} = \frac{1.00 \times 10^6 \text{ W}}{5.00 \times 10^3 \text{ V}} = 2.00 \times 10^2 \text{ A}$ 2. The power *lost as heat* in the cables would be: $P_L = I^2R = (2.00 \times 10^2 \text{ A})^2(10.0\ \Omega)$ $P_L = 4.0 \times 10^5 \text{ W}$ **Summary** Of the 1 000 000 W supplied, 400 000 W or 40% would be wasted as thermal energy at this low voltage.	1. The current in the cables would be: $I = \frac{P}{V} = \frac{1.00 \times 10^6 \text{ W}}{5.00 \times 10^5 \text{ V}} = 2.0 \text{ A}$ 2. The power *lost as heat* in the cables would be: $P_L = I^2R = (2.0 \text{ A})^2(10.0\ \Omega)$ $P_L = 4.0 \times 10^1 \text{ W}$ **Summary** Of the 1 000 000 W supplied, only 40 W or only *0.004%* would be wasted as thermal energy.

Quick Check

1. Why will a transformer not work with DC current?

2. A transformer has 120 turns in the primary coil and 600 turns in the secondary coil. If 120 V is applied to the primary coil, what will the secondary coil voltage be?

3. The primary coil of a transformer has 5000 turns and the voltage across it is 120 V. The secondary coil has 50 turns.
   (a) What is the voltage across the secondary coil?

   (b) What is the primary coil current if the current in the secondary coil is 10.0 A?

Investigation 8.2.1 Back EMF of an Electric Motor

Purpose

To investigate electromagnetic induction in an electric motor

Procedure

1. Connect a small DC motor to a galvanometer. Turn the shaft with your fingers and watch the galvanometer. Turn the shaft in the opposite direction. Try turning the shaft faster.
2. Set up the circuit in Figure 8.2.5. Choose a battery or power supply voltage that will make the shaft turn at its top speed. (Instructions with the motor will say what the maximum safe operating voltage is.)

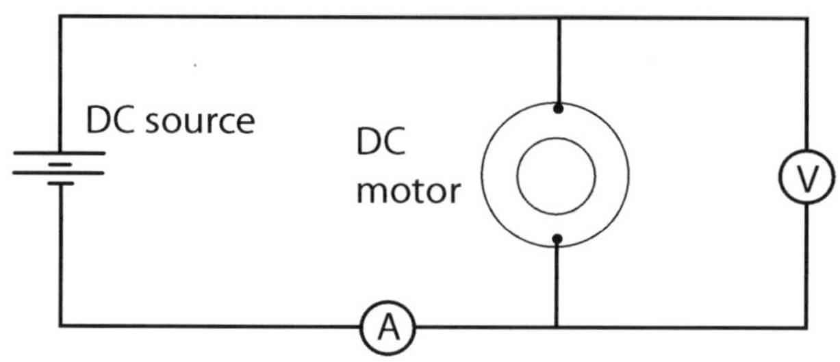

Figure 8.2.5

3. You will need to know the resistance of the armature of the motor. To find out what it is, do the following:
   (a) Stop the shaft of the motor from turning by holding it with your fingers.
   (b) Measure the voltage across the motor and the current through the motor.
   (c) Calculate the armature resistance by using Ohm's law: $R = V/I$.
4. Measure the back emf of your motor while it is running at full speed. To do this, measure V across the motor, which is equal to the terminal voltage of the power supply or battery. Measure I and then calculate $\mathcal{E}_B = V - IR$.
5. Let the motor run, but brake the shaft slightly with your fingers. What happens to the current? What happens to the back emf?
6. To find out how the back emf varies with the frequency of rotation of the motor shaft, use the set-up shown in Figure 8.2.6. A thread approximately 1.5 m long is attached to an enlarged spindle on the motor shaft, and a small mass (washer) is attached to the other end of the thread. This mass will provide a load that will slow down the motor's frequency.

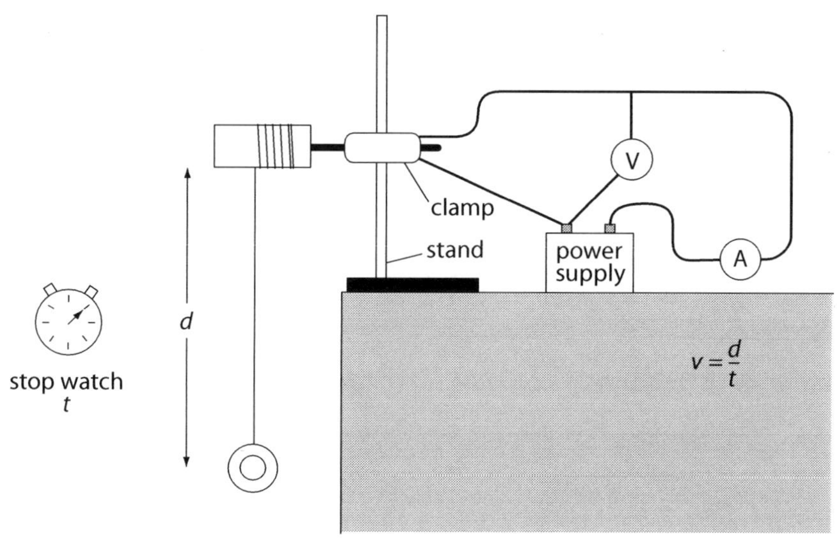

Figure 8.2.6

7. With a load of one washer on the thread, turn on the motor and measure the time it takes the motor to lift the load a measured distance (perhaps 1.00 m). Calculate the speed at which the washer rises ($v = d/t$). Repeat the same procedure with one washer, but record V and I, and calculate $\mathcal{E}_B = V - IR$. Copy Table 8.1.1 and record your data.
8. Repeat step 7, but with loads of 2, 3, 4, and 5 identical washers. Record your data in your copy of Table 8.1.1.
9. Plot a graph of $\mathcal{E}_B$ vs. v using your data from steps 7 and 8.

Table 8.2.1 *Data for Back EMF vs Speed*

Load	d	t	v	I	V	R	$\mathcal{E}_B$
Washers	m	s	m/s	A	V	Ω	V
1							
2							
3							
4							
5							

Concluding Questions

1. When a current exists in an electric motor, magnetic torque makes the armature rotate. What limits the speed at which the shaft can rotate? (Why does it not accelerate indefinitely?)
2. How do you know that the induced current in a motor opposes the current that makes the motor turn in the first place?
3. How does the frequency of rotation of the motor's armature depend on the speed at which the motor lifted the washers? **Hint:** $v = 2\pi R/T = 2\pi Rf$.
4. How does the back emf depend on the frequency of rotation of the motor?
5. Could the back emf ever equal the terminal voltage of the source? Explain.

8.2 Review Questions

1. What is the magnetic flux ϕ through a coil of wire that has an area of 5.0×10^{-2} m^2 and a plane perpendicular to a magnetic field of magnitude 2.0×10^{-3} T?

2. A square coil with 85 turns, measuring 0.15 m on each side, is in a magnetic field of strength 5.0×10^{-2} T. If the coil is removed from the field in 0.20 s, what is the average emf induced in the coil?

3. The graph below shows how magnetic flux through a single loop of wire changes with time. What is the average emf induced in the loops, between $t = 0.25$ s and $t = 0.50$ s?

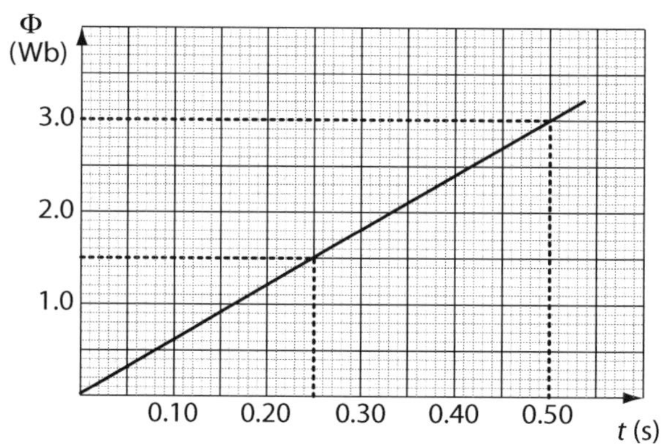

4. The back emf of a motor is 4.2 V when operated from a 6.0 V source. When held stationary, the current in the motor's armature is 5.0 A.
   (a) What is the resistance of the armature?

   (b) What current will exist in the armature when it is rotating at normal speed?

5. Why might overloading a motor actually destroy the armature of the motor?

6. The input power for a motor is IV, where I is the current and V is the source voltage. The power lost as heat in the armature is I^2R. The power output of the motor is therefore $IV - I^2R$. The efficiency of the motor equals the ratio of power output to power input. Show that this ratio reduces to ε_B/V.

7. Is an electric motor more efficient at high frequency or low frequency? Explain.

8. A transformer has 50 primary turns and 2000 secondary turns. The primary coil is connected to a 240 V source. If the secondary current is 2.5 mA, what is the
   (a) secondary voltage?

   (b) primary current?

   (c) power output of the secondary coil?

   (d) power input at the primary coil?

9. Why is a step-down transformer inserted between your circuit box and your doorbell circuit?

10. Find out why the iron core of a transformer is made in insulated layers (laminated) instead of one solid block of steel. What are "eddy currents"?

Chapter 8 Review Questions

1. The magnet in the diagram below is moved to the right toward the inside centre of the solenoid, in what direction will conventional current in the resistor move? Explain.

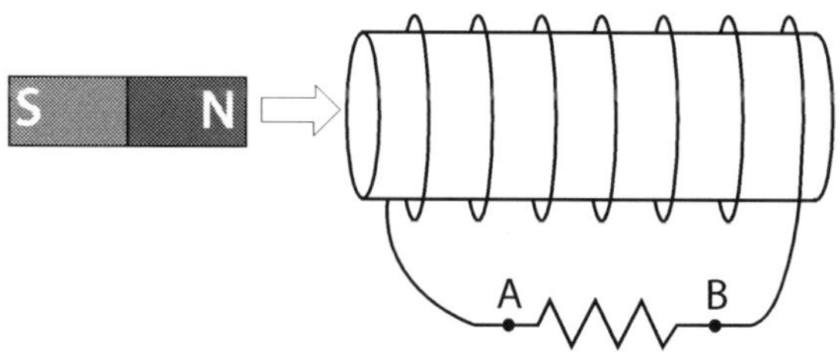

2. A straight piece of wire 10.0 cm long is moved through the poles of a magnet of strength 0.25 T at a speed of 4.0 m/s. What emf is induced between the ends of the wire? What is the electric field strength in the wire while it is moving?

3. What is the difference between magnetic field strength and magnetic flux?

4. What is Faraday's law of induction (a) in symbols and (b) in words?

5. What is Lenz's law?

6. A loop of area 225 cm^2 has 24 turns of wire. It is in a magnetic field of strength 3.6 x 10^{-2} T. To begin with, its plane (face) is parallel to the lines of force of the field. In a time of 0.15 s, it is rotated so that its plane is perpendicular to the lines of force. What is the average emf induced in the loop during the one-quarter rotation?

7. Draw a solenoid with a few representative turns. A permanent magnet is moving toward it from the right, with the south pole about to enter the solenoid. What will be the polarity of the right end of the solenoid at this instant? Sketch which way current will move in the solenoid if it is connected to a conducting path.

8. By how much must the magnetic flux inside a coil of 100 turns change in a time of 1.0 ms to produce an emf of 2.0 V?

9. What is the peak emf of a generator that has a frequency of 60 Hz, a magnetic field strength of 0.64 T, a coil of area 0.120 m^2, and 250 turns in its coil?

10. The diagram below shows how the emf produced by an AC generator varies with time. Show on this diagram how the graph would change if both the number of turns on the generator's rotating armature and the frequency of rotation of the armature were doubled.

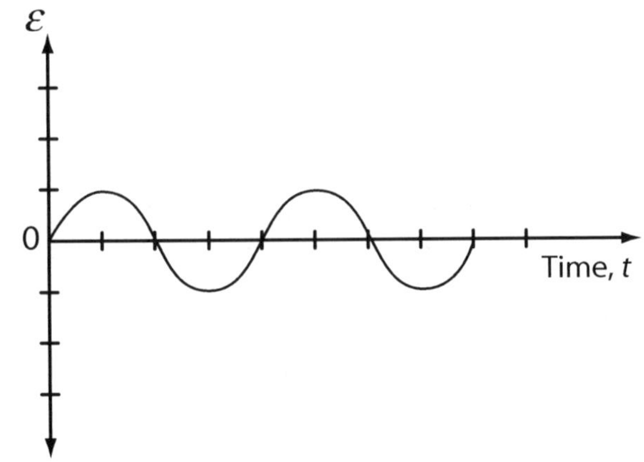

11. The armature resistance of a motor is 1.8 Ω. If the source voltage is 12.0 V, what is the back emf of the motor, which draws 2.0 A when running at full speed?

12. What is the efficiency of a motor if its back emf is 8.0 V when the source voltage is 12.0 V?

13. The back emf of a motor is 6.3 V when the current is 3.0 A. What is the armature resistance if the source voltage is 9.0 V?

14. The armature of a DC motor has a resistance of 5.0 Ω. The motor is connected to a 120 V line, and when the motor reaches full speed the back emf is 108 V.
    (a) What is the current at start-up (before the motor turns over)?

    (b) What is the current when the motor is being used?

15. The primary voltage of a step-up transformer is 120 V. The primary coil has 50 turns and the secondary coil has 800 turns.
    (a) What is the output voltage in the secondary coil?

    (b) What is the current in the secondary coil if the primary coil current is 16 mA?

    (c) What is the power input to the primary coil?

16. A transformer has 400 primary turns and the input voltage to the primary coil is 120 V. The secondary coil voltage is 6000 V. How many turns are there in the secondary coil?

17. A transformer has an efficiency of 98%. A primary voltage of 240 V is stepped down to 12.0 V. If the secondary current is 20.0 A, what is the primary current?

18. A coil of radius 0.072 m and with 36 turns is in a magnetic field of 0.80 T. If the coil is completely removed from the field in a time of 20.0 ms, what is the induced emf in the coil?

19. If the magnetic flux through a coil of wire with 300 turns changes from +5.0 Wb to −10.0 Wb in a time of 0.050 s, what emf is induced in the coil?

20. The magnetic field perpendicular to a coil of wire with radius 4.2 cm and 24 turns changes from + 0.25 T to − 0.25 T in a time of 0.15 s. What is the magnitude of the induced emf?

21. Will the induced current in the conductor below be into the page or out of the page? Explain why.

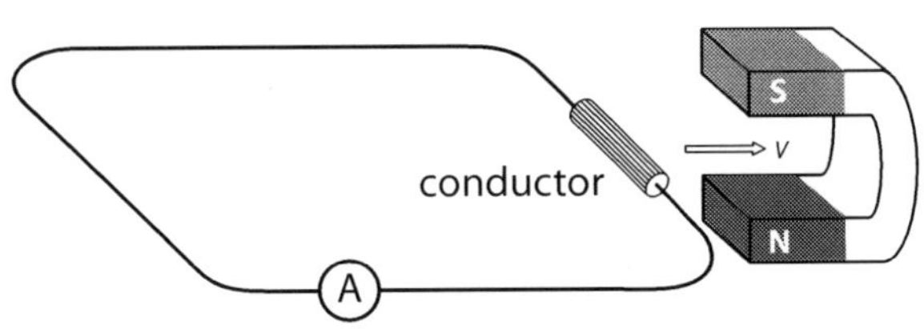

22. A wire 7.8 cm long moves with a velocity of 2.4 m/s through a magnetic field of strength 0.68 T, which is directed into the page on the diagram below. The velocity vector makes an angle of 45° with the wire.

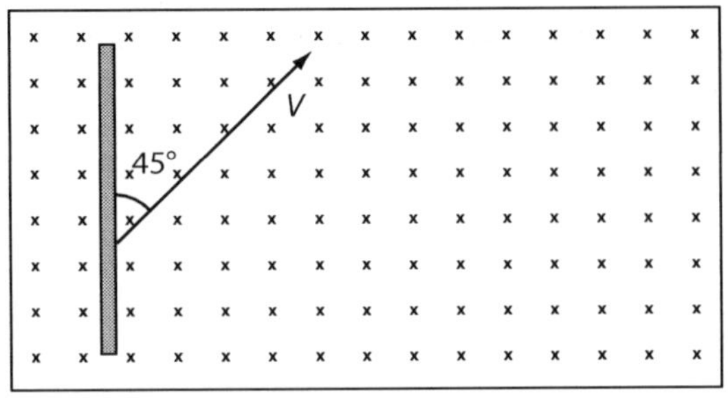

(a) What is the magnitude of the induced emf in the wire?

(b) Which end of the wire will become positively charged?

(c) What is the magnitude and direction of the electric field in the wire?

23. A voltage of 12 V is applied to an electric motor with an armature resistance of 5.0 Ω. When the armature is rotating at its peak speed, the current in it is 0.48 A. When a load is placed on the motor, its speed (frequency) is reduced to one-third of its peak speed. What is the back emf of the motor under this load?

24. A town receives 10 MW of power delivered at 50 kV from a generator over lines that have a resistance of 5.0 Ω. What percentage of the power generated is lost as heat in the lines?

Chapter 8 Extra Practice

1. In what direction in the diagram below should the wire XY move to induce an emf?

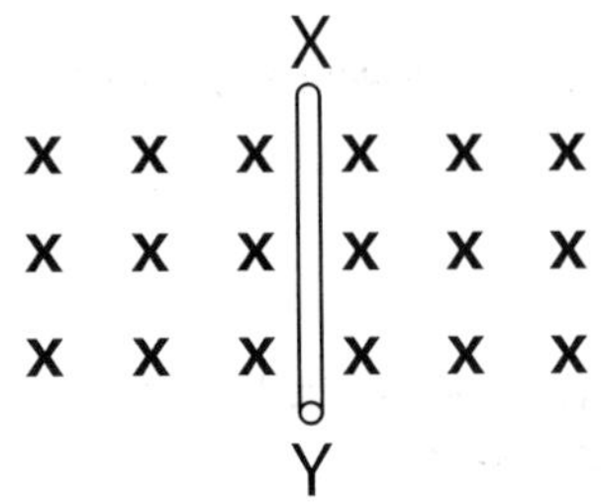

2. A DC motor is connected to a battery. The load on the motor increases, so the armature slows down. How will this affect the back emf and the current through the motor?

3. When the north end of the bar magnet is moved out of the solenoid as shown below, what is the direction of the induced current in the solenoid? What is the polarity of end B of the solenoid?

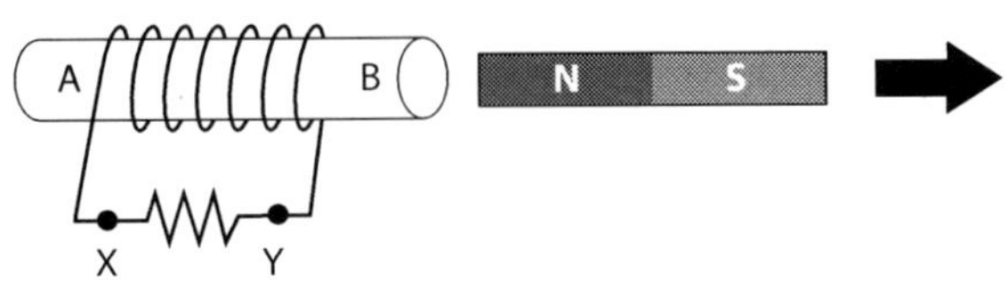

4. What is the magnetic flux, φ, through a coil of wire having an area of 5.0×10^{-2} m^2, whose plane is perpendicular to a magnetic field of magnitude 2.0×10^{-3} T?

5. A generator coil has 2500 turns. It has a cross-sectional area of 2.00×10^{-2} m^2. In a time of 0.20 s, the magnetic field changes from 1.80 T to 2.10 T. What is the average emf induced in the coil?

6. A square coil with 105 turns, measuring 0.20 m on each side, is in a magnetic field of strength 5.0×10^{-2} T. If the coil is removed from the field in 0.15 s, what is the average emf induced in the coil?

7. The airplane below has a wingspan of 12.0 m and travels at right angles through a magnetic field of strength 5.0×10^{-3} T. An emf of 1.5 V is induced between the ends of the wingtips. How fast was the airplane moving?

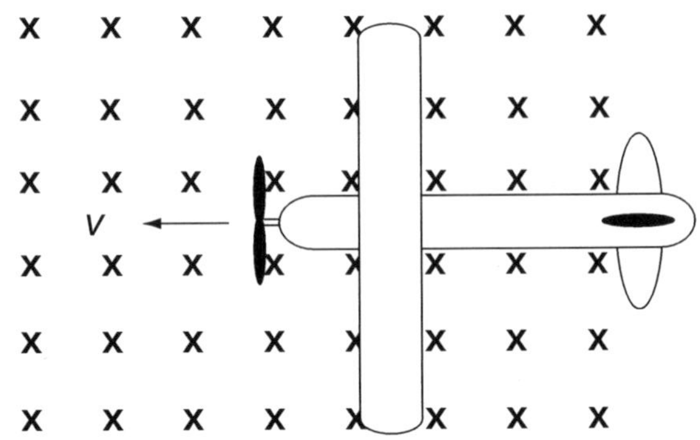

8. A DC motor is connected to a 12.0 V power supply. When the armature is rotating, the current is 3.80 A and the back emf is 10.40 V.
   (a) What is the resistance of the armature?
   (b) If the armature "jams" and cannot turn, what will the current in the armature be?

9. When a 3.0 V battery is connected to a motor with armature resistance 0.20 Ω, a current of 1.5 A exists in its windings. What is the back emf of the motor?

10. A transformer is plugged into a 120 V AC source. It has an output of 16 V AC. If the primary coil has 300 turns, how many turns are there in the secondary coil?

11. A transformer has 600 turns in the primary coil and 120 turns in the secondary coil. If the potential difference across the primary coil is 115 V AC, what emf is induced in the secondary coil?

12. A power station delivers 500 kW of power to a village through lines with a total resistance of 5.00 Ω. The input voltage is 400 000 V. If the input voltage was reduced to 10 000 V, by what factor would the power wasted as heat in the lines be multiplied?

Answer Key

Chapter 1

Page 5, Quick Check
1. the same
2. zero
3. (a) equilateral
 (b) right angle

Page 6, Quick Check
1. six ways
2. no difference
3. 260 m, 37° E of N
4. (a) 3 steps, 37° E of S
 (b) 17 steps

Page 10, 1.1 Review
1. (a) 720 N
 (b) 624 N
 (c) 360 N
 (d) 0 N
2. 5.0 N
3. 130 N, 22.6° E of N
4. 130 N, 67.4° S of E

Page 16, Practice Problems 1.2.1
1. (a) 0
 (b) 0
 (c) 0
2. F_4 is 2 grid squares in length, pointing right
3. F_x = 55 N. This component acts along the road

Page 20, Practice Problems 1.2.2
1. 30 km/h in the direction plane flying
2. 5.2° N of W
3. 316 km/h, 8.99° W of S

Page 21, 1.2 Review
1. (a) v_y
 (b) 12.3 m/s
 (c) 20.8 s
2. (a) v_x
 (b) 8.60 m/s
 (c) 179 m
3. 29.8° upstream
4. 60 N
5. 257 m, 29° E of N
6. 0.49 m/s, 12° to the right
7. (a) 22 km/h, 56° to the west
 (b) 1.5 km
8. (a) 240 N
 (b) 351 N
9. 19 km/h, 51.3° S of W

Page 26, Practice Problems 1.3.1
1. 94 N
2. 55°
3. (a) $1.98 \times 10^3 N$
 (b) So you don't have to include the weight of the beam in the calculation

Page 28, Quick Check
1. 5.00 m
2. Brother should sit half the distance of his little sister from the pivot and on the other side
3. 75 Nm

Page 33, 1.3 Review
1. 5.3 N
2. 37 cm
3. 6.1×10^2 N
4. 5.1×10^5 N
5. 69 N

Page 34, Chapter 1 Review
1. vectors have direction
2. 2.60×10^2 m, 67.4° E of S
3. 5.8 N, 31° W of N
4. (a) 56.0 N
 (b) 10.0 N
 (c) accelerate
5. 545 km/h (W), 779 km/h (N)
6. 852 km/h, 2.42° E of S
7. 5.0 km, 37° E of S
8. (a) 5.9×10^4 N
 (b) 6.9×10^3 N
 (c) 6.9×10^3 N
9. (a) 3.2×10^2 N
 (b) 6.9×10^2 N
10. (a) 250 N
 (b) 354 N
 (c) 500 N
 (d) 2.86×10^3 N
 (e) undefined (infinite)
11. (a) 500.0 N straight up
 (b) F_A=250 N; F_B=433 N
12. (a) 8.0 m/s at 37°E of the vertical
 (b) 2.5×10^3 s (42 min)
13. 1.9 m
14. 2.0×10^1 N
15. 9.9×10^2 N
16. F_A=1.1×10^3 N, down; F_B=2.3×10^3 N, up
17. 385 m

18. 4.7×10^3 km from the center of the earth, or 1.7×10^3 km below the crust of the earth!
19. 34 N
20.

$$F_f L\cos\theta = \frac{1}{2} mgL\sin\theta, \text{ so}$$

$$F_f = \frac{1}{2} mg\frac{\sin\theta}{\cos\theta} = \frac{1}{2} mg\tan\theta$$

Chapter 2

Page 46, Practice Problems 2.1.1

1. 4.0 s
2. 2.0 m/s
3. $-23.1\ m/s^2$

Page 48, Practice Problems 2.1.2

1. $0.102\ m/s^2$
2. 52.0 m
3. 4.71 s

Page 50, Practice Problems 2.1.3

1. 56.1 m/s
2. 92.4 m
3. $156\ cm/s^2$

Page 52, Quick Check

1. (a) $49\ m/s^2$
   (b) $-9.8\ m/s^2$
   (c) $49\ m/s^2$
2. B (time 1.2 s)
3. 5.9 m

Page 53, 2.1 Review Questions

1. 5.3×10^2 km
2. (a) 0.28 m/s
   (b) 14 m/s
   (c) 22 m/s
   (d) 28 m/s
3. (a) 38 m/s
   (b) 47 m
   (c) 1.2×10^2 m
4. (a) Yes, car stops in 47 m
   (b) No, car stops in 59 m
5. (a)

$$v_f^2 = v_o^2 + 2ad, \text{but } d = 0,$$

$$\therefore v_f^2 = v_o^2$$

$$\therefore |v_f| = |v_o|$$

   (b) No, same speed but in the opposite direction
6. $3.0\ m/s^2$
7. 4.1×10^2 m
8. (a) $0.43\ m/s^2$
   (b) 2.6 s

Page 58, Practice Problems 2.2.1

1. (a) 4.5 s
   (b) 1.2×10^2 m
2. (a) 34 m/s
   (b) 6.9 s
   (c) 2.4×10^2 m
   (d) You drive a golf ball farther on the moon!

Page 62, 2.2 Review

1. 4.1×10^2 m
2. (a) 1.0×10^1 m
   (b) 2.8×10^2 m
   (c) Ouch! Yes!
3. 1.9×10^2 m
4. (a) 21 m/s
   (b) 12 m/s
   (c) 2.4 s
   (d) 51 m
   (e) 7.3 m

5i. (a) 17 m/s
   (b) 17 m/s
   (c) 3.5 s
   (d) 6.0×10^1 m
   (e) 15 m

ii. (a) 12 m/s
   (b) 21 m/s
   (c) 4.3 s
   (d) 51 m
   (e) 23 m

6. (c) $v = (10.0\ m/s^2)t + 2.50$ m/s
   (e) $v_x = 2.12$ m/s

Page 65, Chapter 2 Review

2. 39.4 m
3. 34.3 m
4. 41 m (too short for a home run)
5. Misses by 3.0 cm
6. 34.5. It hits the wall 17.7 m above the firing point
7. 12.1 m
8. 27.7°
10. 28.5 m (about 29 m)
11. (a) $v_f = \pm 8.3$ m/s, t = 0.68 s and 2.4 s
    (b) as stone is going up it reaches 8.0 m and then reaches 8.0 m on the way down
12. Remember pebble is dropped from 1.8 m above the top of the window.

$$h_2 - h_1 = \frac{1}{2}a(t_2^2 - t_1^2)$$

$-1.8m = -4.9m/s^2(t_2 + t_1)(t_2 - t_1)$

Since $t_2 - t_1 = 0.25s$, (I)

-1.8m=-4.9m/s$^2(t_2 + t_1)(0.25s)$

$\therefore t_2 + t_1 = 1.47s$ (II)

Add (I) and (II): $2t_2 = 1.72s$

$\therefore t_2 = 0.86s$ and

$\therefore t_1 = 0.61s$

Solve for $d_1 = \frac{1}{2}at^2 = 1.8m$ above the top of the window

Page 72, Quick Check

1. $1.35 \times 10^3 kg$
2. $3.50 \times 10^3 N$
3. $40.0m/s^2$

Page 73, Practice Problems 3.1.1

1. 13.9 N
2. 0.200 m/s^2

Page 77, 3.1 Review

1. 0.17 m/s^2 upward
2. a = 0
3. (a) 3.3 m/s^2
   (b) 6.5 N, No
4. If he allows himself to be accelerated down the rope at 1.3 m/s^2, the tension force in the rope will be lessened from 735 N to 637 N, which the rope can handle
5. (a) 4.66 m/s^2
   (b) 37 m/s
6. 4,5 m/s^2. Constant velocity when F = 0 (Terminal velocity)

Page 81, Practice Problems 3.2.1

1. 5.3 m/s
2. zero
3. 0.57 m/s

Page 82, 3.2 Review Questions

1. 3.0 × 10^{-3} kgm/s
2. (a) 5.4 × 10^2 kgm/s
   (b) -5.4 × 10^2 Ns
   (c) -4.5 × 10^2 N
3. Throw the camera in a direction away from the shuttle
4. Thrust is 6.0 × 10^7 N, which is greater than the force of gravity on the rocket
5. 0.77 m/s
6. The bullet which rebounds has $\Delta p = -\frac{3}{2}mv$. The bullet hitting modelling clay has $\Delta p = -mv$. Since $F\alpha\Delta p$, the rebounding bullet must exert a greater fore.
7. (a) -13.0 Ns
   (b) -1.3 × 10^4 N
8. 3.6 × 10^2 m/s
9. 12 m/s
10. -8.0 × 10^1 Ns, F = -16 N

Page 92, 3.3 Review Questions

1. 2.7 m/s, 37.5° E of N
2. 3.3 m/s, 58° S of W
3. (a) 5.0 kgm/s
   (b) 33 m/s, 37° to direction of first mass
4. Struck proton: 3.0 × 10^6 m/s, 60° from the incident proton's original direction. Incident proton: 5.2 × 10^6 m/s
5. 22 km/h, 12° E of S
6. 259 kgm/s, force exerted 17° E of S

Page 95, Practice problems 3.4.1

1. (a) 1.2 × 10^3 J
   (b) 1.4 × 10^3 J. No, effort force is less
2. 6.8 × 10^2 J
3. Since the ball is moving in a direction perpendicular to the force acting on it, **no work** is done. Since there is no force component in the direction of motion, no work is done.

Page 82, Quick Check

1. 0.72 J
2. 0.41 m

Page 83, Quick Check

1. Doubling speed increases E_k by 4 times, while doubling mass only doubles E_k
2. 42 kJ
3. 180 kJ

Page 104, 3.4 Review

1. 10 N
2. 4.9 × 10^2 J
3. Ball is slowing down, so force and work are negative
4. 3.46 × 10^3 J
5. 215 J
6. Car A as the velocity increases kinetic energy by the square
7. 7.2 × 10^{-2} J
8. 9 times
9. 370 J
10. 2.3 × 10^2 m

11. Both of you are correct. Calculating potential gravitational energy is relative to where you call zero.
12.29.4 J
13. 3.67 J
14. (a) 2.7×10^2 J
(b) 0.36 hp
15. (a) 2.63×10^5 J
(b) 263 kW

Page 107, Practice Problems 3.5.1
1. 0.24 J
2. 5.4 m/s, No
3. 15 m/s, No

Page 110, Quick Check
1. 5.0×10^2 m/s
2. 4.7 kg
3. 5.5×10^2 J, 4.4 m/s

Page 111, 3.5 Review
1. A
2. (a) $E_p = 0$ J; $E_K =$ 3.6 J; $E_T = 3.6$ J;
(b) $E_p = 1.3$ J; $E_K =$ 2.3 J; $E_T = 3.6$J;
(c) $E_p = 3.6$ J; $E_K =$ 0 J; $E_T = 3.6$ J;
3. (a) 10.7 m/s
(b) No
(c) 12.5 m/s
(d) Masses cancel in final calculation
4. 2.2×10^2 J
5. 15 m/s
6. 1.71 m/s

Page 113, Chapter 3 Review
1. 0.467 m/s^2
2. (a) 5.88 m/s^2
(b) 4.70 N
3. 12.5 kgm/s
4. 4.00 Ns
5. 0.37 m/s
6. 2.2 m/s
7. 0.97 m/s
8. 0.59 m/s, 23° W of S
9. (b) 1.04 m/s
(c) 0.60 m/s
(d) 9.0×10^{-4}J
10. 12.3 kJ
11.6.9 kJ
12. 3.1×10^5 J
13. 1.47 MJ
14. Energy is use to change the shape of the modeling clay. Internal friction results in heating
15. The girl. The weightlifter does no work
16. 130 MJ
17. 21 m/s 2.1° W of N
18. 2.9 m/s^2
19. 1.7 m/s^2
20. If the block has a steady speed down the ramp, then $F_f = F_p$(magnitude only)

$$\mu = \frac{F_f}{F_N} = \frac{F_p}{F_N} = \frac{mg\sin\theta}{mg\cos\theta} = \tan\theta$$

21. 7.9×10^2 m/s

Chapter 4

Page 129, Practice Problems 4.1.1
1. 2.4×10^2 N
2. 7.1×10^4 N
3. (a) 9.68 m/s^2
(b) 1.2×10^4 N
(c) Car skids

Page 129, 4.1 Review
1. (a) 12 m/s
(b) 93 m/s^2
(c) 93 N
(d) the rope
(e) No. The force of gravity on the mass will make the rope dip below the horizontal
2. (a) 1.2 m/s
(b) 1.0×10^1 m/s^2
(c) 1.0×10^{-2} N
3. 8.91 m/s^2
4. 19.3 N
5. 27 m/s
6. (a) 3.4×10^{-2} m/s^2
(b) 2.0×10^{-4} Hz (17X faster than normal)
(c) You would feel 'weightless'
7. 2.0×10^2N, 4.5×10^2 N
8. 6.5×10^3 N
9. 7.1 m/s
10. (a) 5.95×10^{-3} m/s^2
(b) 3.6×10^{22} N (gravity)
11. 11 m/s
12. (a) 33 m
(b) Bank the curve towards or facing center. Then a component of F_g provides some centripetal force

Page 135, Practice Problems 4.2.1
1. 1.9×10^8 s
2. 2.8×10^4 s

Page 138, 4.2 Review
1. 12 a
2. At D
3. 4R
4. 27 a
5. 1.02×10^{13} m^3/s^2
6. 4.24×10^7 m

7. (a) 76 a
   (b) $R_{mean} = 2.7 \times 10^{12}$ m
   (c) $R_{max} = 5.3 \times 10^{12}$ m
   (d) Between Neptune and Pluto

8. 0.62 a

Page 142, Practice Problems 4.3.1

1. (a) 7.5×10^{-8} N
   (b) 4 times as uch
2. 113 N
3. 253 N

Page 145, Quick Check

1. a = g
2. 616 N
3. 7.9×10^3 m/s
4. Your weight is primarily due to the gravitational attraction of the massive earth

Page 146, Quick Check

1. 7.35×10^3 m/s. No. $\frac{mv^2}{R} = \frac{Gmm}{R^2}$
2. 7.4×10^3 m/s

Page 148, Quick Check

1. 9.9×10^{21} kg
2. (a) 1.47 N/kg or 1.47 m/s^2
   (b) 2.79×10^3 m/s

Page 149, 4.3 Review

1. 1.72×10^3 N
2. 2.7×10^{-3} m/s^2
3. 1.0×10^3 m/s
4. G appears to be constant anywhere in the universe, but g varies as $1/R^2$, therefore g is constant only at a given distance from the attracting planet
5. (a) 1.62 m/s^2 or 0.17g
   (b) 3.31 m/s^2 or 0.34g
   (c) 1.47 m/s^2 or 0.15g
   (d) 273 m/s^2 or 28g - Mercury
6.

$$\frac{GMm}{R^2} = \frac{m4\pi^2 R}{T^2};$$

$$\therefore M = \frac{4\pi^2 R^3}{GT^2} = 6.02 \times 10^{24}\, kg$$

7. 2×10^{18} N
8. 5.4 m/s
9. 41 m
10. 1.1×10^4 m/s
11. Sun: 6.2×10^5 m/s
    Moon: 2.4×10^3 m/s
    Mars: 5.0×10^3 m/s
12. Venus is easier. To go to Mars you have to move away from the sun. Toward Venus the sun's gravitational pull helps you

Page 151, Chapter 4 Review

1. 3.3×10^2 N
2. 6.0×10^2 N
3. (a) 14 m/s
   (b) 56 m/s^2
   (c) 69 N
4. 5.2×10^3 s (1.4h)
5. 1.8×10^3 N
6. 542 N
7. 90.0 N
8. (a) January (Kepler's Second Law)
   (b) January ($F \propto 1/R^2$)
9. (a) 686 N
   (b) 2.3×10^{-9} N
10. 2.0×10^1 N
11. 3.1×10^6 m
12. 2.64×10^6 m
13. (a) 7.9×10^3 m/s
    (b) $v_{escape} = \sqrt{2}\, v_{surface\ orbit}$
14. 22 m/s
15. 3.4×10^8 m
16. 5.9×10^{23} kg
17. 0.472 km
18.

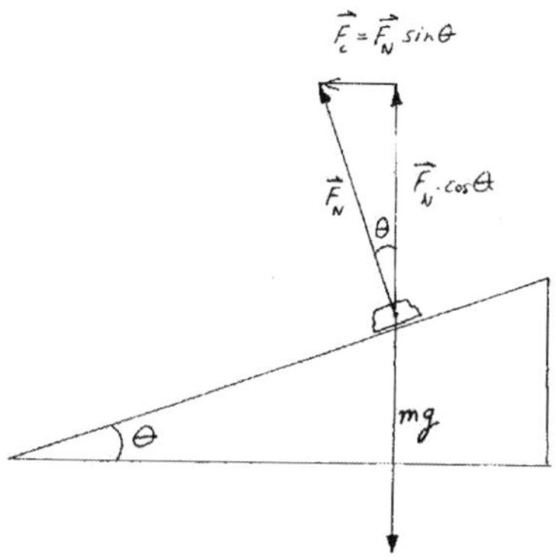

The road is banked so that the force F_N exerted by the road on the car is perpendicular, or normal, to the road surface. Since the surface is frictionless, the only forces acting on the car are the normal force F_N and the force of gravity, mg. A horizontal component of the normal force provides the centripetal force F_c. Note that on a truly frictionless surface, the required angle will only work for one particular speed v! On the diagram $\sin\theta = F_c/F_N$ and $\cos\theta = mg/F_N$

$$\tan\theta = \frac{\sin\theta}{\cos\theta} = \frac{\frac{F_C}{F_N}}{\frac{mg}{F_N}} = \frac{\frac{mv^2}{R}}{mg} = \frac{v^2}{gR}$$

19. $g=\frac{Gm}{R^2}=G\frac{\rho V}{R^2}=G\frac{\rho}{R^2}\bullet\frac{4\pi R^3}{3}=\frac{4}{3}\pi G\rho R$

Chapter 5

Page 165, 5.1 Review

1. Both are charged particles, electron is negatively charged, proton positively charged and heavier
2. Positive charge is a lack of electrons; negative charge an excess of electrons
3. See Figure 5.1.6
4. See Figure 5.1.7
5. Clothes have been rubbing together and this has caused a transfer of charge between the various materials that make up the clothes.
6. Silk/glass: silk negative; Plastic/silk: silk positive
7. The neutral plastic spheres are attracted to the charged rod. Upon contact, spheres take on same charge as rod and are repelled.
8. The acetate strip will attract electrons, which will flow through the metal conductor to the acetate. The metal becomes positive and attracts electrons off the metal sphere of the electroscope. Both the sphere and the rod are positive, so they repel each other
9. Charge an electroscope positive, see if the comb repels it. If not, charge an electroscope negative and see if the comb repels it. Repulsion of like charges is the only sure test.

Page 169, Practice Problems 5.2.1

1. 41.4
2. 0.30 m
3. 5.27 μC

Page 172, Practice Problem 5.2.2

1. (a) 25.5 N, 61.4°
   (b) 188 N, 20.6°
   (c) 126 N, 11.9°

Page 175, 5.2 Review

1. (a) 2F
   (b) 4F
   (c) F/4
   (d) F/9
   (e) F
   (f) 16F
2. 9.0×10^{-3} N
3. 3.2×10^{11} N
4. 9.2×10^{-8} N
5. 1.8×10^{11} C, 2.8×10^{26} N
6. 12 μ C
7. 0.39 N directed along a line bisecting adjacent sides

8a. (i) 2.9×10^{26} N
(ii) 6.7×10^{-17} N
(iii) 4.3×10^{42} N!!!

9. Electrical force is 10^{39} times great than the gravitational force between a proton and an electron in a hydrogen atom
10. 1.5×10^{-8} m

Page 181, Practice Problems 5.3.1

1. 4.50×10^{-5} C
2. 4.5×10^{4} N/C
3. 3.00×10^{-4} N

Page 182, Quick Check

1. 1.4×10^{6} N/C
2 5.69×10^{-11} m
3. 3.5×10^{-12} C

Page 184, Practice Problems 5.3.2

1. III
2. 1.2×10^{5} N/C
3. -5.2×10^{4} N/C, to the left

Page 185, 5.3 Review

1. 2.0×10^{2} N/C, down
2. 1.4×10^{-16} N
3. 4.7×10^{-19} C
4. 1.8×10^{11} N/C, outwards from nucleus
5. 5.9×10^{4} N/C
6. 1.0×10^{10} N/C in a direction away from the charge
7. 4.0×10^{6} N/C toward the 36 μC charge
8. 3.3×10^{2} N/C
9. $E_A = 2.6 \times 10^{5}$ N/C, 11° left of the vertical and upward
10. 6.0×10^{-6} C
11. 9.6×10^{10} m/s^2

Page 189, Quick Check

1. Work is done moving electron to negative plate. High E_P. After release, electron moves away from negative plate and E_P converted to E_K.
2. High E_P at top of hill and near positive plate. E_P converts to E_K as going down hill or away from positive plate.
3. Double the field, hill twice as high. Half the field, half the height of the hill.

Page 191, Practice Problems 5.4.1.

1. -3.1×10^{-18} J (-19 eV)
2. r is the same, charge Q_B twice as much so twice as much electric potential energy
3. 2.44×10^{-9} m

Page 192, Quick Check

1. Increase E_P
2. Decrease E_P

3. Decrease E_P
4. Increase E_P

Page 194, Quick Check
1. 1.8×10^{12} V
2. 8.0×10^{-18} J
3. 5.00 C

Page 195, Quick Check
1. Decreases in half
2. (a) -5.0×10^5 V
   (b) -5.0×10^5 V

Page 196, Practice Problems 5.4.2
1. 1.5×10^2 V
2. 3.6×10^6 J
3. 6.00×10^3 V

Page 197, Practice Problems 5.4.3
1. 6.4×10^{-21} J
2. 20 000 V

Page 198, 5.4 Review
2. 6.0×10^{-5} J
4. 2.8×10^{-1} J
6. 3.0×10^{-4} J
8. 2.3×10^{-17} J
10. (a) No; 1; 1
    (b) Yes; 2; 2
    (c) No; 1; 1
    (d) Yes; 2; 2
12. 60 V

Page 202, Practice Problems 5.5.1
1. 2.38×10^{-3} m
2. 49.0 V
3. $\frac{V}{d} = \frac{\frac{J}{C}}{d} = \frac{\frac{Fd}{C}}{d} = \frac{N}{C}$

Page 207, Quick Check
1. 1.9×10^7 m/s (0.063 c)
2. 4.4×10^5 m/s
3. (a) 1.6×10^7 m/s
   (b) 2.5×10^3 N/C
   (c) 4.0×10^{-16} N
   (d) 4.4×10^{14} m/s^2
   (e) 3.1×10^{-9} s
   (f) 2.1 mm
   (g) 19 mm

Page 211, 5.5 Review
1. 1.20×10^3 V/m
2. 10 V
3. 0.57 m
4. 5.0 N/C from + to - terminal
5. (a) 5.0×10^4 N/C
   (b) 8.8×10^{15} m/s^2
6. (a) 9.8×10^{-15} N upward
   (b) 4.8×10^{-19} C
   (c) Sphere is negatively charged
   (d) 3 excess electrons
7. Proton is heavier so has more E_K as reaches other plate
8. 7.7×10^{-8} kg
9. 3.69×10^5 m/s
10. 147 V
11. 0.60 cm

Page 214, Chapter 5 Review
1. (a) 4 F1
   (b) 4 F1
   (c) 256 F1
2. Electrons on the metal sphere are repelled to ground by way of the body. When the finger is removed, the sphere is left with a deficiency of electrons, so the sphere has a positive charge.
3. (a) 6.0×10^{-5} J
   (b) 3.0×10^2 V
4. 9.2×10^{-16} N
5. 1.5×10^{11} m
6. 1.0 × 103 N/C
7. 4.8×10^{11} m/s^2
8. 9.0×10^5 N/C (to the right)
9. 9.0 × 101 V.
10. (a) 4.2×10^3 V/m
    (b) 6.7×10^{-16} N
    (c) 7.4×10^{14} m/s^2
11. 3.2 cm
12. 2.4 cm
13. 45 J
14. 1.44×10^2 V
15. 0.75 F_1
16. 1.8×10^6 V
17. 2.0×10^{-14} m
18. 6.9×10^{-17} J

Chapter 6

Page 225, Quick Check
1.

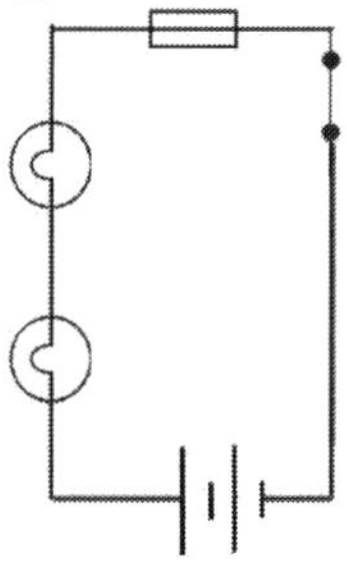

2.

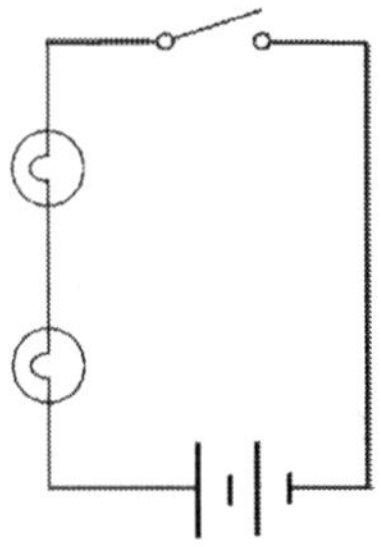

3.

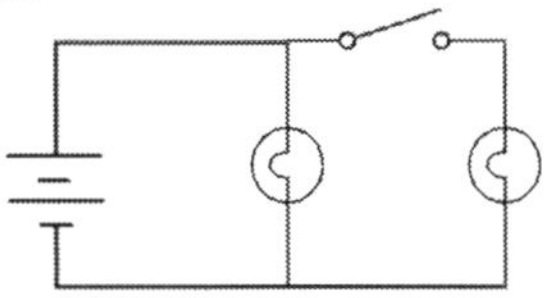

Page 226, Quick Check

1. (a) 100 mA
   (b) 67 mA
2. (a) 16.7 mA
   (b) 6.7 mA
   (c) 3.5 mA
   (d) 0.67 mA

Page 229, 6.1 Review

1. 3.0×10^2 C
2. 1.0×10^1 A
3. 2.7×10^{23} electrons
4. 23 days
5. 1.8 g
6. 4.02 g
8. 80 mA

Page 231, Practice Problems 6.2.1

1. 1.5 kΩ
2. 12 A
3. 25 V

Page 233, Practice Problems 6.2.2

1. 2200Ω ± 220 Ω
2. 10 000 Ω ± 500 Ω
3. 1 500 000 Ω ± 150 000 Ω
4. 470 000 Ω ± 94 000 Ω

Page 234, Quick Check

1. 240 Ω
2. (a) 24 Ω
   (b) 24 Ω, 2.2×10^5 J
3. 4.5×10^5 J

Page 236, Practice Problems 6.2.3

1. 1.20 V
2. 0.030 Ω

Page 239 6.2 Review

1. 5.8 Ω
2. 6.0 V
3. 4.0 A
4. (a) 1.0×10^3 Ω
   (b) 6.0×10^3 A
   (c) 2.0×10^3 Ω
5. 6.0 Ω
6. 110 V
7. 5.0 A
8. 1000 Ω ±5%
9. (a) 320 Ω ±10%
   (b) 20 Ω ±5%
   (c) 85 000 000 Ω ±10%
   (d) 9700 Ω ±20%
10 (a) green black brown
   (b) orange purple orange gold
   (c) brown black black silver
   (d) grey blue red
11. 0.104 Ω
12. 8.1 Ω
13. (a) 3.6×10^6 J
    (b) 72 kWh
    (c) $4.32
14. 0.045 kWh
15. 22 V
16. 5.0 A

Page 245, Practice Problems6.3.1

1. (b) 1.1 A
2. (a) 9.0 Ω
   (b) 2.0 kΩ
   (c) 314 Ω

Page 246, Quick Check

1. 6.0 A
2. R/16
3. 1.5 A
4. (a) 6.0 Ω
   (b) 1.0 A

Page 251, 6.3 Review

1. 1.0 A
2. D
3. (a) 50 Ω
   (b) 1.0 A
   (c) 0.13 A
   (d) 7.3 V
4. 2.0 A
5. 10 V
6. 72 V
7. 0.50 Ω
8. (a) 91Ω
   (b) 0.13 A
   (c)).93 W

9. (a) 16 V
(b) 1.8×10^2 W

Page 254, Chapter 6 Review

2. 4.0×10^1 A
3. 2.7×10^{24} electrons
4. 24.7 g
5. 1.29 V
6. (a) 15 V
(b) 120 V
7. 30 kΩ
8. 80 V
9. 100 000 Ω ± 5 000 Ω
10. yellow, violet, green
11. 33 V
12. 12.5 A
13. 960 W
14. 144 Ω
15. I = 21.3 A; breaker is activated
16. 60 kWh, $3.60
17. 0.25 V
18. 7.5 V
19. (a) 44 Ω
(b) 4.0 Ω
20. 51.28 Ω
21. 3.0 V
22. 0.75 V
23. 18 kΩ, 9.0 kΩ, 2,0 kΩ, 4.0 kΩ
24. (a) 167 kΩ, 0.48 mA
(b) 77 Ω, 0.13 A
(c) 314 Ω, 5.2 mA
25. 3.0 V
26. 0.83 Ω

Chapter 7

Page 267, Quick Check

1. (a)

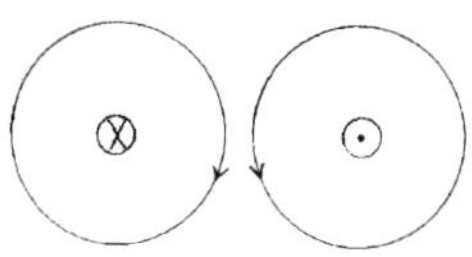

(b) The conductors will repel each other. The lines of force around both conductors are in the same direction in the space between them.

2. The Right Hand Rule predicts that end B is north

Page 272, 7.1 Review

9. 2.0 cm
10. (a) 0.70 cm
(b) 0.35 cm
11. 2.0×10^3 V
12. South

Page 275, Quick Check

1. (a) 8.0×10^{-15} N
(b) 8.8×10^{15} m/s^2, perpendicular to the velocity
2. 1.0×10^{-15} N
3. (a) Up, perpendicular to the magnetic field lines
(b) 1.2×10^{-10} N

Page 277, Quick Check

1. 8.0×10^{-3} T
2. 300 turns
3.159 turns

Page 282, 7.2 Review

1. 7.9×10^{-6} N
2. 3.0 N
3. 0.067 T
4. 0.60 N
5. 0.01A
6. 3.1×10^{-4} T
7. (a) 3.1 N
(b) 125 T
8. 5.3 A
9. 2.36 T
10. 9.1×10^{-3} T

Page 286, Quick Check

1. 9.1×10^{-31} kg
2. 1.7×10^{-27} kg

Page 288, Quick Check

1. 2R
2. 3.0×10^5 m/s; 8.4 cm

Page 293, 7.3 Review

1. 1.1×10^5 m/s
2. (a) R = mv/Bq
(b) 0.13m
(c) 2.9×10^{-21} kgm/s
3. (a) B
(b) 2.00 δ
(c) 0.707 δ

Page 294. Chapter 7 Review

1. iron, nickel , cobalt
2. Electric field. A constant magnetic field will not affect a stationary charged particle
3. Lines of force are clockwise and circular
4. Lines are parallel for the length of the solenoid, going from S to N inside the solenoid
6. Out
7. 2.9×10^{-12} N

8. 6.3×10^{-2} T
9. 1.60 cm
10. 0.32 cm
11. 26 N
12. 1.7×10^{-3} T
13. 3.2×10^{-4} N
14. 1.5×10^{-2} T
15. 6.7×10^{-27} kg
17. attract
18. 6.5×10^{-5} V/m; 3.3×10^{3} V
19. 2.0×10^{6} V/m; 3.8 mm

Chapter 8

Page 302, Practice Problems 8.1.1
1. 0.38 V
2. 0.30 V
3. Into the page

Page 305, Quick Check
1. (a) Use a split ring commutator
   (b)

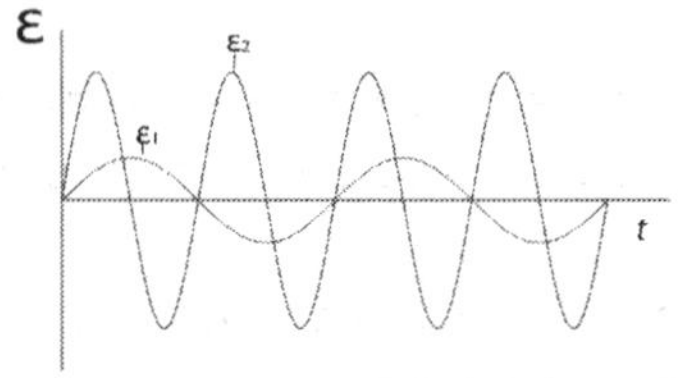

2. $\varepsilon = 4\pi NB\ell fR\sin\theta$
3. $\varepsilon = 2\pi NABf\sin\theta$

Page 309, 8.1 Review
1. left or right
2. Current direction: Y to X; Polarity of End B: S
3. Increase any of N, B, A or f
4. 60 km/s!
5. While switch S is being opened or being closed
6. 25 m/s
7. 5.2×10^{2} V
8. -1.0×10^{1} V

Page 314, Practice Problems 8.2.1
1. 2.5 V
2. - 0.10V
3. - 5.0×10^{3} V

Page 315, Quick Check
1. (a) 1.5 Ω
   (b) 2.4 V
   (c) 1.8 V
2. 11.1 V

Page 318, Quick Check
1. With DC, the rate of change of magnetic flux is zero, therefore the induced emf is zero also.
2. 600 V
3. (a) 1.20 V
   (b) 0.10 A

Page 321, 8.2 Review
1. 1.0×10^{-4} Wb
2. 0.48 V
3. 6.0 V
4. (a) 1.2 Ω
   (b) 1.5A
5. Overloading decreases f, which decreases back emf and increases current I, which may burn out the armature
6. Efficiency $= \dfrac{IV - I^2R}{IV} = \dfrac{1(V - IR)}{IV} = \dfrac{\varepsilon_B}{V}$
7. Since efficiency = ε_B / V, and $\varepsilon_B \propto f$, therefore efficiency increases at higher frequency

Page 323 Chapter 8 Review
1. A to B. Left end becomes north (Lenz's Law) Ampere's Right Hand Rule indicates current is from A to B
2. 0.10 V, 1.0 V/m
3. $\phi = BA$
6. – 0.13 V
7. Right end is south
8. – 2.0×10^{5} Wb
9. 7.2×10^{3} V
10. $\varepsilon_2 = 4\varepsilon_1$ and $t_2 = ½t_1$
11. 8.4 V
12. 0.67
13. 0.90Ω
14. (a) 24 A
    (b) 2.4 A
15. (a) 1.92×10^{3} V
    (b) 1.0 mA
    (c) 1.9 W
16. 2.0×10^{4} turns
17. 1.02 A
18. 23 V
19. 9.0×10^{4} V
20. 0.44 V
21. Out of the page
22. (a) 0.090 V
    (b) Top end
    (c) 1.2 V/m
23. 3.2 V
24. 2.0 %

Glossary

A

accelerating anode (5.5) an anode that accelerates the electrons through a potential difference

acceleration (2.1) the rate at which the velocity of an object is changing; the change may be in magnitude, direction, or both

acceleration due to gravity (2.1) acceleration of a falling object due to gravity in the absence of air resistance; the value of acceleration due to gravity near Earth's surface is approximately 9.81 m/s^2; symbol *g*

accelerometer (4.1) a device used to measure acceleration

ampere (6.1) a unit for measuring current; 1.0 A equals one coulomb per second

anode (5.5) the positively charged electrode in a cathode ray tube

armature (7.3) the coil in a motor

attract (5.1) cause to pull or move together; cause to come close together

average speed (2.1) the rate of change of distance over a given period of time

B

back emf (8.2) the emf produced from a turning armature in a motor; also called counter emf; the counter emf is in the opposite direction to the source emf

bar magnet (7.1) a permanent magnet; usually made of nickel, cobalt, and/or iron

brush (7.3) the point in an electric motor that is in contact with the armature and allows for the transmission of current to and from the armature

C

centre of gravity (1.3) the single point in a body where the force of gravity may be considered to act

centre of mass (1.3) the point where the mass of the object may be considered to be concentrated; for most everyday situations, the centre of mass is the same as the centre of gravity

centripetal (4.1) directed toward a centre

centripetal acceleration (4.1) a centre-directed acceleration that causes an object to move in a curved, sometimes circular, path

charging by conduction (5.1) the process of charging an object through direct contact

charging by induction (5.1) the process of charging an object without direct contact

completely inelastic collision (3.5) a collision in which two or more objects collide and stick to each other

conductors (5.1) any materials that allow charged particles to pass through them easily

conservative (3.5) description of forces that act within systems but do not change their mechanical energy

counter emf (8.2) the emf produced from a turning armature in a motor; the counter emf is in the opposite direction to the source emf; also called back emf

D

deflecting voltage (5.5) the potential difference between two plates responsible for changing the direction of the electron beam

displacement (2.1) straight line distance between initial and final positions; includes magnitude of distance and direction

distance (2.1) a scalar quantity that is the length of a path between two points or locations

drift velocity (6.1) in electrical terms, the rate at which free electrons move through a current-carrying conductor

dry cell (6.1) a voltage-generating cell that has an electrolyte in the form of moist paste

dynamics (3.1) the study of the relationship between motion and forces

E

elastic collision (3.5) a collision in which total kinetic energy is conserved; colliding objects rebound without lasting deformation or heat generation

elastic potential energy (3.4) energy resulting from an object being altered from its standard shape, without permanent change to the object

electric current (6.1) the amount of electric charge that passes a point in a circuit in one second

electric field (5.3) an area surrounding an electric charge in which another electric charge will experience a force

electric field strength (5.3) a measure of the magnitude of the force field that fills the space around every electric charge or group of charges

electric potential (5.4) the electric potential energy per coulomb at a location in an electric field; measured in volts; often called voltage

electrode (6.1) a solid electric conductor through which an electric current enters or leaves a cell or other medium

electromagnet (7.1) magnet that is magnetized only while an electric current flowing

electromotive force (emf) (6.1) a source of energy that can cause a current to flow in an electrical circuit or device

electron (5.1) a subatomic particle with a negative charge

electron volt (5.4) the amount of energy gained by one electron when it moves through a potential difference of 1.0 V

electroscope (5.1) a device that detects excess electric charge

elementary charge (5.2) the charge on a proton or electron

equilibrium (1.1) the state in which two or more forces acting on a body have a resultant of zero

equivalent resistance (6.3) the total resistance of a circuit or the value of a single resistor needed to replace all the resistors in a circuit

F

ferromagnetic (7.1) description of those elements that have magnetic properties; usually iron, nickel, or cobalt, but also neodymium and gadolinium

field (5.3) an area surrounding a mass, electric charge, or magnet in which another mass, electric charge, or magnet will experience a force

focusing anode (5.5) an "electronic lens" that focuses the electron beam into a small spot on the screen

free fall (2.2) motion under the influence of the force of gravity

fulcrum (1.3) the pivot point of a lever

G

gravitational potential energy (3.4) energy of an object due to its position above Earth's surface

grid (5.5) an electrode on the front of the filament in a cathode ray tube

H

horizontal component (1.2) the horizontal vector of a resultant vector

horsepower (3.4) unit used to identify the power output of motors; equal to 750 W

I

impulse (3.2) product of the net force on an object and the time interval during an interaction

inelastic collision (3.5) a collision in which total kinetic energy is not conserved; colliding objects become distorted and/or generate heat

instantaneous speed (2.1) the speed at a particular instant

insulators (5.1) any materials that resist the movement of charged particles through them

K

kinematics (2.1) the study of motion without reference to the causes of the motion

kinetic energy (3.4) energy due to the motion of an object

L

lever arm (1.3) the distance between the fulcrum and the force acting on a lever

lodestone (7.1) common name for magnetite; a naturally occurring magnetic material

M

magnetic field (7.1) the field around a magnetic material

magnetic field strength (7.2) the strength of a magnetic field at a given point; the commonly used unit is a tesla (T)

magnetic flux (8.2) a measure of the strength of a magnetic field over a given area perpendicular to it

magnetite (7.1) a naturally occurring magnetic mineral

mass spectrometer (7.3) a device used to measure the mass of charged atoms

momentum (3.2) the product of an object's mass and velocity; a vector quantity

N

negative charge (5.1) a charge with an excess of electrons

net force (1.1) the combination of forces that act on an object

neutral (5.1) description of an object with an equal number of negative and positive charges

neutron (5.1) a subatomic particle with no charge

nonconservative (3.5) description of forces applied from outside the system that cause the energy of the system to change so that energy is not conserved

north pole (7.1) one end of a bar magnet; sometimes called the north-seeking pole

nucleus (5.1) the positively charged central region of an atom, composed of protons and neutrons and containing almost all of the mass of the atom

O

ohm (6.2) the unit for electrical resistance

P

parallel circuit (6.3) a closed loop that has several paths along which current can travel

peak voltage (8.1) the maximum induced emf in a motor

position (2.1) a vector quantity that describes a specific point relative to a reference point

positive charge (5.1) a charge with a deficiency of electrons

potential difference (5.4) the difference in electric potential between two points; free charge flows between points in a circuit when there is a difference between the points and continues to flow until both points reach a common potential

power (3.4) the rate of doing work or the rate at which energy is transformed from one form to another; (6.2) the rate at which energy is released with respect to time

primary coil (8.2) the input coil in a transformer

projectile (2.2) an object that moves through the air or through space, acted on by gravity (and air resistance, if any)

proton (5.1) a subatomic particle with a positive charge

R

repel (5.1) push away

resistance (6.2) the opposition of a body or substance to current passing through it, resulting in a change of electrical energy into heat or another form of energy

resistor (6.2) a device that offers some resistance to the flow of electric charges

resultant (1.1) the vector sum of two or more vectors or component vectors

resultant force (1.1) the combination of forces that act on an object

S

scalar quantities (1.1) quantities that have magnitude (size) only

secondary coil (8.2) the output coil in a transformer

series circuit (6.3) a circuit that has only one path along which the current can travel

series-parallel circuit (6.3) a circuit containing both series and parallel circuits

solenoid (7.1) a current-carrying coil of wire that acts like a magnet when a current passes through it

south pole (7.1) one end of a bar magnet; sometime called the south-seeking pole

split-ring commutator (7.3) the part of a motor that makes the current in the two halves of the coil on the armature change direction so that the magnetic force is always in the same direction

static electricity (5.1) an accumulation of electric charge on an insulated body

static equilibrium (1.3) the state when the net force of a body is zero and the body is not moving

statics (1.3) the study of the calculation of forces acting on bodies that are in static equilibrium

superconductors (6.2) materials that offer no resistance to the flow of electric charges

T

terminal voltage (8.2) the voltage at the terminals connected to the source of electricity for an electric device

test charge (5.3) a charge so small that it does not affect a source charge and change its electric field

torque (1.3) the product of a force and its distance from the fulcrum, measured perpendicular to the direction of the force vector

torsion balance (5.2) a device used to calculate the force of repulsion between two charged spheres

transformer (8.2) a device designed to alter the voltage in an alternating current (AC) circuit

U

uniform circular motion (4.1) movement of an object in a circle at a steady speed

V

vector (1.1) an arrow drawn to an appropriate scale that represents the magnitude and direction of a quantity

vector addition (1.1) the process of adding vectors together by placing the head of one vector to the tail of another

vector quantities (1.1) quantities that have both direction and magnitude

velocity (2.1) the speed of an object with direction included; a vector quantity

velocity selector (7.3) a mechanism in a mass spectrometer that selects a certain mass of ions to be measured

vertical component (1.2) the vertical vector of a resultant vector

voltage (5.4) electric potential measured in volts; (6.1) potential difference measured in volts

voltaic cell (6.1) a wet cell consisting of two electrodes in an electrolytic solution such as ammonium chloride

W

weber (Wb) (8.2) the unit for magnetic flux

work (3.4) the amount of energy transferred when a force acts over a given displacement

Index

F

G

H

I

J

K

S

T

U

V

W

Z

Useful Mathematical Information

Right-Angle Triangles

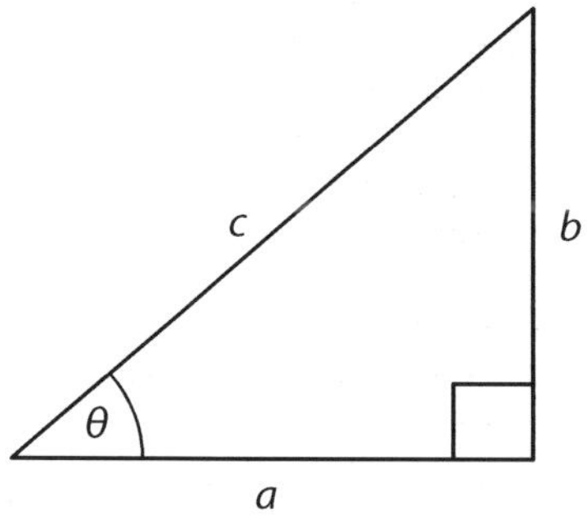

Pythagoras

$$a^2 + b^2 = c^2$$

Trigonometric Functions

$$\sin\theta = \frac{b}{c}$$

$$\cos\theta = \frac{a}{c}$$

$$\tan\theta = \frac{b}{a}$$

$$\sin 2\theta = 2\sin\theta\cos\theta$$

$$\frac{\sin\theta}{\cos\theta} = \tan\theta$$

Area of a Triangle

Area = ½ ab

Quadratic Equation

If $ax^2 + bx + c = 0$, then

$$x = \frac{-b \pm \sqrt{b^2 - 4ac}}{2a}$$

All Triangles

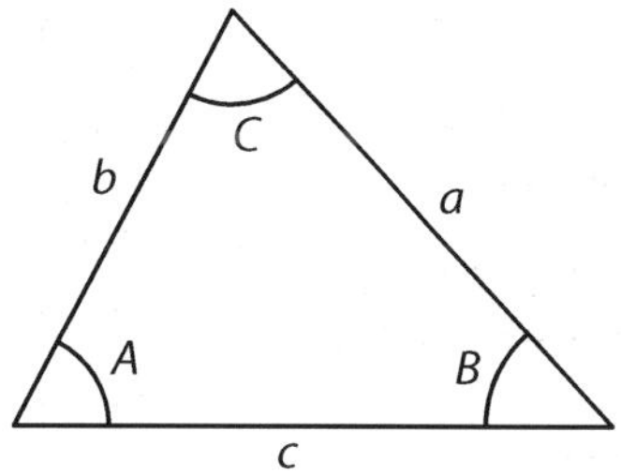

Sine Law

$$\frac{a}{\sin A} = \frac{b}{\sin B} = \frac{c}{\sin C}$$

Cosine Law

$$c^2 = a^2 + b^2 - 2ab\cos C$$
$$b^2 = a^2 + c^2 - 2ac\cos B$$
$$a^2 = b^2 + c^2 - 2bc\cos A$$

Prefixes

centi (c) = 10^{-2}
milli (m) = 10^{-3}
micro (μ) = 10^{-6}
nano (n) = 10^{-9}
pico (p) = 10^{-12}
giga (G) = 10^{9}
mega (M) = 10^{6}
kilo (k) = 10^{3}

Table of Constants and Other Useful Data

Universal gravitation constant	$G = 6.67 \times 10^{-11}\ Nm^2/kg^2$
Gravitational acceleration at Earth's surface	$g = 9.80\ m/s^2$

Earth

Radius of Earth	$R_E = 6.38 \times 10^6$ m
Mean orbital radius about the Sun	$R = 1.50 \times 10^{11}$ m
Rotational period	$T_E = 8.61 \times 10^4$ s
Period of revolution around the Sun	$T = 3.16 \times 10^7$ s
Mass of Earth	$M_E = 5.98 \times 10^{24}$ kg

Moon

Radius of Moon	$R_M = 1.74 \times 10^6$ m
Mean orbital radius about Earth	$R = 3.84 \times 10^8$ m
Rotational period	$T_M = 2.36 \times 10^6$ s
Period of revolution around Earth	$T = 2.36 \times 10^6$ s
Mass of Moon	$M_M = 7.35 \times 10^{22}$ kg

Sun

Mass of the Sun	$M_S = 1.98 \times 10^{30}$ kg

General

Speed of light	$c = 3.00 \times 10^8$ m/s
Coulomb's constant	$k = 9.00 \times 10^9\ Nm^2/C^2$
Mass of electron	$m_e = 9.11 \times 10^{-31}$ kg
Elementary charge	$e = 1.60 \times 10^{-19}$ C
Mass of proton	$m_p = 1.67 \times 10^{-27}$ kg
Mass of neutron	$m_n = 1.68 \times 10^{-27}$ kg
Permeability of free space	$\mu_o = 4\pi \times 10^{-7}$ Tm/A
Electron volt	$1\ eV = 1.60 \times 10^{-19}$ J

Mathematical

Pi	$\pi = 3.14$
Circumference of a circle	$2\pi r$
Area of a circle	πr^2
Volume of a sphere	$4/3\pi r^3$

41828567R10198

Made in the USA
Middletown, DE
24 March 2017